Women's Spirit Bonding

*Behind naming, beneath words, is something else
An existence named, unnamed, unnameable*[1]

*I am a woman come to speak for you
I am a woman speaking for us all
From the tongue of dust and fire
From the bowl of bitter smoke
This is a song for strength and power.*[2]

*I gave birth to a daughter yesterday
The house still feels hushed and holy . . .
and the quality of the light is otherworldly.
It took me a few moments to realize she was there.
The sense of wonder is persistent.*[3]

Women's Spirit Bonding

Edited by **Janet Kalven**
and **Mary I. Buckley**

Mary I. Buckley

Janet Kalven

THE PILGRIM PRESS
New York

Copyright © 1984 The Pilgrim Press
All rights reserved

No part of this publication may be reproduced, stored in a retrieval system, or transmitted in any form or by any means, electronic, mechanical, photocopying, recording, or otherwise (brief quotations used in magazines or newspaper reviews excepted), without the prior permission of the publisher.

The biblical quotations, unless otherwise indicated, are from the *Revised Standard Version of the Bible*, copyright 1946, 1952 and © 1971, 1973 by the Division of Christian Education, National Council of Churches, and are used by permission. Scripture quotations marked KJV are from the *King James Verson* of the Bible.

The lines from "Diving into the Wreck" are reprinted from *Diving into the Wreck, Poems 1971–1972*, by Adrienne Rich, by permission of the author and W. W. Norton & Company, Inc. Copyright © 1973 by W. W. Norton & Company, Inc. The lines from "Natural Resources" from *The Dream of a Common Language, Poems 1974–1977* by Adrienne Rich, are reprinted by permission of the author and W. W. Norton & Company, Inc.

Library of Congress Cataloging in Publication Data
Main entry under title:

Women's spirit bonding.

   Includes bibliographical references.
   1. Women and religion—Congresses. 2. Religion and culture—Congresses. I. Kalven, Janet, 1913–
II. Buckley, Mary I., 1917–
BL458.W6595   1984   291.1'78'088042   84-1865
ISBN 0-8298-0707-1

The Pilgrim Press, 132 West 31 Street, New York, New York 10001

200.82 W842k
Women's spirit bonding

*To Mira, Nora, and all the
other children for whom we are
trying to build a viable future*

Contents

Acknowledgments x
Contributors xi
Introduction xvii
Reflections on a Process   CHERYL GILES, NANCY RICHARDSON   xxii

PART I: Women and Poverty   1

1. Women, Poverty, and Economic Justice/MARY I. BUCKLEY   3
2. Class, Gender, and Religion: A Theoretical Overview and Some Political Implications/JACKIE DI SALVO   11
3. Suggestions from the Working Group on Politics and Spirituality   35

PART II: Women and Nature: Violence or Interdependence   39

4. The Great Chain of Being and the Chain of Command/LETHA DAWSON SCANZONI   41
5. Making the World Live: Feminism and the Domination of Nature/YNESTRA KING   56
6. Litany of Women in Pain   65

PART III: Racism, Pluralism, Bonding   67

7. Racism and the Bonding of Women /JAMIE PHELPS   70
8. A Historical Addendum/REBECCA JOHNSON   75
9. "Las Marías" of the Feminist Movement/YOLANDA TARANGO, ADA MARIA ISASI-DIAZ   85
10. Anti-Semitism: The Unacknowledged Racism/JUDITH PLASKOW   89
11. White Women and Racism/RENNY GOLDEN   97
12. Discussion   106
13. A Black Response to Feminist Theology/JACQUELYN GRANT   117
14. Report from the Working Group on Racism/Classism/Sexism   125

PART IV: Women as Makers of Literature — 137

15 Women as Makers of Literature/DELORES S. WILLIAMS 139
16 Poems/SHARON THOMSON, RENNY GOLDEN, ANN THACHER, JOAN WYZENBEEK, MARY JO GROTE, JACKIE DI SALVO, AND DELORES S. WILLIAMS 146

PART V: War and Peace — 161

17 Political Oppression and Creative Survival/MARY E. HUNT 164
18 Patriarchy and Death/MARY CONDREN 173
19 Why Women Need the War God/KAREN MCCARTHY BROWN 190
20 Feminist Liberation Theology and Yahweh as Holy Warrior: An Analysis of Symbol/CAROL P. CHRIST 202
21 Discussion 213
22 Women Responding to the Arab-Israeli Conflict/MARY BENTLEY ABU-SABA, JUDITH PLASKOW, ROSEMARY RADFORD RUETHER 221
23 Suggestions from the Working Group on Political Strategies 234

PART VI: Lesbianism and Homophobia — 239

24 My Voice... and Many Others/LYNN WILSON 240
25 A Religious Perspective/LETHA DAWSON SCANZONI 243
26 A Political Perspective/MARY E. HUNT 249
27 Discussion 255

PART VII: Resources from Various Traditions — 263

28 Affirming Diversity and Biblical Tradition/MARY K. WAKEMAN 267
29 Reclaiming Our Past/JUDITH OCHSHORN 281
30 Claiming the Center: A Critical Feminist Theology of Liberation/ELISABETH SCHÜSSLER FIORENZA 293
31 Immanence: Uniting the Spiritual and Political/STARHAWK 310
32 Suggestions from the Working Group on Feminist Education 318

PART VIII: Envisioning an Alternative Future — 323

33 Envisioning Our Hopes: Some Models of the Future/ROSEMARY RADFORD RUETHER 325
34 A Feminist Approach to Alternative Enterprises/CAROL COSTON 336

PART IX: **Rituals and Celebrations** **345**

  35 Guidelies for Planners of Rituals/DIANN NEU, JULIA UPTON 347
  36 A Ritual of Water 349
  37 Reflections on the Creation of a Ritual
       Meal/ELLEN M. UMANSKY 351
  38 A Ritual Meal 353

Epilogue JANET KALVEN 357
Notes 373

Sketches CHARLOTTE L. DANIELS

Acknowledgments

THE MATERIALS IN this book developed out of the Women's Spirit Bonding Conference, July 11–17, 1982 at Grailville, Loveland, Ohio. We would like to acknowledge with gratitude those who made that conference possible: the department of theology of St. John's University, Jamaica, New York, which offered the credit option and provided the initial financing and support services necessary to mount a national conference; the panelists and facilitators, all of whom contributed their services without honorarium; the United States Grail, the Episcopal Diocese of Southern Ohio, various friends of The Grail, and members of the Women's Caucus of the American Academy of Religion, all of whom contributed to the scholarship fund; and the members of the Grailville staff, who went to extraordinary lengths to provide a flexible and supportive environment for the conference.

A word about The Grail and Grailville. The Grail is an international movement of women, rooted in Christian tradition, striving to integrate a living faith, the development of the full potential of women, and action for liberation leading toward a just and peaceful world order. The largest Grail center in the United States, Grailville, located in Loveland, Ohio, twenty miles northeast of Cincinnati, is an adult education and conference center. Concerned since its establishment in 1944 with questions of women and religion, in the past decade Grailville has given particular attention to issues of feminism and religion, drawing together women of different religious traditions to theologize out of their shared experiences. This volume continues that work of feminist theologizing.

Our special thanks go to our editor, Marion M. Meyer, for her support and creative suggestions. We are grateful to Frances McLaughlin for her work in typing the manuscript.

Mary Buckley and Janet Kalven shared equally in the work of coordinating the original conference and in making the editorial decisions with regard to the present volume. The major part of the editorial work has been done by Janet Kalven.

Mary I. Buckley
St. John's University

Janet Kalven
University of Dayton

Contributors

MARY BENTLEY ABU-SABA has been a counseling psychologist at the University of North Carolina at Greensboro since 1975. She has been involved with women's issues for the past decade and has become increasingly interested in a feminist religious perspective. She is married to a Lebanese and has two young-adult children.

KAREN McCARTHY BROWN is associate professor of sociology of religion in the Graduate and Theological Schools of Drew University. She has been researching Vodou in Haiti and in the Haitian community in New York City since 1973.

MARY I. BUCKLEY, a native New Yorker, owes her first awareness of social justice issues to her parents and their experience of oppression in rural Ireland. A member of The Grail since 1943, she took a doctorate in theology at the University of Münster, Germany, in 1969, out of her concern for the relation of faith to issues of colonialism, racism, and sexism. As associate professor of theology at St. John's University in New York City, she has developed several courses: Women in the Christian Tradition, Theological Issues in Urban Problems, and Women/Poverty/Justice.

CAROL P. CHRIST, associate professor at San Jose State University in California, is the author of *Diving Deep and Surfacing* and coeditor of *Womanspirit Rising*. She is doing research on symbolism in feminist theology.

MARY CONDREN worked with the Student Christian Movement of Britain and Ireland from 1974 to 1979 as editor of *Movement*, a journal of theology and politics, and as coordinator of the Women's Project of the World Student Christian Federation in Europe. In 1979–80 she was a research/resource associate at Harvard, where she is presently pursuing a doctorate in theology.

CAROL COSTON, O.P., an Adrian Dominican, was an original founder and first executive director of Network, a

Catholic social justice lobby. She was a delegate to the International Women's Year Conference in Houston and attended the IWY mid-decade conference in Copenhagen. At present she is studying organic food production and worker-owned cooperatives.

CHARLOTTE L. DANIELS' thirty-year art career has earned recognition in *Who's Who;* she has produced hundreds of portrait paintings, murals, and other works for public buildings and private collections. Crone Charlotte especially wanted to sketch the life-affirming and bonding activities at Women's Spirit Bonding.

JACKIE DI SALVO is professor of English at Rutgers University and is a literary critic, lecturer, performance poet and political activist in women's, labor, and antiimperialist movements. Di Salvo is a member of The Grail and the author of *War of Titans: Blake's Critique of Reason and the Politics of Religion.*

ELISABETH SCHÜSSLER FIORENZA is professor of New Testament studies and theology at the University of Notre Dame. She is the author of books on ministries of women in the church *(Der Vergessene Partner)* and on priesthood in the New Testament *(Priester für Gott)* and of the following works in English: *Invitation to the Book of Revelation: A Commentary on the Apocalypse* and *In Memory of Her: A Feminist Reconstruction of Christian Origins.*

CHERYL GILES, M.Div., has since 1979 been a chaplain at Boston College, where she is involved in developing social responsibility through programs focused on racism, sexuality, and politics. She is codirector of the Women's Theological Center, which offers a one-year program of study and action from a Christian and feminist perspective.

RENNY GOLDEN is a member of the Chicago Religious Task Force on Central America. She is an assistant professor at Northeastern Illinois University and was a resource/research associate in women's studies at Harvard Divinity School. She coauthored with Sheila Collins *Struggle Is a Name for Hope.*

JACQUELYN GRANT has taught in the Women's Studies Program at Harvard Divinity School and is now on the faculty of the Interdenominational Theological Center in Atlanta, Georgia. She is director of Black Women in Church and Society at ITC.

MARY JO GROTE, a former teacher of English, is a part-time discussion leader, proofreader, liturgist, and poet. She is a member of The Grail.

MARY E. HUNT, after completing her doctoral dissertation on feminist liberation theology at the Graduate Theological Union in Berkeley, California in 1980, served for two years as visiting professor of theology at ISEDET in Buenos Aires. She is now a coordinator of WATER (Women's Alliance for Theology, Ethics, and Ritual) and teaches social ethics at a Washington seminary.

ADA MARIA ISASI-DIAZ was born and raised in Cuba. For the past ten years she has been active in the Hispanic community in the United States as a Christian writer, lecturer, and process facilitator.

REBECCA JOHNSON is president of the board of the Contact Center, a community-based membership organization working on justice issues in inner-city Cincinnati, where she is working out her commitments as a Black Christian feminist.

JANET KALVEN has been involved in alternative education for women since 1942, when she left the Great Books program at the University of Chicago to become a member of The Grail staff. One of the group that established Grailville in 1944, she has coordinated a variety of short- and long-term residential programs for women at Grailville, including Semester at Grailville (1968–75) and Seminary Quarter at Grailville (1974–78). She is coauthor and coeditor of *Your Daughters Shall Prophesy: Feminist Alternatives in Theological Education*.

YNESTRA KING, a nontheist, visionary outlaw, believes in the power of women to shake the world and put it right. She is a founder of the Women's Pentagon Action, a spiritual/political/ecological/antimilitarist group.

CAROL FEISER LAQUE, associate professor of English at the University of Cincinnati, has published *Stone Poems, Sundial Season,* and *Parallel Places*.

DIANN NEU, a coordinator of WATER (Women's Alliance for Theology, Ethics, and Ritual) in Washington, DC, is working on the development of feminist liturgies. She edited the report *Women Moving Church* and compiled a directory, *Women's Base Communities,* both published by the Center of Concern.

JUDITH OCHSHORN is author of *The Female Experience*

and the Nature of the Divine, a comparison of ancient Near Eastern polytheistic and monotheistic attitudes toward the importance of gender and its relation to power and divinity. She is associate professor and director of women's studies at the University of South Florida.

JAMIE PHELPS, O.P., has been a member of the Adrian Dominicans since 1959. Her ministry has included education at the elementary, high school, and graduate levels; psychiatric social work; and pastoral ministry in several Chicago parishes. She has worked primarily among middle- and lower-class Blacks. At present she is studying for a doctorate in theology at Catholic University of America in Washington, DC.

JUDITH PLASKOW teaches religious studies at Manhattan College. Actively involved in many projects pertaining to women and religion, she is coeditor of *Womanspirit Rising* and author of *Sex, Sin and Grace*.

NANCY RICHARDSON served as national consultant on racism for the YWCA, was the first coordinator of Seminary Quarter at Grailville, taught in the Training Women for Ministry program at Andover-Newton, and is coeditor and coauthor of *Your Daughters Shall Prophesy: Feminist Alternatives in Theological Education*. An ordained minister of the United Church of Christ, she is completing a doctorate in theology at Boston University and is codirector of the Women's Theological Center in Boston.

ROSEMARY RADFORD RUETHER is the Georgia Harkness Professor of Applied Theology at Garrett Evangelical Theological Seminary at Northwestern University. She writes about feminist and liberation theology.

LETHA DAWSON SCANZONI is a professional writer on social issues and religion. She is author of *Sex Is a Parent Affair*, coauthor of *All We're Meant to Be*, *Is the Homosexual My Neighbor?*, and a college text, *Men, Women and Change*. At present she is at work on a book about domestic violence.

STARHAWK (Miriam Semos) is a therapist, witch, peace activist, and author of *The Spiral Dance: A Rebirth of the Ancient Religion of the Great Goddess* and *Dreaming the Dark: Magic, Sex and Politics*. She is a faculty member of The Institute in Culture and Creation Spirituality at Holy Names College, Oakland, California, and is a coordinator of Reclaiming, a center for feminist spirituality and counseling in San Francisco.

YOLANDA TARANGO, C.C.V.I., is a Sister of Charity of the Incarnate Word and a member of Las Hermanas. She was a participant in Mujeres para el Dialogo, an international feminist group convened during the Latin American Bishops' Conference (CELAM) in Puebla, Mexico, and is active in Theology in the Americas' National Committee and Inter-Ethnic/Indigenous Women's Dialogue.

ANN THACHER has been married to the same man for forty-one years, has five children, and is active in a variety of community service jobs in seven communities. In her life and writings, she is interested in translating insights gained as a feminist in a sexist society into tools useful for growing old in an ageist society.

SHARON THOMSON is a performance poet and teacher with the New York State Poets-in-the-Schools. Her poems have been published in *Poetry, Pequod,* and *Three Rivers Poetry Journal.* She is the mother of one daughter and a member of The Grail.

ELLEN M. UMANSKY, assistant professor of religion at Emory University, is the author of several articles on women and Judaism. Her book *Lily Montagu and the Advancement of Liberal Judaism: From Vision to Vocation* is published by the Mellon Press.

JULIA UPTON, R.S.M., a Sister of Mercy, is assistant professor of theology at St. John's University in New York. She is a member of the Liturgical Commission of the Diocese of Brooklyn and is doing research on feminist images of God.

MARY K. WAKEMAN is associate professor of religious studies and women's studies at the University of North Carolina in Greensboro. She is active in the American Academy of Religion and the National Women's Studies Association. At present she is working on the relation of monotheism to the affirmation of diversity.

DELORES S. WILLIAMS is a poet whose work has appeared in journals in America, Europe, and Africa. She has taught liberation theology at Boston University and has also taught in the women's studies program at Harvard Divinity School.

LYNN WILSON, after obtaining a degree in fine arts at Indiana University, spent some time working in the Peace Corps and at Grailville. She is now studying political economy and oppression at the University of Massachusetts, Amherst.

JOAN WYZENBEEK has a strong interest in feminist theology, which motivates her work in a Christian church as well as her study of ancient Goddess religions. Through her poetry, Wyzenbeek attempts to give meaning to the lives of women in pain.

Introduction

"WOMEN'S SPIRIT BONDING" brought together at Grailville, Loveland, Ohio, 136 women, two very small girls, and one man for a week of feminist theologizing. In many respects we were a homogeneous group: from all parts of the United States with just a sprinkling, 10 percent, from other countries—Canada, Mexico, Brazil, Holland, Australia; 93 percent White; predominantly middle class; predominantly professional women—university professors, graduate students in seminaries and departments of theology, Catholic nuns, four women ordained in various Protestant traditions; editors and writers (about one third of the group had published some work during the preceding year); a number of members of The Grail, the women's movement which, together with the department of theology at St. John's University in New York City, sponsored the conference.

Yet at the same time our group encompassed great diversities in race, religion, ethnic background, life-styles: we were White, Black, and Hispanic; Jew and Gentile, Catholic and Protestant (ranging from Evangelical to Episcopal to Unitarian), secular humanists and pagans of ancient or modern Goddess traditions; single, married, divorced, widowed, celibate, and lesbian women.

What was the magnet that drew us together and attracted another hundred participants who had to be turned away for lack of space? Our starting point was a shared sense of crisis, a perception that human and global survival are indeed in question. We shared, too, a faith in the potential transforming power that lies in women's bonding. As Adrienne Rich has written, "Connections between and among women are the most feared, the most problematic, and the most potentially transformative force on the planet." But to exercise our transformative power, we must be able to bond together. Therefore the purpose of our conference was twofold: (1) to bring feminist thinking to bear on the crisis that threatens human survival—what analyses can we offer? what alternatives can we envisage? and (2) to look long and hard both at the barriers that keep us apart and at how we can strengthen our bonds. We were particularly concerned with a religious orientation as a source for bonding.

We dismissed as a sexist myth the notion that women cannot work together. We were convinced that women's socialization gives a sensitivity to the needs of others, a willingness to play a supportive as well as a stellar role, a capacity for collaboration. We had had experience of the synergy and creativity that can develop in a group working together freely in a supportive environment. We had experienced the power of a religious orientation to facilitate bonding: a group that celebrates together can often overcome barriers to communication that prove insuperable in a totally secularized context. At the same time, we were concerned about the lack of communication between the different groups of religiously oriented feminists. Women committed both to feminism and to a religious tradition are a minority of a minority, regarded with suspicion by coreligionists as too radical and by other feminists as hopelessly conservative. We were distressed that within this relatively small group there seemed to be so few points of contact between the evangelical feminists, engaged in retranslating and reinterpreting the Bible; the liberationist feminists who find in the prophetic texts a touchstone for their critique of both Jewish and Christian traditions; and those feminists who reject the biblical traditions as irredeemably patriarchal and turn instead to Goddess-centered approaches. Could we open up channels of communication with one another in ways that would enable us to pool our resources, deepen our critiques, and develop visions of an alternative future?

What could we offer in the way of feminist thinking about the global crisis? Implicit in our approach is the notion that feminism is not simply a set of "women's issues": equal pay for equal work, right of entry into various trades and professions, government-supported child-care programs, and so forth. Rather, feminism is an all-encompassing perspective on the whole of reality. To use Mary Daly's phrase, it is a new naming of ourselves, the universe, and the transcendent. It is a fresh perspective on the most fundamental questions—how we conceive reality, what it means to be human, how humans should relate to one another and to the planet, what is valuable, and what grounds our values. Moreover, it is a perspective that men can share. Feminist scholars in the past fifteen years have produced a vast body of work in almost every field, explicating some of the consequences of the feminist vision. The strength of this vision—in an era of extreme specialization and compartmentalization—lies precisely in its all-encompassing character: it is a holistic vision, which seeks to trace connections between theory and action, among different fields of study, among different aspects of our culture. Hence our need to deal with a broad range of topics, even though we were limited to the brief compass of one week: poverty, violence, ecology, racism, identity, war and peace, resources, alternatives. Our aim was not an exhaustive study of any one question but rather a tracing of interrelationships.

As we looked about us, we perceived millions of people mesmerized by images of seemingly inevitable disasters: an arms race stockpiling ever deadlier weapons in prospect of a nuclear holocaust; economic and political forces tending toward greater exploitation and more brutal repression of human beings; a technology out of control, wasting irreplaceable resources, poisoning the food chain, threatening all life on the planet with extinction. We understood the dynamics of self-fulfilling prophecies. If all we are able to see is these images of disaster, we are quite likely to bring these negative possibilities into existence. This understanding gave special urgency to our work. What analysis could we as religious feminists bring to our contemporary world? Could we begin to picture an alternative future in terms compelling enough to grip the imagination and thus help to start a process of transformation?

Characteristic of a feminist method is an emphasis on process as well as product. We conceived the conference as a dialogue, a live meeting of minds that could generate new insights and clearer visions of a sane, healthy, loving way to live with our sisters and brothers on planet Earth. We did not want to sacrifice the vitality and spontaneity of the event to the production of a written record. Therefore, this book is not intended as a record of proceedings. Rather it is the fruit of reflections on a week of intense interaction at many levels: presentations and discussions, intimate sharing in small base groups, keen analysis in small working groups, confrontations and affirmations, rituals and celebrations, singing and dancing, and all the informal contacts that come with living together in Grailville's rural setting of fields and woods, gardens and pond.

Some thirty women, most of whom were present throughout the week, served as resource persons—making presentations, facilitating the general group process, coordinating the planning of the rituals. The panelists spoke informally and at a later date wrote the pieces presented in this volume. The group discussions were taped, and the tapes were transcribed and edited by Janet Kalven. Because of practical difficulties in identifying the speakers and obtaining permission to use their remarks, the comments during the discussions included are presented anonymously except for those of the panelists. The reports from the working groups are also presented anonymously, since no record was kept of the groups' membership. Further details on the means of organizing the conference to combine maximum participation by all present with high input from the resource persons will be found in "Reflections on a Process" by Nancy Richardson and Cheryl Giles.

The book is divided into nine parts. It begins with a consideration of immediate problems in women's lives: poverty in Part I, physical violence against women in Part II. It moves to a discussion of racism in Part III, of war and peace in Part V, and of heterosexism in Part VI, always with concern for the connections between the personal and the political, and between the various forms of oppression—racism, sexism, classism, heterosexism, imperialism. Each topic is explored in its relation to the theme of women bonding. Moreover, as women concerned with theologizing, the writers probe the religious roots of the various forms of oppression.

All the writers, however much they may focus on critique, also indicate positive possibilities. Parts IV, VII, VIII, and IX give particular emphasis to alternatives. Part IV analyzes and illustrates the process of personal empowerment that women are finding through literature. In Part VIII Rosemary Ruether sketches in broad strokes an alternative social order and Carol

Coston details several models for more just economic structures. Part VII explores the resources of various religious traditions, and Part VIII, on rituals, illustrates ways to use traditional materials for healing and bonding. Finally, the Epilogue deals with hindrances and helps to women bonding, offers some images of alternative futures, and suggests practical steps for bringing about change.

As women theologizing, our stress is on breadth and depth of vision—the connectedness of the issues to one another rather than an exhaustive analysis of any one issue. The reader will find that certain themes recur—a nonhierarchical view of the universe, the unity of the spiritual and the political, the interstructuring of oppressions, the value of diversity, the need for mutuality, the importance of image and story as vehicles for insight—approached from quite different starting points by different women.

Mary I. Buckley
Janet Kalven

Reflections on a Process

DEVELOPING A PROCESS for some 136 participants, including twenty-seven resource people, to work together five days in mid-July heat on issues ranging from sexuality to nuclear war presented no small challenge to the two of us who had been invited as "process people" for the conference.

Convinced that process *is* content, we wanted to develop a design for the conference that would facilitate bonding among women, bonding that could reach across differences but not ignore or trivialize these differences. Thus, we were faced with designing a process that would enable participants to name their own reality and the questions with which they were dealing in that reality, that would be participatory, that would facilitate mutuality in dealing with the conference process/content, that would provide opportunities for an integrative physical/intellectual/emotional/spiritual interaction. As we began planning, our questions, therefore, were:

- How could we design a process that would be flexible enough to provide space for women to deal with the questions and issues they brought with them and stable enough to honor commitments to participants who had come to the conference based on preconference agreements and information?
- How could we insure maximum participation in the design of the conference format while minimizing the chaos of trying to plan with 136 people?
- How would we deal with the fact that while the preconference publicity had offered an opportunity for women to meet across faith lines and had identified racism as a major issue to be addressed, the conference participants would be largely White and Christian?
- What kind of process would enable participants to have

Reflections on a Process xxiii

Cheryl Giles   Nancy Richardson

space for group reflection in some depth with an ongoing group as well as an opportunity to meet and discuss issues with a variety of people?

With these questions in mind, we developed a conference design that included the following elements:

- panel presentations, limiting each panel member to thirty minutes for an initial presentation
- responses to the panels through small-group discussions, fishbowls,* and question-and-answer periods

*A "fishbowl" is a discussion format that promotes widespread participation while at the same time enabling even a group of 150 or more to be self-regulating. The fishbowl is an inner circle of not more than ten chairs, with the other participants seated in concentric circles around it. Panelists and responders are seated in the fishbowl, leaving two to four chairs empty. Those in the inner circle begin their discussion. When anyone from the outer circle wishes to join in, she simply moves in and sits in one of the empty chairs. That gesture is the signal to those speaking to yield the floor to the newcomer, who makes a comment and then returns to her place. After the discussion is well under way, and all the chairs in the inner circle are filled, the facilitator may suggest that those wishing to speak tap the shoulder of someone in the fishbowl and change places with her. This format usually maintains a high level of interest in the total group and helps to keep one person from dominating the discussion. The total group feels responsible for fair play and generally enforces the rules in an even-handed and good-humored way.

- small base groups scheduled to meet daily
- liturgies and rituals
- free space for relaxation
- open space for conference participants to develop programs and discussions related to issues that might surface during the conference
- issue groups for dealing with questions identified by participants during the week

In an effort to ensure that the design was workable for the group as a whole, we presented it on the first night, trying to make clear what was negotiable and what was not. For example, the planners of the program had made contracts with speakers about times for their presentations. If all the speakers were to be heard, the scheduling of presentations was not realistically negotiable, as some speakers would not be there at other times. After presenting an overview of the format, we asked participants to gather in small groups and decide whether this design would work for them. Each group was asked to write down suggested changes (if the suggestions were relatively minor), or to send a representative to meet with the steering committee later that night if the suggestions were more complex. A business meeting was planned for the next afternoon to deal with any schedule revisions, with the understanding that we would proceed with the morning panel as scheduled.

Similarly, each group was asked to make a list of questions and issues that members wanted to address during the conference. These, too, were then presented to the total group. We had planned that the steering committee would organize these according to common themes and that base groups would be formed around them. As a result of suggestions made in the total group as well as those discussed in the steering committee, this plan was altered slightly, with base groups being formed around "identity" categories, and work groups being formed around "issues" (recognizing that these two are not entirely separable!).

The steering committee presented the results of its late-night meeting to the total group the next day. Base groups were formed, with some participants choosing to be in groups formed around a common identity: educators, lesbians, Jewish women, Wicca (the Goddess religion, rooted in the pre-Christian tribal traditions of the West). Most participants, however, chose to be in groups whose members were randomly selected from among those left after the identity-based groups were formed. Work groups were also set up around the issues and questions that had been identified. It was agreed that these groups would begin meeting on Wednesday afternoon and that there would be blocks of time for collective work on these issues on Wednesday, Thursday, and Friday, with reports to the total group Friday afternoon and Saturday morning. In order to ensure ongoing input from the total group as the process developed through the week, the steering committee requested that representatives from the total group participate in its daily meetings. The group decided to elect two members who would meet with the committee for the entire week and to rotate two additional members on a daily basis.

With these process questions resolved, at least temporarily, the total group adopted the design and the conference proceeded.

In general, the process for the conference was effective in dealing with three of the four questions we had identified at the beginning: the concerns about flexibility/stability, maximum participation/minimal chaos, and small-group experience. It was less effective in dealing with the racism/anti-Semitism issues.

The only persistent problem in dealing with the flexibility/stability issue was that of timing. There were too many resource people to allow adequate time for presentations *and* ensure listener participation. On one hand, some resource people were not able to work within the thirty-minute limit, with the result that discussion/response time was cut short. On the other hand, the open spaces left in the conference schedule served the purpose of providing time for additional programs and discussions. The program as planned did not address two issues of concern to some conference participants; additional sessions were organized to discuss the Middle East and lesbianism/homophobia.

The participation/chaos question was effectively dealt with through the opening session, the business meeting, and the steering committee process. Similarly, the concern about small groups, which had initially raised some problems, was resolved by forming both base groups *and* work groups as well as providing for responses to the panels in a variety of formats.

As indicated earlier, the racism/anti-Semitism issues were issues from the beginning: most participants were White and/or Christian. Trying to deal with this problem through the conference process proved to be a weightier burden than the process itself could bear effectively. This was true on at least two levels: the failure to deal with the built-in reality "up front" meant that the responsibility for dealing with the problem fell on the panel on racism and on the process facilitators; and the division of leadership between the two process consultants resulted in an unequal distribution of power between us.

In deciding on the division of responsibilities for facilitating the sessions, the process facilitators (Cheryl, who is Black, and Nancy, who is White) decided that on the first night Cheryl would introduce the week by giving an overview of the schedule and then Nancy would facilitate the small-group process and the report-back session. At the steering committee meeting later that night, the group decided that Nancy should complete the process of dealing with the conference design by facilitating the business meeting the next afternoon. The result was that throughout the week the conference participants viewed Nancy as the person with authority in relation to the process rather than seeing Cheryl and Nancy as having shared authority. Thus, although both were facilitators for both panel presentations and responses throughout the week, Nancy was consulted by both conference planners and participants regarding process concerns. Moreover, Cheryl's authority as process facilitator was challenged. For example, when she tried to hold the group to agreed-upon time limitations for discussions, her leadership was criticized by White women (both times in sessions in which racism was being discussed), while Nancy's leadership was not challenged at all.

The issues of racism and anti-Semitism came to a focus in the panel on racism. The panel was scheduled for the third day of the conference. By that time, tension had built up around the panel. First, a conference participant had raised a question about the legitimacy of the presentation entitled "Anti-

Semitism: The Unacknowledged Racism" in view of the Lebanon/Israel situation, which at that time was extremely volatile. In addition, the panel members had had numerous meetings to deal with issues among themselves to prepare for their presentations. Some conference participants had expressed concern about what this meant, since other panels did not appear to be working in that way. At the beginning of the session, Cheryl introduced the panelists and outlined the process for the session: the panelists would each make a presentation and then discuss the issues raised among themselves; after the discussion among panelists, there would be a break, followed by a fishbowl discussion. Five observations about what followed are in order.

1. Many conference participants left the room before the panelists completed their presentations, even though they completed them in less than the allotted time.
2. The agreed-upon process was not followed because so many people left the room immediately upon the completion of the final panel presentation that a discussion among the panelists was not possible.
3. The issue of anti-Semitism in the United States as it was presented was never addressed, because the Lebanon/Israel situation became the focus of the response to the person who had made the presentation.
4. Cheryl's facilitation of the process was criticized by a White woman who had challenged some issues raised by the Black panel member.
5. It was only on the issues of racism and anti-Semitism (this panel and again later in the week in a discussion on Black feminist theology) that panel members were debated by other conference participants.

When a conference participant raised the Lebanon/Israel issue with the steering committee, the committee and the participant agreed that a separate session would provide the best forum for discussion. This decision was reached because the panel as planned was already large and was focused around a U.S. context, and because the Middle East situation was both complex and highly charged; a combination of the two issues appeared to be too much for one panel. A separate session on the Lebanon/Israel issue was organized for later in the week and proved to be very helpful and clarifying. The issue of anti-Semitism in the women's movement as raised by the racism panel was not addressed by the group as a whole, however, nor was the issue of racism. It was only in a work group on racism, classism, and sexism, and through that group's report to the total group, that issues posed by the panelists as well as problems in the planning of the conference and in the process design were addressed.

Clearly, in an event such as this, the issues addressed are determined, at least in part, by those who are participants in the program. Racism and anti-Semitism were not the primary issues for most people present. This fact has important implications for planning and implementing conferences and other educational events: feminists committed to bonding among women must find ways of working together across barriers of race, class, and religion in planning as well as in implementing such events. This will ensure that the questions addressed and the resource people invited will reflect the diversity envisioned in women's spiritual bonding, and will enhance the possibility of a more diverse group of conference participants.

Cheryl Giles
Nancy Richardson
Process Facilitators

Part I

Women and Poverty

MARY I. BUCKLEY'S paper begins with a succinct summary of the devastating economic position of women in the United States: women in dead-end jobs, single mothers, elderly women, widows, Black women, Hispanic women, divorced women, women who are heads of families. Among the proximate causes of women's poverty, Buckley points to the segregated job market; discrimination in wages, insurance, and social security payments; the rapid increase in female-headed households; and the discriminatory character of the Reagan administration's budget cuts. But beyond these immediate factors loom the structural causes of oppression, which Buckley identifies as the interlocking systems of patriarchy, capitalism, and racism. After briefly analyzing each of these systems, she concludes that these systems are not unchangeable, and she suggests steps that women can take, ranging from the immediate work of building an autonomous women's political bloc to the long-term task of developing a Christian feminist theology to challenge unjust traditions and develop a liberating vision.

Jackie Di Salvo puts the question of the economic oppression of women into the broadest possible context: an analysis of the relations of gender, class, and religion from the earliest human societies to the present conservative political administration and religiously inspired right-wing backlash. Boldly sketching a theoretical overview based on the contrasts between matrilineal clan societies and patriarchal class societies, she traces the consequences for the position of women and the character of religion of each of these forms. Bringing her analysis to bear upon present-day problems, she focuses her conclusions around two poles: a political strategy for feminists, and a religious strategy for revolutionaries. Her thesis: an economy dominated by a small elite will tend to find legitimation in a patriarchal hierarchical religion. These mutually supportive institutions combine to create the worst of all possible worlds for women: restriction of women's roles to a private, domestic realm sharply separated from the public sphere; dependence of women and children on a male provider; sexual repression and control of women by their male relatives; demonization of women as sinful and seductive temptresses; introjection by women of a spirituality of docility, guilt, and expiation.

Indicating the applicability of this analysis to the present, Di Salvo insists that a movement focused on consciousness-raising and anti-discrimination, while necessary, is not sufficient. If women are to have choices beyond the current debilitating options of childlessness, marital dependency, or destitution, they must work for a radical restructuring of society that will change both the class structure and the sexual division of labor. To move toward such restructuring, feminism will need to join forces with all women, especially poor and minority women, and with all oppressed groups.

Finally, addressing herself to social revolutionaries, Di Salvo points out that the religion Marx dismissed as "the opiate of the people" was precisely the traditional hierarchical structure that legitimated class society. She suggests that just as capitalism exploits the workers and robs them of the surplus value of their work, so hierarchical religion strips the people of their immanent spiritual powers. In support of her conviction that a religion that is available to the masses and that builds on their own spiritual energies could enhance the revolution, she points to the Jewish prophets, the Christian millennarians, the English Puritans. Finally, she asks to what extent a social movement inspired by prophetic intuitions and using symbolic rituals might rouse and direct popular energies.

Women, Poverty, and Economic Justice
MARY I. BUCKLEY

The growing impoverishment of women in the United States has been called "the feminization of poverty." Many women dislike the phrase, because it hides the fact that women have always been the poorest of the poor. Elizabeth Reid, the Australian feminist, insists that women are the marginal among the marginal throughout the world.[1] If men are poor, women and children are even poorer. If we look at the United States over the last two decades we find overwhelming evidence for the growing impoverishment of women. For vast numbers of women the United States is becoming a workhouse without walls. This condition is growing apace under the Reagan administration. Social programs that despite their inadequacy at least provided a network of help against destitution are now being dismantled by massive budget cuts.

The National Advisory Council on Economic Opportunity in its final report (September 1981) had this to say: "All other things being equal, if the proportion of the poor in female-householder families were to continue to increase at the same rate as it did from 1967 to 1978, the poverty population would be composed solely of women and their children before the year 2000."

Women in Poverty

In preparing this article I examined many studies on the condition of women, especially working-class women, in the United States. The following facts, drawn from the studies consulted, give a picture of the poverty of women in America.[2]

4 Women and Poverty

- Two out of three adults who fall under the federal definition of poverty are women; and more than half the families defined as poor are maintained by single, separated, divorced, deserted, or widowed women. In this affluent country 24 million people fall below the poverty line and 30 million of the working poor barely survive above this line.
- Between 1969 and 1977 there has been a great increase in out-of-wedlock births, especially to teenagers: a 49 percent increase among Black women, a 35 percent increase among White. Many of these young mothers are on welfare.
- The number of female-headed families with children increased by 81 percent during the 1970s. Approximately one third of these live below the poverty level.
- Many women are divorced or deserted and they have the care of children. Divorce for multitudes of women ends membership in the middle class; many must ask for welfare or survive just above the poverty line.
- Courts are punitive to divorced women in granting child support. Forty percent of departed fathers contribute nothing; the remaining 60 percent contribute on the average less than $2000 a year.
- Many women in need do not go on welfare right away. They try to work. But day-care centers for the children are few, and they are now being cut back farther.
- Many of the "workfare" jobs President Reagan talks about would net less than welfare—and who will care for the children?
- The jobs that most women get are dead-end jobs—minimum wage jobs. Most have no fringe benefits and carry no unemployment insurance. They yield low social security benefits when one is old. Women average just over $10,000 dollars a year: men average $21,000. For most women a job is no answer to poverty.
- Most available jobs for women are in a sexual ghetto: clerical work, sales, light manufacturing, a variety of service jobs. Many seem like extensions of work in the home. Jobs that are considered women's jobs are low-paying jobs.
- There is a dual job market and a dual welfare system. In the primary job market, upward mobility is to some extent possible; in the primary welfare system, welfare is considered a

right, e.g., unemployment insurance, health insurance, social security payments. In the secondary job market, jobs are minimum wage or less with little advancement; the secondary welfare system is coordinated with this market: food stamps, ADC (Aid to Dependent Children), Medicaid. The secondary welfare system carries a stigma. It is in the secondary job market and the secondary welfare system that most poor women find themselves.

- Older women face much higher risks of poverty than do men. Two out of five Black elderly women are poor. Women receive smaller amounts of social security because they have been at home or working at poorly paid jobs.

The immediate causes for the growing impoverishment of women are not difficult to identify. First, despite all the efforts to secure equal pay for equal work, women earn, on the average 59¢ for every $1 men earn. Many work part time and therefore receive no fringe benefits. Because women often have less training than men, they are more easily locked into low-paying jobs. Second, the reality of our world is that women are more likely than ever to be on their own, with children to support. Most women work "the double day," first on the job and then at home. Day-care centers are essential for women heads of families, but good day care is hard to find and expensive, and receives little support from public funds.

To this already dismal picture, government budget cuts have added further devasting consequences. There have been cutbacks in food stamps, food programs, school lunches, family planning help, Medicaid and Medicare, educational help, energy assistance, Aid to Dependent Children, legal services, and unemployment funds. A brochure entitled *Inequality of Sacrifice: The Impact of the Reagan Budget on Women*[3] clearly shows that the cutbacks have been most harmful to women.

Why are women so vulnerable? To understand why women are so poor in our wealthy societies, it is necessary to analyze the structural causes of their oppression. Three mighty systems of injustice are locked together, keeping women in dependence, poverty, and powerlessness: patriarchy is one, and capitalism is another. The widespread structure of racial oppression is yet a third framework which ensures that the poorest women will be women of color.

Patriarchy

Patriarchy is the rule of men in the overall shaping of human life, from the public realm to the most personal domain. Adrienne Rich gives the following definition: "Patriarchy is the power of the fathers: a familial-social, ideological, political system in which men—by force, direct pressure, or through ritual, tradition, law and language, customs, etiquette, education and division of labor—determine what part women shall or shall not play, and in which the female everywhere is subsumed under the male."[4]

Is women's subordination God-ordained? A young woman once asked this question in class, so fully established and internalized has the patriarchal order become! Patriarchy has an almost universal presence and is yet historically flexible, adapting itself to different times and economies.

The core of patriarchy is the control of women's sexuality by men and men's institutions. Women are by nature the bearers of children; but that in addition they are often the exclusive nurturers of children (and often the nurturers of men as well) is not something natural but a social and political construction. Motherhood has a biological base, but that women are designated as the nurturers in society is a cultural manipulation of their biology. To keep women in this fixed situation, men control all other options for women. Motherhood as a cultural construction is replicated from generation to generation. Zillah Eisenstein writes:

> The reproduction of gender roles supplies society with the most basic form of hierarchial social organization. The woman as mother reveals woman's role in the reproduction of the species most easily. Derived from this are the most subtle forms of patriarchal organization—the sexual division of labor in the labor force, the division between public and private life, and the divorce of political and family life.... Women defined as mothers structures the "either/or" mentality.[5]

Women are the primary parents, for child-rearing and child-nurturing are seen as women's vocation. Women are seen as caring, emotional, dependent beings. This view of motherhood cuts a woman off from the public domain. Her role is to help and to support a man, and to care for the children and the house. This is not seen as work (or it is seen as a work of love), for she receives no payment for it. If women must work for wages—and more and more women do—the great majority of jobs open to them are extensions of this nurturing task and are minimum wage jobs with little or no upward mobility.

Capitalism

The second framework that fosters oppression is present-day capitalism. Capitalism is an economic system based on the competitive market, and therefore aims at an ever-expanding technology and the maximization of production.

Capitalism enriches the owners of industries while it makes the workers and other wage earners dependent and vulnerable. Capitalism aims at increasing the profit of owners and shareholders and hence remains indifferent to the common good and to the sector of the population that is pushed into poverty. The market serves the strong. The working people, although they constitute the great majority, are highly stratified in terms of income and are also divided in their loyalties. Some are much better off than others, but even the former remain wage earners without ownership of productive property. Capitalism creates classes, an aspect of the economic system that has often gone unrecognized. While capitalism usually favors political democracy, the propertied interests in the United States have worked diligently against the growth of economic democracy. Capitalism is also inimical to democracy in its own organizations. Capitalist corporations are organized on strictly hierarchical lines. For this reason, patriarchy suits capitalism well.

The subjugation of women has been used by capitalism in a variety of ways. It symbolizes hierarchical control. More than that, women represent a labor market that can easily be manipulated. When workers are needed, women are encouraged to take jobs (e.g., Rosie the Riveter in World War II); and when fewer workers are needed, cultural trends are created that urge women to return to the home and the care of their families. Capitalist society, moreover, is in need of vast numbers of menial services for very low pay. Such tasks are likely to be performed by people of low status, people who cannot make their voices heard, among them especially women. At this low level, women find themselves in competition with non-White men. At present, as William Tabb has noted, women constitute a reserve army of workers willing to work even under extremely exploitative conditions.[6] And because of their presence, the people presently employed remain docile, afraid to protest against low pay and poor conditions.

Patriarchy and capitalism have become intertwined. But these systems are not unchangeable. What is needed is the entry of democracy and the dismantling of hierarchy in the economic system itself. As people are now collectively responsible for their political life, they will have to become collectively responsible for their economic life, i.e., the production and distribution of goods. There is more than enough work for all if the cities are to be made habitable again, if there is to be sufficient housing, if people are to work toward a sustainable future in the use of energy and natural resources. It is possible that political democracy can shape an economic democracy, if people become more aware of the injustices they suffer and learn to build effective coalitions that work for change.

Racism

The third grave system of injustice is racism. Some people think this evil has been overcome in the United States, but the presence of the non-White ghettos in every big city of the country proves this is an illusion. What Kenneth Clark wrote in 1967 remains true today: "The dark ghettos are social, political, educational, and—above all—economic colonies. Their inhabitants are subject people, victims of the greed, cruelty, insensitivity, guilt and fear of their masters."[7]

Racism fulfills a special function in the capitalist system. Like women, Blacks and other minorities are also the last hired and the first fired. Racism protects the reserve army of the unemployed. Black and minority women are especially vulnerable, as the three systems of oppression—sexism, classism, and racism—converge on them. More than 45 percent of Black families are now headed by women, compared to 31 percent in 1970. This is not due to Black matriarchy; it is due rather to the skyrocketing unemployment among Black and minority men. Sixty percent of Black teenage males are unemployed. Many Black and minority men are psychically destroyed in an economic situation that puts the White standard of manliness—a steady job to be a provider—beyond their reach. Here society itself does not allow them to fulfill the role that patriarchy has assigned them.

This brief analysis of the interrelationship between sexism, classism, and racism in the subjugation of women demonstrates that the cause of poor women is the cause of all women.

What Can Women Do?

Both immediate and long-range work are needed. Only a few suggestions will be put forward here.
- The work of education and of raising consciousness remains central. The facts are not widely known, and the analysis of the facts must grow deeper.
- The cause of poor women is the cause of all women. While acknowledging the differences among women, we must resist the use of the great dividers—race, class, religion, ethnic background, sexuality—to split the women's movement. We must be on guard against divide-and-conquer tactics arising from racial discrimination, control of women's sexuality, and control of women's economic independence.
- We need an autonomous women's political bloc along the lines of Women USA as organized by Bella Abzug and others. We cannot relinquish the network of social programs that has been assembled in the past fifty years in the United States. Although inadequate, they fend off the worst destitution. An autonomous women's bloc, representing women's issues across racial, religious, and class lines, is essential to save these programs. Such a bloc must also work hand in hand with other coalitions.
- We need to consider a new economic order. It is not enough to affirm day care, affirmative action, and equal pay for

comparable work, as important as all these are. A just economic order that affirms people over profits and that seeks the common good of all must be envisioned and fought for.

- Christian women need to work together with the women of other traditions for these goals. At the same time, there is a need to build a Christian feminist theology that questions all that is unjust and evil in the tradition, while searching out the liberating strands of Christian faith. This work is only beginning. Women's experience must be allowed to challenge the long tradition.
- We need a women's bloc in the churches too, to put forward women's issues and to work in coalition with other groups for a vital church and a relevant theology.

2

Class, Gender, and Religion: A Theoretical Overview and Some Political Implications
JACKIE DI SALVO

> *To the woman [God] said, "I will greatly multiply your pain in childbearing ... yet your desire shall be for your husband, and he shall rule over you." And to Adam he said, "Because you have listened to the voice of your wife, and have eaten of the tree of which I commanded you, 'You shall not eat of it' cursed is the ground because of you; in toil you shall eat of it all the days of your life.... In the sweat of your face you shall eat bread till you return to the ground, for out of it you were taken; you are dust, and to dust you shall return.*
> —GENESIS 3:16–19

In many cultures there is a central story, which has been called a "myth of origins" or "charter myth" because it serves virtually as the constitution of the society, validating its central values and institutions. For several years now, feminist thinkers have produced thousands of books, articles, films, and poems that attempt to unravel the cultural warp and institutional woof of our collective condition. The opposition, significantly, seems to want to rest its rebuttal on a single text—Genesis—which it is attempting to impose, through the public school curriculum, on the imaginations of the majority of American children.

Indeed, the Genesis story of creation and fall (as John Milton instinctively understood when he wrote his epic celebration of the rise of patriarchal, bourgeois society) does provide a legitimizing myth for this society. For there women's inequality, the sufferings of poverty, the miseries of labor, the need for punishment, the repression of sexuality, and the possession of property all find absolute sanction in the will of an all-

Jackie Di Salvo

powerful Creator and Ruler of the universe. Opposition to such conditions appears, therefore, as a futile exercise of the same proud humanism through which the species exchanged a happy for a wretched subordination in the first place. Or rather, of a proud feminism, for the "sin" responsible for all human woe is a woman's remarkable assertion of her right to be herself "as God," in an act of self-determination that confidently dismisses the authority of both an earthly and a heavenly patriarch. Her flagrant violation of their rules can consequently be seen not as criminal, but as revolutionary. In challenging paternal authority and thus the family itself, she is a feminist; in seeking forbidden knowledge, a heretic; in asserting her appetites, a libertine; in consorting with the serpent, a proponent of free love. Since she joins her consort in conspiring against authority, she is a subversive; in appropriating the apple, she indicates her contempt for private property; in defying the Lawgiver, she becomes an anarchist; and in affirming her own divinity, she becomes an atheist—or worse, some kind of pagan witch.

Karl Marx himself explains that the idea of creation presented in Genesis retains its hold on the popular consciousness despite the most massive intellectual critique because it reflects our continuing inability to create and determine our own lives in a society run by powers beyond our control.[1]

Recognizing the biblical Ruler-Creator as the legitimator of a hierarchic and patriarchal social order, William Blake named him "Nobodaddy" and castigated him in his satiric version of the Lord's Prayer.

> Our Father, Augustus Caesar, who art in these thy Substantial Telescopic Astronomical Heavens, Holiness to thy Name or Title, & reverence to thy Shadow. Thy Kingship come upon Earth first & then in Heaven. Give us day by day our Real Taxed Substantial Money-bought Bread & deliver from the Holy Ghost whatever cannot be Taxed; for all is debts and Taxes between Caesar & us and one another . . . & deliver us from Poverty in Jesus, that Evil One. For thine is the Kingship or Allegoric Godship, & the Power, or War, & the Glory or Law, Ages after Ages in thy descendants; for God is only an Allegory of Kings & nothing else.
>
> Amen.[2]

The interrelationships among gender, class, and religion become evident when one looks at the genealogy of this concept of Godhead. I will focus on a feminist and class analysis of religious orthodoxy and then speculate on how a spiritual perspective might enhance or detract from the struggle against oppression. In order to develop a comprehensive paradigm with implications for political strategy, I will assume many things that could not be assumed in an article with a narrower focus. Although I make controversial generalizations, I can point to a significant body of scholarship that attempts to substantiate similar views.[3]

Overthrow of the Goddess: A Babylonian Myth of Origins

A myth of origins that predates Genesis by some millennia has clearly influenced the biblical text. The Babylonian Genesis *(Enuma Elish)* is the oldest of those many mythic analogues in which an upstart King of Heaven conquers an original Mother Goddess of Earth, in direct contrast to Genesis, where a female rebel challenges a preexistent male authority. In the more archaic myths, the institutions and values rendered universal by Genesis's Creator-King appear as the result of a process in which the Royal Father himself emerges as a product of evolution.

According to this myth, in the beginning there was only Tiamat, the Great Mother, identified with the moon, the earth, and the primeval ocean, source of the universe and the Gods, all themselves nature daimons. After she has parthenogenetically conceived all things, including her son-lover, they together give birth to subsequent generations of deities. Eventually these dynamic, younger Gods challenge their parents' cyclical order of nature, and war ensues. Meeting as a heavenly council, Tiamat's rebellious progeny elect Marduk (Sun God and patron of Babylon) as their leader, much as tribal assemblies would confer chieftaincy on temporary military leaders. Marduk, however, demands that the council permanently abdicate their collective powers and designate him as Supreme God, King of the Gods and the universe.

The battle itself provides an interesting contrast. Tiamat is championed by Kingu, a totemic, snakelike monster that traditionally signified the life force itself, and she seems to summon psychic powers for a kind of shamanic duel; she "became as one possessed . . . lost her reason, uttered wild, piercing screams, trembled, shook to the roots of her limbs, pronounced an incantation."[4] Marduk relies on a horse-drawn storm chariot, solar flames, and a new military technology. His victory (which indicated the limits of psychic as opposed to technological power in certain arenas) is used to denounce totally the more intuitive powers. Marduk splits Tiamat in half like a shellfish and claims to create heaven and earth out of her severed body.

Marduk, as alleged Creator of the universe, now asserts his power as owner and ruler of it—much like the God of Genesis, who promulgates laws for Eden and evicts undesirables from his property. Next Marduk creates humanity out of the gore of Kingu to be a race of slaves so that the Gods might live in leisure. In doing so he establishes a divine paradigm for human society, where the aristocracy will claim their own divine origin and the bestial origin of their slaves as justification for class rule.

Marduk then constructs Babylon as a temple city centered around the ziggurat. Enthroned there in its tower, linking heaven and earth, the Priest-King rules as Marduk's representative. Thus, one such ruler, Hammurabi, has written in his divinely sanctioned legal code:

> When they made Marduk great among the gods . . . made Babylon unsurpassable in the regions of the world, and established for him in its midst an everlasting kingdom, . . . at that time Anu and Bel [Mesopotamian Gods] called to me, Hammurabi, . . . to bring about the rule of righteousness in the land . . . to go forth like the sun over the human race, to illuminate the land.[5]

Here, like Marduk, his royal surrogate is a solar figure, and, hence, his domination represents a triumph of reason or a bringing of enlightenment. In the old lunar system time was reckoned by the senses, and human beings sought to align themselves through ritual magic with natural cycles. But the discovery of the solar calendar, through sophisticated astronomy and mathematics, allowed humanity to exert a new power of prediction and subsequent control over the agricultural cycle, particularly where irrigation works sought to harness the power of annual floods. Thus, on one level, Marduk's conquest of Tiamat's dark and fertile forces of earth and sea represents a progressive conquest of nature by growing knowledge. In warfare, city building, architecture, and astronomy (he establishes the zodiac) Marduk, like many other solar deities, is an Apollonian hero of triumphant civilization.

At the same time, however, this victory involves rational control over the dark powers within human beings themselves, powers of procreation, eroticism, intuition, ecstasy, and the magic or imaginative will revered in the fertility cult. An orgiastic culture yields to a religion of reason and law here, as in Genesis, where God creates by his Word, bringing order from chaos, and Adam establishes his dominion over the animals by naming them. Genesis, no less than its Babylonian analogue, must finally be understood as a polemic against the ancient cult of Earth, everywhere signified by a divine woman, by the fruit tree that was the gift of her fertility, and by the snake consort who lived in her womb-tomb and symbolized the cycle of nature. Its celebration of the forces of enlightenment must, however, be set alongside its powerful nostalgia for her lost garden with its evocation of psychic and natural harmony.

Class, Gender and Religion: Two Models

The *Enuma Elish* was not written as history, but as polemic. It was recited at annual reinvestiture rites where the people renewed their vows to Marduk and the king who played his part in the drama of conquest. By establishing the society's authorities in the order of creation itself, such rites warded off challenges from disgruntled forces that might group around images of a happier past. I contend that one can find historical significance behind myths of the overthrow of the Great Mother, namely the breakup of preclass, clan societies, and the growth of a class-divided urban society organized under a theocratic state. Apart from such a historical argument, however, I suggest two paradigms, presented below in a highly simplified and schematic form. These paradigms emerge from my thesis that there is a close relationship between economic class domination, the oppression of women, and the promotion of reactionary religion, whether in ancient or modern civilization, just as one might draw from preclass societies inferences about the interrelationships among class, gender, and spirituality one might seek in a future, liberated society.

Preclass Societies	Class Societies
\multicolumn{2}{c}{General Characteristics}	

General Characteristics

Preclass Societies	Class Societies
• collective, subsistence economy, clan control of the land	• overthrow of the collective economy, control of means of production and of surplus production by an elite
• extended, often matrilineal kinship groups collectively responsible for nonproducers—children, aged, disabled	• development of family unit as responsible for nonproducers
• minimal split between public and domestic realms	• sharp distinction between public and domestic spheres
• no inheritance	• linking of marriage and inheritance

Consequences for Women

- greater variety and value in female roles
- economic independence for women as producers
- greater sexual freedom and autonomy for women
- greater political and ritual participation by women

- isolation of women in family
- economic dependence of women on male providers
- sexual repression and control of women by male relatives
- atomization and impoverishment of masses who lose access to productive resources; enslavement of lower-class men as well as women

Religious Consequences

- reverence for the maternal principle in women and in nature
- spiritual power viewed as immanent in all people

- communal enactment of ritual
- ritual experienced as participation of humans in cosmic energies
- emotional and ecstatic techniques for intensifying individual and group energies
- integration of spiritual, sexual, productive, artistic in ritual

- social and sexual hierarchies projected into a transcendent realm
- supernatural realm detached from experience, God superior to humanity
- God:man = man:woman = ruler:ruled = master:slave = spirit:body = reason:passion
- priestly mediation
- ritual experienced as submission to superior being

- demonizing of the subordinate elements: women, nature, sexuality, lower classes
- introjection into the powerless of a spirituality of asceticism and expiation

The Rise of the State and the Decline of Women

The transition from procreative Goddesses to ruler Gods can be shown to reflect changes in the political and kinship organizations of the ancient world. The reverence offered the Mother of All Living in ancient horticultural societies arose not only from their awe of the procreative forces of nature, but also from the validation in myth of kinship structure based on matrilineal clans composed of all the children of common female ancestors. In such cultures one finds subsistence agriculture under relatively egalitarian and cooperative economic and political arrangements: clan control of the land, some common labor, rule by all the elders, and collective kin responsibility for dependents, particularly children.

With the growth of a surplus, trade, and private property—a trend exacerbated by the waves of nomads with their private cattle wealth, who entered and conquered the region—clan society began to break up. The community divided into atomized families sharply divided by economics, as some became leisured landowners and others impoverished serfs and slaves. Consequently, a strong centralized state emerged to contain the struggles for wealth, to administer a growing surplus, and to represent the powerful class. Ultimately, in Mesopotamia, a class-divided urban society developed under the theocratic rule of aristocratic priests who governed economic, political, military, and religious affairs. Dwelling in the temple-palace, they supervised lands belonging to "the God," oversaw public works and the agricultural and artisan labor of slaves and serfs, and collected from poor farmers the tributes required as sacrifices to "the God."

In this transition, women were particularly the losers. Current scholarship does not support the idea of a lost matriarchal golden age of female domination, or even an era devoid of gender roles. What numerous feminist scholars will contend, however, is that the more egalitarian a society was generally, the greater was the status of women, and that with the rise of hierarchic, class societies women suffered a serious decline. Where matrilineal descent coincided with more equal access to land and subsistence, women's dignity benefited from their greater economic independence, based on their own participation in production and their reliance on siblings for assistance in raising their children. With no husband liable for such support, women were likely to be allowed greater sexual autonomy, since it hardly mattered who fathered the children. Moreover, since there would be little division between a public and a domestic sphere in simpler societies, child-rearing would not bar women from full economic participation. Instead the encompassing nature of the domestic realm often made women the primary producers in gardening and related crafts, such as weaving and pottery. Greater political and ritual participation probably accompanied such economic status. Indeed, one finds a preponderance of female sacred images, derived from the analogy perceived between female maternity and earthly fertility, often accompanied by a celebration of other female functions, as in the association of weaving with many of the ancient Goddesses.

Primitive societies were, nevertheless, characterized by a sharp sexual division of labor, with childbearing inevitably (although not always exclusively) setting the conditions for other female activities. What was defined as male or female otherwise could vary widely between cultures, and, depending on other social conditions, women might be judges, farmers, shamans, priestesses, potters, traders, sometimes even hunters or warriors. Maternal responsibilities were compatible with any number of occupations until the domestic sphere became isolated from the public. This development, through the substitution for household gardens of larger, more distant ox-ploughed fields or the relocation of craftsmen in urban trading centers, undermined the status of women's work. When the breakup of the clan rendered women dependent on individual men for child support, maternity was transformed from an asset to a liability. Women became economically dependent, the work they did less valued.

For poorer men, this process involved a loss of power; the new economic responsibility for wives and children once supported collectively became a terrible burden, reflected in the curse of toil the God of Genesis imposed on the monogamous and patriarchal Adam. The wives of the aristocracy were, in fact, supported by the exploitation of these same laborers. At the same time elite women were themselves reduced to powerless breeders of heirs, and men of all classes sought to control female sexuality and, consequently, female independence in general, lest unwanted bastards lay claim to private resources.

Class Structure and Religious Ideology

Religious ideology came to mirror these new conditions, as the rise of patriarchal Gods and male priesthoods was accompanied by a denigration of the earlier female iconography in hundreds of mythic revisions, which produced Eve, Pandora, the promiscuous and dangerous Aphrodite, etc., ad nauseam. Poor, illiterate men would have had little part in the creation of this new culture, and it is likely that they as well as their wives hung on as best they could to their old, local nature cults against the threats of priestly orthodoxy, whose royal Father God reflected the world view of a tiny elite.

The rise of temple religion led simultaneously to other significant changes in religious experience. The old fertility rites had been more a culture than a religion. The emphasis was on natural forces, not on divine beings, and any anthropomorphizing probably reflected the effect of human actors taking the roles of natural elements in ritual drama. Regard for the earth's fecundity might appear as the honoring of a female Goddess, because a priestess enacted Mother Earth. But the actual worship of beings outside of and superior to humanity probably awaited the experience of such domination in society.

In ancient ritual, the focus was on participation in an energy force believed to pervade nature and humanity, body and psyche. Emile Durkheim has suggested that the religious principle arose from the collective superexcitation of the clan, which was experienced by every participant as an impersonal, infectious power *(mana)* that was presumed to emanate from their sacred symbols. Thus, all the arts—drama, myth, music, dance, and visual icon, as well as various orgiastic and hallucinogenic practices—were used to intensify human energies in ritual. The symbolism of fertility itself celebrated the transformations of *mana* as it passed between nature and humanity in the cycles of birth and death, planting, harvesting, and eating. At the same time, these symbolic rites actually did enhance procreative and agricultural activities, reconciling the inevitable limitations of individual life, death, and sacrifice through a joyous merger with the life force itself. Such rituals united all the aspects of human experience that would become divided and even antagonistic in later civilization, simultaneously celebrating procreation and production, work and art, sexuality, spirituality, and social solidarity. In this context, the spiritual had nothing to do with the separate supernatural realm to which it would later refer; rather it seemed to designate an altered state of consciousness that heightened but did not depart from ordinary life. The connection between the words for spirit and breath in many languages suggests this realm of intensified life energy. No doubt such cultures could achieve more through breathing techniques than later systems based upon mind-body dualism would ever know anything about.

With the rise of patriarchy and the hierarchic, theocratic state, a priesthood seemed to usurp spiritual as well as economic prerogatives and drastically to alter religious conceptions. The myths of this priesthood, as we have seen, proclaim a conquest of the old symbolic totems by a new breed of anthropomorphic, supernatural Gods divorced from human experience or limitation. On a psychic level, the conquest of the animal and chthonic daimons signifies a sacrifice of the powers of participation—the energies of passion, the animal acuteness of the senses, and an intuitive, poetic logic of identification (knowing things by merging with them)—to a new, more alienated knowledge in which both nature and the Gods are deemed separate from self.

Marx has pointed out that the metaphysical inversion in which real life is perceived as derived from the Gods, rather than vice versa, directly parallels social development. Thus elites, like their creator Gods, claimed credit for the civilization building that was, in fact, entirely accomplished by the labor of slaves who had to live outcast and hungry in the world they had made. Thus, for Marx, "Man . . . looked for a superman in the fantastic reality of heaven and found nothing there but the reflection of himself. But man is no abstract being squatting outside the world. Man is the world of man, the state, society. This state, this society produces religion, a reversed world consciousness because they are a reversed world."[6] The religious hierarchy of God over humanity and nature, of spirit over body and reason over passion, in part indicated a new domination of nature by humanity. More pointedly, it signified the new hierarchy of king over subjects, master over slave, priest over laity, and father over wife and children. A reverence for life, perhaps insufficiently anthropomorphic, passed into a debilitating worship of authority.

The triumphant forces in these equations tended to demonize all that had been subordinated: woman, nature, sexuality, emotion, and the potentially rebellious lower class. On one hand, the elites projected their own domination onto the Gods; on the other hand, they encouraged the introjection of social impotence into the people's psyches. Such powerlessness was rationalized through concepts of human sinfulness, the expiatory value of suffering and sacrifice, the virtue of asceticism, and the continual psychic humiliation inculcated by religious practices. This "devastation of the spirit" has been described by William Blake.

> Then Man ascended mourning into the splendors of his palace
> Above him rose a Shadow from his wearied intellect
> Of living gold, pure, perfect, holy; in white linen pure he hover'd
> A sweet entrancing self delusion, a watery vision of Man
> Soft exulting in existence all the Man absorbing
> Man fell upon his face prostrate before the watery shadow
> Saying O Lord whence is this change thou knowest I am nothing. . . .
> Idolatrous to his own shadow words of Eternity uttering
> O I am nothing when I enter into judgment with thee
> If thou withdraw thy breath I die and vanish into Hades.[7]

Despite this cultural and psychological catastrophe, an alternative world view survived as the subterranean basis of new orthodox symbols and practices, as a heretical underground tradition found in various spiritual movements right up to and beyond seventeenth-century witchcraft, and as the secret language of literature and art.

The role of women in such pagan survivals as witchcraft is significant, because the gender split is one of the most spiritually disastrous aspects of an intensified division of labor. Mothering becomes more exclusively a female function, as women are increasingly secluded within a domestic sphere. But mothering as revered in the ancient Goddess cult suggested a whole range of psychological experiences that were symbolized by the symbiotic relationship. The child at the mother's breast remained a symbol of spiritual consolation even under patriarchal Christianity, and the dream of paradise, the garden of the Goddess, has been traced back to the psychic experience of infancy, in which, as Norman O. Brown once put it, the child experiences a tranquil "being at-one-with-the-world" in which "Reality is its mother."[8]

But in clan society, it might be said, the whole community was one's mother, and nature was revered as a loving and maternal force. Within such a framework, human beings pursued a spiritual harmony with the "other" that tapped psychological powers rejected by patriarchy and virtually forbidden to adult men. Women, therefore, as the guardians of the symbiotic experience, may have retained unique spiritual capacities. Perhaps Jesus himself (a remarkably androgynous man) could not even articulate his vision adequately within the patriarchal language of his tradition. Would not the gospel, with its old tribal language of "brotherhood," have been less easily misunderstood and less susceptible to splitting spiritual and material needs if Jesus had simply said, as did the old Goddess culture, "Mother one another"? Has not the problem with much spirituality been that it has been perverted into emotional bankruptcy in the service of socialization into the repressiveness of a subservient feminine role or an either tyrannical or alienating masculine function? The psychic splits engendered in much orthodox Western religion are profoundly rooted in both its gender and its class division.

Some Political Implications

Subsequent history clearly alters many of the factors identified with the development of a patriarchal class society in the ancient world. Specific attributes of the division of labor (including the sexual), forms of economic exploitation and political dominion, the amount of segregation between the domestic and public spheres, the apportioning of responsibility for dependents between family and society, and the forms in which these relationships are reflected in the ideological sphere have been transformed in modern society. Nevertheless, the fundamental relationships of class, gender, and religion remain defined by oppressive hierarchies in the present as in the past. Perhaps because the subjugation of women is one of the earliest oppressions, rooted in circumstances that have prevailed since the breakup of the clan, a consideration of that ancient social structure can illuminate contemporary relationships. In some form, the factors I have pinpointed will continue to define both the status of women and the nature of spiritual life in class society.

The state of the American nation today makes this frighteningly clear. The modern equivalent of the theocratic oligarchy can be found in the tiny elite that owns and runs the multinational corporations which dominate our social existence so completely that the tendency to call the elite "Babylon" in Reggae music appears entirely appropriate. For over a decade the U.S. economy has been in a severe crisis, which that elite has been trying to resolve to its own advantage by what United Automobile Workers president Douglas Fraser once called "class war from above." The slashing of the "safety net"—created during the Depression to prevent the vagaries of a competitive economy from threatening the very existence of those barred from wage labor by old age, disability, or unemployment—represents an almost complete abandonment of social responsibility for people's survival. Women and minorities have become the handiest target of this attack; measures won to promote their greater equality are being dismantled or rendered inoperative. Within this context the resurgence of right-wing religious groups—preaching a biblical fundamentalism of sexual repression, patriarchal family order, the return of women to their "proper place" in the home, and an economic fatalism in which "the poor you have always with you"—was to be expected.

Some general principles of political strategy and spiritual culture can be derived from the above analysis, but a few caveats must be observed on the relationship of theory to strategy. First, in approaching either women's problems or spiritual possibilities, one must locate them in relation to a complex totality of human social experience. Since aspects of that experience exist in dialectical, contradictory, and always-changing relationships, one should not assume, as some feminists do, that men are always oppressors, or, as many Marxists do, that spiritual practices are inherently reactionary. Second, the connection in the ancient world between economic development and social relations indicates that political change cannot be a matter merely of changing minds and hearts, but must presuppose the mastery of productive tasks and social organization. Consciousness-raising should be an adjunct to strategy, not a substitute for it. There are real and changing conflicts between various groups, determined by whether they benefit or suffer from particular social arrangements. It is crucial to differentiate between what have been called "antagonistic contradictions" between the people and the dominant elite and "nonantagonistic contradictions" among the people, which might be overcome with the right political program or social reconstruction. The contradiction between women and nonelite men must, therefore, be kept from becoming an "antagonistic contradiction" by a strategy that can envision elimination of the causes of the battle of the sexes. At the same time, the woman's movement must be wary of allowing the entry of women into the economic elite to divide it from the struggles of all the American people for justice. Finally, history teaches that human fulfillment involving such practical tasks can only be accomplished by stages, and that a political program or a society should be judged not on whether it solves all women's problems, but on whether it can move toward their solution.

The goal, therefore, must be to put people before profits and demand a society in which the needs of the many, including long-ignored women's needs, are placed before the privileges of the few, resulting in an economy that functions rationally to meet all human beings' needs for subsistence and personal development. Such a goal will require a merger between the struggles of women and those of all oppressed people to determine the course of their lives against the obstructions put up by corporate powers. The struggle will involve demands both for immediate reforms and for a more long-range restructuring of society. These two emphases will have to be coordinated under strategies that are grounded in accurate analyses, led by principled people, and carefully chosen to avoid the twin pitfalls of a utopianism that preaches possibility but changes very little and a shortsighted pragmatism wedded to achievements that become irrelevant almost as they are accomplished. Such a movement must be multiissue, multiconstituency, and grass roots in character, and it must be prepared to utilize a wide range of tactics, from elections to militant, direct mass action. Above all, it must be truly independent of the corporations, which are correctly viewed as an opposition that must be pressured into concessions, not a true ally.

Within such an alliance there must be an independent movement specifically for women's rights, which mobilizes the vast political force of millions of women to press their own demands without ignoring the needs of such forces as labor and minorities. This cooperation is mandated by the size of the task. Even the achievements of the women's movement are driving home the conclusion that real liberation requires a transformation of society so vast that it can only become possible through support of a broad grouping of the people. When this recent phase in women's struggle was initiated in the 1960s, it was carried on largely by young, middle-class White women seeking equal access to education and careers and mostly willing temporarily to postpone childbearing and starting families; hence, that struggle focused on consciousness-raising and antidiscrimination. On one hand, women sought access to education and jobs previously monopolized by men; on the other hand, women initiated a huge cultural movement to challenge the traditional ideological supports for their subordination and, through many new kinds of mutual encouragement, to empower them to break out of limited roles.

Such efforts presumed that this society could, in fact, provide new, more satisfying opportunities for women. The movement tended to place less emphasis, therefore, on the deeper resistance to women's advance rooted in society's relegation of child care almost entirely to individual women and in the split between that domestic realm and the sphere of production and public power. Actually, these conditions meant that the majority of women probably experienced changes in their life-styles but very little, if any, improvement. The absorption of more women into the work force in low-skilled, underpaid jobs required by an inflationary economy may have involved, on the contrary, a deterioration in their lives. Moreover, a shrinking economy, recalcitrant sexism, and disintegrating family and community bonds exacerbate the contradictions in women's situation, even for relatively privileged, educated women. Thus, women today suffer from tremendously overburdened motherhood, meaningless and exploitative jobs or lonely and still handicapped careers, and the psychological schizophrenia of functioning in a public, male-dominated realm that is hostile to female experience. In addition, there is evidence of a severe decline in economic status for many women who are now heads of impoverished households, since women's alleged new economic independence and consequent sexual "freedom" seems to have been most successful in liberating many men from the old idea that they need bear any responsibility for children, either individually or collectively.

The women's movement must, therefore, go beyond demands for nondiscrimination to wage an offensive struggle to change the material basis for women's lives. Women might find legitimacy for such reforms in the precedent offered by the European social democratic concept of the "social wage," in which some of the value produced by workers is returned to them in the form of public housing, medical care, and even a token "mother's allowance." While in America such "entitlements" have been limited to public education and a minimum "safety net" for dependent children and those unable to work, there is no reason not to voice demands for such resources for women and children; they offer women some choices other than childlessness, poverty, or marital dependency.

Women should bear in mind, however, that at present corporate politicians claim that even more limited social programs are too expensive and that it is incorrect to presume that the economy should offer continual improvements in the lot of the majority. Instead, sermons are preached about the necessity and godliness of austerity and inequality. The right wing of the corporate elite (which always reemerges in moments of intensified class struggle) is dragging out all the old religious supports for misogyny and impoverishment in this vale of tears, which must be the lot of our largely sinful race. It is unlikely, however, that many people will swallow such cant in the face of the enormous potential of modern industry and the noticeable lack of sacrifice by these blatantly luxurious elites themselves.

The right-wing economists may be accurately describing the constraints on prosperity in the system as it is presently organized. So, if women are not ready to pick up the old prayer books for directions on how to jam their psyches back into the sacrificial niches once allowed them, they will have to begin to pursue analysis and education preparatory to an eventual economic restructuring. Before the present crisis, this proposal might have seemed too radical for American politics; in the present context, even corporate leaders are realizing that some kind of restructuring away from completely unplanned and anarchic free enterprise might be required.

Even if such a revolutionary transformation of society is accomplished, many of women's problems will still remain to be solved. Women will finally have to place on the historical agenda the transformation of the sexual division of labor that has made them primarily responsible for mothering in every form of society, from primitive to socialist. Having barely begun to emerge from underdevelopment, socialist societies have either been necessarily preoccupied with creating the material basis for social change, or have become stuck in the divisions of labor maintained during this accumulation process. Only when women challenge gender roles themselves will the full possibilities of human liberation be imaginable. Feminist psychology is increasingly showing to what degree human neurosis and alienation is derived from how women are split and programmed within the gender conflicts of the patriarchal family. The extension of mothering—that is, loving and nurturing responsibilities to both sexes—holds, as Dorothy Dinnerstein has argued in *The Mermaid and the Minotaur*, the key to psychological wholeness. When women no longer search hopelessly in relationship for their lost "other half," lo! even sexual love, that tantalizing Goddess who has promised so much and often delivered so little, may become possible at last.

Some Religious Implications

At such time human beings may experience that return to Eden, the dream of which it has been the function of religion to keep alive. Until then, however, spirituality will remain highly problematic, bound up closely with the material and psychological boundaries of society. Based upon my argument for these interdependencies, I would like to make a few comments about the role of spiritual practices, negative and positive, in the process of liberating the human majority.

The Marxist critique of religion derived from the idea that worship of a supernatural God and class oppression arose hand in hand, as described earlier. Marx did not give much consideration to spiritual experience in preclass societies because not much was known about it. Neither did he comment on the spiritual dimension of a revolutionized society, because, for one thing, he considered all utopian discussions of the future to be irrelevant, since problems could only be dealt with experientially once the basis existed for solving them materially. This historical humility of Marx is usually overlooked, and his prescriptions for effectively waging the struggle against capitalism are presumed to define all the possibilities of socialism. Existing socialist practice sheds little light on this issue; the socialist countries are either totally absorbed with the basic economic struggle against underdevelopment or, in fact, have gone astray during the tremendous difficulties of that process carried out in an antagonistic international climate and are now socialist in name only. Marx did, however, point to a time when that economic task would be completed and humanity would pass finally into the "true realm of freedom."

> Socialized mankind, the associate producers, regulate their interchange with Nature rationally, bring it under common control, instead of being ruled by it as some blind power, and accomplish their task with the least expenditure of energy and under such conditions as are proper and worthy of human beings. Nevertheless, there is always a realm of necessity. Beyond it begins the

development of human potentiality for its own sake, the true realm of freedom, which, however, can only flourish upon that realm of necessity as its basis.[9]

Since Marxist theory is a generalization from history and changes with new historical developments, its orientation for spiritual and cultural life after the accomplishment of socialist construction cannot yet have been settled. Marxist analysis of religion, therefore, applies to the period of contention against capitalism and construction of socialism.

The objection might be made that Marxism, as a materialist philosophy, offers a total rejection of spiritual experience, whose pursuit is regarded as an idealist delusion. That is true of traditional Marxism, but it should be possible to adopt a slightly different standard and still be consistent with the central concerns of a Marxist world view. My own approach begins with the influence over Marx's materialist philosophy of the mind-body dualism that characterized both traditional religion and the mechanical Newtonian science of the time. He opted for a monist materialism that promised to deprive social impoverishment of ascetic justifications and promote an activist stance toward economic and social problems. Marx's materialism was not concerned with reducing human beings to molecular functions but with analyzing human material activity.

The epistemological possibilities are somewhat different today, since modern science has replaced the old dualism of matter and spirit with a new dialectic of matter and energy, now conceived as interchangeable. Invisible forms of energy—atomic, electrical etc.—provide an entirely new way of conceiving spiritual reality that has as its focus human experiences of consciousness and energy and the relationship between consciousness, energy, and matter, rather than a realm of supernatural beings outside human life. This approach is closer to the concepts of preclass societies, such as *mana*, and to mystical traditions in both the East and West.

Once the focus has shifted to spiritual experience, that experience may be subjected to the same kind of critical challenge to which a class analysis subjects any human experience. The question then becomes the one in which Mao Tse-tung summed up the whole Marxist critique: "For whom?" Who benefits, who loses, if one follows the implications of various spiritual admonitions? The question becomes a practical and strategic one of establishing what spirituality offers toward fulfilling, not a special few, but the majority of the people.

Marx once remarked that his entire theory was a science, an economics of time, an analysis of what human beings were able to do with their own time and their collective history. Here a crucial problem arises with regard to spirituality. Traditionally, the peak spiritual experiences have been reserved for the few whose time is freed from labor (by the labor of others) for contemplation. The masses, on the contrary, are fed various forms of religious practice that reconcile them to their alienating lives of menial labor. In preclass societies the lack of effort to accumulate meant a relatively high degree of leisure, which may well explain the spiritual achievements of simple societies; even when materially poor, they were time-rich. Moreover, as we have seen, their spirituality was bound up with their productive and sexual lives; hence it was a very bodily spirituality; by contrast, the spirituality of elites might seem deformed and repressive. Within an exploitative society whose workers are reduced to mental and physical exhaustion by deprivation or by debilitating or tedious labor, the workers' first goals must necessarily be their liberation from that misery before they can hope for any greater fulfillment. The question of spirituality is in this sense identical to that of art in its relationship to material needs and exertions. The few who have had the luxury of mystical practices, like the artists, have undoubtedly contributed to the understanding of human possibilities, but at this stage of history human beings must not be satisfied with individual witness to that potential but must seek its mass achievement. The reactionary tendencies in ecclesiastical organizations have led Marxists to denounce religion as "the opiate of the people," but the full context of this remark is worth considering: "Religion is the sigh of the oppressed creature, the heart of a heartless world, the spirit of a spiritless civilization. It is the opiate of the people."[10]

Marx suggests that religion has arisen from the denial of human material needs, but one might include here the denial of spiritual needs as well. Instead of seeing all spirituality as a delusion based on primitive ignorance or civilized alienation, one might argue alternatively that just as the development of class society involved an economic and political usurpation of the masses' rights and resources, so too the development of religion involved a spiritual swindle. Thus, the expression of immanent human energies and potentialities of consciousness were systematically denied to the majority by a system that sought their demoralization as a mode of control, and all aspirations to such experience were redirected into the worship of Gods who became a projection of what humanity had lost, or, as Marx himself said:

> Religion is the self-consciousness and self-feeling of man, who has either not yet found himself or has already lost himself again. . . . Criticism has plucked the imaginary flowers from the chain not so that man will wear the chain without any fantasy or consolation, but so that he will shake off the chain and cull the living flower. The criticism of religion disillusions man to make him think, and act and shape reality like a man who has been disillusioned and has come to reason, so that he will revolve around himself and therefore his true sun. Religion is only the illusory sun, which revolves around man as long as he does not revolve round himself.[11]

I find Marx's formulation compatible with the view that religion has been the denial not only of material but of spiritual happiness.

Given the reactionary role that religion has played in justifying the status quo or in offering a temporary consolation that renders it bearable, the strategic problem remains: is there a positive role for spirituality to play for the multitude in our era of oppression, struggle, and gigantic and urgent practical tasks? If one views the spiritual realm as one of collective energy and consciousness larger than the individual—or even, ultimately, than the human species—is it not possible to imagine that such deep stores of energy and consciousness might be brought into conjunction with, rather than opposition to, the attempt to remold our ecological, productive, and social relations?

In fact, the tribal experience of this enlarged energy field was never entirely obliterated but went underground in various religious and cultural movements. Some of these traditions combined a spiritual opposition with a political one, inspiring heroic resistance to the dominant system. Jewish prophets brought their visionary experience to the defense of social justice; Christian millennarians preached a mystical communism; Wicca empowered women and preserved positive images of the feminine, the sexual, and the ecological; various mystical Christian heresies practiced an antiauthoritarianism based on celebration of the divinity of all human beings. In the seventeenth century, the English Puritans brought to their revolution a faith in their providential role and the inspiration to attempt radical social change. Every radical movement has, in fact, produced something of a cultural and spiritual counterpart; indeed, the political unification of the people in these struggles seems to produce a unification of their hearts and souls as well. For many of us, the antiwar, civil rights, and women's movements were a kind of conversion, enlarging our dreams, changing our personalities, and bonding us profoundly to one another. I believe this happens even when there is no explicit spiritual culture, but in both the Black and student movements, with their countercultural explorations, there was a profound and explicit spirituality, which produced both strengths and weaknesses. The women's movement is increasingly evolving its own spirituality, which is why women must think deeply about its implications.

Ultimately, the value or lack of value of such a spiritual component will be demonstrated by experience. I wonder, however, whether the cultural limitations of past radicalism have reflected only the limits of material necessities and the hard facts of politics, or whether something might have been lost when Marxists severed their roots from the underground spirituality that inspired medieval peasant revolts and seventeenth-century Ranters in the past, and Native American and Third World peoples in the present.

I wonder to what extent the intuitive faculties employed in prophetic religion might enhance political understanding, or to what extent ritual, the kind that turned 1960s' demonstrations into mass theater, might arouse and direct popular energies. Movements like puritanism, the Crusades, or Muslim nationalism have also gained confidence from the belief that

"God is on our side." What strength might be possible to a movement that dispensed with this deus ex machina to affirm that to the extent that we unite with the aspirations of all humanity at its psychic depth, "God" *is* on our side? What might life be like when, having conquered the realm of necessity, a community that no longer depends on the discipline of denial can unleash the full potency of its collective passion?

These are theoretical questions, but they cannot be answered theoretically. Let us get on with the more mundane tasks of organizing so that history may sooner provide the answers.

3

Suggestions from the Working Group on Politics and Spirituality

We must visualize the possible, the positive, if we are going to make it happen. If we can see only destruction ahead, that is what is going to come. We need to visualize our strengths in our individual fantasies and in our groups.

One of the things we talked about—and not enough—was the connection between the political and the spiritual. We understand that our spirituality grounds our political activity, and that our political activity feeds our spirituality. This was evident in the fast of seven women in Illinois for the Equal Rights Amendment (ERA). Their act was both spiritual and political; the women who participated felt spiritually nurtured. The fast, women hungering for justice, brought together in a very real way—an integrated way—the spiritual and the political.

We analyzed a number of elements that can bring on or contribute to discouragement and a feeling of powerlessness.

- A purist approach, insisting that there is only one way to do something, only one correct political ideology or religious stance, tends to make us feel that if we are not in line, we are not capable.
- The fear of escalation—if I do this, I will be asked to do more—is very real, and each of us needs to consider what step to take next.
- The fear being coopted: my struggle will be subsumed in this other struggle.
- Personal resistance: what am I going to lose? As White middle-class women, we have a lot to lose. Involvement in this movement, this struggle, will cost us.

We also identified six particular political strategies. Our list is not all-inclusive, but simply sets forth some options as places to begin.

1. Working within the system, within educational institutions, political structures, and existing women's organizations, such as the National Organization for Women and the National Women's Political Caucus.

2. Changing personal life-styles. We need to think about our material life-styles—the air conditioner I just bought, the energy drain and continuing costs that it represents. Our commitment to oppose the nuclear buildup, for instance, is hypocrisy if we continue to pay for those same bombs with our tax dollars. We need to take seriously practical measures—tax resistance, simple living—that will make our life-style (what we eat, buy, do) consistent with our politics.

3. Building alternative structures. No movement has ever succeeded unless it also became a counterculture. We need to build the structures—the food and housing and banking cooperatives, for example—that will sustain and employ us after we have dropped out of or been thrown out of or have destroyed the old (patriarchal, racist, imperialist, capitalist, heterosexist) structures.

4. Building coalitions. If we are to make a difference, we must find the language and the forms that will link poor, working, and middle-class persons together. Direct action seems to preclude participation by people with nine-to-five jobs or jobs where they cannot afford to miss a day. We need to find forms of action that all can participate in, and we need to find the elements of our common struggle and common vision with various organizations and groups.

5. Developing autonomous blocks of women. Women themselves need to come together to strategize and support one another. One model in a university setting brings together women from the faculty, administrators, students, secretaries, and maintenance staff to form a community of women.

6. Direct action. If negotiation, legal approaches, and all else fail, we can move into direct action. We stress that direct action is not an initial strategy, but a last resort when other, less confrontative strategies have failed. It is not useful to de-

velop "civil disobedience junkies" for whom going to jail becomes an end in itself.

In developing a direct action campaign, the following stages are important:
- Identification of the problem, the issue, the point where the myth does not square with the reality. The issue needs to be named in relatively theoretical terms.
- Research to identify the target, some specific entity that people can confront, e.g., a corporation, a government office, a particular nuclear plant.
- Education, of the individuals within the organization and of the general public. In the case of the ERA, perhaps we failed to educate the public sufficiently on the values involved.
- Negotiation, attempting to solve the problem through existing channels on the personal level or on the legal level.
- Preparation for direct action: nonviolence training, formation of small "affinity" groups for both immediate and long-range support, before, during and after the action.
- Direct action.
- Protracted struggle: evaluating the action, planning the next step, recognizing that it is part of a cycle and that the struggle will be a long one. The affinity groups are important as part of the evaluation process, and in giving support to the households of those who may have been jailed.

We talked about children. Those of us with children pointed out how integrally what we do now affects them. We are building the world they will inhabit—it is their future. And we recognized the need for children to be involved in direct action. At the blockade of the Livermore Weapons Laboratory in California an affinity group of children, aged seven to seventeen, took part in the demonstration and were arrested, handcuffed, and kept in a bus for six hours without being allowed to go to the bathroom. That experience allowed the children to participate in an important work that needs to be done in the world.

Finally, each member of the group reflected on the changes she might make in her life as a result of this conference or this working group. What difference will it really make that I have been here, listened to the talks, shared with this group of women?

Lest we become discouraged contemplating the immensity of the problems, someone quoted Mary Hunt: "We are not about building the kingdom, the realm of God; we are about working on the conditions that allow it to come." Perhaps in remembering this, we will be freed to continue.

Part II

Women and Nature: Violence or Interdependence

ANOTHER OF THE concrete issues that women face in their daily lives is violence—the battering of women and children, sexual harassment and abuse, rape, and murder, all occurring with alarming frequency in that supposed haven of peace and quiet, the family home. Research carried on by the women's movement in recent years has revealed both the previously unsuspected extent of violence against women and its occurrence throughout the population. Wife-beating is not confined to low-income groups, but is found at all levels of income, education, and professional standing. Violence against women is one of the issues around which women have been able to bond across the barriers of class, race, religion, and ethnic differences.

To put this issue in a broad context, we chose to pair violence against women with violence against nature out of a sense that the parallels between women and nature—in conceptualization, roles, and treatment at the hands of Western civilization—would prove illuminating. Clearly both women and nature suffer violence under patriarchy. Both parts of this section attempt to trace the roots of that violence. Letha Dawson Scanzoni, writing as an evangelical feminist, follows the notion of a hierarchy of being from its beginnings in Greek philosophy, through its development as the "chain of being" in Christian theology, to its present-day resurgence among leaders of the religious right. She demonstrates how the chain of being legitimates a chain of command that easily deteriorates into a justification of brutal subjection of the inferior. Ynestra

King, a secular feminist concerned with integrating an ecological perspective into feminism, points to the profound psychological and philosophical connections between misogyny and the rape of the earth.

Since feminists seek to be integrative and constructive as well as critical, both writers sketch alternative visions. Scanzoni offers a concept of negotiated order and suggests replacing the chain of being with the image of a cosmic dance, creative, graceful and joyful. King, using the web as an image of the interconnectedness of all living things, develops a theory and politics of ecofeminism, speaking for both women and nature.

4

The Great Chain of Being and the Chain of Command
LETHA DAWSON SCANZONI

The "great chain of being" was a way of conceptualizing the universe in terms of a vast hierarchical arrangement. The cosmic order was compared to a great chain stretching from heaven to earth—a chain teeming with every possible type of created being, from orders of angels down to the most minute particle of matter.

"According to this conception," writes C. S. Lewis, "*degrees of value* are objectively present in the universe. Everything except God has some natural superior; everything except unformed matter has some natural inferior."[1]

Origin of the Chain Idea

This hierarchical notion is not taken from the Bible, but rather owes its roots to Plato and Aristotle. It may be traced through the Neoplatonists of the third century onward, who began organizing such ideas into a coherent scheme of things that came to be called the "scale of nature" or the "great chain of being."[2]

By the Middle Ages and into the Renaissance, this vision of the world was taken for granted, and efforts were made to fit it into Christian theology—even though the two systems of thought were at odds in many respects. The chain idea helped justify the hierarchical ordering of society at that time. And it also fitted nicely into the notion of a hierarchical church with higher orders of clergy over lower orders, and both over the laity.[3] The idea fitted well, too, with keeping women in a subor-

Letha Dawson Scanzoni

dinate place, since a woman's position on the "scale of nature" was considered lower than a man's. "To deny this," wrote Touteville in 1635, "is to resist the Councell of the Highest."[4]

The popularity of the chain of being as a model for social order mirroring the supposed cosmic order continued through the eighteenth century. To leave one's assigned place in society was considered an inversion of the "laws of order." And to go so far as to seek equality was to act in a manner "contrary to nature."[5]

Writing in 1757, Soame Jenyns argued that

> the universe is a system *whose very essence consists in subordination;* a scale of Beings descending by insensible degrees from infinite perfection to absolute nothing: in which . . . the beauty and happiness of the whole depend altogether on the just inferiority of its parts, that is, on the comparative imperfections of the several Beings of which it is composed.[6]

"Inequality of conditions is not to be counted among evils," wrote Gottfried Wilhelm von Leibniz, a German philosopher and mathematician whose lifetime overlapped parts of the seventeenth and eighteenth centuries. He referred to the logic of another writer who challenged those wanting changes in the status quo by asking them why rocks do not have leaves or why ants are not peacocks. "If equality were everywhere requisite," Gottfried Wilhelm von Leibniz warned, "the poor man would set up his claim to it against the rich man, the valet against his master."[7] Such a picture of the world was, of course, very static.

How the Chain Has Been Used

One of the most despicable uses to which the chain idea was ever put was to justify slavery. An eighteenth-century poem announced:

> The meanest slaves or they who hedge and ditch,
> Are useful, by their sweat, to feed the rich.

And the rich were admonished not to disdain even the lowest slave because he or she was "equally a link of nature's chain." Both were fulfilling the role of a wise providence who dispensed "various parts for various minds."[8] Both rich and poor were thus in a sense "equal" by virtue of being a part of the chain!

As David Brion Davis points out in his Pulitzer Prize-winning book *The Problem of Slavery in Western Culture,* the chain idea allowed slavery to be rationalized as an illustration of "a cosmic principle of authority and subordination," which therefore had "a necessary place in the ordered structure of being."[9] The idea of continuity—no gaps in the chain—also entered in, as Gordon Turnbull made clear: "Negro slavery appears . . . to be one of those indispensable and necessary links, in the great chain of causes and events, which cannot and indeed ought not to be broken; or in other words, a *part* of the stupendous, admirable, and perfect *whole* which, if taken away, would leave a chasm."[10] Black people were thus not only chained by physical slavery but also by the chain of being, which gave religious and natural-law legitimation to the practice of regarding and treating Black people as less than fully human.

A confusing set of biological criteria gradually emerged by which peoples could be categorized as higher or lower on the chain. Not surprisingly, given the criteria they had decided upon, the Europeans found they were highest on the scale, while Blacks ranked lowest. As historian Winthrop Jordan writes, "No one thought of the Great Chain of Being as originating in differences in power and social status between human groups; to do so would have been to blaspheme the Creator."[11] A book published near the end of the eighteenth century declared that the theory of racial inferiority was not degrading to Blacks but instead could confirm God's wisdom and omnipotence in providing such variety and making the chain of being so complete through a progressive series "from a lump of dirt to a perfect man."[12]

Sociologist William Wilson defines racism as "an ideology of racial domination or exploitation that (1) incorporates beliefs in a particular race's cultural and/or inherent biological inferiority and (2) uses such beliefs to justify or prescribe inferior or unequal treatment for that group."[13] We could substitute words relating to gender here and define sexism similarly. Thus, today biological arguments are being marshaled to bolster claims of female inferiority (for example, Steven Goldberg's *Inevitability of Patriarchy*[14]), with such arguments often tied in with chain-of-being ideas to show that women have been designed for a different function from men. The "nature" of females is said to be suited to a subordinate, helping position through which they glorify God by staying in their place—just what was said about Black slavery in past centuries. Hierarchy is thus considered built into nature, part of the eternal scheme of things. And one should not tamper with the cosmic order!

Resurgence of Chain-of-Being Ideas

Chain ideas will reemerge in some form at any period when the status quo is being questioned and calls for change are being sounded. A revival seems to be occurring today, especially among conservative Evangelicals. Representative of such thinking are the writings of missionary author Elisabeth Elliot and her brother Thomas Howard, a professor at Gordon College. Howard, for example, suggests "a pattern of things that is fixed by divine wisdom" and "in the hierarchical order, rightly understood and enacted, freedom (or wholeness or felicity) for each participant would be found in a set of relationships reaching *up and down.*" Authority, mercy, and responsibility are exercised in downward relationships ("a man rightly relating to his son or to his dog, say"), with obedience, loyalty, and trust governing upward relationships ("a man rightly relating to his master or his god, say"). The overarching quality demanded by all these relationships is *courtesy,* which Howard defines as "that keen and noble awareness of the validity and splendor of the nature, individuality, and office of every other creature, be that other creature an archangel, a charwoman, a spouse, an elf, or a mole."[15]

On a similar note, Elisabeth Elliot suggests that God has set up a design that "includes a hierarchy of beings under God such as cherubim, seraphim, archangels, angels, men, animals, insects, things like paramecia and microbes and who knows what yet undiscovered beings? Every creature is assigned its proper position in this scale." She emphasizes that "every creature—whether the horned ox or the scaled fish, the man or woman, the clam or the archangel—glorifies God by being what it is, by living up to God's original idea when he made it." Elliot says that she understands that "women, by creation, have been given a place within the human level which is ancillary to that of men, . . . an inferior place within the human locus." She hastens to point out that by "inferior" she is referring to position and not worth.[16]

Another Chain—the Chain of Command

Let us leave for a moment the great chain of being and move on to another chain, the chain of command. This term and others with similar meanings (such as the divine order or the principle of headship) have come into vogue in certain evangelical circles—and often beyond those circles—in recent years. The acceptance of such ideas has come about largely through the influence of certain speakers and writers, such as Bill Gothard (whose Basic Youth Conflicts seminars are attended by thousands) and Larry Christenson (author of *The Christian Family*).

There is, for example, Gothard's grotesque picture of a hand (representing God) holding a hammer (representing the husband), beating on a chisel (representing the wife), which is carving out a diamond in the rough (representing the child).[17]

And there is Christenson's diagram, based on his interpretation of 1 Corinthians 11:3, which shows at the top a box labeled, "CHRIST, the 'Head' of the husband; Lord of the family." Under it is a box labeled "HUSBAND, the 'Head' of the wife; chief authority over the children"; and under that, a box labeled "WIFE, the helpmeet to the husband; secondary authority over the children." At the bottom is a box labeled "CHILDREN, obedient to parents." Connecting these boxes are downward arrows, all solid lines except for a dotted line from the husband through the wife to the children, which Christenson explains graphically illustrates that the only authority a woman has over her children is *derived authority* from her husband. "She exercises authority over the children on behalf of and in the place of her husband," writes Christenson. And she herself "lives under the authority of her husband, and is responsible to him for the way she orders the household and cares for the children."[18]

Clearly the two chains—the chain of being and the chain of command—are intricately connected. This is demonstrated in C. S. Lewis's description of the seventeenth-century conception of hierarchy in his *Preface to Paradise Lost*. Earlier, reference was made to his portrayal of the chain of being, where everything in creation has its natural superior and inferior. In the remainder of that section, Lewis describes what in essence is the chain of command.

> The goodness, happiness, and dignity of every being consists in obeying its natural superior and ruling its natural inferiors. When it fails in either part of this twofold task we have disease or monstrosity in the scheme of things until the peccant being is either destroyed or corrected. One or the other it will certainly be; for by stepping out of its place in the system (whether it step up like a rebellious angel or down like an uxorious husband) it has made the very nature of things its enemy.[19]

This is a kind of social stratification, specifically stratification based not on *achievement* of position but rather on an arbitrarily *assigned* position ascribed to someone by reason of birth into a particular group or category of persons—a position that does not take into account a particular individual's interests, preferences, abilities, or accomplishments.

Many current religious publications favor chain-of-being and chain-of-command thinking. Roman Catholic charismatic Stephen Clark provides one example, in a long, heavily documented book used in many seminaries. Defining subordination as dependence "upon another person for direction," Clark uses the creation accounts to argue for women's subordinate role in life. God's statement that it was "not good for the man to be alone" is viewed by Clark as meaning something different from the man's need for a woman's companionship. Rather, says Clark, the man needed *human society* and "a race to fulfill his commission." The man "needed more people to fill the earth and rule over it, and he needed to be able to increase and multiply." Therefore, reasons Clark, "the man needed a wife with whom he could beget children. . . . One reason that animals will not do as a partner for man is their inadequacy for reproductive purposes. . . . Genesis does not describe woman as a companion to man but as a helper to him. . . . The phrase is not a romantic evaluation of woman. Rather, it describes woman as 'useful' to man."[20] Clark goes on to say that "it is the man who is called 'Man' or 'Human' and not the woman. . . . What we meet at the end of Genesis 2 is Human and his wife."[21]

Why Is the Hierarchical Chain Idea Reemerging Today?

Since we live in a time of rapid change, it is not surprising to see a revival of the chain of being. When people fear change, or when change occurs rapidly, people often yearn for the security of rigid structure. "*Order* is heaven's first law; and this confest/ Some are, and must be, greater than the rest/ More rich, more wise," wrote Alexander Pope in his eighteenth-century best seller, *Essay on Man*, which popularized the notion of a divinely ordained chain of being.[22]

Winthrop Jordan, referring to the eighteenth century, writes, "It was no accident that the Chain of Being should have been most popular at a time when the hierarchical arrangement of society was coming to be challenged."[23] There is a parallel here with the acceptance of authoritarian chain ideas today, when traditional gender roles and the hierarchy implied in them are being increasingly challenged.

New options are opening up for women and men, and this can be frightening, as freedom often is. Thus, Erich Fromm entitled one of his books *Escape from Freedom* and showed how persons can be tempted by totalitarianism as an easy way out of the anxiety of alternatives.[24] Scholars tell us that much of the appeal of the chain of being during the medieval and Renaissance periods related to intense fears of chaos, confusion, and change. The cry was for order, and the only way people seemed to think of order was in terms of hierarchy. Order was assumed to mean a place for everything and everything in its place. The chain of being spelled out that place for each social category; life could therefore seem manageable.

Effects of Chain-of-Being and Chain-of-Command Thinking

"Chain" ideology leads to a climate that accepts, legitimizes, and promotes control, coercion, domination, and even violence in human relationships. Such a climate characterizes militarism with its nuclear muscle-flexing. It is manifest in an irreverent disregard for the natural environment that ruthlessly depletes natural resources. Anthropologist Peggy Sanday writes of nature's "backlash" against human beings (in the form of pollution and other environmental problems) because they have carried the domination of nature too far. She describes the new and different kinds of stress people feel today with the "knowledge that the technology of male dominance has given us the wherewithal to destroy all life on earth."[25]

The effects of chain-of-being, domination/subordination thinking are also seen in exploitative attitudes toward Third World peoples and in violence against women and children.

How Domestic Violence Flourishes Under the Chain-of-Being/Chain-of-Command Philosophy

It is not hard to see how hierarchical teachings foster a climate in which wife-battering can grow. Think of the implications, for example, of the following quotation from a book that many fundamentalist churches are using as required reading for engaged couples:

> Suppose a woman feels God is leading her definitely opposite to what her husband has commanded. Who should she obey? The Scriptures say a woman must ignore her "feelings" about the will of God, and do what her husband says. She is to obey her husband as if he were God Himself. She can be as certain of God's will, when her husband speaks, as if God had spoken audibly from Heaven![26]

The ideology of male supremacy and female subordination fosters a property view of wives that is destructive to the human spirit, hurting both partners in different ways and preventing marriage from being the rich, reciprocal, energizing relationship it was intended to be.

A tragic outcome of one husband's treatment of his wife as property was the wife's suicide attempt. She told me how he would brutally beat her, humiliate her, and rape her. Several times she suffered miscarriages after her husband violently raped her while she was pregnant. One Sunday he beat and raped her and then went off to church. When the woman sought help from pastors and pastoral counselors, she was told she had no right to leave her husband but must submit to him in all things. Both she and her husband were told that the Bible said the wife does not rule over her own body, but the husband does; and thus the husband had a right to do what he pleased with what "belonged" to him. Such counselors were, of course, greatly distorting the message of 1 Corinthians 7:4, to which they were alluding. They ignored the context and the remainder of the verse, which says, "Likewise the husband does not rule over his own body, but the wife does." The emphasis is on mutuality and reciprocity of equal partners in the marital union. Certainly the message is not one of privilege to do whatever one wants with a spouse's body and to think of it in terms of ownership!

Some men have also used chain-of-command thinking in relation to their children, seeking to show their power and control over them. I know of one religious leader who advised parents not to worry if they hit their children so hard that bruises occurred, since Proverbs 20:30 (KJV) says, "The blueness of a wound cleanseth away evil." And I know of one father who sits in prison because he took the words of Proverbs 23:13 as a literal command backed up by a literal promise: "Do not withhold discipline from a child; if you beat him with a rod, he will not die." But his three-year-old son *did* die.

The most bizarre case I have read about is that of a man who set up a throne for himself in his house and forced his three daughters to perform sexual acts with him. Researchers on sexual abuse of children have found it is not unusual for fathers involved in incest to hold rigid religious beliefs and to quote scripture as proof of their place as rulers over the household.

It is clear that distorted religious teachings are being used to justify domestic violence in some cases; and in other cases, such teachings can foster a climate that nurtures its growth. Women's shelters and crisis lines constantly hear from beaten-down women who feel they are caught in a no-win situation. Such women fear their husbands' beatings and bullying on one hand, and fear the displeasure of God on the other hand if they should leave their husbands (since they have been taught that separation and divorce violate God's will as revealed in scripture).

One counseling psychologist told me of the experience of one of her clients who had gone to her pastor for advice, telling him that not only did her husband regularly beat her, but he had recently shaken her so hard that her head hit the brick wall in their apartment. The pastor said, "Can you say 'Thank you, Jesus' each time your head hits the brick wall?"

Another example of such teaching is found in Bill Gothard's special seminars for male ministers only. The handbook for the seminar on divorce and remarriage urges pastors strongly to oppose divorce. The first page of the handbook says, "We will never solve marital problems until we relate 'suffering for righteousness' sake' to the marriage relationship." In response to the question "What if a wife is a victim of her husband's hostility?" Gothard replies, "There is no 'victim' if we understand that we are called to suffer for righteousness."[27]

The rigid, legalistic, and distorted use of scripture in these examples not only fails to take into account human need and human suffering; it violates the overall spirit of scripture with its emphasis on mercy, justice, compassion, and liberation from oppression.

Other Effects of Dominance/Submission Ideology

In addition to encouraging a climate of physical and psychological abuse, an emphasis on male domination and female subordination damages the self-esteem of girls and women. It also polarizes the sexes and blocks deep intimacy and communication between women and men.

In the chain-of-being and chain-of-command philosophies, society requires an imposed order of things, and God is the one who imposes that order. As biblical scholar David Tiede points out, religion *can* be liberating; but it can also be an instrument of oppression when excessive emphasis is put on stability, social control, and the status quo. God is then seen as "the power that keeps people in their place" rather than as a liberator.

What is needed is an alternative way of looking at the scheme of things. To gain such a perspective, women need to begin with themselves; then they must work for change in society.

Constructing Our Own Reality

Scholars who specialize in the sociology of knowledge tell us that what appears *real* to us in everyday life is a socially constructed reality.[28] That is, we see things (including *ourselves*) in a certain way because of interaction with others who view the world in a certain way. In a similar vein, Nelle Morton comments that as women share experiences, raise consciousness, and encourage one another to speak out about our feelings on what it means to be a woman, we "hear each other into speech."[29] By doing this, we are validating one another and defining our own reality rather than being defined in terms of the dominant male culture. Thus, Anne Wilson Schaef speaks of "an emerging female system in the white male society." Her book *Women's Reality* contrasts the dominant White male system, which permeates every area of life, with two female systems—one a reactive, *coping* system for dealing with the roles women have been assigned by the dominant male system, and the other an *emerging* system occurring as women "'get clear' and feel free to express their values and perceptions."[30]

As women we have often doubted our own perceptions of reality because of how we have been regarded. We need to help one another form a new outlook. I am reminded of a cartoon I saw in *New Woman* magazine in which a woman is saying to a man seated across from her, "I've finally found myself, Charles. My problem was that I wasn't looking high enough."* We need to challenge one another to catch the spirit of Kristin Lems's song:

> Women walk more determined than they ever have,
>   Women walk with a stronger stride than they ever did before.
> Take a look, sisters and brothers,
>   'Cause you're gonna find you've got another kind of woman
> Who will ask a lot,
>   And give a lot,
> And live a whole lot more.[31]

Helping Shape an Alternative Societal Vision

We cannot, however, stop with ourselves. Women need to be aware that the hierarchical view of males and females in our society is nothing short of sexual stratification and therefore is marked by the characteristics of any other kind of social stratification. Social theorist Max Weber pointed out long ago that ranking persons in society relates to three realms: the *economic* (one's life chances), the *social* (the degree of honor, prestige and esteem given by society), and the *political* (the power to which one has access). Obviously, women have not been permitted equal access with men to these rewards, either in religious institutions or in society at large. If women are going to effect change and help shape an alternative societal

---

*Reprinted by courtesy of *New Woman* magazine. Copyright © 1980 by *New Woman*. All rights reserved throughout the world.

vision, they need to become part of the political and economic decision-making processes of our societies.

To help bring about change, we must start where people are. We must realize that people need a conception of the universe that provides them with a sense of order, a way of making sense out of things. Without that sense of order, there is a feeling of disequilibrium, a disorientation that seems frightening. Simply disturbing that equilibrium with a new vision of reality is not enough; it may even be counterproductive. We must not lose sight of the fact that people long for certainty, stability, and a yearning to know their world is manageable and predictable so that they can calmly go about their everyday lives.

People also fear questioning the familiar, and this relates to a fear of change. Change can seem inconvenient and stressful and can produce much pain. People do not want their sense of order disrupted. And challenging their perception of reality—their acceptance of "the way things are" as a given—is likely to be met with resistance and denial. "The appearance of an alternative symbolic universe poses a threat because its very existence demonstrates empirically that one's own universe is less than inevitable," write sociologists Peter Berger and Thomas Luckmann.[32]

For persons who are certain that traditional dominance/subordination ideas about male/female roles and relationships are a taken-for-granted part of how the world was meant to be, it is disconcerting and upsets their sense of order to hear such ideas being challenged. In the seventeenth century, King James lamented that "the world is very much out of order" because females were wearing clothing styles and hair styles previously worn only by males.[33] And in our own day, one anti-ERA letter published in the newspaper ended with this sentence: "Long live sexual inequality; for this is what makes the world go round."[34]

If women are going to help change such attitudes, we need to be sensitive to the anxieties many people are expressing; and we need to help them see that chaos is not the only alternative to their perception of order. The familiar order need not give way to *dis*order but rather to another kind of order. An alternative to *prescribed* order is a *negotiated* order in which females and males mutually respect and appreciate one another and care about each individual's preferences, needs, concerns, dreams, fears, pains, interests, talents, and aspirations.

And we also need to help people see that God and good can be seen in change and diversity rather than in static uniformity. This change and diversity can be exciting and exhilarating rather than threatening.

Another image employed during the Elizabethan age, in addition to that of the great chain of being, is the image of the dance. This image has also been recently evoked to describe the cosmic order. For example, Elisabeth Elliot has written:

> For the tremendous hierarchical vision of blessedness—often compared to a Dance in which initiation and response are the movements—the feminist substitutes a vision of blessedness which holds all human beings on a level plain—a faceless, colorless, sexless wasteland where rule and submission are regarded as a curse, where fulfillment depends on the denial of that "graduated splendor" which we see in all creation, of which the differentiation of male and female is earth's most splendid.[35]

I think she misunderstands what feminists are saying. The dance we are suggesting is dynamic and offers far more creative possibilities than any hierarchical vision can ever offer with its rigid, static places for whole categories of persons—whether based on sex or race or marital status or age or sexual orientation or anything else.

Women of faith hold a vision in which the divine Choreographer marks out steps for the *individual,* making for far greater variety than the most complex system that deals with whole groups of people as the basic units. There is allowance for spontaneity and creative improvisation in our vision.

The wind of the Spirit is blowing—that same Spirit who, according to the Christian faith, was poured out at Pentecost on women and men alike as they trustingly waited in obedience to the Risen Christ. "There are varieties of gifts," Paul tells us. "There are varieties of service. . . . There are varieties of working. . . . All these are inspired by one and the same Spirit who apportions to each one *individually* as [the Spirit] wills [1 Cor. 12:4-6, 11]."

This vision throbs with life and excites and energizes. And it frees from the confinement of chains! But it is not a selfish freedom to "do one's own thing." It is freedom to love and serve God and humanity—and, yes, ourselves—out of the fullness of one's own uniqueness. We can join Cris Williamson in singing her "Song of the Soul," following our hearts so that "love will find [us]" and "truth will unbind [us]," and we can experience healing and growth and a true sense of who we are and who we can be.

"Love of my life," I am crying; I am not dying:
    I am dancing,
Dancing along in the madness; there is no sadness,
    Only a Song of the Soul.
And we'll sing this song; why don't you sing along?[36]

The dance goes on. And we can all be part of it, moving with joy and grace and beauty as those who have been unbound.

5

Making the World Live: Feminism and the Domination of Nature

YNESTRA KING

Feminism is not an issue, but a woman-identified perspective on the whole of life. It involves the challenging of social domination in all its forms, and it views the different forms of domination—sex, race, class, and the domination of nature—as interconnected and mutually reinforcing. The relation between the domination of nature and the domination of human beings suggests a theory of ecological feminism, ecofeminism for short.

In a feminist perspective, humanity is part of the larger nonhuman nature on which humanity is wholly dependent. Nature can get along without us, but we cannot get along without it. Moreover, from a feminist perspective it is of the first importance to understand the connection between the misogyny and violence against women in our culture and the contempt for nonhuman nature that has resulted in the rape of the earth by men, especially White men. Women and nature are the original "others" in patriarchy—those who are feared, the reminders of mortality, those who must be objectified and dominated.

Woman/Man = Nature/Culture

Our culture is defined against nature and the biological or natural world. In *The Second Sex*, Simone de Beauvoir puzzles over why nature is seen as the other and why women are

Ynestra King

identified with nature. For de Beauvoir "transcendence" is the work of culture, the work of men. It is the process of overcoming immanence, a process of culture-building that is opposed to nature and that is based on the increasing domination of nature. It is enterprise. Immanence, symbolized by women, is that which calls man back, that which reminds him of what he wants to forget. He must forget and overcome his own naturalness to achieve manhood and transcendence.

> Man seeks in woman the Other as Nature and as his fellow being. But we know what ambivalent feelings Nature inspires in man. He exploits her, but she crushes him, he is born of her and dies in her: she is the source of his being and the realm that he subjugates to his will; Nature is a vein of gross material in which the soul is imprisoned, and she is the supreme reality; she is contingence and Idea, the finite and the whole; she is what opposes the Spirit, and the Spirit itself. Now ally, now enemy, she appears as the dark chaos from whence life wells up, as this life itself, and as the over-yonder toward which life tends. Woman sums up nature as Mother, Wife, and Idea; these forms now mingle and now conflict, and each of them wears a double visage.[1]

Women, because of their biological possibilities and their socially constituted mothering roles, are believed to be closer to that nature against which culture is defined. For de

Beauvoir, patriarchal civilization is about the denial of men's mortality, of which women and nature are an incessant reminder. Women's powers of procreation are distinguished from the powers of creation—the accomplishments of culture by which men achieve immortality. Anthropologist Sherry Ortner finds in the identification of women with nature the basis for the well-nigh universal phenomenon of the subjugation of women.

> What could there be in the generalized structure and conditions of existence, common to every culture, that would lead every culture to place a lower value upon women? Specifically, my thesis is that woman is being identified with—or, if you will, seems to be a symbol of—something that every culture devalues, something that every culture defines as being of a lower order of existence than itself. Now it seems that there is only one thing that would fit that description, and that is "nature" in the most generalized sense.[2]

For de Beauvoir—and for Ortner, who draws extensively on de Beauvoir—a woman's physiology, her social role, and her psychology are the basis for her being perceived as closer to nature, or as an intermediary between nature and culture. Ortner says that women are "situated between the two realms."[3] Defining culture in opposition to nature has also resulted in defining culture in opposition to life, devaluing life-giving functions and life itself. Ortner says, "We realize it is not the killing that is the relevant and valued aspect of hunting and warfare; rather, it is the transcendental (social, cultural) nature of these activities, as opposed to the naturalness of the process of birth."[4] Women are not more natural than men, but are simply perceived as being closer to nature. Because of women's experience, because of the lives we have led, we tend to have a certain viewpoint that makes an ecological perspective easier for us.

Two Directions for Feminists

The recognition of women's bridgelike position between the realms of nature and culture poses two possible directions for feminists. One direction is the integration of women into the world of culture and production, defined as the overcoming of the natural and the biological. Both de Beauvoir and Ortner see this integration as the purpose of feminism. Ortner writes, "Ultimately, both men and women can and must be equally involved in projects of creativity and transcendence. Only then will women be seen as aligned with culture, in culture's ongoing dialectic with nature."[5] Many socialist feminists have adopted this view, perhaps because they have accepted the socialist goal of integrating women into economic production as the route to liberation. The National Organization for Women and other liberal feminist groups also seek equality with men "in the mainstream" without closely examining male values in contemporary culture and the structures of production and ownership.

Other feminists, who have brought an ecological perspective to their feminism, want to use women's position on the dividing line between nature and culture to create a feminist culture that recognizes the dependence between humans and nonhuman nature. They challenge the tenet that women's lifegiving functions are somehow lower than culture or lacking in creative or transcendent dimensions. Constitutive of their feminism is a challenge to the definition of culture as opposed to nature. Rather than severing the woman/nature connection, they would use it as a vantage point for creating a different kind of "culture" that transforms the nature/culture distinction itself. Poet and feminist Adrienne Rich shares this view.

> We have been perceived for too many centuries as pure Nature, exploited and raped like the earth and the solar system; small wonder if we now long to become Culture: pure spirit, mind. Yet it is precisely this culture and its political institutions which have split us off from itself. In so doing it has also split itself off from life, becoming the death culture of quantification, abstraction, and the will to power which has reached its most refined destructiveness in this century. It is this culture and politics of abstraction which women are talking of changing, of bringing to accountability in human terms.[6]

But the only way to ground a feminist critique of "this culture and politics of abstraction" is to apply a self-conscious ecological perspective to all theories and strategies, much as race and class insights need to be taken into consideration and applied every step of the way. Women need to maintain their otherness outside male-dominated culture, to guard it voluntarily, and to use it as a political vantage point to resist domination of nonhuman nature and to envision an ecological way of life.

What does it mean for women to resist the domination of nature as practiced in our culture? It has two parts: resistance to the domination of our own sexual natures, and resistance to the domination of nonhuman nature. The first domination has to do with our inner, sensate, sexual natures, with the repression of eros in ourselves, which is necessary to maintain authority relationships and hierarchy, and which alienates us from ourselves and from one another. The fear of eros is behind the attacks by the new right on women's right to choose an abortion and on lesbianism. The new right wants to keep sexuality restricted to reproduction; the only sexual expression allowed to women under patriarchy is in marriage, in order to conceive children. The new right would like to force women back into our naturalized social roles, thwarting women's sexual nature, potential, and freedom. The flowering of our sexual natures and the freeing of our sexuality (including a freely chosen celibacy) has a potentially subversive power that the new right, I suspect, recognizes more clearly than we do.

The second domination is the drive to control nonhuman nature, which has brought about the ecological crisis. Ecology is a science that recognizes the interdependence of all life, including human life. It offers principles, which if integrated into feminism will broaden and deepen our vision.

Ecological Principles

Ecology teaches that life is an interconnected web, not a hierarchy; the idea of a hierarchical chain of being, as we have seen in Letha Scanzoni's discussion in the previous section, has been invented by humans and projected onto nature as a convenient justification for social domination. So persuasive is this projection that the rule of some people over others appears natural. Feminism asserts that the original domination in human society, making way for all the others, was the domination of women. Ecofeminism draws on an ecological perspective to assert that there is no hierarchy in nature—among persons, between humans and the rest of the natural world, or among the many forms of nonhuman nature. The human species is only one of millions. But the human species, in its patriarchial form, is the only species that holds a conscious belief that it is entitled to dominion over all the other species and over the planet itself. An ecofeminist culture would emphasize the interconnectedness of all forms of life and would itself be antihierarchical.

Another ecological principle: diversity in nature is enriching and necessary. Environmental simplification is as much a problem today as environmental degradation; a richly diversified and differentiated natural situation has the potential to support life that a simplified environment does not. The Amazon forests before and after exploitation are one example. The Amazon region is the source of much of the earth's oxygen, and it is being defoliated, with long-term consequences we can only surmise. Many species are simply being wiped out, never to be seen on the face of the earth again, and the rate of annihilation is accelerating. At present, one species disappears every day; if the acceleration continues at the same rate, by the year 2000 one species will disappear every hour. Similarly, in human society, commodity capitalism is intentionally simplifying human communities and cultures so that the same products can be marketed anywhere, to anyone: McDonalds in China, Coca-Cola in Africa. There are probably no indigenous peoples left whose lives have not been changed by industrialization and technology. Ecofeminism as a social movement celebrates the rich diversity of women while embodying politically the principle of oneness in diversity. Ecofeminism tries simultaneously to resist racism, classism, heterosexism, and the domination of one nation over another. This is a tall order, but ecofeminists and other feminists are moving toward a politics that will confront all forms of oppression without ranking them, a politics that affirms as a basic belief that ultimately no one is free until everyone is free.

A third ecological principle: everything humans do to nature has a reaction somewhere, has consequences later—acid rain,

DDT in the food chain, depletion of the ozone layer by aerosol sprays. We literally have the power to wipe out all life on earth, either instantly through military violence or gradually through pollution and misuse of the earth's resources. This generation has even to consider the awesome possibility that we may permanently alter the gene pool.

An Ecofeminist Politics

Taking account of these ecological principles will mean broadening feminist theory and politics. It is significant that as we face the prospect of the end of life on planet Earth two social movements have emerged: ecology, speaking for nature, the "other" who has had no voice and certainly no subjectivity in our civilization; and feminism, representing the refusal of women—the original "other" in patriarchy—to be silent any longer. Ecofeminism is the voice of both "others," women and nature. In struggling to bring together these two movements, ecofeminists are developing both a theory that spells out the connections between the oppression of women and the hatred and exploitation of nature, and a politics that would resist all forms of domination simultaneously. To accomplish this, ecofeminist politics needs to take a variety of directions.

Ecofeminists need to develop a strongly woman-identified culture and politics (theory and action) that draw on the life-affirming aspects of traditional female socialization and provide us with political outlets, avenues for making public some of our so-called private virtues. Motherhood, female religious imagery, and lesbianism are all sources for culture-building.

Ecofeminists need to build new models for human society—nonhierarchical, valuing diversity, living in harmony with nature—and not be afraid to draw on the most utopian imaginings in developing visions of what is possible. Such an ecofeminist culture is beginning to emerge. Women are learning holistic health and alternate technologies; women are living in communities that are exploring old and new forms of spirituality that connect people to one another and to the rest of life. Harmonious, diverse, decentralized communities, using only those technologies that take into consideration ecological principles, are now the only practical solution for the continuation of life on earth, and there are already groups of women engaged in bringing these imagined communities to life.

Ecofeminists must build bonds between women cross-culturally and globally. While celebrating the rich diversity of women, we recognize that most of us are complicitous in one another's oppression, depending on race, class, sexual preference, and nationality. To oppose the ways these differences separate us from one another, we need face-to-face dialogue, and we must take conscious account of all the connections in our political actions.

Ecofeminists cannot back down on issues of sexual freedom. The right of a woman to have an abortion and the right of a woman to express her sexuality however she chooses are basic to feminism. We have quoted Adrienne Rich: "Connections between and among women are the most feared, the most problematic, and the most potentially transformative force on the planet."[7] We need to examine lesbianism as a model for connections between and among women. Lesbians have a powerful experience of women bonding that is important to all women. When we speak of threatened peoples, we must always include lesbians and gay men.

Ecofeminists need to develop empowering, imaginative forms of feminist direct action, as part of an ecofeminist reconstructive/resistance movement. These political actions can embody a nonhierarchical, personalizing way of acting, linking all the issues as one particular issue is highlighted.

Examples of ecofeminist direct action are multiplying: in the June 1982 disarmament demonstration in New York City, where a group marched under the banner "A feminist world is a nuclear-free zone"; in California, where women surrounded the Bohemian Club, a male-only playground for corporate, government, and military elite; in England, where thirty thousand women, standing shoulder to shoulder, "embraced" the U.S. military base at Greenham Common and blocked access to it.

To illustrate this approach in some detail, let me describe the Women's Pentagon Action, in which 2,500 women took part in November 1981. We asked ourselves, "What is a feminist form for a national political action at the Pentagon?" We chose not to have speakers addressing a crowd from high on a platform; we wanted no separation between organizers and participants. Together, we wrote a unity statement, reflecting our multiple origins and our common concerns. The statement expressed our understanding of militarism as a reflection of a much more pervasive cultural and political situation, connected with rape, genocide, imperialism, the poisoning of the environment, the pall of fear that hangs over the people of the world. It pointed out that women suffer particularly from war, as spoils to victorious armies, as refugees, as victims of dwindling social service budgets looted for military buildup. It sketched our vision of a feminist future, for we are in all things critical, integrative, and reconstructive!

The action was developed in four stages: mourning, at Arlington Cemetery, where we placed tombstones for victims of patriarchal violence; rage, in which we vented our anger; empowerment, in which we encircled the Pentagon, singing and weaving a web of yarn; defiance, in which we blockaded the entrance and were arrested in an act of nonviolent civil disobedience. (Not all the women who participated in the action committed the civil disobedience; that was an individual choice made without pressure from the group.)

The kind of politics ecofeminists are creating draws on women's culture, builds on women's differences, organizes in an antihierarchical, small-group mode, is visually and emotionally imaginative, and strives to connect all the issues. One of the women at the Pentagon action told us that she had never been to a demonstration in her life, but that she had come all the way from California to place a tombstone that read: "For the three Vietnamese women my son killed." Her action demonstrates the working out of a new kind of politics that will touch women's hearts and lives so strongly that even though they have never before engaged in political action, they will be moved to do whatever is necessary to make the world live.

6

Litany of Women in Pain*

We have had enough silence. We gather now to name the oppression and pain that we have known, to speak out for ourselves and for all those not here whom we represent. We have not tried to speak for all the oppressed, but only to name our own pain. We ask you to respond, "We stand with you."

—I am the voice of the woman who has been beaten, threatened, and abused. I am afraid you will blame me for the choices I have made, even when I felt I had no choice.
—I speak for the elderly woman. I feel our society wants to throw me away—no one will hire me.
—I speak for those women who have been manipulated and coerced by suicide threats, emotional blackmail, psychological and verbal abuse. My capacity to love has been turned and used as a weapon against me.
—I am the voice of the woman abandoned after a marriage of many years. I'm still trying to figure out what happened.
—I speak for the woman who is a victim of the medical establishment. Doctors I trusted to heal me have seduced me or committed me. Others have performed unnecessary surgery or refused to tell me what was happening to my own body.
—I speak for the physically handicapped woman.
—I speak for the woman who was called a lesbian in an attempt to control her, and for all who have recognized more deeply the communality of our separate oppressions when we were being stepped on ourselves.
—I speak for the child who grew up in a household where we all had to walk on eggs and keep a long list in our heads of the things we had to do, or not do, to keep my father from exploding in anger.

*Composed by Kathy Eickwort from the input of the Women in Pain Working Group.

—I speak for the woman who was blackmailed and manipulated into having an abortion she did not freely choose.
—I speak for the battered children, for the victims of incest and rape, and for the children of battered women.
—I speak for the women, lay and religious, who have had no voice and no choice, no respect and little compensation in their service to the community, for all who have suffered from clericalism and legalism.
—I speak for the woman who has taught her children to live a spiritually and socially responsible life, and shares with them the difficulty of radical insecurity and of not fitting in.
—I speak for the mother who, out of fear, is reluctant to let her daughter have the freedom her son has.
—I speak for the woman who cannot speak about the pain in her family because of her position in the community.
—I speak for the one who attempted suicide after her husband left her.
—I speak for the one who was "raised-poor." My mother taught me always to finish the chores before I could sit down and read—even today I have to go out of my house to read. My father was afraid I might become too well educated and surpass him.
—I speak for the unemployed, the underemployed, and the impoverished woman.
—I speak for the woman who turned to her religious community when she was hurting and found herself blamed for her pain.
—I speak for the woman who grew up in a home filled with violence and confusion, and found a place of safety and love with other women.
—I speak for the one who was too shy to be heard, and for all women who are afraid to speak out, who block the pain from their memories, who hide their pain from others.

We stand here also to celebrate those who have found healing through the support of other women, through music, through prayer or meditation, laughter, liberating spiritual experience, working with our dreams, or a myriad of other ways. We have learned to respect the divine within ourselves, and have found new strength, new sensitivity, new solidarity with all the victims of sexism, heterosexism, racism, and classism through our struggles.

Part III

Racism, Pluralism, Bonding

RACISM IS A major obstacle to women's bonding, both nationally and internationally. The familiar maxim that those who do not learn from history are condemned to repeat it could well serve as the theme of this part of the conference. Over and over again, speakers referred to a history of monstrous injustices, etched into the memories of the oppressed and known scarcely, if at all, to the oppressors: a history known to Blacks and forgotten or covered up by Whites; known to Jews and pushed aside by Christians; known to Chicanos and ignored by Anglos. The issues are complex and highly charged; the discussions during the conference were filled with the immediacy of personal pain: the suffering of a Black woman seeing her family repeatedly denied education, housing, employment; of a Jewish woman whose relatives had died in Nazi concentration camps; of a Chicana, who after five generations is still not at home in her native Texas; of an Italian immigrant's daughter fighting fiercely against the racism of her blue-collar family.

Under the immediate pain lies a long history full of ironies. To consider only the relations of Black and White women in the United States, it is ironic that White women did not discover their own oppression until they began to speak out against slavery and found they were denied the right to speak in public. Nevertheless, the organizers of the women's-rights movement, who were White, discouraged the participation of Black women, fearing "lest every newspaper in the land will have our cause mixed up with abolition."[1] Even those who opposed discrimination at a personal level (Susan B. Anthony dismissed a secretary who refused to take dictation from the

Black leader Ida B. Wells) still adopted racist policies at the organizational level.

We may debate the details of this history, but as Rebecca Johnson's addendum makes clear, it has shaped feminist attitudes and left its mark on the women's movement today. Other factors besides a history of racism have contributed to the predominance of White middle-class women in the feminist movement: single professional women have more leisure time to devote to organizational activities; suburban women with children feel more keenly the dependency and constraints imposed by their life-style; the media, unsympathetic from the first action at Atlantic City in 1968, play up the conflicts. More crucial, however, has been the difficulty of developing and disseminating an analysis of the interlocking character of the oppressions. One of the contributions of this book is to highlight how racism, sexism, classism, and imperialism form a web of oppressions, interacting and supporting one another. Feminists have frequently been blind to issues of race and class. Even in women's studies (and Black studies), as the title of a recent book points out, *All the Women Are White, All the Blacks Are Men, But Some of Us* [the hitherto invisible Third World women] *Are Brave*.[2]

This part examines racism from Black, Hispanic, Jewish, and White perspectives. It also includes some materials that were not part of the original panel. To supplement Jamie Phelps's succinct account of Black/White relations in the United States, Rebecca Johnson has contributed an addendum, filling in the historical background on racism in the women's movement and on the values of Black culture. Jacquelyn Grant, who spoke on the panel on alternative futures, devoted her talk to a critique of feminist theology; it relates so closely to some of the points made by the speakers on racism that we have included it in this part.

In women's heritage is our power. If we come to terms with our history, we free ourselves to move toward a better future. The working group on racism/sexism/classism was the largest working group and produced the longest paper. Since it attempts to model an approach of respecting differences, each subgroup has defined itself and its concerns. Since it also attempts to unite theory and practice, it evaluates the conference and offers some guidelines for the future. It asks planners to test their practice of mutuality by asking themselves these questions: Who is naming the problem? Who has access to the resources? Who sets the standards for appropriate behavior? Who has power to make and enforce decisions?

7

Racism and the Bonding of Women
JAMIE PHELPS

> RACISM . . . is a systematized oppression of one race by another. In other words, the various forms of oppression within every sphere of social relations—economic exploitation, military subjugation, political subordination, cultural devaluation, psychological violation, sexual degradation, verbal abuse, etc.—together make up a whole of interacting and developing processes which operate so normally and naturally and are so much a part of the existing institutions of society that the individuals involved are barely conscious of their operation. As Fanon says, "The racist in a culture of racism is therefore normal."[1]

Black women are often invited to participate in coalitions of White women in the feminist movement with the assumption that as women they share a common oppression. While not denying the presence of sexism in the Black community, its root cause and implications within the context of the Black freedom movement suggest the necessity of a different set of strategies for the liberation of Black women. Black women's liberation must be within the context of the liberation of the Black community, that is, within the context of the liberation of Black families, males and females, adults and children.

The suspicion with which many Black women approach the White feminist movement is well founded, given the history of Black-White alliances. Reviewing the attempts at Black-White alliances as long as 2,500 years ago in Africa, John Henrik Clarke notes that Black people have a history of allowing others to come among them, solicit their help and get it, only

Jamie Phelps

to turn away and betray them.[2] Arabs, Hebrews, Asians, Greeks, and Romans all attempted such an exploitation. Happily, not all such attempts were successful. Clarke, a Black historian, underscores the fact that in every alliance between Afrikan and non-Afrikan people made by an Afrikan woman, the Afrikans got the best of the deal.[3] Among these wise women were queens Hatshepsut and Cleopatra of Egypt and Candace of Ethiopia. Characteristic of this exploitative pattern is the arrangement of a "partnership" in which the Black person is always in the position of junior partner whose participatory power does not include a genuine alliance and a genuine friendship. The senior partner alone decides how, when, and what goals and strategies will direct the alliance. Clarke's analysis echoes the declaration of one of his Black predecessors, Martin Delany, in 1858.

> As men and equals, we demand every political right, privilege and position, to which the white are eligible in the United States, and we shall either attain to these or accept nothing. . . . As a people we will never be satisfied nor contented until we occupy a position where we are acknowledged as a necessary constituent in the ruling element of the country in which we live.[4]

The history of the Black movement in the United States suggests that efforts to secure Black freedom have always been co-opted by those who exploited the Black tendency to be inclusive by recruiting Blacks for their needs and self-interest.[5] This is clearly evident in two periods of our history, which take on the appearance of unhealthy repetition of error: the period of the Civil War, and the period of the civil rights movement of the 1960s.

The Civil War period signaled the demise of a very flourishing movement of Black abolitionists who, in allegiance to the needs of the nation, set aside the direct question of abolition to participate in the war—which from the perspective of the North and Lincoln was fought to preserve the Union, and from the perspective of the South was fought to preserve states' rights and slavery. Blacks assumed that this conflict among Whites was God's hand of deliverance ushering in freedom. But neither the Whites in the North nor the Whites in the South shared their view. Lincoln's Emancipation Proclamation was only an auxiliary decision to support his attempts to save the Union.[6] After the war the efforts at reconstruction were quickly undermined as both North and South returned to business as usual. Black slave status as a commodity shifted to the slave status of underpaid labor for the industrial development of the period.

Sensitized to their own "pedestal" slavery, White women from the abolitionist movement had begun in the middle 1800s to organize to acquire suffrage. Prominent Blacks in the abolitionist movement acknowledged the legitimacy of the White women's efforts, Frederick Douglass and Sojourner Truth among them. Yet White women excluded Frederick Douglass's daughter from attending a New York school and were resentful of Sojourner Truth's presence and participation in the women's movement.[7] The former had been present at the Seneca Falls Convention in 1848, while the latter had been present at another women's convention in Worcester, Massachusetts in 1859 and delivered her famous "Ain't I a Woman" speech at a women's rights meeting in Akron, Ohio in 1851.

Despite this active presence and support, some of the most prominent leaders of the suffrage movement who had participated in the abolitionist movement, when challenged with the prospect of the Black male vote preceding their own access to voting power, articulated a deep-seated racism.

> If the two million of Southern Black women are not to be secured rights of person, property, wages and children, their emancipation is but a form of slavery. In fact, it is better to be a slave of an educated white man than of a degraded ignorant black one.[8]

This from the mouth of Elizabeth Cady Stanton in 1865. Susan B. Anthony shared her racist sentiments.

Fortunately, the Grimké sisters saw the integral connection between the quest for Black rights and their own. Angelina Grimké stated in 1863, "I want to be identified with the Negro. Until he gets his rights, we shall never have ours."[9]

The civil rights movement once again found Blacks and Whites, males and females, struggling together for Black rights. White flight from this movement seems to have occurred with the cry of Black power, which signaled the Black participants' decision that it was time to claim the privilege of senior partnership, that is, the right to decide on the tactics, goals, and locations of the struggle. As Blacks assumed their adult roles in a self-determining community, Whites could not, it seems, work as equal partners or as followers of Black leadership in the Black community. The women, once again awakened to their oppression by participation in a movement against Black oppression, turned to the women's movement. Once again both movements were submerged when the nation's focus turned to the Vietnam war. Few made the connection between the oppression of Blacks in the United States and the oppression of People of Color in Vietnam (except Martin Luther King Jr.). Black rights movement, women's movement, war seems to be the cycle of the historical pattern.

To break this vicious cycle of alienation, mutual defeat, and frustration of efforts for freedom and justice, several lessons must be learned from history.

- An alliance of Blacks and Whites in which the former are viewed as inferior and dependent partners is counterproductive for both the Black and White communities.
- Failure to attend to the unique features of the oppressions of other groups prohibits any real, lasting, or effec-

tive coalition for liberation. White women still persist in varying degrees in denying the perniciousness or reality of racism as the determining factor in Black oppression. While racism did have an economic root, once it was established, as Sidney Wilhelm tells us, "racism assumed a determining character in its own right: it must now be taken for a dominant autonomous social value which, when linked with economic considerations, establishes an elaborate network of social relations between Blacks and Whites."

- The Black community, as does any community, posits a variety of interpretations of Black life based on a heterogeneous reality. White women must resist the temptation to pit one Black interpretation against another, assuming that neither is correct or inclusive enough, thus justifying an astute, all-inclusive, superior analysis to which Blacks as junior partners should dutifully acquiesce.
- White women must respect the rights of Black women to select the manner in which they will address the issue of sexism in the Black community and to work collectively with their Black brothers for the liberation of the Black community. Such respect does not mean that White women should fail to address the issue of the debilitating effects of racism on themselves and their Black brothers and sisters.
- White women need to learn how to celebrate differences and to build coalitions not only on the commonalities Blacks and Whites share as human beings but to seek honestly to enrich church and society with the gift of Blackness.

The Black value system not only can serve to unify the Black community, but may also prove an interesting base out of which to attempt a coalition of a multicultural, ecumenical movement.

Oppression anywhere is oppression everywhere.
—Martin Luther King Jr.

Until all are free, none are free.
—Martin Luther King Jr.

8

A Historical Addendum
REBECCA JOHNSON

At Jamie Phelps's request, I have enlarged on the historical background presented in her paper, with particular reference to the issues raised by the discussion on racism. In each case, I have included some reflections on the significance of these issues for Black and White women today. Among the issues: (1) the presence of racism in the women's suffrage movement and how that racism affects Black/White relations in the feminist movement today; (2) what issues inform the concern of Black women for the liberation of their families as a necessary condition for their own liberation; and (3) how the Black woman's search for personhood in a hostile culture speaks to the revisioning of womanhood in the feminist movement.

1. Racism in the Suffrage Movement

White women, especially middle-class women, came to the abolitionist cause out of a deep conviction of the immorality of keeping slaves. Thus Sarah Grimké writes in her diary in 1827:

> Slavery was a millstone about my neck and marred my comfort from the time I can remember myself. . . . I believed their bondage inconsistent with justice and humanity. . . . Deprived of ability to modify their situation, I was as one in bonds looking on their sufferings I could not soothe or lessen.[1]

The women's attempts to involve themselves actively in the movement were met, however, with great resistance by the White male leadership. When the leading abolitionists met in Philadelphia in 1833 to form the American Anti-Slavery Society, they permitted a few women to attend, but not to join the society or sign its Declaration of Sentiments. The women, led by Lucretia Mott, immediately formed the Philadelphia Female Anti-Slavery Society. Male resistance to their antislavery work was for many White women the first time they felt the need to break out of the straitjacket of "woman's role." Soon middle-class White women began to identify their own oppression with the oppression of the slaves. "What then can woman do for the slave, when she herself is under the feet of man and shamed into silence,"[2] wrote Angelina Grimké, after the clergy of Massachusetts in 1836 had condemned her public speaking against slavery as "unwomanly and unchristian." Admonished that women ought not to concern themselves with a political issue like slavery, Angelina replied, "The denial of our duty to act in this case is a denial of our right to act; and if we have no right to act, then may we well be termed 'the white slaves of the north,' for like our brethren in bonds, we must seal our lips in silence and despair."[3] And Sarah Grimké, in her letters on the equality of the sexes, denied "the distinction now so strenuously insisted upon between masculine and feminine virtues," and emphasized the great benefits to men and women both of "equality of the sexes."[4] Moreover, as White women worked in the abolitionist movement, they accumulated invaluable political experience and skills—in fundraising, writing and distributing literature, calling and presiding at meetings, public speaking, organizing. Without this experience, they could not have effectively organized the campaign for women's rights a few decades later.[5]

In the early days of women's suffrage, Frederick Douglass was one of its staunchest supporters. Present at the Seneca Falls Convention in 1848, the first women's rights convention in the United States, he supported women's suffrage editorially in his newspaper, *The North Star*, and introduced the issue to the American Anti-Slavery Society and the Black Liberation Movement.[6]

Elizabeth Cady Stanton caught her first glimpse of the relation between slavery and women's oppression when women delegates were refused seats at the London Anti-Slavery Convention of 1840. In fact, it was while she and Lucretia Mott angrily paced the streets of London after this refusal that they conceived the idea of the Seneca Falls Convention. Stanton often blurred the two issues in her speeches, as in these remarks to the American Anti-Slavery Society in 1860: "No, the mission of the Radical Anti-Slavery Movement is not to the African slave alone, but to the slaves of custom, creed and sex, as well."[7]

The women's suffrage movement wanted universal voting rights. During the Civil War they discontinued their own conventions, and under the leadership of Stanton and Susan B. Anthony formed the National Women's Loyal League, which campaigned effectively for the passage of the Thirteenth Amendment, abolishing slavery. After the war, in 1866, many of the men and women who had fought the abolitionist and women's rights battles formed the American Equal Rights Association (AERA) to bring together the struggles for Black and women's suffrage into a single campaign. Anthony insisted on the need "to broaden our Woman's rights platform and make it in name what it has always been in spirit—a Human Rights platform."[8] And Angelina Grimké declared, "I want to be identified with the Negro. Until he gets his rights, we shall never have ours."[9]

From 1866 to 1869, the AERA struggled to incorporate both Black and women's suffrage into law. But these principles were not shared throughout the movement. When the suffrage issue came before the Congress, it was not phrased in terms of universal suffrage but of suffrage for Black men. The Fifteenth Amendment stated that the vote was not to be denied because of race, color, or previous condition of servitude (but not sex, as the women had wanted). The AERA split over the issue of whether to campaign for the Fifteenth Amendment. The old-line abolitionists insisted that it was "the Negro's hour" and that they could work later for women's suffrage. They saw Black suffrage as imperative to protect the fragile rights the former slaves had just acquired. Douglass made an impassioned appeal to his White sisters to support Black suffrage as a strategic priority.

> When women, because they are women, are dragged from their homes and hung upon lamp-posts, when their children are torn from their arms and their brains dashed upon the pavement,

when they are objects of insult and outrage at every turn, when their children are not allowed to enter schools, then they will have [the same] urgency to obtain the ballot.[10]

The women who had worked for decades for abolition and for universal suffrage were deeply disillusioned by this change of course, particularly on the part of men like Douglass, William Lloyd Garrison, Wendell Phillips, and Charles Sumner, who had been among their staunchest supporters. Stanton and Anthony immediately struck back. Stanton wrote in the columns of her newspaper, *The Revolution:*

> Manhood suffrage? Oh! no, my friend, you mistake us! we have enough of that already. We say not another man, Black or White, until woman is inside the citadel. What reason have we to suppose that the African would be more just and generous than the Saxon has been? Wendell Phillips pleads for Black men; we for Black women, who have known a degradation and sorrow of slavery such as man has never experienced. . . .
> How insulting to put every shade and type of manhood above our heads to make laws for educated, refined, wealthy women. Horace Greeley thinks that Patrick and Sambo would appreciate the ballot more highly than the women of *The Revolution*.[11]

She warned that the advocacy of manhood suffrage "creates an antagonism between Black men and all women that will culminate in fearful outrages on womanhood, especially in the southern states." And Anthony in 1869 pledged: "I will cut off this right arm of mine before I ever work for or demand the ballot for the Negro and not the woman."[12] Clearly, Stanton did not scruple to cast doubts on the intelligence of Blacks; the human worth of Blacks, Chinese, and other immigrants; or the ability of Black men to render fair judgment in a court of law. Nor did she hesitate to play on the sexual fears of White women with regard to Black men. She and Anthony accepted support from any advocate of women's suffrage, including the avowed White supremacist George Brooks and the even more dubious racist Democrat George Francis Train.

In their disappointment, Stanton and Anthony moved quickly from their earlier equal rights/universal suffrage position to the advocacy of "educated suffrage," with all its racist and elitist overtones. Under Anthony's presidency, the National American Women's Suffrage Association promoted a literacy qualification for suffrage and assiduously courted the support of southern Whites. A southerner, Belle Kearney, in 1903 bluntly stated the position:

> The enfranchisement of women would insure immediate and durable white supremacy, honestly attained; for upon unquestionable authority, it is stated that "in every southern state but one, there are more educated women than all the illiterate voters, white and black, native and foreign combined."
>
> Just as surely as the North will be forced to turn to the south for the nation's salvation, just so surely will the south be compelled to look to its Anglo-Saxon women as the medium through which to retain the supremacy of the white race over the African.[13]

There was a lack of political sophistication on both sides. Frederick Douglass overrated the power of the ballot to protect the freedmen. Stanton and Anthony believed their help in securing the passage of the Thirteenth Amendment, abolishing slavery, had secured a commitment from the Republican Party to push for women's suffrage. Neither side fully grasped the depths of cynical opportunism in both political parties—the Democrats taking up the cause of women's suffrage in order to oppose Negro suffrage; the Republicans pushing suffrage for Black men in order to gain two million votes in the South.

Ellen DuBois sums up the effect of this troubled history on the women's movement: "After the [Fifteenth] Amendment's ratification, Stanton's outright racism subsided, but the more subtle habit of seeing women's grievances from the viewpoint of white women had been firmly established within the suffrage movement."[14]

The suffrage movement of 1868–69 was clearly racist and did not shrink from the use of racist tactics. Was the abolitionist movement sexist? The evidence suggests that it was.

The issue for feminists of the late twentieth century is not really whether a fledgling movement of the late nineteenth century was capable of being any different from the cultural milieu from which it grew, but whether White middle-class feminists can face their race/class prejudice today and give up their race/class privilege in order more fully to identify with the sufferings of their Sisters of Color. Equally important is whether feminists can learn from the mistakes of the early years of the movement and discover viable strategies for working with other liberation movements.

What Issues Inform the Concern of Black Women for the Liberation of Their Families as a Necessary Condition of Their Own Liberation?

"We cannot be concerned just with our own liberation as women. Only when Black men, women, and children are free will we be free. Our concern is with the black family." This statement has been made repeatedly by Black women during this conference. Where does this position originate? What values undergird it, and what does it say about the meaning of liberation?

In looking at the experience of Black people under slavery, Angela Davis, in her book *Women, Race and Class,* points out that slave women were expected to do the same hard labor in the fields as slave men, to bear the same harsh punishments. If a pregnant slave was sometimes treated humanely, it was only because the slaveowner appreciated the value of a slave child born alive in the same way that he appreciated a newborn calf or colt. Slave women were also confronted with rape at the hands of owner or overseer. Their children could be sold away from them; families were often forcibly disrupted by indiscriminate sales.[15]

In the midst of this dehumanizing environment, Black families survived. They did more than survive they overcame the slaveholders' attempt to reduce them to so many subhuman labor units, managing to create an ongoing system of family arrangements and kin networks. Domestic life became very important, for it was the only place where the slaves had any autonomy, but their family life did not correspond to the matriarchal stereotype of some social scientists. Rather, says Davis, the slaves were men and women of exceptional strength who did a remarkable thing: "They transformed that negative equality which emanated from the equal oppression they suffered as slaves into a positive quality: the egalitarianism characterizing their social relations."[16] Black women could never be regarded as mere housewives. Domestic labor—the work the slaves did for their own sake and the only work not done directly for the master—was the only meaningful work in the slave community. According to Davis, it was carried out on terms of equality between men and women.

Harriet Tubman, Sojourner Truth, Mary McLeod Bethune, and countless others provide a picture of slave women as strong, self-reliant, proud of their roots and of their ability to survive, convinced of their right to a place in society through the liberation of all Black people. Equally oppressed as laborers, equal to their men in the domestic sphere, they were also equal in their resistance to slavery, participating in work stoppages and revolts, fleeing north and helping others to flee.[17] They knew that the survival and enhancement of Black women, first as slaves and later as freedwomen, depended on the survival and enhancement of Black people through the same egalitarian means by which Black families had survived slavery and the turbulent antebellum period.

The ability of Black people to cope in a hostile society has endured into the twentieth century; studies of Black women in inner-city situations show that the means by which Black families survived slavery still enable Black women and their families to survive today.

Within this historical framework, Black people would naturally perceive values in the liberation struggle differently from Whites: domesticity was not seen as entirely oppressive but rather as a vehicle for building family life under slavery; male/female relationships were more egalitarian; there was less emphasis on women's work as different from and inferior to men's; slaves and freed persons, male and female, tended to rebel against the sexual oppression of women and the emasculation of men. It is easy to understand why many Black people see the feminist movement as an attempt to divide Black people. Contemporary Black feminists caution against espousing the more radical feminist stances because they leave out Black men, Black children, Black families.

Is it possible to work for the liberation of Black people and the liberation of women at the same time? Can one liberation movement support the other? What is the most fundamental liberation necessary for the continued survival of the human race?

How Have Black Women Seen Themselves?

How might this vision of self inform the re-imaging of women through the feminist movement?

In the face of overwhelming odds, the slave community managed to maintain a sense of Africanness, of family, of personal autonomy that enabled them to undermine the efforts of the slaveholder to strip them of their dignity. Women of exceptional strength and ability emerged from the Black community to take the lead in the struggle for freedom, education, employment. At the women's rights convention in Akron in 1851, in her famous "Ain't I a Woman" speech, Sojourner Truth spoke of women's strength: "If the first woman God ever made was strong enough to turn the world upside down all alone, these women together ought to be able to turn it back, and get it right side up again! And now they is asking to do it, the men better let them."[18] Frances D. Gage, who was presiding at that meeting, described the effect of Sojourner's words: she had "taken us up in her strong arms and carried us safely over the slough of difficulty [i.e., the arguments and ridicule of the men] turning the whole tide in our favor."[19]

At another convention in 1853, Sojourner revealed her self-image.

> I am a citizen of the state of New York; I was born in it, and I was a slave in the state of New York, and now I am a good citizen of this State. I was born here, and I can tell you I feel at home here. . . . I know it feels a kind o' hissin' and ticklin' like to see a colored woman get up and tell you about things, and Woman's Rights. We have all been thrown down so low that nobody thought we'd ever get up again; but we have been long enough trodden now; we will come up again, and now I am here.[20]

I think of the message passed on to me by my mother and my grandmothers, one northern, one southern. Grandma Finney, my mother's mother, is eight-nine, a thin, nut-brown woman with long gray-black hair who worked all her life in White women's houses, washing their floors and taking care of their children. She is dying now, and will soon join the spirits of long-forgotten African ancestors who still watch over us. She knew the oppression of a society that denied her existence as a human being, yet all the grandchildren she ever touched heard the same message: "You are Black, you are good, you are strong. There isn't anything you can't do. Don't let no White folks put you down."

Grandma believed the race would die out if we ever forgot these truths. White women as a group will not die out in the same sense my grandmother thought Black folks might. But the way Black women image themselves can speak to other women. Perhaps this imaging is one of the principal gifts we bring to the women's movement—a clear sense of who we are and what oppresses us, a history of struggle that gives us strength for the long march toward freedom. If White women will listen, perhaps these gifts can be shared and used in the struggle to free all oppressed people . . . including themselves. Maya Angelou writes[21]:

> You may write me down in history
> With your bitter, twisted lies.
> You may trod me in the very dirt
> But still, like dust, I'll rise.
>
> Does my haughtiness offend you?
> Don't you take it awful hard
> 'Cause I laugh like I've got gold mines
> Diggin' in my own back yard.
>
> Does my sexiness upset you?
> Does it come as a surprise
> That I dance like I've got diamonds
> At the meeting of my thighs?
>
> Out of the Huts of history's shame
> I rise
> Up from a past that's rooted in pain
> I rise
> I'm a black ocean, leaping and wide,
> Welling and swelling I bear in the tide.
>
> Leaving behind nights of terror and fear
> I rise

Into a daybreak that's wondrously clear
I rise
Bringing the gifts that my ancestors gave
I am the dream and the hope of the slave.
I rise   I rise   I rise

9
"La Marías" of the Feminist Movement
YOLANDA TARANGO, C.C.V.I. AND ADA MARIA ISASI-DIAZ*

The plight of Hispanic women is best illustrated by a current practice followed in the big cities of Mexico. The indigenous women who come down from the mountains to work as domestics and servants in the urban areas are simply called "Las Marías." These women are so insignificant that their employers do not have to bother learning their individual names; the women are all called simply "María." To the dominant group, they are all alike.

This custom reflects the mentality of the culture regarding women. It is a custom that could easily be transferred to this country, for it captures the experience of Hispanic women in American society. We are invisible, insignificant, and, to many, indistinguishable. Hispanic women are at the bottom of the poverty scale, lower than White women, lower than Black women. We perform the most deadly of the secondary-sector jobs, and we are voiceless in the social and political areas.

As feminists, we are familiar with the concepts of men's and women's cultures. We talk about women having to live in a male system, abide by male values and rules, and speak male language. And what do men know about women but the myths they concoct and perpetuate to keep power balanced in their favor? This imbalance also applies to dominant and nondominant cultures, to colonizing and colonized groups. As bilingual Hispanic women, in order to survive in the dominant culture, we have to abide by the American system, by American values;

*Used by permission of the authors.

Yolanda Tarango

Ada María Isasi-Díaz

and we have to speak English. What do most people know about us except the myths and the stereotypes?

One of the dynamics of oppression is that those in the dominant position have little need to know anything about those in the dominated position. The dominated have to know a lot about the dominators to survive within this system. Hispanic women believe that if White women want to explore bonding, then they also have to examine what keeps Hispanic women and White women apart: we all have to talk about racism and imperialism. We have to go beyond the stereotypes. That will not happen in any situation where the ratio of Hispanic women to Anglo women is disproportionate.

Has there been progress over the last three generations? Our grandmothers might have worked as domestics and later graduated to work in a restaurant or a cafeteria. Our mothers might have had some formal education, maybe up to the seventh or eighth grade, and they probably worked at a clerical job or in a factory. Hispanic women today are still doing the same kind of jobs. Young Hispanic women are still aspiring today to the heights of being secretaries!

As Hispanic women, we often reflect on the source of our feminist analysis. We are so overwhelmed with what it means to be Hispanic in the American culture that it is hard to look at what it means to be a woman in the Hispanic culture. In the feminist movement we often find ourselves living the same experience that we live as Hispanic women in the dominant society—an experience of silence and voicelessness.

As Hispanic feminists we suffer the great pain of not knowing where home is, of not feeling at home anywhere. If we go back to visit or attend meetings in our countries, we are not considered to be true natives. Because we live in this country, the people back home believe we are not faithful to our cultural identity and values, that we profit from the imperialistic system of this country and thus participate in oppressing them. When we are among our own people here in the United States many of them feel that we are betraying them by being feminists, that our priorities are not correct. And among feminists, we feel you do not know us because you do not need to know us. We need to know so much about the dominant culture that we come to know intuitively what pleases you—it is a survival mechanism. But what do you know about us?

We know what Anglo feminists mean by the word bonding. We know what their expectations are from those they are bonded with. But do Anglo feminists take time to understand what we Hispanic feminists mean by bonding? In our culture, the relationships within our families are the paradigms for all other relationships. The bonds within our families are very strong. When we call an Anglo feminist sister what we mean by it—the expectations we have of those we call sisters and the obligations we feel toward them—are different from those of the Anglo feminists. And what we ask is that you take time to be with us, so you can come to understand us.

You ask what you can do in order not to oppress Hispanic feminists. Our answer is: get to know us. For example, the dominant culture massifies us by using the term Hispanic. Such terminology obliterates the rich cultural diversity of the different nationalities we represent, creating competition among the different Hispanic groups. We feel the need for recognition of our specificity, and since we do not get it from the dominant culture, we engage in horizontal violence among ourselves. Do Anglo feminists know anything about the history of different Hispanic countries other than the paragraph in their seventh-grade history books that refers to the Alamo or to the Rough Riders?

When we as Hispanics engage in dialogue with other Women of Color, there is a conscious awareness of the differences among us, of the need each of our cultural groups has to respect the others' sacred symbols, sacred space, different cultural identities. Among ourselves we do not try to dominate one another, we do not wonder why there are differences, or point to the disvalues of our different cultures. Among ourselves we experience a sensitivity that we do not experience with White women. White women are quick to tell us about the disvalues in our culture. We are oppressed by the use of the word machismo, as if it was a greater problem within our culture, or one we created. The word is Spanish, but we do not hold exclusive rights to it! What we ask and what we need from White women is deep respect for who we are, for our feelings, emotions, ideas, and values.

In our dealings with the Anglo feminist movement we feel like an oppressed group. We experience the paralysis of voicelessness and invisibility. We feel that we constantly have to insert ourselves. We are a parenthesis, an issue within the movement. We are tired of having constantly to say to Anglo feminists, "No, my name is not María. My name is Yolanda, my name is Ada María." We will work in the feminist movement, but only if we can keep our cultural feelings, our needs, and our ideals intact. We are going to be in charge of our own destiny, and we will keep our unique identity.

10

Anti-Semitism: The Unacknowledged Racism
JUDITH PLASKOW

The subject of anti-Semitism frightens me. It does so not because anti-Semitism frightens me, but because the discussion of it threatens to separate me from other women. It reminds me of our differences rather than our similarities. It reminds me that the women's movement, in appealing to women as women, frequently erases important cultural differences among us. It reminds me that sisterhood, while powerful, is not powerful enough to eradicate deeply seated prejudice. The very process of trying to organize these remarks reminds me that I belong to different communities. As a feminist addressing other feminists, I want to be honest about the contradictions I see in Judaism and Jewishness. As Jew, I do not want to be misheard or provide ammunition to the anti-Semites among my Christian feminist sisters.

Perhaps these conflicts are appropriate to my subject: complexity. As feminists, we are forced to acknowledge the complexity of oppression. We are aware that race, class, and sex oppressions are interstructured in the lives of many women.[1] They interlock not in an additive way—so that one is oppressed as a Woman *and* a Black, for example—but in an integral way that alters the total experience of oppression.[2] We recognize that the complexity of oppression makes it possible for the same person to be both oppressed and oppressor, and that as American feminists many of us are in both categories. But these insights, which are easier to assent to than to integrate fully into our analysis and practice, become particularly clear in the situation of the Jewish woman. To be a Jewish woman in

Judith Plaskow

America is to experience many aspects of the complexity of oppression, only a few of which can be discussed here.

It is necessary to admit at the outset that Jews hardly appear oppressed in the United States today. Anti-Semitism in the United States, never as virulent as in Europe, declined in the decades after World War II to the point where many were predicting its disappearance.[3] Such prejudice as there was did not, in any event, prevent the economic integration of Jews into American life. Contrary to all the stereotypes, there are poor and working-class Jews, but the majority of American Jewry appears comfortably ensconced in the middle class. Indeed, one might say Jews are exhibit A for the upward mobility possible in American society. Many an immigrant toiling in poverty on New York's lower East Side had the privilege of seeing children or grandchildren go to college and enter the professions—a fact that has occasionally been used against other minority groups.[4]

Moreover, since the vast majority of American Jews are White, we share White-skin privilege and have assimilated racism along with other American values. The disproportionately high percentage of Jews involved in the civil rights movement never represented a majority of American Jewry, most of whose attitudes toward Blacks are indistinguishable from those of other Americans.[5] In the last fifteen years, the Jewish and

Black communities have come into conflict on a number of specific issues. That Jews have sometimes been the last group to leave an area before Blacks move in has meant that in certain Black neighborhoods, a disproportionate number of storekeepers and landlords are Jews. This makes Jews the buffer group, the representatives to Blacks of the exploitative White community. In New York City, the underlying tensions created by this situation were exacerbated by the school crisis of 1968. Jews who had "made it" in American society through the school system perceived Black insistence on community control as a threat to their livelihood and place in society. For many Blacks, the crisis marked the beginning of the Jewish community's backing away from commitment to racial justice. This feeling, fanned by President Carter in the Andrew Young affair, was reinforced by the recent and ongoing role of a number of major Jewish organizations in opposing affirmative action. That this last turn of events is deeply disturbing to many Jewish feminists only illustrates the complexity of our situation. Whatever we may feel, in all these cases the Jewish community appears as oppressor, not as oppressed.

Yet to be a Jew in the United States is to know that there are forms of oppression other than economic oppression. Acceptance comes in many shades; although Jews can and have entered the professions in this country, they are closed off from the avenues of real power. Again contrary to the stereotypes, Jews are not the bankers in America, nor the corporation heads. There has never been a Jewish President, and there are not very many Jews in Congress. To be a Jew in the United States is to have enough money to live in certain parts of town or to join certain clubs, and yet not be permitted to live there or join anyway. It is to have a cousin or uncle or sister who went to an inferior medical school or did not get to go at all because of anti-Jewish discrimination. It is to be aware that in the name of what is now euphemistically called "geographic distribution," certain colleges still take care not to admit too many Whites from New York City, lest the school have too many Jews.

Such forms of discrimination, while less than life-threatening, take a psychic toll. I recall as a child not liking people to ask me my religion and, indeed, viewing the question as "impolite." I would never deny my Jewishness, but I was uncomfortable acknowledging it. I was aware quite early that it was not the preferred thing to be! This feeling is certainly related to the unwillingness of many Jews to press their own Jewish concerns and to the more subtle forms of self-contempt that come with not living up to particular standards of beauty, manners, or discretion. Other Jewish feminists have written of attempts to iron their dark, kinky hair or to stop being "pushy" or shooting off their big mouths.[6] The epithet pushy need not be explicitly accompanied by "Jew" for the message to be conveyed that Jewish ethnic mannerisms do not conform to American norms. (Of course, many other American ethnic groups have this same experience.)

There are also more important determinants of the American Jewish experience. To be a Jew in the United States is to live in an overwhelmingly and often unself-consciously Christian country. One's school vacations are scheduled around Christian holidays, one learns Christmas carols and participates in Easter-egg hunts, all the while being assured that these customs and holidays are not really Christian but American, that "they belong to everybody." When I lived in Wichita, Kansas, the local newspaper had a big picture of a sunrise on its cover one Easter with a caption remarking that the coming of Easter brings a smile to the face of everyone, whether or not they are Christian. Such blithe cultural imperialism masks not only the indifference of most of the world toward Easter but also the Jewish historical experience of Easter as a time of fear, a time when Christians could be expected to take revenge on their Jewish neighbors for the death of Christ. This cultural imperialism is part of the broader phenomenon that Tarango and Isasi-Diaz have discussed (" 'Las Marías' of the Feminist Movement," pp. 85–88): the oppressed must know about the oppressor's culture, but the oppressor need know nothing about the oppressed.[7] Ironic as this is, given the Jewish roots of Christianity, American Jews necessarily acquire a surface knowledge of major Christian beliefs and celebrations, while—particularly outside New York City—Christians are often totally ignorant of Jewish holy days and their meaning.

It is hardly surprising, given this Christian dominance, that to be a Jew in America is to meet anti-Semitism in its particularly

Christian formulations. It is to learn that one is a Christ-killer, and perhaps be beaten for being one, at a time when, without being quite sure who Christ is, one knows quite well one never killed anybody. I remember standing on the opposite side of the street from the Catholic children on my block throwing bluestones back and forth while they yelled, "You're going to burn in hell!" I did not know why I was going to burn in hell, but I recognized an insult when I heard one. A more subtle form of Christian anti-Judaism, one that ties in with the issue of cultural imperialism, is the Christian perception of the essence of Judaism as rejection of Christ. From the Jewish perspective, this makes almost as little sense as the idea that the essence of Buddhism is rejection of Christ. Judaism has nothing to do with Christ. It is an independent tradition that did not end with the Old Testament but, in a sense, began in the same period that Christianity did. This fundamental misunderstanding of Judaism denies its integrity and legitimacy as a living religion at the same time that it supports a Christian interpretation of reality.

On another theme, to be a Jew in the United States is to know as a fundamental part of one's identity that in this century, a third of world Jewry was exterminated simply because they were Jews. Hitler's war against the Jews was not part of the wider war effort; in fact, it may even have lost him the war.[8] But anyone who had one Jewish grandparent, even if the family had been Christian for two generations, was exterminated as vermin. To be a Jew in the United States is to know that one *is* a Jew in the United States because parents and grandparents came here fleeing pogroms at the turn of the century. Had they not come fleeing other persecutions, they would have been part of the statistics of the Holocaust. Therefore, to be a Jew in the United States is to be a survivor. Jews are sometimes accused of seeing anti-Semitism where it does not exist and bringing it into being by their expectations. I do not doubt that this is sometimes true. But it is all too easy for non-Jews to discount or tire of the scars that come with knowing even third hand the impassioned hate directed at one's people within or almost within one's lifetime.

This is all just background, however, to what many Jews perceive as a new escalation of anti-Semitism in this country as part of the right-wing backlash of the last few years. Reports of anti-Semitic incidents such as vandalism and cross-burnings have recently risen dramatically. And whether this is new or not, the women's movement has had its share of anti-Semitic incidents and feeling. Indeed, it is ironic that women who had abandoned their Judaism because it was sexist, seeking community in the women's movement, are now being forced back to Judaism because of feminist anti-Semitism. As Jean-Paul Sartre said in his book *Anti-Semite and Jew,* "The Jew is one whom other [people] consider a Jew."[9] Jewish women are learning the truth of this in a very painful way.

Certain forms of Christian cultural and linguistic imperialism in the women's movement cannot really be called anti-Semitism. It would be nice if feminists were immune to attitudes that pervade the culture, but there is no reason to expect they will be. Thus when the supposedly interreligious Feminist Theological Institute is initially called the Institute for Theology and *Ministry,* or when one of its organizers speaks of "giving birth to this baby [i.e., the institute] and baptizing her," or when there are only five Jewish women at the Grailville conference, these things can be understood simply as everyday thoughtlessness.

Other reports coming out of the women's movement are more disturbing. Jewish feminists have reported having to listen to anti-Semitic jokes. Their concerns have been trivialized and treated as "Jewish paranoia" in contexts where every other form of oppression is taken seriously. Anti-Semitic stereotypes have been used to silence or discount feminist Jews: she's just a Princess/Jewish intellectual/rich Jew/pushy Jew/cunning Jew, etc.[10] Most upsetting are stories about the women's conference at Copenhagen, where American delegates found the anti-Semitism overt and intense. Novelist Esther Broner, for example, had a United Nations staff person remark to her, "Denmark is wonderful, but the Germans take it over in the summer, and I hate them. They only did one thing right: they killed the Jews." When Broner started to choke, the woman said to her, "Oh, did I hurt your feelings? Are you German?"[11]

Little in an American Jewish upbringing prepares one to deal with such remarks. In a spring 1982 issue of the *New York Times Magazine,* Jewish historian Lucy Dawidowicz had an article on American Jewry's response to World War II.[12] She argued that, contrary to the dominant view, American Jews did everything they could to try to save European Jewry; they simply lacked the power to be effective. In the following weeks, there were several letters to the *Times* disputing her interpretation of events. I do not know who is right. But it strikes me that it is easier for the Jewish community to beat its collective breast saying it did not do enough than to accept the fact of powerlessness. As an American White middle-class woman, that powerlessness terrifies me.

Nowhere do Diaspora Jews experience this powerlessness more strongly than in relation to Israel. An important element in the anti-Semitism at Copenhagen, and in the American feminist movement, is anti-Semitism in its new and "genteel" form of anti-Zionism. I do not consider criticism of the Israeli government anti-Semitism. I deplore its policies as strongly as anyone. But I think the Jewish community has a right to ask itself why, when other peoples kill, lie, maim, or steal, the world closes its eyes or legitimates their deeds in the name of self-defense or national liberation. When the Jews behave as a "normal" nation, however, the moral outrage of the world is focused upon them. From this I can only conclude that the world wants to see the Jews remain victims. In that status, we *may* be allowed a place among the world's people, but for us to seek to determine our own destiny is unacceptable.

But I learn something else from Israel, which brings me back to my initial point: to be oppressed does not protect one from being an oppressor. To be a Jew and not a Nazi is, in a sense, a moral privilege, but it guarantees nothing about who the Jew will be when she or he comes to power.

A number of years ago, I wrote an article on anti-Judaism in Christian feminist treatments of Jesus. In it, I discussed a problem that had disturbed and angered me for some time and that I felt Christian feminists had an obligation to address. Several months after I wrote the piece, I read an article by Alice Walker on racism in White feminist writing.[13] Essentially, she was saying about White feminists what I had said about Christian feminists, and every point she made applied to me. The article frightened me because it made me wonder whether we are all locked into our own experience of oppression, wanting other people to hear and know us, but unwilling to undertake the difficult process of trying to know others. How can we use our experience of oppression, I wondered, not to wall ourselves in but to build bridges to one another?

Thinking about this question sends me back to a basic affirmation of the Jewish tradition, its insistence on remembering that "we were slaves in the land of Egypt." Every Passover, the telling of the story of the Jewish people begins there. Several years ago, in the context of an anthology on Jewish feminism, Esther Ticktin suggested that the knowledge that we were slaves in the land of Egypt should become the basis of a new Jewish law governing the relationships between Jewish women and men. Just as Jews have the right to expect that a decent Gentile will not join a club that excludes Jews, so Jewish women have the right to expect that decent Jewish men will not participate in any Jewish institution or ritual that excludes Jewish *women*.[14]

But as women from many different backgrounds, each of us in her own way has been a stranger or slave in the land of Egypt. Could not Esther's sensitizing and consciousness-raising device become the basis for our ethical dealings with one another? As Cherríe Moraga put it, "We don't have to be the same to have a movement, but we *do* have to be accountable for our ignorance. In the end, finally, we must refuse to give up on each other."[15] Can we learn to value our differences instead of being threatened by them? Is this not part of what it should mean to be a feminist? Is this not part of what it should mean to be a Jew?

White Women and Racism
RENNY GOLDEN

While for black people the lessons of colonialism have been driven home with unmediated force, white women have been caught in the middle.
—MICHELLE RUSSELL[1]

The Reagan camp, flashing the new right's slogans like a sleazy neon sign, has managed to illuminate, albeit in murky light, the underside of North America's nascent racism, sexism, and class blindness. Practically every civil-rights gain accomplished at the human cost of bloodshed, hosings, and police-dog attacks is being eroded, while white hoods of terror, once again, poke boldly into southern skies.

Deft budget transfers have taken money from mothers and children in this country to build a military junta in El Salvador responsible for the deaths of 34,000 people in the last two years, the majority of whom were women, children, and the elderly. As the women's movement mourns the demise of ERA, has it mourned these deaths, which are tolled nightly on our TV sets as consistently as the Dow Jones average? Can the women's movement make the connections between racist, imperialist human-rights policies toward poor countries and the lives of women in this country?

As White feminists we must examine, not simply national racist policy, but our own racism, in light of the challenge of Women of Color whom we have failed to acknowledge. We must probe deeper into our feminist practice to discover our past failures, lest we repeat our two primary mistakes: speaking for the women's movement as if it were all ours and all White, and separating racism and sexism. The identity of Women of Color has been invisible. They are rarely recognized as a group distinct from the men of their race, and they are not included in the White culture's definition of women.

Renny Golden

Bell Hooks, author of *Ain't I A Woman: Black Women and Feminism,* comments on the separation of race and sex in the women's movement: "I was disturbed by the white women's liberationist insistence that race and sex were two separate issues. My life experience has shown me that the two issues were inseparable, that at the moment of my birth, two factors determined my destiny, my having been born black and my having been born female."[2]

But just as we cannot understand women's lives if we separate race and sex, so we cannot separate issues of class and heterosexism. We cannot talk about racism if we do not talk about imperialism, because we will not be talking about the majority of Women of Color in this world and the primary force that exploits them.

I have learned about my own racism from Women of Color. I worked for fourteen years in the Black community in Chicago, and I have spent the last two years with Salvadoreans, Guatemalans, and Nicaraguans doing solidarity work. Therefore, I will limit my discussion to White women, Black women, and Hispanic women struggling for liberation in Central America. Absent from my comments will be attention to the lives of Latina, indigenous, Jewish-American, Arab-American, Asian-American, or other Eastern women. The enormous complexity of racism means that any discussion will be incomplete; I intend simply to offer a few points for reflection.

Michelle Russell, a friend from whom I personally have learned a great deal about the lives of Black women, has written:

> While for black people the lessons of colonialism have been driven home with unmediated force, white women have often been caught in the middle. As a victimized accomplice population in this process, they have been confused. Your oppression and exploitation have been more cleverly masked than ours, more delicately elaborated. The techniques, refined. You were rewarded in minor ways for docile and active complicity in our dehumanization.
>
> At base, the risk of your complete alienation from the system of white male rule that also exploited you was too great to run. While your reproductive function has been the only reason for your relative protection in the colonizing process, ours, on the contrary, has sharpened the knife colonialism applies to our throats and wombs.[3]

These words of Johnnie Tillmon, the former leader of the National Welfare Rights Organization, extend Russell's point.

> Welfare is like a traffic accident. It can happen to anybody, but especially it can happen to women. For a lot of middle class women in this country, women's liberation is a matter of concern. For women on welfare, it's a matter of survival. [Welfare] kills your illusions about yourself and where this country's really at. You learn to fight, to be aggressive, or you just won't make it. . . . It gives you a kind of freedom, a sense of your own power and togetherness with other women. . . . Maybe it's we poor welfare women who will really liberate women in this country.[4]

These reflections from Black women challenge White women who, in encountering the forces of their own oppression, must face their own structural complicity in the oppression of Black women. The confusion, guilt, and resentment of middle-class White women are symptoms of the problems that emerge when they begin to deal with their privileged silence about the lives of *all* women.

I agree with Tillmon's hunch that it is the historical destiny of the poorest class to be liberators, despite the past weight of their invisibility and silence. It is the force of the working classes, and especially the awakening voice of poor women, which, like river waters, will carry liberation to the mouth of freedom. This trust in the revolutionary destiny of women oppressed by race and class is both a scientific conviction based on a critical analysis of their socioeconomic structural position and a paradoxical intuition based on faith. I believe that God is revealed to us through the suffering and courage of those whose lives bear witness to a hope in life against all possible odds. They are the locus of God's presence in history.

I do not believe, in holding out this hope in the poorest of women, that we White middle-class women must wait around, discounting our own oppression until the really oppressed rise up. Measuring our suffering is a *quantifying* of our pain (capitalistic estimation of value), and it continues to focus us on our victimhood. We need not to describe how bad our condition is or how awful it has been, but to change it. While transformation of the systemic structures of oppression of women is a goal, the historical moment still requires that our stories be shared, our grief and anger about our condition be told, as well as the basis of our distrusts. I believe, further, that sharing, confronting, and seeking a deeper perception of our mutual struggle is liberating and a sign of hope. I believe this hope, discovered in sisterhood, forged in the struggle of oppressed peoples, is a trust in liberation that will bring about a new woman, a new earth.

Women of White middle-class backgrounds have had to bear a challenge of elitism from Women of Color, from poor and working-class women who have historically been the voiceless ones. Their question has been: Whose language do you speak? Whose experiences do you articulate when you speak of women's experiences? Such a challenge has had, at times, paralyzing effects on White women, whose vulnerability historically has been guilt, internalized through a patriarchal socialization process aimed at keeping them passive.

This guilt is one of the dimensions of White women's experience that keeps them caught by keeping them reactive and defensive. Their guilt has historical roots, and they remember it uncomfortably. In the 1800s the Negro male was enfranchised by the Fourteenth Amendment, and women were disqualified from the vote. Although many women in the movement had worked tirelessly for abolition causes and the enfranchisement of women and Blacks, this blow to their cause severed their solidarity with Blacks. Angry militant feminist leaders tried to stop the amendment until it included women. Elizabeth Cady Stanton, despairing that women would receive any consideration or rights from enfranchised Men of Color (as if they had any power), demanded that White daughters be enfranchised, thus ignoring Black women. Stanton argued:

> If Saxon men have legislated for their own mothers, wives, and daughters, what can we hope for at the hands of Chinese, Indians and Africans? . . . I protest against the enfranchisement of another man of any race or class until the daughters of Jefferson, Hancock, and Adams are crowned with their rights.[5]

Lest we repeat failures of the past we must resist the systematic imperative to separate issues of race, class, and sex, which leads to goals focused on White women's agendas in the name of all women. Black women, in much the same way as did Black women's-rights advocates in the nineteenth century, assumed that a women's movement concerned with the lives of women would confront race as a primary contradiction dividing women, and would be determined to confront racism and classism as forces that thwart solidarity and suppress revolutionary potential. Throughout the 1970s, however, if Black women participated in women's groups, conferences, and coalitions, they found their trust betrayed. A similar process seems to be operative for Latina women, with tragically the same conclusion emerging. According to Bell Hooks, Black women

> found that white women had appropriated feminism to advance their own cause, i.e., their desire to enter the mainstream of American capitalism. . . . White women liberationists decided that the way to confront racism was to speak out by consciousness-raising groups about their racist upbringing, to encourage black women to join their cause, to make sure they hired non-white women in "their" women's studies program or to invite one non-white woman to speak on a discussion panel at "their" conference.[6]

Certainly I am one of the women Bell Hooks is talking about, because I assumed that working in the Black community "covered me," and I have not listened carefully enough to the experience of Women of Color. So I do not stand outside the feminist movement's failure when I say the following: the failure of the White woman's movement to enter into the struggle of Women of Color and of poor women is a failure to live up to its revolutionary potential. It is why our movement is labeled bourgeois, why the original inspiration and force of the movement has waned for me. It is not interesting to argue endlessly in women's groups that separatism will get us nowhere because forces that oppress are not simply men, that racism cannot truly be addressed unless women can talk about imperialism and not simply about patriarchy.

At this historical moment, when our nation actually colludes in the slaughter of the poor of Central America, we as women must act, even though White males dominate foreign and domestic policy. Given the current U.S. interventionist policy, one would expect Central America and the Caribbean to be on every feminist agenda. But, sisters, they are not.

In El Salvador and Guatemala, 80 percent of the fleeing refugees are women and children. Six hundred women and children were massacred or drowned as they frantically tried to swim the Río Sumpul. "Huey" helicopters supplied by the U.S. State Department to the Salvadoran military strafed the river with machine-gun fire, turning the Río Sumpul red with the peoples' blood. In Guatemala, recent reports of the massacre of women and children in the province of San Francisco have received little press coverage. Because the three hundred peasants were Indians, their deaths have not alarmed the international press. Under the "moderate" government of Ríos Montt, the Guatemalan military threw dead bodies of mothers onto burning village pyres with their still-living babies tied to their backs.

Meanwhile, President Reagan's destabilization plans for Nicaragua involve a $19 million CIA-sponsored "covert action" objective with a similar high human cost for the poor of that country. Already counterrevolutionaries involved in this plot have killed almost three hundred Nicaraguans. While I was with a North American group in Nicaragua in March 1982, we met with AMLAE, the mass women's organization. The women took us into the camps near the Nicaraguan border to show us the buildings they had constructed for child-care centers. For the mothers of those children, the cotton pickers of Chinandega, such centers were a small miracle the revolutionary process had provided. We asked the mothers, who arise at 4 A.M. to begin picking in the relative coolness of the early morning, what they did with the infants before there were child-care centers. They pointed to the side of the cotton fields, where no shading grew for miles, and explained that they had placed babies there with a sheet cover for protection from the sun and snakes. Knowing our government's complicity in these wars, whose victims have been women and children, why has there been no outcry from the women's movement?

If White women, although faced with daily erosion of economic and political options, do not enter into solidarity with Women of Color and women fighting to live in underdeveloped nations, then the women's movement will continue, in spite of rhetoric to the contrary, to offer Women of Color and poor women only apologies. The argument that women cannot take on the burdens of others as they have been socialized to do, that they must each do their own work excellently, and so forth, misses the point. The point is simply that our struggle is against the oppression of all women, and that colonialist oppression must be confronted because not only is its knife at our throats and wombs, but in this nuclear age its big gun is cocked (so to speak!) and poised at the heart of the earth itself.

The murder of Mother Earth is planned, the slaughter of mothers and infants is accomplished before our eyes, the slow erosion of poor women in this country is happening clandestinely. We cannot allow it. If the liberation struggle of Women of Color, of poor women, is not a binding force in the women's movement, then I am not interested in our spiritual bonds.

I would like to conclude by celebrating the lives of four White women raped and assassinated in El Salvador, whose roles as religious women relegated them to a patriarchal social stereotype of humble handmaidens. They were pictured as martyrs who bumbled into a revolution, content to feed hungry refugees. Their death was interpreted as a catastrophe occurring because these innocent victims happened to be in the wrong place at the wrong time.

But the facts confront these stereotypes. Ita Ford, Maura Clark, Dorothy Kazel, and Jean Donovan freely and consciously chose, not simply (as we have been told) to accompany the people, but to support their insurrectionary struggle. Two of the women, in fact, were living out their choice to enter the context of death that is the reality of El Salvador, when they took their last flight from N_____ to the San Salvador airport. They had spoken with a Maryknoll psychiatrist on leaving Nicaragua about their daily fear of death, and reclaimed their determination to be with the people with whom they had cast their lot.

I would like to offer my poem *"¡Adelante!"* ("Forward!"), which I wrote on the occasion of their murder.

¡Adelante!
for Ita, Maura, Dorothy, and Jean

> Do not remember us then,
> violated, blood darkening
> an earth strewn with bodies,
> broken egg shells discarded,
> silent as Victor Jara's lost fingers.
> Listen to the wind
> shaking these fields,
> the poor's voices whispering
> into North American ears,
> "We are dying while
> you are our assassins."
> Hearing this voice, act
> to hold back the hand that fires.
> Remember us then as ones
> the people taught courage.
>
> Remember us when
> they sing again.
> Sing of innocence
> soaring like doves
> against the night fire,

silver cracks of rifle shots.
The death each morning when
mothers dig their children's graves.
Sing of the insolence
of the dead, brushing
the stars above Chalatenango,
when we gringas
stayed with the people
until we broke with them,
like fingers from a hand.
Then sing compañeras,
sing with the people,
   ¡Adelante!

12

Discussion*

REBECCA JOHNSON: I am struck by the similarity among the three minority speakers—Black, Hispanic, and Jewish. We are all called to be biculturally competent; I can talk one way here and another way down in the street. We can all operate across cultures and make ourselves understood in both cultures. That has to happen for the minority to be accepted, but it is not an expectation for the majority. Jews tend to cross over a little more; our ability to be biculturally competent may help minority women to coalesce more easily than White women.

JUDITH PLASKOW: If I go to my own culture, I feel alienated as a feminist, but when I come to the feminists, there is also the sense of not being 100 percent there. Jews have always felt this schizophrenia throughout the centuries: a connection with the state of Israel or with the place of Israel before it was a state, and an identity with the culture in which they lived. I feel that way, but even more so, because feminism is so strong for me. I want to feel totally there in the feminist space and totally there in the Jewish space, but I can't come up with a place that is really home.

ADA MARIA ISASI-DIAZ: There is a tremendous problem of finding a place where we really feel at home. We have difficulty with our men, who feel we are betraying them in being part of the feminist movement. We need to know a lot about the dominant culture; for generations we have learned all we could about the oppressor so that we could survive in that world. Our relationships of friendship are based on the relationships in our families. Those bonds are

*This discussion followed the presentation of the panel on racism. The comments of the various participants are indicated by letters of the alphabet, except for the panelists, who are identified by name.

very strong, so "sister" means more to me than it might to someone in another culture. We need to have a dialogue about this.

JAMIE PHELPS: We miss in this conference some other Women of Color—the Native American and Asian women. Given the historical origins of the master-slave relation, White relations with Blacks will be different from those with other People of Color. With Native Americans, the relation was extermination. With Blacks, it was slavery—the relation that is most frightening to Whites because the implication of guilt is stronger. The Black man is the object of extermination in the present system. Because Black women are devalued as females, the White male is comfortable with us. Just look at the secretaries when institutions begin to integrate, and watch the rapport. Sometimes it has sexual connotations, but they are not coming from the woman. Black women can have the illusion of access to that power structure because we are not threatening as women. We are viewed as objects, either sexual objects or pawns to be pitted against the Black man. I refuse—as do most black women I know—to be pitted against Black men for alliance with White women or women of any other color. When you pit us against our partners, we are dead, because the extermination of the Black community is the extermination of all Blacks, male and female, adults and children.

PLASKOW: I can identify with other White feminists as my primary community, and then all of a sudden, wham! But I have the illusion that I can identify with that feminist community.

PHELPS: That has to do with the assimilation scale and the fact that you can pass over. We can never pass over unless we truly pass, and then you don't know we are there.

ISASI-DIAZ: The dominant culture puts all Hispanics together in one group, and totally obliterates our differences. We feel all the more need, therefore, to emphasize our differences; we bicker among ourselves. We are refugees of the right and of the left, from different cultural backgrounds.

JOHNSON: Blacks are not all alike, but we have suffered from a more unified form of oppression. What does unify us is the attempt to eliminate the Black family. One of the defects of the feminist movement is the inability to see that the family is an overriding concern for Black folks. Family is an important African value. We have to structure our other values around that. Black women have always worked and raised the children; they have always had freedom of movement. But none of that was by choice. Where we differ from the feminist movement is that for Black folks liberation is for families; it happens to us together, and the problems we have in male/female relations are our own to work out. You can't really understand these relationships, because the defects in the relation are caused by White oppression.

YOLANDA TARANGO: Women of Color are conscious that each has her sacred space and symbols and is interested in preserving that cultural identity. That makes us sensitive to the culture of others, a sensitivity that I do not find with White women. White women are quick to tell me about the disvalues in my culture and all the ways that I am oppressed by machismo. We may have named it, but we don't have exclusive rights to it! We will work in the feminist movement only if we can keep our own cultural heritage intact and find it respected.

A: I had occasion to do some work on contemporary sources on the suffrage question. The quotations you have heard from Elizabeth Cady Stanton and Susan B. Anthony are certainly accurate, because we all live in a racist culture. For me as a Jewish woman, historical anti-Semitism must be acknowledged loudly and clearly when we talk about what Christianity stands for, and that is not often done. So I am particularly sensitive when lateral anger is directed toward other victims of oppression, as even White middle-class women were victims of oppression in the mid-nineteenth century. Stanton and Anthony formed a universal suffrage association to work politically to open up the ballot to everyone, Black and White, male and female. They saw that if the vote was not extended to everyone, then to extend it to Black men would be useless and worthless, and that is what happened. The vote proved useless; the ballots of Black men were torn up. Blacks were victimized by all sorts of brutal racism. I do not deny that Stanton and Anthony expressed racism, but this should also be added.

PHELPS: Two things: First, I think Freudian slips are important, and that quotation may have been Stanton's Freudian slip. It says something about the suffragists' fundamental perception of Black men. Second, the Black men were wrong. That is exactly what I have been pointing out. You have to allow Blacks the luxury of making their own mistakes. If their goal was the Black male vote and it turned out not to be the right answer—it became an empty thing—that is O.K. The Black male analysis was not astute enough; they did not understand that if they got their vote before the women, it would solve neither their problem nor the women's problem. We have to make our mistakes, and we will learn from them. Let us choose our own goals and tactics. If we fall on our faces, fine. Then we can move on to the universal by discovering it.

A: Stanton never saw the failure of Black male suffrage as the fault of Black men. She saw Black male suffrage as a dispensation from the power structure, which was controlled 100 percent by White men. Black men did not have the power to get the vote for themselves. All she was saying was that so long as White men chose to give the vote to Black men, they could also take it away, and that is what they did in fact do.

PHELPS: We agree that it was necessary for everyone to have the vote. We disagree about what strategy would achieve that. Stanton and Anthony should have sat down with Frederick Douglass and Sojourner Truth as equal partners, but that didn't happen; it was a senior/junior partnership. We are all sinners and saints. Stanton had her faults even though she had her richness.

B: I'm angry. I come from a working-class home that was full of racism. I've been in jail, not for a political demonstration but because I was arrested for petty thievery. I feel uncomfortable among bourgeois White women and among bourgeois Black women. I'm not a college graduate. I am ready to move and I want to know how.

ISASI-DIAZ: One thing you can do is to get to know us better, but here we are only two Hispanics among 140 people.

C: There are several things I want to say. To all of us Blacks, I say, guard against accepting sociological and mythological accounts of our history. Don't mythologize what Africa was and is or what its relevance is for Black people in the United States. As to Stanton, I don't think we can hide what she was about under the rubric of trying to get the vote for everybody. If we know anything about the relation between southern and northern feminists of that period, we know there was a lot of racism over certain issues. Northern White feminists thought it very important to make alliances with southern White women and therefore sacrificed their relation to Black people. They used racism as a political tool to get the vote. A White southern feminist in 1903 said that some day White American males would appreciate the women's movement because it would be the instrument by which Blacks would be kept oppressed in America. Many of us Black women have feared over the years, and still fear, that that is the national policy of the women's movement. Emancipation was the same: Abraham Lincoln had nothing to do with us; he wanted an instrument to support White supremacy. The kind of assumptions the women's movement has made are not realistic. We Black women are not here because we trust White women. We know the research, we know the history of relations between Black and White women. We are here because we want to know whether any transformation has taken place in the way White people relate to Black people when the agenda is feminist. I trust some White women in a one-to-one situation, but not in groups. White folks' racism is not my problem. White supremacy is my problem. If you work in a White institution, what are you doing to get jobs there for Black women? That is something you could do. The women's movement must set up structures for internal critique. Let's avoid the business of victims making victims.

D: I want to ask the Hispanics about their culture. We Mexicans do not call ourselves Hispanic; we are Spanish and Indian and are proud of both parts of our heritage. Do you want to create your own culture, or to share in our Mexican culture? The research that Yolanda Tarango quoted on "las Marias" was done by a Mexican woman. It is important for you to define your culture. Do you want to be Mexicans living in the United States? or Cubans? I think it is better for the movement to take advantage of the cultural developments in Mexico. Machismo is not our invention—it is the Mexican translation of patriarchy.

MARY BENTLEY ABU-SABA: I am experiencing computer overload. I have so many things to respond to. I have heard the words "annihilation" and "extermination" bandied about. My feeling is that in the past month my family has been annihilated and exterminated, and though I realize that many of the things I have to say belong to the topic of war and peace, I am going to separate them out and try to speak only to the issues that confront us in this culture in the United States.

In the United States "anti-Semitism" is erroneously used to mean anti-Jewish. Semites are people that have originated in a certain area of the world. My daughter Leila and my son Khalil are Semitic, but they are also Arabs. Arabs are Semites. When we Lebanese talk about our pain, frustrations, and grief, about the agony of twelve thousand people being killed in one month, we are Semitic. We are not being anti-Semitic when we ask that people try to understand that problem. It is unhelpful in this culture to be accused of being anti-Semitic when we ask Americans to understand who the Palestinians are. Accusing us of being anti-Semitic only perpetuates the pain and the suffering.

In response to how can we accuse the Israeli government of doing dastardly deeds when they have just been doing what everyone else has been doing in order to achieve their own freedom, I would say that the same thing has been said about the Palestinian freedom movement, that they have been fighting for survival; they are pushed out of their land, they don't have a home, and they will not give up. The carnage that is being perpetrated in Lebanon this month is only the tip of the shovel that will dig the grave of untold numbers of Semites. We are all cousins.

E: I grew up with four sisters, but I don't always trust them. I am not always at home in my sisters' homes; we differ in values and life-styles. I am not ready to trust all White women here simply because they are White or Christian or Catholic. I am Irish and German, Catholic with some Scottish Presbyterian, and those identities are stronger for me than being White. Part of racism is judging someone on the color of their skin, and that is a problem for me when I hear things about White Catholic women. Because one is in a conference of White Catholic women, one doesn't necessarily feel at home. An assumption is made that because one is White in a conference of White women, one will feel at home, and that is not true.

IsASI-DIAZ Culture is dynamic and ever-changing. I am a second-generation Cuban of Spanish background. My culture has had new elements added to it because I live in the United States. I feel welcome in Latin America but not totally. In Mexico I am told to keep a low profile because I am not Latina, since I live in the United States. In the United States, when I try to define myself according to what I see in this country, I am told, "Why do you make differences when we are from the same culture?" We have difficulty in allowing one another to define who we are. In the development of cultures, the next generation will have a culture different from mine.

TARANGO: I am a fifth-generation Mexican from Texas, where my family lived before Texas was part of the United States. I do not have a home. In the United States, I am not quite American; in Mexico, I am not Mexican and am considered a cultural illiterate. There needs to be a dialogue between Chicanas and Mexicans about this. Mexicans and U.S. Hispanics need to avoid being manipulated against one another. Right now there is an enchantment in this country with Latin Americans, and that makes the U.S. Hispanics still more voiceless, because we constantly have to import the Latin Americans to articulate our experience when we are capable of speaking for ourselves.

F: I have many things I want to say, but I feel that Mary Edith's remarks were directed to Judith Plaskow, so if you promise me that I can speak before this fishbowl is over, I would like Judy to speak next.

PLASKOW: The term anti-Semitism was coined not by the Jews but by a nineteenth-century German anti-Semite as the new racial anti-Semitism was emerging in Germany. It is true, of course, that Arabs are Semites, but that in no way changes the long history of anti-Judaism in the West, which continues into the present.

The other things you say are difficult to respond to, because I feel I am speaking to someone whose family has been killed by my brother. Yet, my brother is still my brother, even as I, an American Jew, say with other American Jews and with Israelis marching in the streets of their country, "This is not our war. We ought not to be fighting."

My question is: Where are the Palestinians who for the past ten years have been marching in their streets, saying "We want to sit down and talk to Israel"? At the International Women's Conference in Copenhagen, Shulamith Aloni was asked, "Would you talk here with Palestinian women?" She said, "Yes, absolutely. I would talk with anyone so long as we can have peace." When the same reporter went to the Palestinian delegate and asked her, "Would you talk with Shulamith Aloni?" the Palestinian replied, "I will talk to her with a gun in my hand."

F: Women's meetings are usually too utopian. I'm glad we are confronting each other here. We are in a dilemma and a contradiction because, on one hand, if we want to solve our problems, we must represent among ourselves all the elements of the dilemma we find ourselves in in America. On the other hand, we cannot reflect accurately the composition of the American people in our group here, but only out there. Therefore it is more important to look at what goes on out there than at what we are able to achieve among ourselves here. If we all feel terrific after this week, that would still be tokenism.

I am concerned with interracial dialogue so that we understand how bad it is out there. I don't feel guilty at all. I hate the backwardness of the White working class. They will cut their own throats. It is the worst in the South, where racism has created nonunion shops. It is stupid, ignorant, and self-destructive. I don't feel guilty; I feel hatred and resentment toward the racism in the White working class. I don't share it. I have found that White working-class people who have experienced a change in their thinking are ashamed that they almost got locked into that prison. I am willing to follow the leadership of Black men when it is the clearest in articulating goals. Our strategies have to come from the same enemy, the same fights and contradictions, the same practical solutions—otherwise we don't get anywhere. My criticism of feminism has to do with the bourgeois co-optation of feminism in the United States, like the co-optation of the unions. Just as there were Uncle Toms in the Black movement, there is opportunism in the trade union movement and in the women's movement, cadres of leadership that want token gains and don't want to wage a full fight. Basically, they accept getting some concessions and being included in the ruling class. Class struggle is necessary but not sufficient for the liberation of women and minorities. I will not follow Black men who support the corporate structures. I have a right to choose among leaders in the Black community. I will follow Black working-class or Black middle-class leadership with an anticorporate strategy, but I will not follow opportunists in any movement. Why hasn't there been a struggle for jobs in the Black community? There have been gains in token representation of Blacks in the professions versus no gains for the Black working class because of opportunist leadership. I am for Black leaders who use strategies that can work.

PHELPS: I have said over and over that the three main Black issues ever since the Civil War have been housing, education, and employment. In terms of the internal fight, whenever we choose one type of leadership over another, we end up by co-opting and making the movement fail. The strategy is not either/or; it is both/and, and you have to deal with it according to your natural gifts.

There is a romanticization of the grass-roots Black woman, presuming that I am not grass roots. You don't know what I am. Blacks are not as divided classwise as Whites would like to believe. Whether you are a Ph.D. or whatever, you are Black and will be exterminated. Every Black knows this, whether or not they deny it. When you choose whether you are going to listen to the house nigger or the field nigger, that is plantation politics. My political strategy is to deal with the divisions within the Black community inside the community. I am not going to hang out the dirty washing. If you know it, you know it. If you don't, I'm not going to tell you.

G: Christians do not talk enough about anti-Judaism as a strain within Christianity. I am not a Christian, although I come from a Christian background. My decision was made as much on the anti-Judaic as on the sexist aspects of Christianity—the opposition between the law and the gospel, the idea of the Jews as Christ killers. In her book *Faith and Fratricide*, Rosemary Ruether shows that the stronger the proclamation of Christ became in the early church, the stronger the anti-Judaism became. Anti-Judaism is intrinsic to Christianity; we need to think and write and talk about it much more seriously.

JOHNSON: The issue isn't whether or not White people support and criticize Black leadership. We critique our leadership and determine our leadership. You can join us if you want to. On the issue of the vote, when universal suffrage came, it didn't matter for Blacks. My mother and father had the vote because they belonged to the minority of Blacks who could pass the test. I didn't hear any White women saying that that was wrong.

When you say you don't call everyone sister, don't water down the issue. For some Black women in Cabrini Green, a municipal housing project in Chicago, the issue is whether their children will live to be productive. Their existential problem is surviving long enough.

H: I want to talk about labels and transcending labels. In Miami I am now called an Anglo. I don't consider myself an Anglo. I am a Swedish American. Do we have to wait another hundred thousand years before the empathy we feel for one another can transcend that? In Miami there is a lot of anti-Arab sentiment, but not a lot of anti-Jewish sentiment. The label bourgeois bothers me; the label seems to mean enemy. If you are going to name an enemy, look at the one or two percent who control the world. Some of the Black women here have said that if it is a choice between their men and feminism, they will choose their men. I think the same choice faces all women at this point in history. For many White women, for me, it is a constant balancing act between the movement and my husband. In the Western world, the first oppression comes from Genesis, from male/female relations.

I: I have to cope with anti-Semitism on my part; it's not just religious, it is cultural conditioning. There are undefined ways that Blacks and Jews use one another. If you want to do something, support Black institutions. *Essence* is in financial difficulties; we read *Working Woman*, but you don't read *Essence*.

PHELPS: The fundamental necessity is the freedom to name your oppression and to strategize for your own solutions.

A Black Response to Feminist Theology

JACQUELYN GRANT

Any liberation theology has a threefold task: (1) the critical, because we must critique what has been done; (2) the compensatory, because we have to collect our IOUs for what has been left out of the history; and (3) the constructive, because a theological system must be developed. I have begun work on the second and third stages, but here I will focus on the first one, the critical task. How do Black women criticize other theological perspectives?

At this point in our history, we as Black women find ourselves at a crossroads between the Black liberation movement and the feminist liberation movement. The primary point of departure of one movement is racism, and of the other, sexism. This does not mean that we ignore the struggles against classism; certainly it is no accident that a disproportionate number of Blacks in general, and Black women in particular, are poor. The effects of racism and sometimes of sexism often produce conditions that thrust one into the class struggle. But here we want to examine racism and sexism. I have dealt with the Black woman's critique of the Black liberation movement elsewhere;[1] here I will discuss the Black woman's critique of feminist theology.

Sometimes we get tired of hearing the same things over and over again. I am reminded of these lines by Langston Hughes.

> Seems like what drives me crazy
> Don't have no effect on you,
> But I'm goin' to keep on at it
> 'Til it drive you crazy too.[2]

Jacquelyn Grant

Sometimes it seems that as we critique one another, our words have no effect in terms of concrete programmatic developments. We must keep on raising the issues until it drives all of us crazy—not an insane craziness, but a craziness that forces us to responsible living. It is the kind of craziness that leads us to lay our all on the line for the sake of justice, particularly if it has to do with someone else's immediate situation rather than our own, realizing that justice for "you" is tied up with justice for "me." So I seek to drive us all crazy for the sake of justice.

Walter Rauschenbusch has remarked, "Ascetic Christianity called the world evil and left it. Humanity is waiting for a revolutionary Christianity which will call the world evil and change it."[3] Feminist theology has called the world evil in identifying sexism as a major and universal form of oppression, but has not dealt adequately with changing the world. It has failed to bring about adequate participation of Black and other Third World women in the movement. I am impressed by the issues feminist theologians are raising, but when I return to Black groups such as Black Women in Church and Society at the Interdenominational Theological Center, where we are trying to define our own issues and agenda, I find that the issues are somewhat different; even when the issues are the same, the approach and the interpretations are often different. I am always aware of these differences, and that helps keep me accountable to my community, so that I am not guilty of imposing on my community something that comes out of your community.

The feminist movement is on to something. We still have to figure out what it is on to and how it is going to get to where it says it is going. But there are some very serious problems that need to be dealt with if the feminist movement is to be what it claims. In *Women, Race and Class*, Angela Davis says that the women's liberation movement is in trouble because it has not taken seriously the issues of class and race.[4] We have talked about it in consultations and conferences and have tried to deal with a multifold analysis, but we have not been able to get beyond a stage of talking about the problems. The reason for that has to do with the differences that exist between the communities. We have a tendency to overlook the differences and to talk about our commonalities, but that is problematic because it attempts to move toward reconciliation without liberation. This is the way many Black women interpret some aspects of the feminist movement, particularly the eliciting of Black women's participation. The Black representation at this meeting—4 percent—is indicative of that reality. The primary problem is the differences in the way we perceive our struggles. Historically, Black women have been defined primarily by racism. Therefore, it is not easy for us to align with our former mistresses, who often added insult to injury in their treatment of us. We have not always suffered the same pains and sorrows. Black women's agenda and goals are different from White women's. Black women's agenda has been defined by our pains and sorrows, very few of which White women have shared. As Deborah Harmon Hines writes,

> Black women find it difficult to align themselves with those who have not been a part of the solution, but in fact have been a part of the problem. Black women find it extremely difficult to align themselves with those who say, "we have all suffered the same," when we know it isn't so. Black women find the situation intolerable when we are *told* (by white women) *what* we should do in our struggle rather than asked what we need to do. . . . We are

being told that apples and oranges are the same, when we can see that they are not. You cannot easily substitute one for the other in a recipe. Their odors are different. They appeal to people differently. Even a blind person can tell them apart. Yet, a steady stream of rhetoric is aimed at convincing black women how much alike their lives, wishes, and desires are to those of our stepsisters.[5]

This passage reflects the general attitude of most Black women about the feminist movement. The poem "To Ms. Ann," by the Black poet Lucille Clifton, capsulizes this point.

> I will have to forget
> your face,
> when you watched me breaking
> in the field,
> missing my children.
>
> I will have to forget
> your face,
> when you watched me carry your husband's stagnant water.
>
> I will have to forget
> your face,
> when you handed me your house
> to make a home,
> and you never called me sister,
> then, you never called me sister
> and it has only been forever and
> I will have to forget your face.[6]

Many Black women are making a radical connection between the Miss Ann of the nineteenth century and the Ms. Ann of the twentieth century. Miss Ann was the mistress, the slave owner, the slave-owner's wife. Ms. Ann is the privileged one, the liberated woman, the corporate executive. Suddenly, White women want to be considered sisters. Yet they are still the privileged, and Black women still represent the underclass.

The notion of sisterhood in the feminist movement is problematic for Black women. It is difficult to accept being called sister when for so long we have been called by other names. Every theology emerges out of a community. The community out of which feminist theology emerges is the community of sisterhood. But it is a sisterhood of White women's experiences. How do we achieve real sisterhood? That feminism has not dealt sufficiently with racism and classism makes it difficult for the feminist movement to develop this sisterhood. Black women have not responded to the feminist movement in great numbers because from its beginning it was labeled a White middle-class women's movement, with questionable interests. Toni Morrison describes this distrust on the part of Black women: "They look at white women and see them as the enemy for they know that racism is not confined to white men, that there are more white women than white men in this country, and that 53% of the population maintained an eloquent silence during times of greatest stress."[7]

Feminist responses to Black women's cries have been varied. I will not forget a scene in a northeastern seminary in which I was invited to do a presentation on Black women and feminism for a class on women in ministry (the class consisted of White women plus two or three White men). When I finished my presentation, one of the students asked, "Why is it that Black women do not join us in the struggle? These are issues that are relevant to all women." I tried to explain the historical problems that have existed between Black and White women that make it difficult for Black women to jump on the feminist bandwagon. I explained that while we have some commonalities as women that perhaps should enable us to talk to one another, the differences keep us apart. The student persisted, saying that Black women needed to join the feminist movement, as that is where their salvation lay. When I refused to accept this premise, she told me politely where to go. Needless to say, the exchange ended. White women do not take seriously other women's agendas. Black women hear White women saying, "If you don't join us in 'our' struggle, if you don't join us where the 'real issues' are, then we don't have time for you." One would not say this to a sister. Women in the dominant culture do not understand the complexities involved when they ask other women to join them as sisters in the movement.

Sisterhood requires trust, and trust has to be earned. Black women have been the nonhumans, the maids, the prostitutes, the slaves and nannies. Too many Black women, and men, have been unemployed or underemployed, unable to obtain the bare necessities, while White women are working in order to obtain luxuries. This is not to denigrate the need for any woman to work. Michelle Russell concretizes the point.

> What perpetuates the tunnel vision that leads White feminists to pressure their corporations for child care facilities so as to maximize their vocational opportunities without regard for the wage scales, welfare legislation and institutionalized values that will ensure that third world women will be there to take care of their children? By what feminist criteria do White women celebrate token jobs as truck drivers, when not only the mob connections but the racism of the trucking industry are legendary, and the unemployment rate in the Black community as a whole continues to be twice that of the white?[8]

Racism and sexism have caused such divisions among women that it is unimaginable that a mere call to sisterhood will be enough to usher in the kind of reconciliation, not to mention liberation, that we generally talk about. For this reason sisterhood is not enough, because sisterhood is just not powerful enough to bridge the gap between races and classes of women. I think a feminist theology is an oppressive theology rather than a critical tool of liberation if it fails to develop an adequate doctrine of sisterhood, which challenges the universalizing of the perspectives of White middle-class women. What happens in the feminist movement is really the same as what happens in the world at large. The critique that feminist theologians make of the classical theologians, namely that they have taken one culture—that of White males—and universalized it, can be turned against them. Feminist theologians have taken one experience, that of White middle-class women, and made that the norm.

The strength of feminist theology lies in its vision of wholeness. We need a wholistic theology, as feminists insist, but we will need the experience of all women to develop it. We have *talked* about it, and that makes us think that we are doing it.

At a World Council of Churches consultation on the community of women and men in the church, held in Sheffield, England, an intense effort was made to deal with international issues in terms of classism and sexism; but in most of the analysis, racism was left out. I thought I would give the participants the benefit of the doubt by assuming that perhaps it was just an oversight, because the World Council of Churches has long had a commission to combat racism. Just in case they were thinking that that commission had combatted racism out of existence, I reminded them that racism was still alive and well. The point was immediately picked up, but that I had to raise it suggests that we do forget easily. I was the only North American Black woman at that consultation. There were no North American Black men; there was one Black man from the Caribbean. We are anxious to deal with international issues, but why do we tend to forget or ignore what is in our own backyard?

Black women see this. When we see that White women continually ignore our questions and analysis, then joining you in your struggle is more than problematic, it is downright impossible. How can we identify with a group that ignores our oppression, even if their rhetoric says differently? Until there is radical change in the feminist movement, feminist theology is perpetuating the very dichotomies it claims to discard. Just as White women have been throughout history, Black women will continue to be on the passive, weak side of those social dualisms that Rosemary Ruether examines in her work: rational and irrational, logic and imagination, mind and body, superordination and subordination. White women are beginning to be on the active, strong side of these dualisms. Feminists are successfully instituting just what they claim to reject. The strength of feminist theology lies in its vision of wholeness, which envisions all women, and ultimately all men, in a manner that leads to real liberation. Its claims can be accepted only in the context of a prophetic vision.

A revolutionary dimension is needed to actualize that prophetic vision. This revolutionary dimension will be possible only when those at the bottom of the totem pole—Black and other Third World women—become empowered to change the oppressive structures of the church and society. Only as these women begin to participate in the theological process will the revolutionary character of the enterprise become visible.

Myrtle Gordon uses an African folk tale to illuminate the problem.

> A small boy is going to the mission school. When he comes home, his father asks, "Son, what did you learn at school today?" "How the great white hunter kills the lion," the boy replies with puzzlement. "What troubles you about that story?" asks the father. "Well," the boy answers, "they tell us how brave and strong the lion is. It seems to me that every now and then the lion would kill the white hunter! After all, the lion is King of the jungle." The father shook his head sadly, "Son, until the lions learn to write books that is always the way the story will end."[9]

Until Black women have equal access to writing books and doing theology, a wholistic theology will be impossible. The kind of coalition we need to build is one that shares the little bit of access that White women have already gained, and strategizes for more. Black feminists, even though they are not afraid at this point to call themselves feminists in spite of all the negativism that the word carries in the Black community, still refuse to accept any feminist analysis uncritically. Until the feminist movement shows a serious interest in the liberation of Third World women (which means also the liberation of Third World people), Black women and White women can never be sisters. Black women want to be included in the process *before* the point of coming to conferences and listening to papers—at the point of agenda-setting, where we determine if in fact a conference is needed or if we should be actively engaged in something else.

As feminists, you White women can say, "We will just go along to do our thing without them. Who do they think they are? Black women and other Third World women can't tell us what is legitimate." If you choose to do that, then you must change your rhetoric. No longer can you say that you participate in a movement for the liberation of all women; you have a movement that advocates instead the liberation of the women of the dominant culture.

14

Report from the Working Group on Racism/Classism/Sexism

We agreed that the Women of Color would set the goals for this group. These goals were (1) a critique of this conference as a microcosm of the larger feminist movement, and within the critique some suggestions of strategies for change; and (2) an analysis of racism, sexism, and classism in an international context.

This report deals with the following topics:

- definitions of "racism" and "People of Color"
- learnings from the conference
- strategies for developing mutuality between White women and Women of Color, as formulated by White women
- strategies from a Hispanic perspective
- strategies from a Jewish perspective
- strategies from a Black perspective
- critique of the conference
- racism, classism, sexism in an international context

Definitions

We find the term racism is inadequate because in current usage it seems to include only the oppression of Blacks. A term needs to be developed that will include Hispanics, Jews, Blacks, Asians, and Native Americans.

We use the term People of Color to mean primarily Hispanic

Americans (i.e., Chicanos, Puerto Ricans, Cubans, Central and South Americans), Black Americans, Native Americans, and Asian Americans. We include Jews under this category. While acknowledging that most American Jews are White, identify themselves with Whites, and participate in racist structures, we recognize that the worldwide Jewish family includes many people whose experience is rendered invisible by a European-centered understanding of the Jewish tradition.

Learnings

It is apparent from the history and experience of Black, Hispanic, and Jewish women that there is a long tradition of oppression of People of Color by White men and women. White women, by omission and commission, have contributed to this tradition of oppression. White women, whether feminists or traditionalists, have shared a propensity for at best ignoring Women of Color and at worst excluding them from equal participation in the feminist movement and in the wider community.

The lack of a radical understanding of the interconnectedness of racism, sexism, and classism means that Women of Color have at best been marginalized in the feminist movement. More often, they have chosen to absent themselves from the movement.

What are the conditions that eliminate Black, Hispanic, and Jewish women from the contemporary expressions of the feminist movement? The following limitations have been raised in this conference:

- the inability of White women to deal with Women of Color as equals in the process of liberation
- the inability of White women to see Hispanics, i.e., relegating them to a position of invisibility by their language and analyses
- the inability of White women to respect and cherish family and community as basic values of People of Color
- the latent anti-Semitism of White women, which refuses to acknowledge the different historical experience of Jewish women, and which too easily identifies itself with

the anti-Israeli (anti-Zionist) stance of part of the American left
- the inability of White women to recognize the right of People of Color to set the agendas for their own communities
- the inability of Women of Color to perceive themselves as sisters to those who are still in great measure contributing to their oppression

In the light of these reservations expressed by Women of Color, it is essential to develop a theoretical framework for feminism that defines mutuality as the enabling of all women to participate in the liberation of all peoples within their respective communities and in the world at large.

The group believes this framework must involve the following elements:

- an honest inclusion by White feminists of the history of Women of Color in the feminist movement
- the integration into feminist theologizing and strategizing of the dynamics of liberation as set forth by Mary Hunt in "Political Oppression and Creative Survival" (pp. 164-72)
- A radical redefinition of sisterhood in the light of an analysis of race and class; also a redefinition of the value of the family in the light of the experience of People of Color
- a commitment to the praxis of liberation as well as the theory—in this case, affirmation by the feminist movement of the right of Women of Color to determine the agenda for their own liberation
- a commitment of the feminist movement to deal with its own racism, thus moving toward a real celebration of differences and the possibility of mutually enriching coalitions for the liberation of all oppressed people

Toward Mutuality: Strategies from a White Perspective

In our country at the present time, we perceive a strong feeling in many sections of the White community that racism ended with the civil rights movement of the 1960s and the grape boycott of the early 1970s and that now the nation needs to move on to other, more pressing issues. But the facts remain that Whites have the power, that racism is pervasive, and that racism, sexism, and classism are structurally interrelated. On the part of White people, there is evidence of

- growing anti-Semitism
- noninvolvement with the problems of Mexican-American farm workers
- resentment at the plight of Cubans on the East Coast, Asians on the West Coast
- insensitivity to the plight of Haitians
- a general tendency to blame the victim for violence between working-class Whites and People of Color in many cities

The list could go on and on. The conclusion is inevitable: despite the presence of People of Color in visible positions in business and other institutions, racism is very much with us. The system by which White people dominate People of Color is basically unchanged.

Where do we White women fit into this ugly picture? We believe we cannot separate ourselves from it. Our stereotypes may not match the gross exaggerations of an earlier day, but too often we assume

- that all Blacks and Hispanics are poor and uneducated
- that all Jews are well educated and rich
- that differences in language or customs are threatening
- that People of Color are without gifts
- that People of Color must be the object of White generosity

Sometimes we secretly harbor expectations of gratitude—if not of canonization—for our most superficial or short-lived involvement with any People of Color. Unconsciously, we assume that our models of family and community are normative, that the color symbolism and value systems of Western civilization are universally accepted and valid. Above all, we dissipate our energies in proving our personal guiltlessness for racism rather than accepting our responsibility for enjoying White privileges.

Our vision: We envision a relationship between White people and People of Color marked by mutuality rather than oppression. Oppression presumes a hierarchical society, since the oppressed are necessarily lower on some scale than the oppressor, and the chain of being becomes in reality a chain of oppression. Mutuality presumes relationships of equality, a balancing of gifts and vulnerabilities. The differences themselves become gifts rather than obstacles or barriers. In relationships of mutuality, all have equal access to the resources of the community, and true self-determination can become a reality.

Lest we regard this vision as a utopian dream, we see the following steps which we as White women can take in the immediate future to facilitate relationships of mutuality with Women of Color. We can

- develop a sense of our own self-esteem, so that our relationships with People of Color are cooperative rather than competitive
- actively seek out the means of educating ourselves on the concerns of our sisters of color through books, periodicals, consciousness-raising, personal encounters, and friendships
- refuse tacit as well as overt approval of racial and ethnic slurs, even when our disapproval causes tension in our families and communities
- actively share our concerns on racism and our information about people who are different from us with other Whites, in awareness that we are not the norm
- participate in cultural and religious events that will help us to experience the cultures of Women of Color and give us the experience of being in the minority
- provide financial support and publicity for cultural and educational events sponsored by People of Color
- make structural arrangements so that People of Color come into situations with Whites with a sense of strength rather than of isolation and weakness

- refuse to enjoy the privileges of Whiteness unless these privileges can be used to facilitate the liberation of Women of Color
- recognize that racism is a vital feminist issue, knowing that until all women are liberated, no woman is liberated

Strategies from a Hispanic Perspective

The use of the word racism makes Hispanics invisible because of its connection with skin color. Racism is understood to mean a structural system of oppression based on the prejudices of the dominant White culture. It allows those who have the power to establish their prejudices as normative and to devalue such Hispanic cultural values as personalism, community, respect for old age, etc.

Conditions for our continued Hispanic collaboration and participation in the feminist movement include:

- The relations between feminists of the dominant White culture and Hispanic feminists must be characterized by a sense of mutual empowerment.
- White feminists must assume responsibility for the systemic analysis of racism instead of depending on Women of Color to raise the issue and aggressively pursue it.
- The Hispanic concept of theologizing is one of organic reflection based on participation in the life of the community; this participation, rather than academic degrees, is what validates theologizing. Due to language difficulties and economic discrimination, very few Hispanic women have the opportunity for graduate education.
- Hispanic women do not understand themselves as a minority nor as a marginalized people who seek fuller participation in the dominant culture. Rather, their stance vis-à-vis the dominant culture is prophetic, calling for systemic change rather than inclusion in the present system.
- Because of the values inherent in their culture, Hispanic women ask to be included in the feminist movement at

the level of conceptualization and planning and not simply at the level of implementation.
- As a colonized people, Hispanics have internalized their oppression to a considerable extent, making it difficult for them to develop a sense of initiative and self-determination. Hispanic women ask acceptance of their sometimes slower, nondirective way as valid. They ask not to be judged by U.S. standards of accomplishment.
- Hispanic women ask that, out of their sense of justice and their commitment to the process of liberation, feminists express a preferential option for Women of Color. In practical terms this means making it economically possible for greater numbers of Hispanics to attend conferences, providing translation when necessary, and in general creating an environment in which the culture and personality of Hispanic women can be fully expressed and valued.

Hispanic women urge that the following qualities be considered as values of the Hispanic culture that can enrich the feminist movement in the United States:

- Due to their geographic proximity to their lands of origin and to their continued use of the Spanish language, Hispanics have been able to preserve their culture.
- Their understanding of the need for integration and their resistance to assimilation offer a prophetic critique of the dominant "Americana" culture.
- Hispanic values of personalism and *carnalismo* (physical contact, touching) offer a valuable corrective to the depersonalization and alienation present in the United States today.
- Hispanics cherish their children and old people as valuable, refusing to recognize as important only those who produce.
- The sense of fidelity based on trust bridges differences in Hispanic families and communities, helping the people to be a constant support for one another.
- The religious sense of Hispanic culture, based on a deep familiarity with the divine, obliterates the unreal separation of the material and spiritual worlds.

Strategies from a Jewish Perspective

Anti-Semitism has at least two elements: a specifically Christian element, and a social/cultural element. The social/cultural element can be subsumed in large measure under a general critique of racism. Religious anti-Semitism, however, poses a distinct challenge to Christians to examine and rethink their own tradition, relinquishing its claims to absoluteness. To confront anti-Semitism is to confront the fact that Christianity is not *the* authentic continuation of the so-called Old Testament tradition, but that Judaism is a continuing, living tradition and that the Jews are a living people with the right to define and determine their own destiny.

Jews are largely absent from the religious feminist movement. They are present in large numbers in the wider feminist movement, including its leadership, but not as Jews. One reason for this is that while Jewish women are perceived as rich, powerful, and smart, in fact they fear to claim their own Jewishness in a Christian society or have lost it, finding it easier to disappear into the homogeneous mass of White middle-class feminists. Thus, while the feminist movement may not need to seek out Jews, it does need to become a movement in which Jews (along with the women of other oppressed peoples) can be who they are, contributing the richness of their experience to the total understanding of women's historical experiences and present agenda.

Strategies from a Black Perspective

Operative assumptions: White women must accept and not debate the reality that many Black women perceive racism as the fundamental basis of their oppression. However, it is clear that racism, sexism, and classism must be addressed together to ensure that the feminist movement facilitates the liberation of all women.

If it is to be inclusive, the feminist movement must opt for a strategic, privileged focus on the agenda of Women of Color—Blacks, Hispanics, Asians, and Indigenous Women. It must make this option evident by facilitating the processes by which

Women of Color seek to contribute to the unification and liberation of their own communities.

Recommendations for action:

- A dialogue of Women of Color should be sponsored to identify issues within their respective communities that could properly be seen as aspects of a universal feminist agenda. Such a conference would be designed, staffed, and participated in by representatives of Women of Color.
- Those feminists wishing to make their resources available for the liberation of People of Color should identify these resources and put them at the disposal of Women of Color to be used as the latter determine.
- Out of their experience of the interrelationships of racism, sexism, and classism, Women of Color should continue to facilitate the clarification of these relationships with their White sisters.
- From a Black perspective, certain aspects of the White feminist movement in the United States seem ultimately self-destructive. Because of their insistence that liberation be community based and inclusive of the family, Women of Color should help correct the current inattentiveness of the White feminist movement to these issues. In addition they should assist White feminists to broaden their goal of liberation to include other oppressed groups, such as Men of Color, and the indigenous people of Africa, Haiti, and Latin America.

Critique of the Conference

Racism exists when members of the dominant culture are in control of

- naming the problem
- access to resources
- setting standards for appropriate behavior
- making and enforcing decisions

Using these criteria, the group made a critique of the conference.

Naming the problem:

- An all-White planning team named the problems to be addressed by the conference.
- Those consulted for input into the format and program as the original ideas were developed and refined were all White.
- When Women of Color began to name the problem during the conference, they were met with resistance, particularly evident during the panel on racism; some people walked out, others debated the naming of the problem and the perceptions of the Women of Color. (Cf. "Reflections on a Process," pp. xxii–xxviii, for details.)

Access to resources:

- White women had access to the resources—St. John's University, The Grail, the Women's Caucus of the American Academy of Religion.
- The channels of communication used by the planners made connections with resources of White women but not Women of Color.
- The absence of Women of Color on the planning team resulted in few Women of Color at the conference.

Setting standards for appropriate behavior:

- Shared participation during the conference was seen by planners and process facilitators as appropriate behavior, but because of the difference in access to resources and decision-making power, this goal was not realized as fully as intended.
- The concept of preferential option might have been a more appropriate standard, but this approach was not considered.
- There was some evidence of "plantation politics," i.e., attempts by White women to set up Hispanics against Blacks, educated Blacks against poor Blacks.

- Some of the language used during the conference—e.g., light/dark, white/black connoting good/bad—had racist overtones.

Making and enforcing decisions:
- The structuring of the process was intended to share decision-making among planners, process consultants, and participants.
- The initial division of tasks between the process consultants contributed to a perception of the White facilitator as having greater authority than the Black facilitator.
- The authority of the Black facilitator was challenged by participants several times.

Racism, Sexism, Classism in an International Context

The group realizes that this conference was not intended as an international gathering; as U.S. feminists, however, we understand that racism in this country cannot be separated from U.S. racist and imperialist attitudes toward People of Color across the globe. Therefore, the group offers these suggestions for use in conferences that are international by design.

U.S. feminists must be on guard against setting up their experience of sexism, as well as racism and classism, as normative. White middle-class feminists need to identify bridge people who can be links to the experiences of races and cultures different from their own. Such bridge people are not necessarily representatives unless specifically designated by their home groups. Similarly, U.S. feminists must avoid generalizations from the U.S. context. Rather, they must take care to qualify their statements, acknowledging that all of them are partial, limited, and contextual.

The group urges that conferences which seek to be international consider the following:

- The agendas of such conferences should be developed by representatives of races, classes, ethnic groups, and nations who will participate. Agendas will include topics,

formats, and styles that reflect the diversity of the participants.
- Efforts should be made to invite groups with which U.S. groups either already have or will commit themselves to have ongoing relationships and communication.
- Scholarships, facilities for translation, and other resources should be provided so that a rich variety of participants can live and work together comfortably and creatively.

By committing itself to work toward international gatherings, this group hopes that its efforts can contribute to addressing and abolishing racism in all its forms.

Part IV

Women as Makers of Literature

THERE IS OFTEN greater wisdom in the condensation of a story than in the abstraction of a logical argument, writes Karen McCarthy Brown in her essay in this volume. Certainly, in their search for meaning and wholeness, women today are telling their stories, to themselves and to one another, finding in the process a way to clarification, healing, and empowerment. Paying attention to the images that rise out of our experience—in daily life, in dreams, through methods of meditation and visualization—becomes a means of generating and focusing energies. Most of our formal education confines itself to the linear and abstract, although perhaps as the current research on right- and left-brain patterns reaches the schools, they may begin to pay more attention to the imagination. In any event, feminists have long been finding strength and wisdom in the works of the imagination—whether poetry, fiction, music, dance, or the visual arts. There are great talents, of course, who have enriched us all, but every women has the power to name her world in poetry and in prose in ways that make new meanings for herself and others. Out of the sharing of these meanings comes mutual understanding, and with the understanding, bonding.

In this section, Delores S. Williams develops the theme of woman inventing herself as it is found in the work of contemporary women writers, White and Black, who have given us vivid models of women coming to awareness of oppression, undertaking the painful voyage of self-discovery, and learning the joys of independence and mutuality. She shares some of her own process of self-invention, voiced in her poetry, as she moved from the assessment of her past, to lamentation, to a freedom nurtured by her bonds with her foremothers and other women. Many of the women present at Williams' talk, having also found in the writing of poetry a means of clarifying their experience, shared their poems, some of which are collected here.

15

Women as Makers of Literature
DELORES S. WILLIAMS

There is at least one thing Black people and feminists agree on: story-telling is important.

I learned this from one of my Black foremothers living across the street from the house where I grew up. In this small, southern Black community, Miss Tillie stayed on her front porch day and night. In fact, she slept there. Whenever I came home late at night, Miss Tillie would holler across the street: "Where you bin, girl? Yo momma know you out this late?" Miss Tillie always asked for explanations. She once said to me, "Tell your story, child, and you'll see who you are." If I have anything to say about myself as a maker of literature, it is that I tell stories to myself in poems and prose to see who I am, to explain the world to myself.

This reason for making literature connects with Black writer Toni Morrison's description of how Black women have come to be. Morrison says, "Black women have neither real nor natural access to power in this country. Whiteness and maleness are the symbols of power in America. *Being neither white nor male, the black woman may well have invented herself.*" Many Black women writers (and some White feminist writers) often make literature in order to see and understand who they are in the world. This process of woman's self-invention makes a woman real to herself.

Hurston, Atwood, Truth, and Lessing

In some women's literature this process of self-invention often begins when the protagonist realizes her understanding

Delores S. Williams

of herself has been determined by social customs, myths, and gender-role expectations designed and assigned to her by males dominating the culture in which the woman participates. Certainly this is true of Zora Neale Hurston's female protagonist in *Their Eyes Were Watching God*.[1] Once Janie steps outside the role the Black male-dominated community has designed for her, she begins to shape herself into an autonomous, self-reliant woman capable, for the first time, of relationship with a man on mutual terms.

In *Surfacing*,[2] Canadian writer Margaret Atwood presents the central female character shedding the skin of custom and dependence. This woman begins the process of self-invention as she separates from forces dominating her—her family traditions, the role expectations of her society. She experiences wholeness when she establishes a creative and sustaining mutual relation with nature.

Sojourner Truth, a former slave and a maker of oral literature, described the self-invented woman when she made her statement at a women's rights convention in the nineteenth century. Within the context of her question, "ain't I a woman?", she drew sharp distinctions between the Anglo-American model of femininity and the femininity invented by her own faith and the institution of slavery. She observed,

> Dat man ober dar [a white clergyman on the rostrum] say dat womin needs to be helped into carriages and lifted ober ditches, and to hab de best places everywhar. Nobody ever helps me into

carriages or ober mud puddles, or give me any best place! And ain't I a woman? Look at my arms! I have ploughed, and planted and gathered into barns, an no man could head me! And ain't I a woman? . . . I have borne thirteen chilern, and seen 'em mos' all sold off to slavery and when I cried out with my mother's grief, none but Jesus heard me! And ain't I a woman?[3]

Sojourner Truth made this statement after she had thrown off the yoke of slavery and was living beyond the role expectations designed for her by White patriarchs.

Doris Lessing, in her book *The Summer Before the Dark*,[4] presents a domesticated housewife whose thoughts and actions have been controlled by the needs of her husband and children. She discovers she has no identity beyond them. She breaks away from her domestic routine and begins to shape her "self." It is difficult for her to transcend the old "sustenance role" she has played in all her relations with men and young people. She experiences many transformations before she shapes a "self" who can return to her family whole.

The Anatomy of Self-invention

When women realize the inadequacies of the "selves" designed for them by patriarchal social, political, religious, and educational institutions (inadequacies they often passively accept), they can begin to shape themselves. But this is not easy. The process of self-invention often involves an encounter with an abyss, when the old forms of identity no longer get women beyond the hurt, the pain, and the feeling of nothingness oppression creates.

In my case, the process of self-invention began when I realized I had no props to support my yearning, my voice, my action on behalf of a free Black womanhood in America. I had mistakenly believed that my participation in the Black civil rights struggles in the 1960s had something to do with the freedom of Black women. When Stokley Carmichael said, "The only position for a woman in the movement is prone," I was shattered. To me, his statement validated the southern White man's historic rape of Black women (I am a southern woman). I indeed faced an abyss. I suddenly realized if I, a Black woman, was going to be free and liberated, I had to create myself *into* that freedom. The process has been continuous. It is full of mistakes, of being knocked down and getting up, of bending but being determined not to break, of delving into the innermost reaches of my spirit. It is full of discovery: of discovering a strong and resilient faith in God, of finding support from that deity and from communities of women—Black and White— and from my family.

For me, however, the process of self-invention has involved three actions: an assessment of the past, lamentation, and an affirmation of faith and hope. When I assess the past, images of ancient pains and tragedies emerge, and remind me that racism has affected Black male/female relations in America. When I bring the past before my eyes to weigh its significance, I can understand the tensions between my responsibility to my collective Black history and my responsibility to female "herstory." Once I wrote a poem called "Little Girl Talk," voicing out loud this aspect of my woman experience. It begins this way.

> my grandpaw was a smooth black,
> before black discovered beautiful
> he was pretty
> he had pearly white teeth and
> a skinny mustache he slicked down
> with a black wax stick
>
> on Sunday he dressed up in
> his dark blue suit
> white stiff shirt
> wide blue tie and
> strutted down to the Presbyterian Church
> where he argued over how to spend
> white folks' mission money
>
> on week days: overalls
> he worked in a factory
> 'till some white boss talked down to him
> then he'd quit to another factory
> talk union talk to Negroes
> get laid-off
> on the way home
> buy me a big box of crayons
> 'cause I spelled iron "i-roam"

my grandpaw was smart!
didn't go to college
said white folks wouldn't let him
but he worked algebra and trig
and read Gladstone's law and science books
he told us kids there wasn't no heaven

my grandpaw said
I was the sugar in his coffee
yes indeed, I remember my grandpaw!

the day the siren screamed into
our street ball game and
stopped at our house
we kids scattered into an uneven line
across the street and
watched two big red neck white men
in white uniforms
stuff my pretty grandpaw into
something called a straight jacket
dump him into the back of their wagon
jump into the front themselves
and shriek off into the distance

my grandmaw stood perfectly still
her eyes looked deep and sore and hollow
my mother, unmoving, cried softly
I tried not to feel anything
the tears that wouldn't come
swelled to a fist in my chest
big, brave, girl-boy me
shoved the weight of my ten years
on two flat feet and
strolled to the middle of the street
screaming as loud as I could,
"Throw the ball, shitty."
The game was on . . .

Then there was/is the second aspect of my process of self-invention: the lamentation. I come from a people who have created a musical form of lamentation called the Blues. Lamentation came not only because of things I could not do or was denied. As a Black woman, I "sang" lamentations for the times I'd given too much because I did not know better. One of these laments, entitled "A Sister Song," talks about

> Things I've shut my life to
> growin-up fast like quick rain and summer sun
> gettin use to hindsight stead of foresight
> youth, beauty, wantin and dreamin
> fadin into aunti, mamma and hard times
>
> Gettin use to this man
> promisin the best he can halfway
> loving and bleedin and achin like a tooth
> that never gets fixed just right
>
> I've shut my life to things
> like love and candy and flowers
> meetin at a just-right time.

Affirmation and hope were/are important as I tried/try to shape myself into freedom. Invariably this act of affirming, this hope, led back to communities of women, to the women who taught me love and support. I wrote a poem called "My Mother's House."

> I believe in my mother's house
> the skinny rooms pressed together by
> kitchen smells in sun soaked drapes
>
> a Sunday room for God with
> sugar-stiff doilies
> shutoff cold all week
> pot-bellied heat stored in us
> loving and paining and old-aging into
> grandmaw or child womaning into me
>
> learning food stamps and extra candy
> separated by broken toilets and
> hungry Kentucky nights
> summered by our longing
> the no man in this house became my faith
> in white dolls with button eyes staring—
> staring a place where feeling ought to be
>
> under patched quilts and no rain summers
> playing house with make believe fathers
> just my size doing it doing it doing it
> feeling an age explode in
> space shapes of Ghana
> darshekies and half-good 'fros

from raps to ripoffs and who I really am
I returned to my mother's house without a God
but believing—believing space ain't my problem
and all room is too skinny to
hold what life really is
in kitchen smells and

God-will-take-care-of-you Sundays of
no-man-in-the-house love
so bountiful
so painfully, painfully bountiful
it is the strength
for what I live with . . .

All these movements in my process of self-invention are partial. Shaping oneself into freedom is a continuous act that always involves telling one's story. I tell my story so other women can share and participate. From this sharing and participating—this participating in my story and my participating/receiving their stories—we women bond. Community happens.

Yet bonding is neither simple nor automatic. It takes time, pain, negotiation, and transformation. From my effort to bond has come a multitude of questions, some of which are posed in the poem *"Mud Flowers"* (see page 159).

Poems

Mosadi

1.
See how she stretches her fingers to the sun
She is a green grass dancer—Mosadi—
Body swelling muscle rivers running.
She is a runner trying for passage beyond
The sky, she races and weeps in celebration
Each spring when she takes as her lover the earth;
For the autumn she chants hours to the wind.
Mosadi means Woman, she thunders
And she stretches her fingers to the sun
She is a green grass dancer—Mosadi—
Body swelling muscle rivers running.

2.
Ain't no one can boogie like Mosadi.
She is smooth. She is cool. She maintains
Control of every motion goin down
She is a master of the boogie.
Mosadi means Woman, she laughs
Deep and she orders another drink
"I am the keeper of the power, you see
What I mean? I can do anything.
I got no sympathy for people moanin
An' groanin in their misery.
They gotta be like me."
She laughs, she grabs a partner for the dance.
Ain't no one can boogie like Mosadi.

3.
When hard times hit Mosadi
She pretended not to notice
Her legs gone wooden, her motions graceless,
The sun a cold yellow patch on the sky

Waiting to crush her in a sandwich
Between sky and earth, she pretends to laugh
When people say Mosadi's dance
Is not what it used to be. Mosadi means
Woman, she hums remembering the sound
Of drums no longer pounding.

4.
Mosadi has moved to the sea this summer.
She roams deserted beaches, collecting ocean artifacts,
Studying the eating habits of ocean birds
She watches for changes, wonders at her anguish,
Each sunset she climbs to the highest dune
And presses her head down to the sands. Mosadi is afraid.
She prays and waits through the night.
She would like to understand the meaning of the moon.

5.
Mosadi is learning to play the flute.
Friends notice her voice a little softer,
She moves a little slower, speaks less;
Sadness in her eyes
She boogies even better than before.
Mosadi means Woman, she laughs
Deep and she orders another drink.
"We are the sharers in the power
And the moon is quietly inevitable."

6.
See how she stretches her fingers to the sun
She is a green grass dancer—Mosadi—
Body swelling muscle rivers running;
See how she settles her palms upon the earth
She is a moon light disciple—listening—
Mosadi means Woman, she whispers
And she stretches her fingers to the sun.
—Sharon Thomson

The Dressmaker

I been pinnin up other women's dresses all my life since I was
16 years old which was when I first hired myself out to Miss Faye
whose original 9 by 12 oil portrait hangs in the back of this shop

which that woman was kind enough to leave to me at the time
 of
her death a . . . bout 25 years ago it was that the pox got her,
kind of a queer thing for this day and age, don't ya think?
Anyway
even though I wasn't workin for her for very long, Miss Faye,
she left me this store since she didn't have nobody else
to leave it to so here I been ever since and every day the ladies,
they come to me "Oh Willa, will you make this pretty for me?"
 and
I do. I bend down and start pinnin, give 'em loose
where they need loose and tight where they need tight
make their bodies better than anything they were ever born
 with
and the ladies, they appreciate me for it in their own way
offer me a little somethin
like one day
I was on my knees pinnin a hem for this one lady, she was so
 antsy
wouldn't stop movin, wouldn't stop talkin either, till finally
I had to tell her to be quiet and keep still so I could concentrate
on my work but let me tell ya, that dress she had me hemmin
it was a *nice* dress, real delicate, not like all those cottons
and linens I'm so sick of by the middle of August
I'm about to scream if I see one more cute little gingham thing.
No. This was a nice dress. Had turquoise flowers printed
all over it and each of the flowers had a deep blue center
and when you held the material up in the air it sort of
stayed there awhile before it came back down so I got
 fascinated
by this dress and I began to play with it a little, you know,
I'd hold it up to the sunlight so I could see
how the blue flowers looked with the sun comin through them
 and
then I'd let go of the edge I was holdin and watch it
hang in the air for just a second before it floated on down and
then I'd start all over again and it got to where I completely
forgot that I was supposed to be workin on that thing, let alone
that there was somebody standin inside it
till the next thing I know
I felt a hand on my head
strokin me
so I looked up. And that lady, she had some of the ends of my
 hair
balancin on her fingertips and she said to me

"Willa, you got such pretty har." Now that was kinda nice,
her noticin me in that way. Don't you think?

—Sharon Thomson

The Hypnotist

You won't believe the things they tell you. You will hear
only the sound of my voice telling you
there's nothing to cling to. Gone are the arms
of the people who raised you. Gone are the friends
who descend for you like a flock of birds
and then disperse. Gone is the lie of the one beside you
in the darkness whispering. You've gone too far.
They no longer flatter you. They can no longer fool you
with their fits of kindness, the grace of their loving gestures

Don't fall
for the tender moment: it will swallow you. Don't be surprised
when the hand stroking you suddenly snaps
into a fist. And when you see a thing of beauty
remember it is only that: a thing of beauty and not a sign
not a prophecy, not a revelation of a benevolent maker.
You are the god. You are the devil. You are the life
locked inside, life swelling inside. You are whatever it is
that is making you sick. This is a hard path
a lonely path. Of course, you miss a sense of home
the feeling of belonging. You torture yourself with memories
that picture of your sister going on in a yellow kitchen.
You think you need to believe in someone. Get over that.
The universe is rolling out before you.
This is the unveiling. Look

From here on
there's nothing to cling to. It's as open
as the desert. You're free.

—Sharon Thomson

Women Behind Walls
(for the women in Cook County Jail and Dwight Prison)

Sisters, is conspiracy our crime,
that song of dolphins who tell each other danger
across oceans of silence?

Our knowing hammered to the heart mute and bloody.
Every women who does not shut up is guilty.
Every silence unremarkable as a dark lagoon. Dangerous.

One by one we're seized: colored women
with low cards, who sneer at their dealers;
welfare shuffles the deck, the hand is predictable as hunger.
They call these thieves who bounce food checks at Jewel and
    A&P.
This gathering of mothers,
like wounded blackbirds in cages for a year without trial.
The state "places" their children
like the dumping of soiled laundry.
The white ones rot like decayed teeth
in the stink of mental wards.
Their breath was bad, their floors weren't waxed,
their husbands' collars were grey, grey.
These turn state's evidence against themselves;
like frightened animals they sense violence
rising like a Kansas twister, then they give away their minds.

Ancient justice is the blind scorekeeper:
"She's not a real woman, she's a whore,
she's not a good momma, lock her up, she's crazy."
Who judges us condemns themselves,
Our freedom is your only way out.
On the underground railroad
you can ride with us or you become the jailer.
Harriet Tubman never lost one of those entrusted to her.
Neither will we.

—Renny Golden

Raising Up the Revolution
(for the women cottonpickers of Chinandega)

Here on the bin floor of border mountains
that once rolled fields of orange groves
as far as Leon, I work a land
that cannot remember its own gilded orchards;
the time before Somoza's growers
levelled all the chocolate dust cottonfields.
In the measure of time when our mountain ridge,
that dark cluster of old women,

wears silver shawls of dawn on purple hunches,
I arise with the silent women.
Before daybreak spills the last
morning star from Nicaragua's violet sky,
before fishermen of Bluefields prepare nets,
before newsboys scuffle barefoot
into Esteli's chalky Streets,
before the women open Market Oriental
like a paper umbrella.
before long arms of sunlight
pull Managua cement workers
onto rickety buses,
before this compañero, a sleeping
braid of muscle and sinew awakens,
before our people's feet
touch their prodigal earth,
we, mothers of Chinandega,
gather into that crack of opening light.
Hours before its searing turns the fields
to a white whistle of heat,
we begin our work.
—Renny Golden

The World of Women

The world of women
is a round world.
Leaning from windows,
sighing along earth's
curve in our encirclement,
we apprehend that
world in an embrace.

We have no ladders
leading to heaven or
corporate board rooms.
Our ladders reach
apples, peaches, pears
which cling on branches just
above our heads.

The bodies of women
are curved bodies:

some limned like Rubens'
ladies; some, like mine,
angular as chairs, but
rocking chairs, for
we too curve.

Women's words have rounded
edges to ricochet off
corners and return when
they are not received. My
words so often roll from
the mountain of your inattention
they are worn to small, round pebbles.

Our anger too
is circular.
Fury contained
is a tornado's
whorled spring which may,
if grounded, cut
a swath of death.

The circular ways of women,
women's paths,
return, and start again,
imperceptibly widening as
a tree, each year,
adds yet another ring.

The world of women
is a round world.
Sometimes, on April mornings,
you will find us, under
the blue rotunda, tossing
that round world, gently
from one to another.
—Ann Thacher

Blessing

John Paul,
clothes cut from
archetypal fathers' cloth
is a fine father
of a man. Of course
he is the Pope.

He speaks long
and often. I agree to
nothing, crying sometimes
when I think about it.

But
he blesses
the people. He blesses
and blesses the people like
a mirror making them
larger and handsomer, like
sun on their shoulders,
melting them
into a warm world,
he blesses.

I want to be the Pope.
So I can bless you,
bless you, and you
accept my blessing,
sun-warm and mirror-bright.

Because
(in this cul-de-sac
of history, I think
I can say this and
not be burnt or racked up)

because
I can reach out and
put my hands
against the morning
as he can,
because
I can go down and
draw from that deep river
where he draws.

because
blessing is
as near as
we are
to each other

if you will

if I will.
   —Ann Thacher

Letter to My Mother

Dear Mama,
I never called you that before—
I always called you Mom or Mother.
I guess I always had to be grown up.
Sometimes I don't feel grown up.
I just feel like crying Mama Mama—Hold me, let me cry.
    You couldn't stand for me to cry.
You cried a lot—Did you call your Mom Mama?
It's good you are dead—I would be embarrassed if you heard
    me call you that.
Oh! I am embarrassed—maybe you can hear me now.
Are you free to hear me now that you don't live in the land of
    Our Fathers?
I have some things I want to tell you—in case you can hear.
Mama, I'm sorry I cashed the milk bottle and bought the piece
    of baker's chocolate.
I ate the whole thing myself—I was hungry—but Mama, so were
    you. I'm sorry.
Mama, when I was 10—you remember—I quit sucking my
    thumb.
You thought you had finally broken me.
I want you to know what really happened.
It was a Sunday night just like most Sunday nights.
I lay in bed unable to sleep. I just couldn't get my arms and legs
    to stop shaking.
I knew Dad would come home drunk and beat you up.
I was so scared I prayed to God—please don't let him beat her
    tonight—
I'll never suck my thumb again if you stop him—oh please—I
    promise.
That night he came home and went to sleep. I never sucked my
    thumb again.
Would you have believed me if I had been able to tell you?
You liked to tell it was because you embarrassed me by sucking
    your thumb in public that I quit.
Mama, remember how you always told me to straighten up my
    shoulders.
You even bought me a brace to wear and made me walk with a
    book on my head.
Remember you also said I was too tall. Men don't like tall girls,
    you said.

You said my girlfriend Caroline was so cute because she was
    pixie like.
You said you wanted petite girls and what did you get—
    Amazons.
I took every opportunity to prove to you you were wrong. I
    showed you articles about women who were tall. I called to
    your attention stars and Miss Americas who were tall.
You just said OK but no man would want to take them out or
    marry them.
Mama, if God is not a Father, please, please tell me it is fine to
    be tall.
You always wanted me to write to you—I just couldn't.
Why is it so easy to write to you now?
Somehow I feel you can hear me now and understand me.
You are free, out from under their control. No more of their
    poisonous semen penetrating your mind and body.
Now you don't have to kill me in the name of The Father, The
    Son and The Holy Ghost.
If God is love, Mama—Love me tall.

Your Daughter
—Joan Wyzenbeek

My Mother Mary

My mother Mary was like the original Mary in many ways.

When she was just a little girl she submitted to being raped by
    her father.
When she was married she submitted to being beaten by my
    father.
When she had emotional problems she submitted to shock
    treatments by her psychiatrist.
When she was physically ill she submitted to surgery by her
    surgeon.

Now she is dead—I hope God is not a father.

My mother Mary married Joseph when she was 20 in 1929.
She gave birth to me when she was 21 in 1930.
And Mary she rocked me every four hours just like Our Fathers
    said.
In between times her heart screamed with pain to hold her
    crying baby.

But alas, the laws of Our Fathers had penetrated her brain so
   deeply—she thought her heart was a liar.
Mary died when she was 70 in 1979.
I held her hand and told her she would be free when she
   stopped breathing Our Father's air.
Her last breath was a long gasp—followed by a look of peace,
The kind she had when she rocked me.
Now she knows her heart is not a liar.
She has escaped Our Fathers.
Please God let it be true.

—Joan Wyzenbeek

Partner

Silent, unseen
Robbing me of control
Stealing, bit by bit
Pieces of the paths over which my messages flow
Blocking my signals to myself
Flooding me with fatigue
After such puny effort.

You own the greater share of me now
Even when you are quiet
I wonder what mischief you are planning next
Even when others say, "But you look so well"
I can only smile
Knowing your betrayal is invisible
I can not dismiss you
We are bound together
Inseparable.

—Mary Jo Grote

Mother-in-Law

Holy sounds, those words to me
Blasphemous, the jokes
You were my Naomi
Until you slipped away
Coming to you for celebration
Finding you gone, so quietly

Ten years now
Bittersweet memories still surfacing
Flickering tapers in your brass menorah
Recall flashing blue eyes
Regaling grand-children with escapades of your school days
Tasting season's first honeydew with lime
Evokes the bringer of many gifts
Re-reading last book intriguing us
Recaptures shared search
Retracing our spring paths
Finds you uncovering your beloved wild flowers

That last week
So unaware of the pain
Of your loneliness
Failing to make one daily call
I missed you altogether

You finished your quest alone
        —Mary Jo Grote

Portrait of Rosa Luxemburg

Such is my life
such slits of time
opening onto hopes of such immense horizons
the rinngggg rinngggggg of a hope totally out of proportion
makes me run run
back to my office in time to catch the sun
burning beyond my window with such enormous promise
it was no wrong number
it was you i missed
yanking my perennially obstinate ankle in the hallway
calling me out to embrace the sun
ringing through months of silences
accepting me my promises and a casual invitation to a
  sunset.

Above my desk I look
and Rosa knows
you haunt me, hunch-back old woman
Rosa, Rosa shall I wave you, a chinese red flag, against the
  slatening sky
the sky has seen nothing burn as red as you

and I am now tormented by those eyes
no revolutionary man has such a look
your eyes magnetize my trivial desires into an iron clutch in my
    throat
choke on the courage they have learned in the bloody streets
the patience day after dying day surveying the world from your
    narrow prison window
the sadness they speak
an old worker dragging his humanity home at nightfall out
    through the factory gates
a young soldier draped in his patriotic delusions
a lover lost to the underground
and friends gone to their graves
or reaction
your eyes tell me that you know in all your flaming red rhetoric
that everyone does not make it to the revolution
some tire   some betray   and so many die without even
    knowing
sometimes I look up into those eyes and think I see a kind of
    fear in them
and yet i know they'd never dart away
you are a woman, Rosa, and your eyes hold me with a calm
    intensity
learned revolving inwards over the horizons of your own
    anxieties
you take up my trivia and make it your own
you are a true Red Rosa
and your lonely eyes assure me there is nothing in them
that cannot be experienced as common.

I take no peace in solitary meditations by the lake anymore
only the promise of some tremendous insurrectionary dance
    around the sun-fire
that will burn   burn   the old forms of this world away
so someday   that alien crimson wonder out there
will no longer be a god
no longer the horsepower for the armored chariots of Empire
no longer a papier-maché guillotine for the lovelorn
the sun will whisper nuances of day
and we in our communal work and play will some of us pause
to catch its bronze illuminations in each others' eyes
it will be a Red sun
full of energy and power

and it will set
in human arms
at last

—Jackie Di Salvo

Mud Flowers

How will I walk this rope?
   My foot size ten
   Broad careening woman
   I am black
I have held her in my gaze
   White woman
Smile slashed across her face
   Like the great pumpkin
   Friendly
Asking to know me and
   I her
Should we together probe ourselves
   Mythed in the strength of
   Men we've forgotten
Should I say fuck the guilt
Should she say fuck accusing
   Should we say to each other
Your people will be my people
Where you go I will go
   Shall we together
   Admit
   Alone
We are the people?

—Delores S. Williams

Part V

War and Peace

IN DEALING WITH the issues of war and peace from a feminist perspective, the writers in this section touch again and again on the theme of patriarchy. At times, they take for granted that we know what patriarchy is: a cultural-historical-structural framework of long duration and universal scope in which men exercise leadership and decision-making power and women are always subordinate. At times male is identified with patriarchy and man rather than woman is denigrated. In a careful reading, however, it becomes clear that all the writers affirm co-humanity and seek a world in which women and men can live together in greater freedom and harmony. At bottom, all share a religious vision, but a religious vision that can never be separated from its impact on the concrete public and political world.

Does the patriarchal-hierarchical order finally culminate in a struggle for the dominance of the world? Is this its end, whether consciously or unconsciously sought? Does domination (which is the bottom line of patriarchy) lead to the destruction of human life, the destruction of the planet itself?

In "Political Oppression and Creative Survival," Mary E. Hunt speaks out of her experience among poor women and men living in Latin America under highly oppressive regimes. She speaks too out of her experience of oppression as a lesbian in the United States and her knowledge of the lesbian and gay movements. Hunt describes six marks of the dynamics of oppression and sets against them six strategies needed for creative survival. If a more human world is to emerge for multitudes of people today, it will not just evolve; it cannot be achieved without struggle. Hunt finds sources of strength for the struggle in supportive networks, "spiraling nonviolence," and "unlikely coalitions."

Mary Condren, a feminist from Dublin, centers her discussion, "Patriarchy and Death," around deep-seated differences between men and women, which she perceives in both the present and the past, and which she traces back to the understanding humans have had of paternity. For Condren female creativity is essentially related to the giving and the nurturing of life, while male creativity is linked to death and death-defying risks and tasks. As a result she perceives patriarchy as a mighty system that moves almost inevitably today toward war and destruction. In nuclear power and the neutron bomb she sees the ultimate patriarchal symbols and weapons of annihilation. Even as patriarchy destroys itself all else will be destroyed, unless women with revolutionary patience find ways of bonding beyond all differences.

Karen McCarthy Brown adds an entirely new note in "Why Women Need the War God," which at first glance appears to be in total contradiction to Condren. Personal anger at grave injustice in her own life had confused her until she realized that she had to claim this anger and use it. From her long study of Haitian culture and Vodou practice, she had come to know of the War God, Ogou. In bonding with him and with many Haitian people, she found a transformative experience. The bond with the War God also highlighted for her the grave injustices to the Haitian people and the need to strike out against them. While standing against all nuclear war, she points to the terrible injustices in life that make her unwilling to condemn all war in principle. Her tragic vision of life contains much ambivalence, even as she embraces the feminist vision of an end to domination and injustice.

Contrasting with Brown's approach is "Feminist Liberation Theology and Yahweh as Holy Warrior: An Analysis of Symbol" by Carol P. Christ. For many liberation theologians the story of Exodus and the writings of the Hebrew prophets have been an inspiration for social justice, as have Jesus' relations to the poor and the outcasts of his society. Christ devotes her attention especially to the Hebrew Bible, traditions she knows well, but in criticizing them she has no interest in "perpetuating Christian anti-Judaism." While acknowledging the liberating aspects of Exodus and the prophets, she points to the consequences of the exodus, the uprooting of many peoples so that the Jewish tribes might enter the promised land. In the prophets, too, other faiths are deemed idolatrous, worthy of death and the sword. Carol Christ sees Yahweh as a God of war whose justice for some leads to grave injustice for others. In the end she would cast her lot not with this powerful God, Yahweh, but with the multitudes of people who *without any great power* work long and patiently, building the world ever anew throughout the centuries.

The three papers that complete Part V respond to the issues of war and peace: a discussion by the total group on feminism and war, the necessity for violence, the possibilities of nonviolent direct action, and the need to bring feminist and Black liberationist perspectives to the peace movement; a panel dealing with a specific war, the Arab-Israeli conflict, as it emerged in the experience of certain of the group members; and finally, a set of suggestions for action, developed by the working group on political strategies.

Political Oppression and Creative Survival

MARY E. HUNT

Economic and political realities of the 1980s indicate that political oppression is on the rise on many fronts, not the least of which include women, the poor, and people from Third World countries. At the same time the necessity for creative survival increases.

Certain elements are present anywhere oppression lurks, whether it be racism, sexism, heterosexism, imperialism, or any other systematic discrimination against people. Similarly, the dynamics of liberation are present wherever people struggle for freedom, to overcome oppression, and to build new structures of inclusion and community.

The examples used to describe the dynamics of oppression and the dynamics of liberation arise from experience. I have worked and studied in Argentina for the past two years. Argentine life and culture provide a helpful way to understand the dynamics of oppression. The reality of heterosexism in North America provides another lens on oppression, another way to focus the many-faceted combination of sexism and homophobia that result in the oppression of lesbians and gay men.

Argentina is a resource-rich country ruled since the coup in 1976 by a military junta. Many North Americans are familiar with the various periods of rule by Juan Peron, thanks to the popular musical *Evita*. But it is important to note that the lyrical life of the musical has been replaced by an ugly reality called "the disappeared"—people who have been rounded up, taken off, kidnapped by night, beckoned from their jobs. The president of the country has called them "the logical consequence

Mary E. Hunt

of a dirty war." Reports indicate that twenty thousand people have disappeared in the last six years. They are probably not injured or imprisoned; they are probably dead. They were probably dropped from airplanes flying at such a speed and velocity that their bodies disintegrated on impact with the river that separates Argentina and Uruguay.

This violent reality is but the logical and most far-reaching effect of oppression; although other forms of oppression differ in degree, they do not really differ in kind. Oppression is a contemporary way of dealing with the age-old theological problem of evil. Oppression is another way of understanding those negative forces in the world that make it impossible to actualize the best of what it means to be human. In order to move beyond oppression, to move toward liberation, it is necessary to understand that oppression is like a round balloon that can be punctured from a variety of angles with a variety of implements, all of which will result in the same thing. Thus, racism can be seen as having one trajectory, sexism another, and imperialism another, but each leads to oppression. Understanding one form of oppression, therefore, is helpful in appreciating and working toward the alleviation of another form.

Once one sees that all forms of oppression work the same way, it is easy to see that they are connected. For example, poor women in Argentina who have lost their children to the national campaign against so-called terrorists, which resulted in the disappearances, understand oppression not only in terms of their experience of imperialism but also in terms of their experience as women. They act out of the necessity of their own lives, not on the basis of some ideology. And they connect one experience with another, demonstrating the integral link that bonds all forms of oppression.

The Mothers of the Plaza de Mayo have been highlighted in the media as leaders of the fight against oppression in Argentina. They are distinguished by their white kerchiefs, on which are written the names and dates of the disappearances of their loved ones. They cross class, age, religion, and race lines in Argentina. I recall vividly marching between two women, one wearing a lovely velvet jacket and the other a tattered old sweater. We symbolized the diversity that will unite over oppression in any and all forms. From any single experience, such as the loss of children, one learns how and why people will fight to the death for their liberation, and it becomes easier to imagine motivations and strategies that arise when oppression worsens, intensifies, borders on the unsolvable.

Lesbian and gay oppression in North America proves that one does not have to go abroad and engage in theological exotica by studying a culture and a people far from one's own experience in order to understand how oppression works, how strategies for liberation are formulated. Since 1969, when the first gay men fought back at Stonewall, the now-famous gay bar in New York City, against police who raided the establishment, the lesbian/gay movement has been part of American culture. This means not that Middle America has welcomed lesbians and gays with open arms, but that they have found so many gays and lesbians in their churches, work places, and even in their families that one of the major fears of a heterosexist patriarchal society has come true. But it has been far less traumatic than expected. People have slowly come to realize, with the help of social scientific, theological, and even biological data, that not only is a good percentage of the population homosexually oriented, but also that many homosexuals, indeed the vast majority, lead healthy, good, and natural lives. Still heterosexism, or the normative value on heterosexuality to the exclusion of homosexuality, is so deeply ingrained in the culture that lesbian/gay oppression is one of the most subtle, violent, and pervasive forms in the 1980s.

All forms of oppression/liberation are not the same; they cannot be homogenized. Poverty, for example, is so damaging to life that economic oppression demands a certain priority. But it is necessary first to recognize one's own oppression as it is related to other forms, and then to begin to pursue the logical progression of oppressions in order to build coalitions for action. This process of creative listening, listening to others' stories in order to act together, results in strong networks.

The first element of oppression is that it is always and everywhere irrational. Those who oppress can rarely if ever explain their actions in terms that satisfy even the most rudimentary canons of rationality. For example, in Argentina the disappeared—among them old women, young children, and pregnant women (and thus their fetuses)—are often dismissed as terrorists. Likewise, when pressed about why they discriminate against lesbians and gay men, most people will be forced to conclude that it is because they are homosexual, no more, no less. The irrational character of oppression makes it difficult to confront, but knowing it is irrational can make it easier to understand.

A second dynamic of oppression is structural and systemic. Oppression is never simply a private matter, something individual or unique to an individual. Rather, people participate in structures of oppression which guarantee that in any fixed situation some people will always come out on top and others on the bottom. In Argentina Jews and poor people have disappeared in numbers that far exceed their respective percentages in the population and certainly in the political life of the country. In North America, lesbians experience greater economic disadvantage than gay men. And heterosexism/homophobia is part of the social and cultural fabric of the country. Marriage contracts (which make legal dealings easier), insurance benefits, hospital visiting privileges, etc., that are reserved for relatives and spouses are not permitted to homosexual partners.

A third element or dynamic of oppression is that it always has physical and psychological consequences. In Argentina this manifests itself as fear, self-censorship, a lack of trust between individuals. Oppression is debilitating for a culture and counterproductive for an economy. In lesbian/gay circles the physical and psychological effects of oppression range from risk of injury or death to fear and self-hatred that can render one invisible in the culture. There is self-censorship too. Lesbians and gay men are taught not to "come out," not to mention whom they love, and not to rock the family boat by being themselves. There is a high rate of alcoholism (reportedly one out of three homosexuals is alcoholic or bordering on it) and suicide within the lesbian/gay community that confirms this dynamic.

A fourth dynamic of oppression is the horizontal violence that is found within every oppressed group. It is Argentines who kidnap, kill, and/or torture Argentines. It was the Argentine military that sent young Argentine boys to fight an unwinnable war in the south. For lesbians and gays in North America, horizontal violence takes a variety of forms. Recent evidence suggests that some of the most virulent critics of lesbians and gays are actually homosexual themselves, including some members of the so-called Moral Majority.[1] Further, the horizontal violence so well documented in the women's movement has carried over into the lesbian movement, where struggles over coping strategies are beset with the extra pressures of intensified fear and the sense of having more to lose. The veiled and not-so-veiled charges that lesbians have "caused" everything from the defeat of the ERA to the need for all women to move beyond feminism[2] reveal horizontal violence.

A fifth characteristic of oppression is its interstructured nature. One form is never experienced in isolation from another form, never found without a companion that makes it worse for those who suffer both forms. For example, in Argentina women suffer the double oppression of being female and of living in a country dominated by outside economic interests and plagued by Third World status. In the lesbian/gay community Spanish-speaking and Third World lesbians and gays find oppression within their own communities just as difficult as it is outside, and often more so. The same applies to People of Color, and of course the oppression of lesbians, even White, middle-class, well-educated lesbians, is usually far more damaging than what occurs for their White male counterparts.

Sixth, all forms of oppression are based on a certain appeal to the transcendent for justification. It is thought to be God-ordained that certain persons are meant to be on the outside. In Argentina the claim that God is on the side of the military is nurtured by frequent news photos of junta members receiving communion, for example. And of course on the lesbian/gay front it has been made clear over and over again that heterosexuality is normative (although some are beginning to dispute the claim that God is not gay).

A footnote to the dynamics of oppression (which perhaps ought to be the opening paragraph, but in any case deserves mention) is that oppression is always and everywhere perceived as a joke by the oppressors. In turn, the oppressed, unable to laugh at the humor directed at them, are often branded as humorless. In Argentina crude and cruel jokes are made by the authorities about the Mothers of the Plaza de Mayo. They are often called "the crazies" and are seldom taken seriously. In the lesbian/gay community the jokes are endless, from Archie Bunker lines to sick cartoons. But here liberation has taken its first stand: the humor has been turned around and made to reflect the uproarious joy that has become synonymous with gay self-discovery.

It is important to note that oppression means an unequal power dynamic is at play. The powerful need to know little if anything about the powerless, while the powerless have to know everything and then some about the powerful. For example, few Argentines would hesitate if asked about the unit of currency used in the United States or the name of its capital. Very few citizens of the United States, however, know what unit of currency is used in Argentina, much less what the exchange rate is, and even fewer could name one major city other than Buenos Aires. This lack of information about the oppressed is a luxury; the overabundance of information about the oppressor country is a necessity in an imperialist setting.

The dynamics of liberation are really a recipe for creative survival. They are an effort to move out of well-established patterns into coalitions for ongoing work. In Argentina this effort is characterized by the formation of groups like the Mothers of the Plaza de Mayo, Servicio Paz y Justicia, the Permanent Assembly for Human Rights, and the Ecumenical Movement for Human Rights, in which people work and play, party and pray so as to make life in the moment bearable and even enjoyable. The dynamics of liberation begin now; living differently in the midst of oppression is a sign that something different is possible. In the lesbian/gay community new definitions and self-understandings are emerging. A new sense of hope rooted in community is emerging. A resolution that "never again" will a people be annihilated is being made and kept.

The dynamics of liberation parallel the dynamics of oppression. First, if oppression is always irrational, then liberation will be rational—not the linear, cerebral rationality of a patriarchal culture, but a multileveled, experientially understood rationality that builds respect for other peoples' experiences by valuing one's own. Understanding on its own terms—and in its own language, if possible—an experience quite different from one's own makes it possible to appreciate how diverse and complex liberation will be, and to internalize that liberation is for all of us or for none of us.

Second, if oppression is structural and systemic, then liberation demands the building of new social/spiritual structures, the ongoing formation of new communities in which liberating values can be embodied. It is a long-term task that needs to be invested in the young.

Third, if oppression has physical and psychological ramifications, then liberation will involve people protecting themselves, taking precautions against the worst of the oppression, as well as fashioning creative cushioning that will ensure longer lives and protect against burnout. It will involve spiritual and physical healing, as well as ongoing nurture. Finally, it will mean psychic and spiritual preparation, a continued conditioning through supportive networks that enable people to rest and renew their energies in the midst of the long haul.

Fourth, if oppression includes horizontal violence, then liberation invites us to spiraling nonviolence. Tactical nonviolence that comes from a variety of sources (e.g., Gandhi, Martin Luther King, Dorothy Day, the Mothers) promises to evoke reaction. It also builds community and cements bonds for the new structures that emerge from liberating praxis. The ERA fast in Springfield, Illinois was an example of spiraling nonviolence that showed how the tactic, when used prayerfully and strategically, spirals into many and various manifestations of new life and renewed resistance.

Fifth, if oppression is always interstructured, then analyses of liberation will demand not only a sophisticated understanding of how the whole works, but also will invite the formation of unlikely coalitions. As people build the new structures, they will bond with others whose primary agenda may be different from their own, but whose collective agenda includes their issues or entrées into the experience of oppression. This is difficult at times when one is seemingly asked to provide support without receiving support. But clearly the unlikely coalitions, as represented by the nearly one million people gathered in New York City for the antinuclear march on June 12, 1982, will be brought together in international, ecumenical, multiethnic constellations that will get the job done. These unlikely coalitions provide the space and time for issues to assume their interstructured character and for people to blossom into the complex individuals they are. These coalitions are the hope for the future.

Sixth, if an appeal to transcendent reality is made to justify oppression, then some appeal to transcendence must appear in the essence of liberation. This could be simply a counterappeal—your God says one thing and mine another. Or it could involve getting rid of transcendence altogether, deciding that religion is a drag on the revolutionary process and therefore must go. But a third, more creative, solution involves placing a moratorium on God and Goddess language for a time, and instead appealing to the universal experience of transcendent mystery that surrounds humanity. The appeal to concrete values and actions makes that mystery real, grounding the commitment to love and justice as values regardless of religious traditions.

Finally, just as humor plays a part in oppression, so too it has its place in liberation. Humor reveals the other side of oppression, the joyful, funny, ironic, delightful side that beckons all to participate. Humor is the domain of little children just learning to manipulate the language. It is the home of the elderly whose wisdom is often cloaked in witticisms. Not taking oneself too seriously is a key to understanding and withstanding the struggle from oppression to liberation.

The dynamics of oppression are political in that they have an impact on the whole community. And their counterparts, the dynamics of liberation, are a recipe for creative survival in that they are the best hope for the future. Gatherings like Women's Spirit Bonding, full as they are with discussion, disagreement, and promise, provide a first step toward a time when, in the words of Sheila Collins, we can "restore to the young that season when all things LEAP and sing."[3]

18

Patriarchy and Death
MARY CONDREN

Picture the scene as Socrates, surrounded by his disciples, prepares to drink the hemlock. One of his disciples, Simmaeus, asks him how he feels about dying. Socrates replies:

> It is a fact, Simmaeus, that true philosophers make dying their profession and that to them of all men, death is least alarming. Look at it this way. If they are thoroughly dissatisfied with the body and long to have their souls independent of it, when this happens would it not be entirely unreasonable to be frightened or distressed? Would they not rather be glad to set out for the place where there is a prospect of attaining the object of their lifelong desire, which is wisdom, and of escaping from an unwelcome association? Will the philosopher not be glad to make that journey? We must suppose so, my dear boy, that is if he is a real philosopher, for then he will be of the firm belief that he will never find wisdom in all its purity in any other place. If this is so, would it not be quite unreasonable, as I have said just now, for such a man to be afraid of death?[1]

The sentiments expressed in the above passage from Plato's *Phaedo* reverberate throughout Western culture and philosophy: preoccupation with death; dissatisfaction with nature and the body; the pursuit of wisdom, even, or preferably, beyond the grave; and death as a means of attaining one's lifelong desire. This understanding of human existence is primarily patriarchal; the cultural forms whereby men establish and maintain their power in society revolve around the theme of death. Death plays a major part in the way men come to individuation, in the development of the male mind, and in patriarchal rituals and ethics. War—and even the ultimate holocaust—is not simply an aberration of an otherwise healthy social order, but may

Mary Condren

in fact be the logical consequence of how that social order has been constructed.

The terms "male" and "patriarchal" are almost synonymous. Individual women have benefited enormously from the privileges of patriarchy, however, and individual men are now seriously troubled by their realization of the far-reaching ramifications of patriarchal culture. Patriarchal culture ultimately benefits neither men nor women. Nevertheless, instrumental power in this society is still held predominantly by men; the male life-principle has overextended itself to such an extent that life on this planet is seriously in jeopardy. Not all men are bad, and not all women are virtuous; it is not necessary to make way for a romantic matriarchy. Such a stance is at best simplistic and at worst dangerous. Everyone has a negative side, which it is her or his responsibility to acknowledge. Owning one's anger or negative side must be distinguished, however, from the cultural edifice predicated on a preoccupation with death and death-defying activities.

Whereas female creativity takes place in relation to giving and sustaining life, male creativity takes place in relation to death and death-defying activities. The passion behind this thesis comes from several sources: an attempt to work on the reasons (both sociological and subliminal) for the historical exclusion of women from the Catholic priesthood; a concern about the relationships between sexual repression, clericalism, and violence in the Irish culture from which I come; a suspicion that these issues are intimately related to the threat of nuclear war, which daily hangs over our heads; and the search for a common basis on which women can come to self-understanding politically and to bonding internationally.

This analysis is based on the profound envy, contempt, and imitation of women's creativity that is evidenced historically in patriarchal culture. This envy/contempt ambiguity is rooted in the uncertainty of paternity, a problem expressed pathologically in desperate attempts on the part of patriarchal ethics, academic life, ritual, and philosophy to overcome the limitations of biology, nature, and earth itself.

Paternity as a Cultural Construct

It is difficult to date precisely when men discovered their role in procreation. Elizabeth Fisher relates the discovery to the domestication of animals and in particular to the more sophisticated process of animal breeding.[2] But even after this discovery there remained a fundamental insecurity. On one hand, a male could not be sure of his fatherhood other than by confining the female. On the other hand, the practices of animal breeding, which were highly selective and permitted only the most perfect males to copulate, did nothing to reassure the male. It became apparent that only one male was necessary to impregnate many females.[3] A more secure and fundamental basis for paternity had to be established. Moreover, the act of procreation itself was a profoundly alienating experience for men. As Mary O'Brien points out in *The Politics of Reproduction*, "Man is negated not as lover but as *parent*, and this negation rests squarely on the alienation of the male seed in the copulative act."[4] Paternity, according to O'Brien, is a social product, whereas motherhood is essentially physiological.[5] The historical development of paternity represents a "real triumph over the ambiguities of nature."[6] In other words, men had to establish a cultural form to transcend their experience of alienation and firmly claim their paternity.

Cultural paternity, although it makes use of biological metaphors, is not primarily biological. Rather, it is the way men have translated the uncertainty of paternity into the cultural edifice of patriarchy. It is a compensatory activity for the many inadequacies of physical paternity.[7] Unlike maternity, biological paternity cannot finally be proven; its fruits are finally subject to death; it is not constant but depends on uncontrollable factors—impotence, nature, women, and death may all intervene to eradicate the male contribution to biological existence; and it is an inadequate power base for male ambition, as it limits control to the fruit of one's seed. Fatherhood must transcend these limitations to take in states, countries, nations, and, if possible, the whole world. "God the Father" and the "Holy Father" are perfect metaphors for this enterprise.

Cultural paternity has several elements. It establishes an order of being that is volitional rather than natural. Creation is transferred from the womb to the mind (where there is more control over it), and the male mind becomes sacred. Ultimately, cultural paternity is concerned with giving birth to a higher order of existence, to which, so far as possible, only men will have access. This realm will transcend natural facticity and will endure beyond the individual life of its creator. In religious terms, this is expressed by the preoccupation with immortality, but the secular versions of immortality are equally potent. While the language that describes the bringing forth of this new order replicates the language of motherhood, there is one aspect of patriarchal birthing that differs radically from its female counterpart. Patriarchal birthing takes place primarily through death: the death defiance of the hero; the hazardous trials of male initiation rites; the mythic slaughter of the Goddess; the life-negating spiritualities of ascetics; Hegel's journey into human history by overcoming the fear of death; or Freud's oedipal conflict in which the father is murdered by the sons. It is perhaps best expressed by Hegel.

> It is solely by risking life that freedom is obtained, only thus is it tried and proved that the essential nature of self-consciousness is not bare existence, is not merely the immediate form in which it

at first makes its appearance, is not mere absorption in the expanse of life. Rather it is thereby guaranteed that there is nothing present but what might be taken as a vanishing moment—that self-consciousness is merely pure self-existence, being-for-itself.[8]

Simone de Beauvoir, drawing on Hegel's paradigm, asserts:

> It is not in giving life but in risking life that mankind is raised above the animals. That is why superiority has been accorded in humanity not to the sex which brings forth but to that which kills.[9]

The Sacred Male Mind

In the patriarchal order, the power of creation is transferred from the female womb to the male mind. Reason rather than nature becomes the final arbiter of existence, a theme found in the mythologies of many cultures.

In the Babylonian creation myths, Marduk, in his efforts for supremacy, first slaughters Tiamat, the Goddess, and cuts her in half to create heaven and earth. His real test for kingship, however, comes when he is required to create "by word alone," that is to say, out of his mind.[10] Similarly, in Greek mythology, Zeus gives birth to Athena from his head. In Egyptian mythology the creator god is Ptah who simply pronounced the "name of all things."[11] The Stoic philosophers went so far as to call creative reason *logos spermatikos*.[12] Plato expresses the superiority of male birthing.

> So those who are pregnant in body turn to women and are enamoured in this way, and thus, by begetting children, secure for themselves, so they think, immortality and memory and happiness, "providing all things for the time to come"; but those who are pregnant in the soul, for there are some who conceive in the soul more than in the body, what is proper for souls to conceive and bear, and what is proper? Wisdom and virtue in general. To this class belong all creative poets, and those artists and craftsmen who are said to be inventive. But much the greatest wisdom . . . and the most beautiful is that which is concerned

with the ordering of cities and homes, which we call temperance and justice.[13]

The male word rather than the female womb is the basis for the creation of whatever is worthwhile.

In the concept of the male word one can begin to see the assertion of man's autonomous mental power over woman's physiological material creativity. As long as creation was from the body or from the earth, these were held sacred: "It is a sin to wound or cut, to tear or scratch our common mother by working at agriculture. You ask me to dig in the earth? Am I to take a knife and plunge it into the breast of my mother? But then, when I die, she will not gather me again into her bosom."[14] When creation was by word or from the male mind, then the body became a mere vehicle and even imprisoned divinity. It certainly presented obstacles to it. Life-negation, enforced celibacy, spiritual masochism and sadism, and avoidance of women (who are identified with nature) were the general prescriptions for full entry into this new order of being. Men could be admitted at various levels, but for women the story was different. It seems as though the sentiments expressed by the Zoroastrian God, Ormazd, were fairly typical of the view of women.

> Had I found another vessel from which to make man, never would I have created thee. . . . But I sought in the waters and in the earth and in plants and cattle, in the highest mountain and deep valleys, but I did not find a vessel from which the blessed man might proceed, except woman.[15]

A similar theme is found in Christianity. Thus, Jerome writes: "As long as woman is for birth and children, she is as different from man as body is from soul, but when she wishes to serve Christ more than the world, then she will cease to be a woman and will be called man."[16] The question was by no means settled, however. As late as 1595, fifty doctoral theses were presented at Wittenberg in which women were denied the dignity of human personhood.

Along with the denigration of the body, there was an exaltation of spirit and reason. Indeed for secular culture, reason became almost synonymous with what had previously been called Spirit, and performed many similar functions. Thus Hegel asserts:

> The highest point of a people's development is the rational consciousness of its life and conditions, the scientific understanding of its laws, its system of justice, its morality. For in this unity (of subjective and objective) lies the most intimate unity in which Spirit can be with itself. The purpose of its work is to have itself as object. But Spirit can have itself as object only by thinking itself.[17]

Given the seriousness of what was at hand, it is not surprising that the male mind was afforded the same kind of reverence that had previously been accorded the natural processes of childbirth. The male mind was protected in several ways: the dissociation from the trivia and distractions represented by home and children; the exclusive corridors of academe until recently closed to women; the myth of objectivity, which assumed that it was possible to "know" without being passionate or selectively intentional; the denigration of the intuitive or inductive sciences, such as herbalism and midwifery; and the freedom from social responsibility given to scientists and their "creations." The male mind was seen as sacred regardless of its products. As a president of Harvard once said, commenting on the possible appointment of someone who had advised the Chilean junta, "I would appoint a Nazi, if he had the right academic qualifications."[18]

Rituals of Rebirth

Patriarchal birthing is replete with rituals, usually celebrating some form of birth, rebirth, or initiation. Essentially this birth is, according to Nancy Jay, "birth done better, on purpose and at a higher, more spiritual level than ordinary mothers do it."[19] Men are birthed not into mortality but into culture, by means of rites from which women are systematically excluded. O'Brien explains:

> Males not only became adults, they became citizens, in a strange tangle of sacred rite and secular bureaucracy. They were symbolically and sometimes mimetically reborn. The conditions of this

second birth, given powerful symbolic expression in the myths of the Second Coming, which are an integral part of many male dominant religions, are very different from the conditions of the first birth. They are conditions created and controlled by men both human and divine, and no female reproductive labour is required for this significant genesis.[20]

Often the rites imitate the female reproductive processes. In some areas, men emulate women by slitting their penises into a symbolic vulva. Others simulate menstruation by cutting their penises on a monthly basis and letting some blood flow out.[21] Hysterical "pregnancies" are common.[22]

Sometimes in these rites the initiate is killed. The mother is not told until afterward; the explanation given is that her son was taken by a spirit or swallowed by a monster whom the other novices managed to escape. There are certain parallels in the lives of young men today. In working-class neighborhoods young male adolescents prove their manhood by such means as riding a motorcycle at 100 miles an hour through crowded streets, carrying switchblades in their pockets, or joining the Provisional I.R.A. In middle-class areas racing cars, hazing, and Russian roulette provide comparable initiation rites. Central to all these rites of passage is that the activities involved must be death-defying. Contempt for women and for natural limitations usually plays a major part in the background discourse.

Women must be kept in ignorance of these rites: "If a woman . . . were to see these things, or hear what we tell the boys, I would kill her."[23] Secrecy is essential: "Until now you have been in the darkness of childhood: you were like women and you knew nothing."[24]

Not only are women excluded from the rites, but in many of them the express purpose is to create a sacred space free of women. In older initiation rites, according to Mircia Eliade, the ceremonies are commonly explained as being necessary to "release the bad blood accumulated since [the initiate] was in his mother's womb, his inheritance from the woman."[25] Among some people, says Eliade, the initiate is allowed to insult and "even manhandle his mother in token of his emancipation from her tutelage."[26] In others, "the novice walks over his mother's belly, deliberately stepping on her belly and this gesture confirms his definitive separation from her"[27] Eliade explains that ultimately "to annihilate the profane human condition in order to gain absolute freedom means to die to this conditioned mode of being and to be reborn to another, a mode of being that is transcendent, unconditioned."[28]

In initiation rites—modern as well as ancient—are found many of the central elements of patriarchal culture, that is to say, the envy and imitation of women's reproductive powers; the simulation of these powers by means of rituals that involve extreme tests of endurance, ritual death, or dangerous death-defiance; the strict exclusion of women from religious rites or from the higher, more transcendent forms of knowledge; and the creation of a sacred space, a universal currency of patriarchy, within which men can function free of the limitations of biology and women.

Patriarchal Ethics

The new patriarchal order brought with it a changed notion of ethics, as Carol Ochs points out.

> In matriarchy, the most important relationship is between mother and child, a relationship that carries with it an absolute obligation. The worst crime is infanticide; the second worst, matricide. In other words, you have an absolute obligation to your blood line. In patriarchy, the concern is not for blood line; rather it is for absolute ethical principles. In matriarchy God is a mother frantically trying to save her child. In patriarchy God is a father who is both creator and destroyer. He is the one who can save you, but he can also condemn you.[29]

The necessity for absolute obedience to ethical norms, especially those coming from the "word of God," is best exemplified in the story of Abraham and Isaac. Abraham had to prove his obedience to God in an ultimate test. God asked him to sacrifice his son Isaac: "Take your son, your only son Isaac, whom you love, and go to the land of Moriah, and offer him there as a burnt offering upon one of the mountains of which I shall tell you [Gen. 22:2]."

At the point where Abraham took his knife and was about to sacrifice Isaac, an angel of Yahweh appeared and told him not to slay his son: "For now I know that you fear God, seeing you have not withheld your son, your only son, from me [Gen. 22:12]." Tradition has it that when Sarah heard the news of what Abraham had proposed to do, she fell dead.[30] Her death was the symbolic death of matriarchy and its ethics in favor of the new faith that was being born, whose ultimate test was the willingness to sacrifice even one's own son, or to go without biological descendants, which in Judaism was equivalent to personal death for oneself. Immortality was located in the new sacred sphere rather than in the fruits of one's biology.

The sacrifice of the son by the father recurs in patriarchal literature. The sacrifice usually takes place to appease or prove the father's sense of "justice" or obedience, or in feminist terms, to ensure the integrity of the realm of command that is being established and the "sacred space" that is coming to birth. This theme recurs constantly in Christianity. Anselm's *Cur Deus Homo* is perhaps one of the clearest expressions of this theme in the redemptive literature of Christianity. The predominant motif in the redemptive literature is that of submission to the will of the Father. Charlotte Perkins Gilman writes:

> Submission is pushed so far . . . that we were taught we must be willing to be damned—for the glory of God! Why should so much mental activity have stopped there, and not inquired what glory there was in an omnipotent being torturing forever a puny little creature who could in no way defend himself? Would it be to the glory of a man to fry ants?[31]

The daily sacrifice of women in the service of their families is too trivial and unimportant to deserve mention in the realm of "higher" ethics. In fact, for Hegel the household was "the arena of death."[32] What is important is the kind of sacrifice that will lead to the building up of the "moral" community, or that will,

> transcend particularity to become the ethics of universal man and the socio-historical realities in which this universality is expressed. . . . Male supremacy is therefore ethical and rational rather than biological, for men have this capacity to struggle for universality, to disregard particular life in the affirmation of a more rational whole.[33]

Ernst Troeltsch has written:

> The group, starting from its natural basis, is thus to develop into a special moral community through the union and interconnection of its members; and the members are to feel their devotion to this community, not merely as an instinct of nature or of habit, but as a duty in which the individual grows to a height above himself, even to the *sacrifice of himself for the Whole*, when that becomes necessary.[34]

In this passage Troeltsch suggests that the pinnacle of ethical endeavor, the culmination of the transcendence of self, or at least the confirmation of it, lies in self-sacrifice. This is a common theme throughout Western philosophy and morality; in fact, as we have seen, for Hegel risking life and overcoming the fear of death are the preconditions for culture itself.

Even when the processes of secularization threaten patriarchal mythology with collapse, faith in the rationality of the patriarchal order can still be established through one's willingness to die on its behalf. Thus Oliver Wendell Holmes wrote:

> I do not know the meaning of the universe. But in the midst of doubt, in the collapse of creeds, there is one thing I do not doubt, that no man who lives in the same world with most of us can doubt, and that is that the faith is true and adorable which leads a soldier to throw away his life in obedience to a blindly accepted duty, in a cause which he little understands, in a plan of campaign of which he has no notion, under tactics of which he does not see the use.[35]

From a feminist perspective, however, this ethical stance is problematic. Elizabeth Fisher writes:

> Evolutionists are changing their minds. They are coming to realize that co-operation, mutual aid, and kindness have been more conducive to survival than the 19th century battle mentality projected onto nature. . . . The price of having a civilization largely recorded by men has been the glorification of what men are, do, or have and the denigration of women's occupations, faculties and physiology. Only child care, which involved the upbringing of males, was spared to some extent.[36]

Physical self-sacrifice in Western society is usually something that takes place in war. For an individual, it may well involve a supreme ethical decision. But this decision takes place in the context of the *failure* of the real ethical endeavor, that of harmony between communities. As such, war is a substitute for the tiring, mundane, protracted business of human relationships. If the final act of ethical endeavor lies in self-sacrifice, as Troeltsch suggests, does this mean that the precondition for ethics is a perpetual state of hostility between peoples? This notion of ethics has been sharply criticized in recent years by a feminist ethicist.

> The blind willingness to sacrifice people to truth has always been the danger of an ethics abstracted from life. This willingness links Gandhi to the biblical Abraham who prepared to sacrifice the life of his son in order to demonstrate the integrity and supremacy of his faith. Both men in the limitations of their fatherhood stand in strict contrast to the woman who comes before Solomon and verifies her motherhood by relinquishing truth in order to save the life of her child.[37]

The myth that women have no sense of justice or ethics has been used for centuries to keep women from having any kind of instrumental power in society. Schopenhauer reflected,

> It will be found that the fundamental fault of the female character is that it has no sense of justice. This is mainly due to the fact, already mentioned, that women are defective in their powers of reasoning and deliberation, but it is also traceable to the position which Nature has assigned to them as the weaker sex. They are dependent, not upon strength but upon craft and hence their instinctive capacity for cunning, and their ineradicable tendency to say what is not true.[38]

In the nineteenth century, the opposite argument was used: woman's spiritual and moral nature was so superior to man's that it should not be tainted by the rough-and-tumble of political life.[39]

The message to women at the end of Vatican Council II was: "Women of the entire universe, you to whom life is entrusted, it is for you to save the peace of the world." Women had not been allowed to speak especially on the subject of saving the world.

The Rituals of War

As we have seen, the initiation rites of various cultures involve the real possibility of death, either in the rituals themselves or because the ritual has been made possible by a previous death, usually the sacrifice of the son by the father. The primordial patriarchal rite, which must be regularly reenacted or threatened in order to maintain or sharpen patriarchal ideology, is war. "War is menstruation envy," say the popular graffiti. The rhetoric of war makes clear the inversion of women's energies, for while excluding women from this sacred sphere, the rituals use the language of intercourse and birth by way of imitation or contempt.

War brings new birth to warrior, nation, and culture. Some writers go so far as to claim that death in war is at the heart of the triumphs of the whole patriarchal cultural enterprise.

> Germany lost three-fourths of her population during the Thirty Years War, the Netherlands suffered a similar fate during the Wars of Liberation, England during the War of the Roses and France during the Wars of the Huguenots. But within a century after the worst slaughters, Goethe and Kant were born in Germany, Shakespeare and Bacon in England, Molière and Bayle in France, while Grotius and Rembrandt appeared in Holland even before a century had passed.[40]

The death of the male in warfare is itself a kind of birth to immortality.

> In the German language men never die in battle. They fall. The term is exact for the expression of self-sacrifice when it is motivated by the feeling of comradeship. I may fall, but I do not die, for that which is real in me goes forward and lives on in the comrades for whom I gave up my physical life.[41]

In his *Anti-Memoirs*, André Malraux said that "facing death was the illuminating experience analogous to childbirth for the female."[42] Or, as Mussolini put it, "War is to the man what maternity is to the woman." War also assists the process of separation from the world of the mother, a fact that may account for the strange pride some women take in watching their sons "become men" as they march off to be killed.

In war, the creation of the "sacred space" of patriarchy is made very clear. But this space is so tenuous that in some cultures menstruating women are believed to "pollute" or render harmless the weapons of war. Among the Crow Indians, menstruating women were not allowed to approach either a wounded man or men starting on a war party, nor were they to come near sacred objects.[43] Among the Nuer, contact with women is believed to weaken a man's spear arm, the highly symbolic agent of sacrifice.[44]

Although one of the major students of initiation rites, Eliade, does not see their contemporary equivalent,[45] I maintain that the functional equivalent of these rites is ever present in our society. Certainly, we are using the language of procreation and birth to speak of the death-dealing rituals of war. Listen carefully to the language used about the military buildup in the United States. On the night the attempt to rescue the hostages in Iran failed, people talked of an "abortive attempt"; the only way for the American government to demonstrate its willingness to "save" its citizens would be by demonstrating a willingness to "lose them"; the attempt was foiled by a "precipitous withdrawal"; and, finally, the United States was "being held impotent by a handful of fanatics."

Turning to military equipment we can see similar parallels. Machine guns have "nests"; giant birds hover over cities dropping their eggs of untold destruction; the penis-shaped missiles wreak havoc wherever they land. In its reversal of life, patriarchy is sure to use appropriate language to justify itself. Thus war-mongering becomes "protection"; male ego-insecurity is translated into the necessity for "national security"; one "penetrates" the enemy camp.[46]

At the Syracuse Research Corporation, a company with large military contracts, a plaque hangs on the wall. It reads as follows:

> I love you because:
> • Your sensors glow in the dark

- Your sidelobes swing in the breeze
- Your hair looks like clutter
- Your multipath quivers
- Your reaction time is superb
- Your missile has thrust; it accurately hones in on its target
- The fuse ignites, the warhead goes;
  SWEET   OBLIVION.[47]

The first atom bomb was designed and built at Los Alamos, New Mexico. Writers have referred to the "secret gestation of the bomb";[48] one "felt as though he had been privileged to witness the Birth of the World"; another heard the "first cry of the newborn world."[49] When the scientists who had been working on the project wanted to communicate to President Truman that the tests had been successful, they chose the following phrase: "Babies satisfactorily born."[50]

Nuclear Power: The Ultimate Patriarchal Symbol

We have seen in the initiation rites how important the element of death-defiance is for entry into the sacred sphere. The development of nuclear power is the ultimate symbol of this death-defiance. It is the pinnacle of academic and scientific endeavor; it is a technology available only to the chosen high priests, and it provides the occasion par excellence for a death-defying war with nature itself. One single error in a nuclear plant could wipe out untold millions of people. Nuclear plant operators are therefore in a daily war between nature and the brilliance of male technology.

Nuclear weaponry is the ultimate tool in the hands of those who would cleanse the earth of undesirable elements. A war could start at any moment because of economic threat or national insult. Ultimately, however, it is a war of competing ideologies—Reason pitting itself against other Reasons—in the name of Truth. As one sociologist put it, "In the past it would seem that men were often mercenaries calculating the gain and loss of military activities; now they fight for ultimate objectives. War has become a sacred activity."[51] And one might add that nuclear destruction has become the ultimate patriarchal sacrament. A military general predicted, "The first world war was a conflict of armies, the second world war was a conflict of nations, and the third world war will be a war of conflicting ideologies."[52] The general was President Galtieri of Argentina.

Even patriarchy at its most cynical realizes that extraterrestrial immortality cannot be guaranteed or may not even be desirable. A secular version, so to speak, of nuclear weaponry was developed, called the neutron bomb. Its distinction is that while leaving intact the offices, buildings, technologies, and property of patriarchal society, it destroys all animal, human, and vegetable life. In other words, all that is born of the earth, nature, and woman would be destroyed, and all that is of male culture and technology would remain.[53] Germany has already begun to record its cultural achievements and to place them in radiation-proof containers in preparation for this eventuality. With the use of this bomb, the ultimate patriarchal initiation rites would take place.

Nuclear warfare is not an accidental feature of an ideology that would otherwise promote the growth of the human spirit. Nuclear weaponry and destruction is intrinsic to the spirituality generated by Western culture. As Hegel himself says:

> The Spirit, devouring its worldly envelope, not only passes into another envelope, not only arises rejuvenated from the ashes of its embodiment, but it emerges from them exalted, transfigured, a purer Spirit. It is true that it acts against itself, devours its own existence. But in so doing it elaborates upon this existence; its embodiment becomes material for its work to elevate itself to a new embodiment.... But even when it perishes, it does so in the course of its function and destiny, and even then it offers the spectacle of having proved itself as spiritual activity.[54]

This view of spirituality and regeneration was shared by the French Jesuit philosopher Pierre Teilhard de Chardin. After the first test explosion of the atomic bomb in New Mexico, Teilhard wrote that

> it disclosed to human existence a supreme purpose: the purpose of pursuing even further, to the very end, the forces of Life. In exploding the atom we took our first bite of the fruit of the great discovery, and this was enough for a taste to enter our mouths

that can never be washed away: the taste for super-creativeness.[55]

This taste for "super-creativeness" was not daunted in the least when the atom bomb was finally dropped on Hiroshima. Upon receiving the news of the destruction the bomb had wrought upon defenseless men, women, and children, President Truman remarked, "This is the greatest thing in history."[56]

We may have more of this "super-creativeness" to look forward to. President Ronald Reagan, at the end of the speech he made accepting the Republican nomination, having enumerated a glorious list of changes he hoped to make—including drastically increasing the budget for "defense"—closed with the following line: "We have it in our power to make the world over again."[57]

These patriarchal forms, and the religions, philosophies, and psychologies that sanction and sustain them, are so serious that they must be questioned radically and in absolutely all their elements. In the light of the threat of nuclear destruction, patriarchy is a terminal disease. It is not enough to clamor to be included in patriarchy's spurious benefits and privileges. At the same time, our cure cannot drive alienated men to further extremes in their efforts to find value, worth, depth, and meaning in their precarious universe. While rejecting the solutions of patriarchy, women must take seriously the profound existential problems that lie at its root.

Women must bond, so that they can begin to articulate a new feminist culture beyond the ethnic, religious, and nationalist boundaries that presently divide them. Many of the old certainties will disappear; they must not be too easily replaced with the Ejaculatory Politics of the Easy Solutions. Rather, women must learn to be patient, as their sisters of old, in the beautiful task of becoming midwives to the new creation they must usher into being.

Why Women Need the War God[1]

KAREN MCCARTHY BROWN

Locating and naming the legitimate sources of authority in our lives is a central and continuing problem for feminists. For those of us involved in religion, the quest for the authoritative is especially problematic. We have had to face the deep misogyny of scriptures, traditions, institutions, and leaders. We cannot easily go back to a naive acceptance of any of these as authoritative on its own terms. Context and content, we have found, are too bound up with each other. We discovered that the antiwoman bias could not be removed from our religion in a once-and-for-all-time feminist chemical bath. Women have learned that the critique must be ongoing and the watchfulness constant. In order to do this we have had to locate an authoritative voice within ourselves, within our own experience. This is what gives us a place to stand as we carry on that critique. Thus, the authority of experience has emerged as one major tenet of feminism.

Out of this has grown a second: the personal, the political, and the spiritual are understood as dimensions of, or perspectives on, one reality. For me, these first two tenets of feminist thought have led to a third—the need for radical or deep pluralism. By deep pluralism, I refer to a style of understanding that holds multiple truths in dynamic tension. Deeply pluralistic thinkers eschew the grand systems, creeds, and philosophies that Westerners have traditionally used as safety nets under their varying experiences in the world. If truth begins in experience, then there must be many truths, for there are many life stories and many stories within a single life. Furthermore, many truths, held in creative tension and rooted in

Karen McCarthy Brown

the deepest parts of one's being, may better equip one to handle the challenges and dangers of contemporary life than those great philosophical, political, and religious systems that, historically, have been able to define themselves only in opposition to other systems. Radical pluralism is not an easy stance toward the world, for there is no place to go "home" to when the crises of one's life demand security before anything else.

To some, this rendition of the basic tenets of feminist thought may appear to paint a picture that is internally inconsistent. On one hand I argue that life is one, while on the other I claim that its truths are many and in tension with one another. Rather than dismissing such a reaction as a misunderstanding needing clarification, I claim the paradox as central to my understanding of feminist vision. As a feminist, I have learned that life is whole and that there is a steady flow of the same life energies and human dynamics across cultures, and within one culture from the bedroom to the boardroom to the temple. Yet I argue equally strongly, and also out of my feminist perspective, that the wholeness of life does not surrender to rigorous thinking. Such thinking is always a sacrifice of fullness of vision in favor of clarity of perception. Ideally, to see the whole, both ends of that spectrum are needed, with each developed to the fullest possible extent. Practically speaking, human beings can never reach that full way of knowing, yet in stretching toward it, the aesthetic appears to carry us farther than the rational. Whatever harmony can be called forth from the many voices of deep pluralism seems more likely to come from a compatibility of ethos than from a consistency of logic.

At this point in history women are well qualified to map out this approach to life's big questions. Living in a world defined by male experience, we have always had to be, at minimum, bilingual—socially, psychically, and spiritually. We know in our bones how to negotiate among conflicting world views and how to dance a meaningful life in the interstices. This is an appropriate model for beginning to articulate a style of thinking-acting-living in the face of the most troublesome moral issues of our time, including nuclear war.

From this outlook comes an appropriate way of communicating about it. I, like many of my sisters, have come to prefer the condensation of a story to the abstraction of a logical argument. Stories do not make other people wrong the way arguments, creeds, and theories do, but they succeed more or less at illuminating the situations in which they are told. There is always room for another story. Story-telling is commonly used in much of the Third World as a means of resolving conflict. Imagine what would happen if at the next summit meeting on nuclear arms control, the participants began by telling their life stories! What if they dared to acknowledge that their politics are rooted in their experience?

With this prologue and in the context of a feminist critique of war, I relate a small, personal story, the story of my marriage to the Haitian Vodou God of war, Ogou.

I am not Catholic and never have been, but, for a period of my early life my parents preferred the local Texas parochial schools to the public ones. And so at age seven, I got to crown the Virgin in the school May procession. I was confirmed in the Episcopal Church at age twelve, but in my teenage years, the life energy began to flow in other directions. I attended Friday-night revivals with my Baptist friends. There I sat, full of sexual charge, watching immersion baptisms.

When I left Texas to study at Smith College my world expanded, and social causes began to claim more of my energy than religion. Nevertheless, religion was my major in college, and I went on to get a master's degree in philosophy of religion. In those days I was far too sophisticated to think that the academic questions I pursued had much to do with my life as I felt it day to day. With this attitude it is no wonder that doing philosophy spun me into arid places, and I began to ache for something that felt more connected to life. I did not know where I would find it, but I knew I had to stop my headlong rush at a Ph.D. So I took a temporary teaching job at a small college in Ohio.

One summer, the college sent me to Brazil, and on the plane going from São Paulo to Rio de Janeiro I sat next to a reporter from Associated Press. He invited me to go with him to a Macumba ceremony that evening. Macumba is a general name for a range of African-based, Catholic-influenced traditional religions in Brazil. When I walked into the temple and saw the altar, I was riveted. The power of that moment had something to do with a paradoxical feeling that I was at home and yet in a place I had never been before. On the altar were statues of Lazarus, the Virgin Mary, St. George, and St. Barbara. That much was familiar. These particular saints, however, had been costumed with cloaks, stars, half-moons, and feathered headdresses.

That experience started me on the main journey of my past decade. I went back to school to study anthropology and sociology of religion and picked a dissertation topic that included field work in Haiti. When the dissertation was completed, the work continued in Haiti and in the Haitian Vodou community in Brooklyn.

I have been doing research on Haitian Vodou for ten years. I began as a Ph.D. candidate, questions in mind, paper and pencil in hand. Gradually, I began to put away these things and let the Haitian community formulate questions as well as answers. More gradually I let go of my need to have verbal equivalents at all levels of understanding. When the rituals began to speak to me in their own language, I found myself, from time to time, drawn into the role of participant. People often ask me if I believe in Vodou. My response to that sort of query is: "That is a question no Vodouisant has ever asked me." Vodou is not about assent to propositions and neither is it about beliefs that can be neatly and succinctly formulated. Furthermore, no Vodouisant has ever asked me to give up whatever other spiritual truths I think I have learned and swear allegiance only to Vodou. Nor do they ask such a thing of one another.

Vodou itself is a mixture of several distinct African traditions and Catholicism, although mixture is not exactly the right word to describe how they all came together. Vodou is mainly an African religion. Some theorists argue that the slaves put a mask of Catholicism on their own spiritual traditions in order to perpetuate them in the hostile atmosphere of the slave plantation. This may be an accurate description of how the presence of Catholicism in the New World African religions actually functioned, but it misses something important.

Every teacher has a favorite typology. Here is mine, with all its outrageous generalizations. There are two types of religious systems: wall-builders and amoebas. Wall-builders use words such as orthodoxy and heresy. Judaism, Christianity, and Islam are the great wall-builders. Each has moved through periods of greater and lesser intensity in this wall-building, and it should be noted that such a posture has rarely prevented them from borrowing from those whom they sought to repress. Nevertheless, the amoeba response is basically different in the initial stages of encounter. The amoebas encounter another religious system and say, "Goody—more!" When confronted by a foreign substance, they put their pseudopods around it and digest it, turning it into food for their own process. West African religions are amoeba religions. That is how they operated with one another and with Catholicism, and that is how Vodou operates today with the values and perspectives that come along with the modern industrial age just now breaking into Haiti. These days, in the Vodou temples of Port-au-Prince, Vodou spirits are served who are identified as automobile mechanics, government bureaucrats, dentists, and physicians.

Vodou is an ecstatic religion. It centers on trance and possession by the Gods. (By the way, I use the term Gods because I do not care for diminutives to distinguish female from male. I can be moved by and participate in Goddess religion, but in my language to myself, I talk about the Gods, and by that I mean spirits, female and male.) In Vodou, one has contact with the Gods. They are available. They give advice, they hug; they can discipline and chastise. They are immediately present in possession-performance. By linking the word performance so closely to possession, I do not intend to signal that I think Vodou trance is not genuine. The trance state the worshiper experiences during possession is quite genuine, but Vodou possession does have a certain theater quality, in the best sense of theater: it is an acting out of a shared tradition. The roles are well known; the personae of the Gods are shared by all who participate. Whoever is possessed by a spirit improvises on a core understanding of who that particular spirit is.

The God I married is Ogou,[2] and he comes from the Yoruba culture of Nigeria. He began as a spirit associated with iron workers. Smiths often had to travel great distances and fend for themselves in foreign territories. Ogou thus became a God associated with "the mobile, the marginal and the isolated,"[3] and his shrine, the smithy, became a place of refuge where enemies could not enter and local police forces could not arrest or seize. Out of such practices came the Ogou cult of modern Nigeria, which is perhaps the most rapidly growing traditional religion of contemporary Africa. In addition to his connection with iron workers and the smithy, the African Ogou has taken on a variety of other areas of life: war and weapons, anything having to do with metal, and so all machines and modern technology. For instance, the modern Ogou cult has become important to the many Nigerians drawn to the cities by the oil industry. Ogou teaches them how to meet change. Ogou awakens the spirit of assertion, personal power, and individuality needed to negotiate with the modern world. Like the smiths of earlier times, the oil workers are forced to travel far from the homes and highly enmeshed family networks that previously provided their identity. Ogou guides them into the modern age. Yet he also embodies the wisdom that the modes of action so necessary for survival in the contemporary world, and so beneficial in many ways, also contain seeds of destruction. The Ogou cult in Nigeria has a trenchant ecological critique of modern technology and of what its ethos does to people and the land on which they live.

Ogou came to Haiti along with the Yoruba slaves who were brought there, most of them in the eighteenth century. Haiti has not experienced much of modern technology, however, and so the Ogou found in contemporary Haiti is different from the one found in contemporary Nigeria. The possession-performance of Ogou in Haiti is an in-depth exploration of things military.

In Haiti, as in Africa, there is not just one Ogou, but many. Haitians say there are seven or twenty-one or several hundred. Attempts to make an exact accounting are pointless, since the Gods vary from one region of Haiti to another, and even from one temple to another within the same region. These many personae of the war God are distinct and yet they are one. These many and this one are all soldiers and all male. They are pictured in elaborate uniforms, and those possessed by them don the same sort of military attire.

The different Ogou explore all aspects of hierarchy, war, and anger; of the mentality of us-against-them; of the uses and abuses of power, aggression, and self-assertion. For example, one Ogou embodies the charisma of the successful hero returned home to advise the people whose safety he has ensured; another embodies the opposite end of the spectrum: a pathetic alcoholic, unreliable in his social relations, a soldier whose power in the world has proved ineffective and who has turned his destructive energies against himself. It is the way (and the wisdom) of Haitian Vodou to encompass oppositions within even the smallest units of meaning. Each and every Ogou, regardless of which dimension of the war-making spirit is dominant in his character, also embodies something of the other side of the coin.

This pervasive quality of Vodou symbolization works especially well in relation to Ogou, because any military presence evokes the same ambivalence in Haitians that the presence of modern technology does in Nigerians. Haitian military history is profoundly mixed. It contains not only Pierre Dominique Toussaint L'Ouverture, the leader of the only successful slave revolution in the Western hemisphere, and Jean-Jacques Dessalines, the first Haitian head of state, but also the American marines, who began an extended occupation of the island in 1915. In turn, each of these historical war-making types conveys mixed messages to the Haitian people. They were creative and destructive, liberating and oppressing. Dessalines, for example, proved to be a man as arrogant and power-hungry as the French leaders he replaced. He liberated the slaves who worked the giant sugar plantations and then introduced a sort of forced-labor system that left their lives little changed. The people of Haiti and their African forebears have had extensive experience with war and those who wage it. The various personae of Ogou are condensation points for this cumulative wisdom. The possession-performances of Ogou allow Haitians to keep the lessons of their experience alive before their eyes.

When people are possessed by Ogou, any of the Ogou, they do a kind of theologizing with the body that is remarkable. It proceeds in three stages. In the first stage, the Ogou are handed ritual swords, and they attack, raging and bellowing around the temple, clanging their swords against pillars and doorposts. In the second stage, those standing closest to the Ogou become potential targets. While the Ogou do not actually harm anyone within the temple in this stage of the possession, they do threaten them by swinging their weapons perilously close to noses and buttocks. In the third stage, the Ogou take the sword and turn it toward themselves. The first stage is attack outward; the second threatens harm to the immediate community; the third threatens the self. This is the basic choreography of war-making as understood by Haitian Vodouisants, and it is reiterated in myriad guises throughout the various and complex rituals performed for Ogou, God of war.

This is the God I married. Spirit marriages are common events in the Vodou world. On my wedding day I wore a bright red dress and a red satin kerchief on my head. There was a wedding cake, a marriage license, and plenty of champagne. I wear his ring on my left hand as a reminder of the pledge I made to Ogou that day.

My relationship with Ogou has become a problem for some of my feminist friends. One in particular has pushed hard: "Karen, what are you doing? How can you have this relationship with—of all things!—a male War God?" I chose this relationship and it chose me intuitively, for reasons that were not articulate at the time. I had always said I would not participate in Vodou out of anthropological curiosity alone. I felt that would show a lack of respect, although that was not the only reason I wanted to find a link between Vodou and my own life. I knew that the Vodouisant brings her or his life with all its knots and loose ends to the system, and unless I did the same, I would not understand anything of its ability to take up a life and weave designs from it. I came to a crisis in my life, an abyss, a dark night. My marriage of eleven years was breaking up, and I was involved in a tenure battle at my university. I was furious and hurt. I was angry at my husband and at the institution of marriage. I was angry at some of my colleagues and at the academic world. I was angry at myself and at women's position in the world. One day I found myself saying: "Karen, stop trying to get rid of this anger. Marry it!" I telephoned a Vodou priestess I knew in Brooklyn and said, "I am ready." And so I married Ogou. I stopped trying to be good, to be understanding, to get over my anger, to be superior to it. I claimed it as mine. It was a transformative experience.

It seems to me that the Gods of war are necessary as long as there is anger in our hearts and war in the world. I am drawn to religious systems that take up all the stuff of life, whole cloth, and bring it into a central, well-lighted place for mutual negotiation. This type of spirituality works for me because it is rooted in an essentially tragic vision of life, and I feel at home there. I do not think humanity is ever going to do away with war, although I can imagine it taking on quite different forms. I fervently hope we can avoid nuclear war. I will work for that. I do not think we are ever going to be rid of hierarchy, another of Ogou's central elements, but I hope we can learn to use hierarchy more responsibly, make hierarchies more flexible, make our critique more trenchant. I doubt we will ever have a world not characterized by some form of us-against-them thinking, although I hope we can find ways to understand one another better and to have more humane exchanges across the boundaries. I am thankful we will most likely not have to live in a world without self-assertion, anger, and energy. For me, the tragic vision is energizing, but not everyone must experience it my way.

There are idealistic rather than tragic visions; such spirituality can be very moving, very compelling, and of great transformative power. Women working with traditional Jewish and Christian models, as well as those who have recently reclaimed the Goddess tradition, most often—although not always—speak from this idealistic, prophetic place. As those who have raised the children who have been victims of war, women are in a good position to condemn the values of the empire builders and assert their own more life-centered value system. The privilege in women's oppression is that we have not been, by and large, those responsible for death and destruction through war. Yet it would be a mistake to think that those who wage war do so out of a humanity essentially different from our own. I have held that particular truth in my own world through my marriage to the male God of war, Ogou. It would be a mistake in a feminist critique of war to paint women as only nurturers, only creative, just as it can be dangerous to attribute only goodness and light to the realm of the spirit. If we go too far in that direction, we put the shadow behind us and put ourselves in a position to be grabbed from behind when we are least suspicious.

The danger of the tragic vision is resignation: "Well, that's life, and I simply have to accept it." The danger is that religion becomes an panacea, a substitute for responsibility in the world. For me, however, the greater danger lies in not acknowledging that part of the spirit, that part of the human community, and that part of my own psyche that is anger-filled and war-making. I prefer to name it, to own it, and, from that place, to work to transform it.

I found a way to deal with my own anger in the context of a discussion of war, but not all warfare is a simple or direct expression of anger. Many different kinds of human energy flow into war-making. Just as no Vodouisant would serve only one spirit, so one spirit is never enough to explain any slice of life. Ogou gives us one lens. We must look through many. Jonathan Schell's *The Fate of the Earth* should convince anyone that the great obscenity of nuclear war lies not in its passion but in its abstraction. Those with the power to start a nuclear war think of it in terms of megatons and epicenters and hundred-mile radii. They think on a scale far removed from individual human experience. Yet, as Schell argues so well, suffering and death have no meaning except at the level of individual human experience. One would think that a good and wise deity would have made a world in which the power of a person could never overrun his or her ability to comprehend the results of using that power. Alas, we do not live in such a "fair" world. The possibility of nuclear holocaust, however, has taken us quantum leaps away from a position where our leaders can imaginatively grasp the havoc they are capable of causing in the world. Humankind is in grave danger. Religions such as Vodou provide a tug in the other direction, toward keeping our powers and their potentialities comprehensible.

There is a difference between honoring a War God and waging a war. This difference is crucial to an understanding of the religions of tragic vision. The power of Ogou is not simply destructive. His capacity to energize and sustain those who live in a changing world does not come from a separate part of his being. Tapping the life-enhancing qualities of Ogou does not require that the worshiper edit parts of Ogou's being out of the picture while emphasizing others. All Ogou power is the same, and there is a choice as to how one uses it. Making that choice well demands that all possibilities be kept in view and that none of them be ruled out in principle.

Logic alone moves me easily to a pacifist stance, but experience has taken me in other directions. Haiti has one of the most corrupt and inhumane governments in power today. The average annual income in the country is $260. Haiti has a 50 percent infant mortality rate in some areas, and roughly one third of the people are dead before age thirty. Eighty percent of the people are illiterate; in the cities, about 50 percent are unemployed.

As feminists—as self-reflective and self-honoring women—we are in a unique position to critique our society and its warmaking drives. Yet if we do so through formulations that condemn war in principle, we move toward that very same realm of abstraction that characterizes common public thinking about war. Who am I to sit in the relative comfort of my life situation and rule out, *in principle*, the possibility of revolution for the Haitian people, or for any other people seeking liberation? War is part of the human tragedy, part of the human comedy, part of each of us. Our job is to stay conscious of what it is, to keep our cumulative wisdom about it alive before our eyes. We must fight against the deadening of the mind and heart that comes from thinking about war at a remove from the individual human lives it touches. The task in thinking about war is to keep our imaginative and empathic skills fully engaged at the level of our experience. If feminists critique warmaking from a position that claims it is essentially foreign to our being as women, we cannot do that.

Given this view, nuclear war emerges as the obscenity it is because, by definition, no one—neither those who wage it, nor those who stand to be its victims—can imaginatively grasp it. Where imagination fails us, responsibility is impossible. From this it follows that the very existence of nuclear weapons in our midst dehumanizes life for all of us. By having to factor the possibility of nuclear holocaust into our thinking about the future, we are robbed of the capacity to create our lives in responsible ways.

While the consequences of nuclear war may be beyond human imagination, the process that made it a possibility is not. We have been brought to the brink of nuclear obliteration by thoroughly human needs, drives, and failings that exist, at least potentially, in all of us. Women simply cannot afford to define the one who makes war as the Other. It will take considerable courage to face the demon of nuclear war and tear off its mask. It will take a strong and large heart to recognize the face beneath the mask as one that resembles our own. Yet I sense this is what we are challenged to do. If women can face this demon and claim its energies as our own, we will be in a far stronger position to suggest how such energies might be turned in more creative, life-supporting directions. Women have a longer and richer history of creatively transforming Ogou energy than any other group of persons. Our task is to understand that this experience is supremely relevant to the greatest challenge of our age, the prevention of nuclear war.

Feminist Liberation Theology and Yahweh as Holy Warrior: An Analysis of Symbol

CAROL P. CHRIST

It has been alleged by some feminist Christian liberation theologians that if feminist critics of the patriarchal elements in biblical religion did their homework more carefully, they would find a liberating vision in the Bible. This vision is said to be found in the Exodus liberation of the Hebrew slaves, in the prophetic call for social justice, and in Jesus' preaching to the poor and outcasts of his society.[1] Some feminist theologians have also stated that the combination of liberation theology with feminist theology provides a more comprehensive vision than either of the two alone. (The implication that feminist theology is inevitably class-bound and/or not concerned with larger social issues is false.)

Why might a socially concerned feminist theologian reject the so-called liberating vision to be found in Exodus and in the

---

Carol Christ's contribution to the panel was a slide-tape show, "Genesis/ Genocide: Women for Peace," which she produced together with Karen Voss and Marcia Keller. The thirty-five minute presentation combines images, music, and speech in a powerful statement of the need to bridge the public/ private split in this culture if humanity is to escape nuclear holocaust. It makes vivid the patriarchal socialization process that leads males to equate manhood with violence and war and leads females to restrict the values of life-giving and nurturance to the private domestic sphere. It is an urgent and moving plea to women and men today "to make primary the values and labors traditionally tendered to civilization by women, the creating, nurturing and celebrating of life and love." It was not possible to do justice to the presentation in book form; hence Christ has set forth major elements in her thought in the following essay. The entire slide-tape presentation can be obtained from Peace Productions, 1735 Grove Street, Berkeley, CA 94709.

Carol P. Christ

Prophets? As someone whose background is Christian, I feel a certain discomfort in focusing my criticism on traditions that come from the Hebrew Bible, because I do not want to perpetuate Christian anti-Judaism in a post-Christian guise. I focus my criticism on the Exodus and prophetic traditions only because I know them better than I know the Jesus traditions, and because in my own religious history Yahweh in Exodus and in the Prophets was a far more powerful figure than Jesus. I do not find the Jesus traditions liberating; the apocalyptic traditions of the New Testament could be shown to be a continuation of the Yahweh war tradition. Moreover, that Christianity became accepted as the official religion of the Roman Empire through Constantine's alleged vision of a flaming cross in the sky, inscribed with the words "In this sign shalt thou conquer," suggests that the Yahweh war tradition has continued in Christian history.

The reasons feminists choose to work within or outside the Jewish or Christian traditions are highly complex and have to do with history, commitment, judgment, and choice as well as with the sorts of issues discussed here. There are, however, negative elements *within* the very traditions feminist Christian liberation theologians cite as liberating.

The image of Yahweh as warrior in Exodus and the Prophets needs to be examined more directly than it has been to date by feminist theologians. It is true that the Exodus tradition of liberation from oppression and the prophetic call for social justice have inspired social liberation movements. Clearly these traditions have provided hope to Jews in Diaspora, to Blacks, in slavery and racist America, to Latin Americans in poverty and destitution, and also to feminists in both the nineteenth and twentieth centuries. Nevertheless I, as a feminist concerned with social justice and peace issues, cannot find these traditions adequate expressions of my spiritual-social vision.

My understanding of the potential scope of feminist theology was shaped in the late 1960s and early 1970s. I became convinced of the wrongness of the Vietnam war some time before I consciously became a feminist. Adrienne Rich's poem "The Phenomenology of Anger" expressed my understanding of the close relationship between patriarchy and war, feminism, and my concern for peace.

> I suddenly see the world
> as no longer viable:
> you are out there burning the crops
> with some new sublimate
> This morning you left the bed
> we still share
> and went out to spread impotence
> upon the world
>
> I hate you.
> I hate the mask you wear . . .
>
> Last night, in this room, weeping
> I asked you: *what are you feeling?*
> *do you feel anything?*
> Now in the torsion of your body
> as you defoliate the fields we lived from
> I have your answer.[2]

I believe that many of the attitudes and behaviors associated with the male image and role are at the root of the threat of global destruction. Human survival depends in part on our examining the relationship between power and violence in the male psyche. My feminist work has focused on women's experience with the hope that it contained a web of values with which we could reconstitute the world: a world without war, without violence as we know it today in patriarchy.

I do not attribute war to the male nature, nor do I argue that women are incapable of warlike action, but I do believe that as feminists we must examine the equation of "manhood" and power with war that has been the legacy of patriarchal cultures. In his brilliant book *The Male Machine*, Marc Feigan Fasteau has shown that boys in our culture must learn to test their manhood through violence in sports and fighting, and he has shown the devastating consequences of the rhetoric of masculinity in shaping U.S. foreign policy with regard to the war in Vietnam. We cannot afford to ignore his message.

My rejection of the image of Yahweh as warrior in Exodus and the Prophets is further shaped—but not dependent on—a historical hypothesis about the relationship between patriarchy and war: patriarchy and large-scale warfare arose together, *although not by simple cause and effect*. Warfare is not a major part of life in preagricultural and early agricultural societies. It is widely accepted by classical scholars that settled matrilineal and relatively peaceful societies in Greece and the Mediterranean area were conquered by and/or assimilated with patrilineal, patriarchal, and warlike invaders during the second, third, and fourth millennia B.C.E. The warlike Zeus was the God of these patriarchal peoples.[3] I do not believe that the warrior Gods and/or Goddesses of this era should be models for feminist theology.

The God of Exodus and the Prophets is a warrior God.[4] My rejection of this God as a liberating image for feminist theology is based on my understanding of the symbolic function of a warrior God in cultures where warfare is glorified as a symbol of manhood and power. My primary concern here is with the function of symbolism, not with the historical truth of the Exodus stories, with questions of how many slaves may or may not have been freed, nor by what means, nor with questions of the different traditions that may have been woven together to shape the biblical stories. Since liberation theology is fundamentally concerned with the use of biblical symbolism in shaping contemporary reality and the understanding of the divine ground, this method is appropriate here. As Clifford Geertz has shown, symbols act to produce powerful, pervasive, and long-lasting moods and motivations in the peoples influenced by them. In a world threatened by total nuclear annihilation, we cannot afford a warlike image of God. The image of Yahweh as liberator of the oppressed in Exodus and as concerned for social justice in the Prophets cannot be extricated from the image of Yahweh as warrior.

In Exodus Yahweh is imaged as concerned for the oppressed Israelites. Exodus 3:7–8 is a good example. "Then Yahweh[5] said, 'I have seen the affliction of my people who are in Egypt, and have heard their cry because of their taskmasters; I know their sufferings, and I have come down to deliver them out of the hand of the Egyptians.'" People in oppressed circumstances and liberation theologians find passages like this inspiring. I too have been profoundly moved by the image of a God who takes compassion on suffering, but this passage has a conclusion I cannot accept. The clause that begins "to deliver them out of the hand of the Egyptians" continues "and to bring them up out of that land to a good and broad land, a land flowing with milk and honey, to the place of the Canaanites, the Hittites, the Amorites, the Perizzites, the Hivites, and the Jebusites." Here Yahweh promises "his people" a land that is inhabited by other peoples. In order to justify this action by Yahweh, the inhabitants of the land are portrayed in other parts of the Bible as evil or idolators (a term which itself bears further examination, as I will show). More recently liberation theologians have portrayed these other peoples as ruling-class opponents of the poor peasant and working-class Hebrews. However that may be, the clear implication of the passage is that Yahweh intends to dispossess the peoples from the lands they inhabit.

In the so-called Song of Moses in Exodus 15:1–18 (which includes the so-called Song of Miriam [Exod. 15:21], which many scholars believe is very ancient), Yahweh is celebrated as a warrior.

> I will sing to Yahweh, for he has triumphed gloriously;
>   the horse and his rider he has thrown into the sea.
> Yahweh is my strength and my song,
>   and he has become my salvation;
> this is my God, and I will praise him,
>   my father's God, and I will exalt him.
> Yahweh is a man of war;
>   Yahweh is his name. . . .

> Who is like thee, O Yahweh, among the gods?
> Who is like thee, majestic in holiness,
> terrible in glorious deeds, doing wonders?
> Thou didst stretch out thy right hand,
> the earth swallowed them.
>
> —Exodus 15:1–3, 11–12

This passage is a celebration of Yahweh as the most powerful warrior imaginable, more powerful even than the legendary Pharaoh and his armies. Yahweh accomplishes the liberation of his people through a magnificent act of war, made all the more magnificent, if we are to believe the story as it is told, by Yahweh's clever act of setting up the Pharaoh not to negotiate peacefully with Moses by "hardening his heart" (see Exod. 4:21 and passim). In Exodus 15:3, Yahweh is explicitly called "a man of war," a line paralleled by "Yahweh is his name." The poem details Yahweh's killing of Pharaoh's chariots and armies and continues with a prophecy of his victories over the inhabitants of Philistia and Canaan, the chiefs of Edom and Moab.

Clearly the image of military victory over one's foes is attractive to oppressed peoples. I myself have sometimes fantasized violent ends for certain selected patriarchs; still I must say "This is not my God. This God of war stands for far too much that I stand against." I must say with Adrienne Rich, "I . . . cast my lot with those/who after age, perversely,/with no extraordinary power,/reconstitute the world."[6]

A second tradition that feminist liberation theology has put forward as an example of the liberating vision of the Bible is the prophets' concern for social justice. This vision of social justice, however, is also embedded in the tradition of Yahweh war that was present in Exodus; further, it is intertwined with a tradition of religious intolerance that has been the source of a great deal of suffering. The prophetic vision of social justice is well expressed in Amos 2:6–7.

> Thus says Yahweh:
> "For three transgressions of Israel,
>   and for four, I will not revoke the punishment;
> because they sell the righteous for silver,
>   and the needy for a pair of shoes—

they that trample the head of the poor into the dust of the earth,
and turn aside the way of the afflicted."

This is an eloquent vision of divine concern for the poor and the needy. There was a time when I considered it both the finest poetry and the highest moral ideal. The passage portrays Yahweh as prepared to punish his own beloved people because they have not upheld social justice within their own community. It reflects a social or corporate rather than an individual notion of salvation, which is attractive because it holds all responsible for the ills of the social body.

On closer examination, however, even this admirable vision must be seen as embedded within the larger structure of a theology rooted in the image of Yahweh as warrior. Ironically, the two chapters of the book of Amos in which this passage is embedded build up to Yahweh's judgment of Israel just quoted. In the earlier verses Yahweh tells how he has punished or will punish Damascus, Gaza, Tyre, Edom, the Ammonites, Moab, and Judah. Yahweh says that just as he has punished or will punish other peoples for their transgressions, so will he punish Israel. Yahweh's method of punishment is fire, mentioned seven times (Amos 1:4, 7, 10, 12, 14; 2:2, 5); exile, mentioned twice (Amos 1:5, 15); and slaying, mentioned twice (Amos 1:8; 2:3). These are typical images of warfare. This passage can be interpreted as an example of the covenant lawsuit in which Yahweh declares his mighty acts, in this case his acts against the other peoples, and his act of deliverance of the Hebrews from Egypt, which is mentioned in Amos 2:10–11. The prophetic call of justice within Israel is not simply a moral injunction presented by a kind and just God, it is a threat that the warlike nature of Yahweh will be unleashed against his own people as it has been unleashed against other people. While I admire the ethical statement that a people is a social unit within which social justice is to be maintained, I do not find the threatening warrior God who makes the ethical statement a liberating vision of the divine power.

I have a second quarrel with the prophetic vision. In this passage in Amos there is an example of the pervasive prophetic intolerance toward other religions that has produced, among other horrors, a climate in which witches could be put to death in Europe, in which the genocide of Native Americans could be attempted by Europeans claiming their promised land, and in which genocide of Jews could be attempted by the Nazis. The passage immediately following Amos's castigation of the Israelites for selling the needy for a pair of shoes reads:

> A man and his father go in to the same maiden,
> so that my holy name is profaned;
> they lay themselves down beside every altar
> upon garments taken in pledge.
> —Amos 2:8

This is Amos's version of the charge of idolatry, which is sprinkled even more liberally throughout most of the other prophetic books, for example in Hosea.

> My people inquire of a thing of wood,
> and their staff gives them oracles.
> For a spirit of harlotry has led them astray,
> and they have left their God to play the harlot.
> They sacrifice on the tops of mountains,
> and make offerings upon the hills.
> —Hosea 4:12-13

Several years ago, as a Christian brought up with little knowledge of other religions and rituals, I could read passages like this and think "Of course, what could be worse than turning away from God?" It never crossed my mind that the prophets might be referring to people who were sincere about their religious rituals and symbols. It never occurred to me that the people inquiring of wood might be addressing the Goddess Asherah symbolized as a wooden pole or living tree, or that the rites celebrated on mountaintops and hills could have been celebrations of the divine manifest in nature. Now I am troubled by a spirit of religious intolerance that condemns the followers of other faiths as idolaters and labels their rituals abomination.

I find the intolerant form that monotheism so often takes in the West—whether preached by extremists like Jerry Falwell or the Ayatollah Khomeini or by "cultured" theologians who insist that salvation is only in Christ—utterly repugnant. And even though I want to avoid saying anything that could be construed as anti-Judaic, I find that spirit of intolerance implicit in Exodus and vividly expressed in the Prophets. The story of the enactment of a passion play that ended in stoning a Jewish boy as Judas, the Christ-killer, in Elie Wiesel's *The Gates of the Forest*, made me face squarely the roots of Christian intolerance toward Judaism in the New Testament. In *Faith and Fratricide*, Rosemary Ruether convinced me of what I had suspected—that the anti-Judaism in the New Testament is not incidental to the preaching about Jesus as savior, but must be recognized as an integral part of the Christian message. This insight prepared me to recognize this same spirit of intolerance toward other faiths in the Hebrew Bible, even in the Prophets, whose ethical vision I had once admired. This recognition became yet more devastating when as a feminist I began to understand that the prophetic criticism of idolatry was in part an attempt to solidify patriarchy, patrilineage, and the exclusively male priesthood through the elimination of female images of the divine. As a woman from a Christian background, it is important for me to make clear that my reasons for rejecting the patriarchal God of the Bible are not limited to his sex, or even his warlike nature, but include as well my rejection of a form of monotheism that spawns religious intolerance and a climate in which destruction of peoples who practice other religions can be countenanced.

I would like to examine the implications of my contention that the image of Yahweh as liberator in Exodus and in the Prophets is part of an image of Yahweh as divine warrior which I as a feminist and peace activist reject. Some feminists have appropriated the image of warrior reflected in figures like the Amazon or Maxine Hong Kingston's Woman Warrior. While respecting my sisters who make this choice, I must ally myself with the long tradition of feminist peace activism represented by the Women's International League for Peace & Freedom, Women's Strike for Peace, and recently the Women's Party for Survival.

I have also been asked whether my repugnance for violence and war stem jointly from my victimized powerless position as a woman and from my privileged position as a White American.

Perhaps my valuing of peace does stem from a heritage of female powerlessness, a heritage in which I was not taught that I had to test my "womanhood" through fighting, hitting, kicking, football, or boot camp. But if that is so, I affirm the power of women as peacemakers and my own power as a woman and a peacemaker. At the same time, I disaffirm the tradition of female powerlessness that has led women to say, "War is men's business; I don't know anything about it. If they say it has to be, then I guess it has to be." From that standpoint I also reject the image of the divine warrior as female. To change Exodus 15:3 to read: "She is a woman of war; Yahweh is her name" would mean that women had adopted the patriarchal male equation of power and violence. I also reject Goddesses of war such as Ishtar and Athene. I do not believe that the images of warrior Goddesses grew out of experiences, values, and cultures created by women. But even if they did, I would not view them as liberating images for us today.

A second response to my rejection of Yahweh as warrior is to assert that my revulsion for war images arises out of my privileged class and national position. The argument here is usually that if I were a starving peasant woman in Latin America I would realize the necessity of revolutionary war—of fighting back against the violence initiated by oppressive governments and military regimes.

I do not know what I would think if I were a poor woman living under an oppressive regime. I do believe that the horror of war, especially from the point of view of a woman who is likely to be raped by soliders, is much greater than I can imagine. I am certain that oppressed women have a wide variety of feelings and views about the destruction wrought by war and whether or not their situations can be improved by violent revolution. As a woman and as a feminist, I am wary of adopting a prowar position—even a pro-revolutionary war position. I am suspicious of any man who says violence and war are the solutions to any problem, because I know that almost every man in almost every culture has grown up learning to associate manhood with violence, fighting, and war. I am even suspicious of women who advocate revolutionary war because it seems to me that women in patriarchal cultures are not immune from equating power with war.

I do not know whether my stand for peace against war is relative or absolute, because I do not know how I would react if I were in a different historical and social situation. But if I cannot urge all feminists absolutely to reject war and warrior God/Goddess images, perhaps I can at least encourage those who find the symbol of Yahweh in Exodus and the Prophets liberating to examine the roots of that image in the God of war and to acknowledge that the liberating God of Exodus and the Prophets acts through war. Instead of referring to that God only as the relatively safe and sanitized liberator of the oppressed, I urge them to think about how they feel about referring to him as a "Man of War" and perhaps even to "her" as a "Woman of War" I hope they will also carefully examine the implications of the symbol of a warrior God/Goddess in a nuclear age. I cannot find that God liberating. I choose to "cast my lot with those/who age after age, perversely,/with no extraordinary power,/reconstitute the world."[7]

Discussion*

A: As a pacifist feminist I encounter a lot of questions about the legitimacy and empowering effect of women's rage and anger. What do we do with that? There are some feminist insights that I don't want to see abandoned as we talk about our nurturing qualities. How can we talk about that dialectic for ourselves? Because we do exist as women, as individuals who need to develop some power, at the same time we dwell on the nonoppositional part of our identity.

B: We need to talk strategically about world problems. We need a material analysis of the causes of war in order to come up with adequate solutions, because cultures derive from structures. Part of the solution is cultural, part is not. As women, being isolated in the reproductive realm and defined by it—while that is a strength—is also a limitation of our understanding of the hard political realities and of the existing battles in the world and how to relate to them.

I like what Brown has said about claiming our anger, but there is a difference between anger and war, between claiming anger and claiming war. I do not accept a tragic view of life. Right now we must accept means that are angry and sometimes violent, but I do not believe that that is always going to be part of life. Violence can end violence. I support the violent struggles for self-determination now going on around the world. I believe that defensive violence—violence to disarm an oppressor who uses violence as a tool of the state to maintain injustices that are the source of violence—is valid and necessary. I believe in minimal violence,

*This discussion followed the presentation of the panel on war and peace. The comments of the various participants are indicated by letters of the alphabet; the panelists are identified by name.

temporary, purgative, absolutely necessary, and I want to be a woman warrior. The defensive use of violence first of all very clearly and narrowly targets the causes. It uses violence because violence has been used against it and not as a substitute for political action. It is not violence by a few as a substitute for mass political organization. It embraces the creative cultural strategies. Pacifist ideals can become a tool of the state and be used as effectively as violence in bringing about repression. In Chile delusions about being able to make revolution without arming the people led to more terror and violence than there would have been if a mass uprising had occurred at the time the junta took power.

I want to say something about working-class machismo. My brother has had his teeth kicked in and his nose broken four times; he works in factories where his personality is degraded. He must build a psychic defense system against the oppressor. Part of machismo is appropriated by the oppressors to seduce the men of the masses into joining their oppressive bullying; the other part of machismo is a defense against the oppressor. Women are going to need more of that second kind of strength along with our capacities for nurturance and openness. Audre Lorde looks forward to a day when men don't expect women to do their feeling for them. I look forward to a day when women do not expect men to do their fighting for them—when there are nurturant men and women warriors! We need to look hard at the realities that require a certain kind of violence and join in it when it is just, defensive, and purgative.

C: What do we actually do to say "No"? I think the discussion of whether we support violence in Third World countries is nonsense. I'd like to know how many of the women here are currently thinking of taking up guns and rifles in the struggle. A few days ago, we talked about direct action, mostly in terms of what happens when you go to jail. But we did not bring up the real reason for direct action: unless we are willing to act by putting our bodies in the way of the war machine, we are not going to stop it, and no women's agenda is going to work in this country. Direct action has been part of the nonviolent movement. There are different approaches: some people think of it as a way of life, some people see it as a tactic. I don't think the differences matter much; the point is to do it. Those of us who are not on the line constantly because of poverty or race have the responsibility to start putting ourselves on the line in other ways. We can undertake direct action at minimal risk compared to the risks people are taking all over the world, compared to the actual risk that we are all in with the guns of nuclear war pointing at our heads and the heads of people we love.

D: I have some questions for Brown about the relations between African religious traditions and the religious experience of African diaspora people, e.g., in Haiti and in the United States. Where is liberation in the Haitian Vodou system? The transformation of the God of war, the spirit of war, can be traced in the African-American religious construct. That construct has taken the best of the memory of Africa and the best of the Christian tradition, and in its ideal form becomes the church where liberation takes place. That process fuels the various civil rights movements—the Black-rights and Black-power movements. If liberation is expressed in transcendent realities through values and acts, there must be some selectivity. Is the Haitian system too broad and too open? In the African-American religious system, there is selectivity, and that makes it possible to approach liberation. And my third question: Where does the matriarchal character of African women come into play in the evaluation of that Haitian system and the Black African-American system?

KAREN BROWN: Let me take your last question first. The use of the term matriarchy for West African cultures is problematic. There are matrilineal cultures, where descent is traced through the mother, but that means the woman's brother, rather than her husband, makes the decisive choices. There is a kind of female power in African culture, however, that has carried over into Haitian Vodou and is reflected in the network of temples headed by women. I was given some advice when I was considering initiation: "If you decide to be initiated, don't ever do it with a man. Go into the women's temples—we do things differently." There is a women's tradition, and if we had more time, I could develop some of the differences.

Where is liberation in Haitian Vodou? It is impossible to reconstruct what happened in Haitian religion in the latter part of the eighteenth century, since the only records come from the planters and the missionaries, for whom African religion was mere superstition. It is clear, however, that Vodou played a major part in instigating and spreading news of the revolution; the old networks held together and functioned to that extent at least. How does it act today? To use a psychological framework, Vodou is about the process of getting to know oneself, owning that self as a whole being, and being empowered out of that wholeness. As a Vodou priestess said to me when I asked why I should get initiated, "Look at me. I got plenty confidence. You want it too?"

On the question of selectivity, let me return to the image of the amoeba. It turns things into food for its own system, it does not take things in indiscriminately. What was taken into Vodou from Catholicism was what fit in with the life view from Africa. There is a sense of openness to the new but also a persistence of structure. The process of encountering and assimilating the new is not indiscriminate.

E: Vodou as Brown has described it is a different kind of reality, another way of seeing, another kind of religion. In the past year I have had a similar kind of experience. My friend goes into a trance state in which she sees things and hears different entities, spirits speaking. Since both of us come from Christian backgrounds, we have been struggling with what this experience means. But part of my experience has been getting a new sense of reality and of wholeness. Part of the vision we have received is an inclusive vision of people of all races, cultures, and sexual orientations living together in peace.

F: As a matter of liberation we have to overcome our fear of death, and this is different from the death defiance that Mary Condren spoke about. In Revelation 12, those who overcome the dragon that is about to attack the child do so because their love for life did not make them fear death. As feminists, we have to be careful that that doesn't lead into a negative theology of martyrdom.

MARY CONDREN: We cannot sit here and debate violence and

nonviolence in the abstract. The decision must be made by the people in the particular situation. Death-defiance can express itself through nonviolence as well as through violence. The Irish hunger strikers used a nonviolent method to achieve a violent end. Their action was patriarchal death-defiance, and it is part of a culture of death and death-defiance that is enshrined in Ireland. In the stories of Irish liberation struggles, only the heroes who met violent death are honored and commemorated. Constance de Markevitch was an important figure in the struggle, but she died peacefully in bed; she is not commemorated, her story is not part of the tradition handed on to the children. But it takes immense courage to be nonviolent. The Irish peace women had the courage to expose themselves to death; they put their lives on the line by following a nonviolent strategy, not by the death-defying strategy of going out to kill.

CAROL CHRIST: It is important to confront death as part of the life cycle. If we do not, we are living in a false reality. In working on the war and peace slide show, I became deeply depressed, and it took me several months to realize the cause: I was facing for the first time my fear that we do not have a future. I am part of a movement to embody feminist values that will take more than my lifetime to achieve its goals, and I don't know if we have even five years. I was negotiating a contract to buy a house—the loan was to be paid off in five years—and my immediate reaction was, "Take it—we won't be here in five years." Finally, after living and dreaming my despair for many months, a voice in me said, "Whoever promised you that this universe would survive?" I had to admit that nobody promised me that. I don't believe in that kind of God and I don't necessarily have a reason to believe that the universe will survive. Accepting that realization gave me a freedom to act—it liberated me to face the possibility of the ultimate destruction of everything I feel is real, and freed my energy to work for our survival and the survival of this earth.

G: We must promote peace from a feminist perspective. The urgency of the peace movement co-opts us from our feminist understanding of strategies. Many people say, "Why worry about feminism? If we don't worry about peace, we won't be around to have a feminist movement." I don't think I want to be around in a world where women will continue to have an oppressed status. Therefore, I will not participate in strategies that do not come out of a feminist approach.

MARY HUNT: Talking about peace under patriarchy is putting on a Band-Aid when major feminist surgery is required. Studies are being made of children in this generation who do not think they have a future; they do not expect to live to grow up and retire; they think the world will end. I think that some parts of the peace movement come out of the anti-Vietnam war movement, from the younger brothers of some of the men who formed the antiwar movement. They have become so nervous about the radical implications of the women's movement and the lesbian/gay movement that they have turned to the peace movement in a way that relativizes all other movements before the horror of the nuclear threat. I urge us to demand that feminist values not only be brought to bear in the peace movement, but that feminism be understood as one of its foundations. The peace movement is co-opting itself when it claims to relativize all other issues. Instead, it can be better understood in the light of women's issues, lesbian/gay issues, racial and economic issues, imperialism, etc. Because we understand these issues and seek to change them, we have a sense of the nuclear threat and how we can begin to respond to it. This helps feminists to build coalitions in the peace movement.

C: The West Coast peace movement has been working on nonviolent direct action organized with deep concern for feminist process and values. The peace movement is a strategy for building unlikely coalitions. It touches people who would not be touched politically in any other way, people who have never involved themselves politically before. What makes people feel powerless is not having any possibility for action. We need to make a line people can put themselves on! In terms of world struggles, we have an opportunity to give support by building a mass movement here that will take action on questions like El Salvador. Those of us who are not so oppressed need to be responsible to take what steps we can.

HUNT: How can we bring together the two notions of the transcendent dimension and the importance of concrete values and actions? The transcendent has been used negatively against women, Blacks, and others confined to their "God-ordained" place. But it is unhelpful to deny any transcendence beyond the human. The discussion of Vodou and some of the other comments made here indicate that a great many things are going on in that sphere that have meaning for us. Historically and personally, I find the transcendent dimension to be a very important part of human experience. In Latin America, for example, political strategies must include a religious dimension. In groups like this conference that include people from a variety of religious traditions, it becomes very difficult to talk meaningfully about the transcendent, very difficult to talk about God or the Goddess. This is understandable. But from a strategic point of view, it is helpful to acknowledge the dimension of mystery beyond, within, throughout, among us. Then as we develop communities of struggle and action, which I call communities of accountability, we can act on our commitments rather than argue about them. Thinking and theorizing ecumenically and internationally can be balanced by acting and praying locally.

H: Once we have peace, will society be any less racist? I cannot march in an antinuclear movement because the racists are marching too and will destroy me after peace is attained. We have different entry points into oppression—racism, sexism, heterosexism. We need to hear and to empathize with the other at least to some extent, to develop the understanding that is the basis for building coalitions. There are two ways of perceiving universalities: one is looking for the lowest common denominator, e.g., not talking about God, Goddess, or Jesus for fear of giving offense; the other is knowing your particularity so well that you know its good and its evil, so you can unite with others on the good and transcend the evil. The question for me is whether I submerge my nationality by projecting a White middle-class norm or whether I can be a Black feminist with unique qualities, a different language and history, but still be feminist with you. If I can't speak from my Black feminist perspective, which is unique, then I can't coalesce with you, because you are saying, "Come with me on my universal plane, which is a White, middle-class feminist plane."

CONDREN: The best definition of universality I know comes from Hunt's thesis, where she calls for a new universality that will mean the greatest possible toleration of the most divergent points of view.

When I call for a new universality that will transcend ethnic, racial, national, and religious differences, I want an understanding of women that is not reductionist, not a matter of a lowest common denominator, a kind of uterine theology. I want a new understanding of the very real differences between men and women. The work of Carol Gilligan on ethics, *In a Different Voice*, is relevant here. She points out that male moral development has been seen as normative for generations. The more abstract one becomes, the more highly moral one is. She studied women making a decision about abortion, and she found that for women this is not the case. The most highly ethical decisions for women were based on interfamilial responsibility; it was only in freedom, and only at a much later stage, perhaps not relevant to the immediate situation, that they could talk about abstraction; and then the fundamental principle was not abstraction but nonviolence. You may not agree with Gilligan's work, but there is a new consciousness on the part of women that has to be explicated and worked on to the same extent that Marxists work on production, production relations, and the epistemology that comes out of production relations. We have to develop a systematic theory, based on our experience, and explicated with the same degree of seriousness that Marxists have given to explicating their theory in the last hundred years. We need to talk about the kind of experiences we have as women and build our theory on that basis. I think we will find that we have more in common with other women throughout the world than with our own brothers.

22

Women Responding to the Arab-Israeli Conflict

The Arab-Israeli issue emerged suddenly and sharply during the discussion that followed the racism panel (pp. 106–16), presenting itself in terms of the personal experiences of various group members: an American strongly identified with her Lebanese husband and extended family and suffering the agony of watching the invasion of Lebanon; a Jewish woman experiencing anti-Semitism even in the women's movement and longing for a place on earth where any Jew could claim a refuge; another Jewish woman, seven of whose aunts and uncles had died in Nazi concentration camps; an American Catholic whose insight had been sharpened by a recent visit to the Middle East. The issue severely tested our ability to bond as women across the chasms created by our diverse histories and loyalties. Mary Bentley Abu-Saba explains how the panelists attempted to build a bridge of understanding and empathy across these divisions. "After I spoke in the fishbowl discussion that followed the racism panel, Judith Plaskow and I got together and talked. It was an emotional encounter. We were trying to understand each other's point of view. Then we began to talk about how to present our understanding to the conference. Our plan was for the two of us to alternate speaking three different times. Each of us would speak for approximately five minutes at a time. We would make an effort not to argue the other's points but to concentrate on presenting our own. Then we asked Rosemary Ruether to comment at the end, which she agreed to do. Our intent was to express our various viewpoints without the volatile feelings that come from arguing the 'correctness' of these viewpoints."

Mary Bentley Abu-Saba

JUDITH PLASKOW: I want to talk on what Israel in Jewish history means to me in theory and then about the reality of the modern state. What I feel about Israel is rooted in a long history, so I can talk about my own feelings only in the context of Jewish history.

Christians have a tendency to identify Judaism with the Old Testament and to think its development came to an end with the birth of Christ. One of the reasons among many that this represents a profound misunderstanding is that the Old Testament is the history of a people who have a land. The law articulated in that book governs a people who have a land. The history describes different stages of the people's life on that land. In 70 C.E., when the Romans captured Jerusalem and destroyed the temple, the Jews lost their land. That was a major turning point in Jewish history. True, it had been prepared for, but it still forced a profound restructuring of the tradition. Mircea Eliade talks about an Australian aboriginal tribe that saw the center of the world as a pole that they carried around with them. One day the pole broke and the whole people lay down around the pole and died. That could have happened to the Jewish people in the year 70, but it didn't. It was at this point that Jews became the people of the book. The Torah, elaborated in law, homily, and narrative, became the center of Jewish life, and the land became a second center, a longing, and a hope. Every synagogue is oriented toward Jerusalem; Jews face Jerusalem when they pray. There is no prayer that does not express longing for the land, for the restoration of the temple. The Passover Seder ends, "Next year in Jerusalem!" It is a central theme of Jewish liturgy and life. At the same time, for two thousand years (although in every period individual pious Jews have gone to live in Israel or returned there to die), Jews have been landless people, people who have had to come to terms with increasing isolation within Christian or Islamic culture.

To skip over many centuries, along came emancipation. With the French Revolution, the Jews of Europe began to be granted rights of citizenship. That was another important turning point in Jewish history, one we are still living out and trying to come to grips with. It was an ambiguous event. On one hand, for the first time Jews were offered citizenship, access to public schools, etc. On the other hand, these things were offered on the condition that Jews cease to exist as a people. For the Jew as a man, everything; for the Jew as a Jew, nothing. If one agreed to be a Frenchman of the Israelite persuasion, everything was fine. But if one wanted to be a Jew as a member of a people, that was outside the agreement. Many Jews were willing to assimilate and to be Jews as a religion. But Judaism is not just a religion; it is a peoplehood, so the compromise was finally impossible.

Emancipation also gave birth to a new form of anti-Semitism, or rather one that harked back to anti-Semitism in its pre-Christian form. Greek anti-Semitism had centered around the Jews as a foreign body in the polis. They did not want to worship the Greek gods, to do what everyone else was doing. With emancipation, this accusation was revived. Jews were a foreign body in Western Europe.

Then, in the mid-nineteenth century, as nationalism became an increasingly important phenomenon in Europe, proto-Zionists began to ask: "Why not for the Jews too? Why not be a people like every other people?" Theodore Herzl saw Zionism as a solution to the Jewish problem in Europe. Give us our own state, he said, and we will leave you alone. We will all go there and the Jewish problem will be solved. That was Herzl's vision, and it depended on the Jews' going to Israel so that they would no longer be a thorn in the side of the nations. In Herzl's vision, the land had to be Israel's historic homeland, not because he was religious but because he thought it was the only land that could sufficiently excite the passion and yearning of the people to get them to get up and move there. "Territorialists" felt no particular connection to Israel and said, "Give us a piece of land anywhere." For a while there was discussion of a possible Jewish homeland in East Africa, but Zionists won the day.

MARY BENTLEY ABU-SABA: The message that is most difficult to say because people do not want to hear it is that while Jews were longing to go back to the land, a people was already there. The Zionists did not go to a vacant land. In making the Jewish people a national entity, grave injustice was done to the Palestinians. Both Muslim and Christian Palestinians see themselves as part of that land. It has been their home for thousands of years. They have great love for that land and no other desire but to go back to it. This is the basic reason for the present crisis, because in affirming the state of Israel, the Jews drove the Palestinians out. The terrorism the Palestinians experienced was seen from the Jewish point of view as freedom fighting. The Palestinians went to Lebanon, Syria, Iraq, and Jordan and set up camps that multiplied. The expulsion of the Palestinians is the basic crux of the problem.

My own involvement in this question began when I started my political career in the civil rights movement in Virginia at the age of twenty-one. At the age of twenty-two, I married an Arab after a long and passionate courtship. At that time we had agreed to live in his home country, Lebanon. That was a challenge for me. We moved there in 1962, when our first child was an infant, and stayed two years. I taught school there and my husband worked as an engineer for the Lebanese government. We lived in Mia Mia, which is about half a mile from the city of Sidon. I heard Palestinians tell their life stories: "We used to live on the land near Haifa. We had olive groves, and then came these people, and they pushed us out, but one day we will go back." I heard that story over and over. Our apartment faced the Mediterranean and was approximately two city blocks from the edge of the Palestinian camp of Mia Mia, one of the camps that was bombed repeatedly during the summer of 1982. From my dining-room window I could see the comings and goings of the people in the camp. There was never a day that passed when I lived in Lebanon that I was not aware of the transient status of the Palestinian people in the camp.

After two years in the Middle East we returned to the United States for my husband to go back to school and for us to have our second child. My husband went to the Pacific School of Religion, not as a minister but as an engineer. He was an involved layman in religion and higher education and was one of the first recipients of the Clarence Prouty Shedd fellowship for persons involved in higher education in religion. It was very difficult for me to discover on my return to the United States that so few people wanted to hear what I had learned about the Palestinian story in the Middle East. It was difficult to tell people about it. During the 1967 war I felt very isolated from others in my own community because of my perspective on what this war was all about. As a WASP I was not accustomed to feeling that kind of alienation and isolation. We were simply not able to say that the reason there is fighting is that there are Palestinians who have been kicked out of their homes. One of the horrifying experiences, however, was to discover that there were some unsavory people who did want to listen to our story and to get us on their team. I first experienced this in Illinois at a meeting we were invited to. The villainous talk about Jewish people made me understand very quickly that we were in the wrong place. We excused ourselves immediately. We were often approached by people who simply wanted to be on the Arab side of the war because they were against Jewish people.

Seven years ago we went to North Carolina to live, for me a return to my native South. My husband teaches in a Black school, and I found a job at a sister school, which is White. For seven years I have again been involved in dealing with the racism of the South—both the racism between Blacks and Whites and the kind of racism my family experiences in being "foreign." Members of my husband's family have moved here to go to school, and we have been helping them understand a more egalitarian life-style. For instance, we have a niece and three nephews studying engineering. We have often explained to them that our niece is here to be a student as well as our nephews and is not supposed to do all the cooking and cleaning for her brothers. Thirteen of our close family live near us in Greensboro. We have spent many summers in Lebanon. Our children know Arabic fairly well. There are thirty people in our extended family in Greensboro. When tragedy strikes Lebanon as it did this summer, we are all greatly affected, because there are so many of us living in this community together.

PLASKOW: Mary Edith asked me, "Why is Israel important to you?" That is an important question, one I have thought about only recently. I grew up in a non-Zionist family. Israel was a place to go on vacation, not to live in. But I always had a sense that Israel was different for me from any other country in the world. I can imagine what it is like for an Irish or an Italian person growing up in the United States. When I began to teach, I taught a course on Jewish identity, which had a section on Zionism. It was then I became aware of the conflicts in the Zionist movement and began to identify with themes in that conflict.

World Zionism grew out of Jewish history; it also represents a significant break with that history. The Jews always believed they would be restored to Zion, but that God was going to do it. Herzl said that if you will it, it is not a dream. That fits into the language of self-determination of the nineteenth century much better than it fits into the language of Jewish belief in the ultimate restoration to Zion. Therefore, there are ultra-Orthodox Jews living in Israel who do not acknowledge the existence of a Jewish state and do not recognize its authority—because it was created by human beings, and un-Orthodox ones at that! But even within the Zionist movement, there was a conflict of vision. Herzl saw the Jewish state as a refuge. That is how I have always seen it, growing up after the Holocaust. For me, Israel is a place where Jews can go when the rest of the world does not want them. In the Nazi period Jews were given passports to leave Germany, and no state would take them. This dramatizes for me the need for a place where any Jew could go. That has always been an element of my thinking about Israel. It has always been in the back of my mind that if there were a resurgence of anti-Semitism in this country, I could go to Israel. Maybe I would die in Israel, but at least I would die as a Jew determining my own destiny, and not as a victim. That is one element in the conflict.

Herzl wanted the Jewish state to be a normal state like every other, a people in the political arena. Jews would go there, it would solve the problem of anti-Semitism in Europe, and Israel would be a state among states. Others—among them Ahad Ha'am and Martin Buber—wanted not a state of Jews but a Jewish state, founded on Jewish values. That did not mean a state founded on Orthodox law as in the National Religious Party. It meant socialism, equality for women, an ethical relation to the land itself, to the Arabs on the land and in the surrounding countries: a light unto the nations. In this vision, it was not important that all Jews go to Israel, but that Israel would be a Jewish state that would be a beacon to the Jews in the Diaspora and an example to the world.

Part of what has prevented the fulfillment of this dream is that Israel has been at war with its Arab neighbors from the moment of its birth. The Palestinians, encouraged by other Arabs, not Israelis, to leave their homes "temporarily" in anticipation of the early destruction of Israel, have become pawns in a struggle in which no one is concerned with their interests.

For me the notion of a Jewish state has enormous power. It is parallel to the notion that women, out of their experience of oppression, have the power to change the world. That was the vision of the early Zionists: that out of the experience of their oppression, they could create a state that was different from all other states. And it was an opportunity to interpret Jewish law so that parts of it that had stagnated for centuries or been wildly theoretical for two thousand years—such as the year of Jubilee when there was no land to give back or let rest—could be made alive on a plot of land.

I feel strongly that non-Jews have no right to ask the Jewish state to be different from any other state. It would be like a man saying to a woman, "You go out and save the world from war. You're nurturing; you do it or you have no right to exist." But to me as a Jew, Israel has meaning only if it is a

Jewish state, just as feminism has meaning only if it is culture-transforming.

One other thing Israel means to me and to a lot of American Jews is a place where one can be wholly Jewish. My four-and-a-half-year-old son came home from nursery school and said to me, "You know, Mommie, I think my school likes Easter better than Passover." To live in Israel is not to have to deal with that. It is to live in a country where rhythms and holidays are Jewish, whether one is observant or not. In Israel I can really be a Jew; but I am also an American, so I could live out one part of my identity in Israel but not the other part. For me, it seems easier to be a Jew in America than to be a feminist in Israel. I am a Jew committed to the Diaspora and believe that Jewish life is viable in Diaspora, but I have a relationship with and feel committed to Israel.

ABU-SABA: The Israel I know about from living north of the border in Lebanon is imperialistic. The maps of the last twelve years will bear that out. Israel has grown with each war, getting bigger and bigger. Now there are settlements on the West Bank, and there are those in Israel who claim that southern Lebanon should be part of Israel.

The emotions of the past month have been wrenching. Something awful was happening in our lives. We watched the television screen night after night; places where I lived, schools where I taught, were being bombed. We were frightened for the grandparents and aunts and uncles and cousins. The children would turn to us and ask, "You think they'll be all right, don't you?" and we had no answer. It is an experience of absolute terror, night after night. On June 7, 1982, we were invited to a dinner party at Jeanette Stokes's home. In the car after watching TV my husband was in an absolute rage at the violence he saw committed in Lebanon by the Israelis. Most families would simply have gone home, but Jeanette was big enough to hear our rage. We expressed our grief and began to regain our equilibrium. Never before that evening had we felt such madness.

Each time we try to speak about it, try to talk about the Arab viewpoint, we are accused of anti-Semitism. We speak on panels, I as a psychologist, my husband from a political

point of view, and we are often met with silence. Our experience has been one of great voicelessness and fear.
I have had a problem in relating to this conference. Obviously I did not check the calendar to see whether there would be a war going on when I decided to come. Had there not been a war I would have had an entirely different agenda, around feminist therapy and religious experience. I have had difficulty in finding a way to speak out at this conference about a war that is happening right now. It is still in progress. It is not just a theory. I had tried to find a way to say, "Look, there is a problem here." The response was, "Don't talk about it now; it's not appropriate." I could have screamed: "When *is* it appropriate for me to say what I have to say about the rape of Lebanon? When *can* I say that if we don't figure this out soon, this is the way the world will end? All the ingredients are there." I don't have any trouble understanding that males are doing the killing and that theoretically this war is a product of the death-ridden patriarchy, but they are killing us *all*. They are our sons, husbands, and brothers—*your* sons, husbands, and brothers. We keep coming back to this central issue: there are Palestinian people who no longer have a home, and they are angry. If I were a Palestinian I would be right with them. I know what I would do with my rage.

These past weeks I have had difficulty doing therapy with people. I can't deal with others' issues when mine are eating me up. I don't know what to do about it, but I am trying to find a way. This discussion was the most sensible thing I could find to do today. I don't know what I will do tomorrow.

PLASKOW: I want to echo Mary Edith's question: What happened to the vision of the early Zionists? What we have today is not a Jewish state, but a state of Jews. I was in Israel in 1967 right after the war. It was an incredible time in Israel. It wasn't that there was a sense of triumphalism—quite the contrary, although there was an incredible religious power in having Jerusalem back. A book came out at the time called *The Seventh Day*. It was a conversation with Israeli soldiers talking about their experience of the war and asking whether even the recovery of Jerusalem was worth it, whether the loss of life was worth it. There was a sense on everyone's part at the time: we have achieved this, and now we have a bargaining chip; now we can give it all back and make peace. Now what I see happening—particularly with the election of Menachem Begin, but his election already reflects that change of mood—is the sense that no, we won't give the land back. For me, again it is like having a brother who is going out killing people. You can't separate yourself. The peace movement in Israel is not having any influence, so what influence can we have as American Jews? In 1967 there was a real counting of life and a real awareness of what war meant. I don't see that any more.

I also see the interstructuring of different forms of oppression. Israel is becoming more intransigent toward the Arabs and more and more sexist as the religious party asserts its influence. It is also racist internally because the Jews from Arab countries, while they are keeping Begin in power, have no economic power in the country. So there is racism, classism, and sexism from an Israeli perspective. Unless Israel recognizes the existence of the Palestinians and the justice of their cause, Israel cannot survive. There can be no settlement, no Israel, until that reality is faced. Jews have been powerless so long, they don't know what to do in a situation of power. I don't know; that's too easy to say. The pain for me is that there are two rights here. What to do with two rights?

ABU-SABA: My understanding of racism came from the awful segregation I grew up with in the South. Because of my understanding of this racism, I have made a commitment to finding an integrated way of life with all kinds of people with various kinds of religious beliefs. I no longer consider myself a Christian, because I find it wall-building. It is more inclusive to be more amoebalike with people. A Jewish state with all Jewish people is wall-building; it is a racist nation; I would never be able to accept that as appropriate. I ask myself to give up my "White" views and to be inclusive of other people. I can't imagine making a whole nation an exception to this way of life.

One of my deepest fears is that I will have to put away my idealistic notion that this situation can be settled in my lifetime. I fear that the rest of my life will be punctuated with these awful happenings.

The worst fear is that there is no way the Jewish people in Israel can win, that we will again have to experience what happened in Europe during World War II. Israel may indeed be the final solution for the Jewish people. With each of these warring events they dig their own graves deeper. No matter how much they spend on armaments there is no way, surrounded by that many Arabs, that they can extricate themselves. I don't want to experience that tragedy for them either.

PLASKOW: This points to another conflict among Zionists: what does it mean to say that Israel is a Jewish state? There are those who want a theocratic state, controlled by the rabbinate according to Jewish law. The government has depended for its ability to stay in power on a coalition with the religious party. A lot of negative aspects of Israeli society are the result of that coalition. There are also Jews who envision Israel as a secular democratic state living according to the Jewish calendar. But I must say I do not see a Jewish state as any more wall-building than an Italian state or a Russian state. It is not Jews who walled themselves into ghettoes for hundreds of years. As Andrea Dworkin put it, "In the world I'm working for, nation states will not exist. But in the world I live in, I want there to be an Israel."

ABU-SABA: The superpowers are feeding each other, using this war for their own ends. Americans don't care if both Jews and Arabs are wiped off the face of the earth—that is a reality that both Judy and I experience.

ROSEMARY RADFORD RUETHER: I became involved with this question through my book *Faith and Fratricide,* which I wrote some years ago after studying the roots of Christian anti-Semitism. I saw my work as a Christian self-critique rather than a means to "dialogue with Jews." My conclusion was that Christians must do this internal critique and accept the autonomy of Judaism as a people and a religion in its own right, not one that needed to be involved with Christianity.

In the book I showed how Christianity has grown out of Judaism. I traced the way that Patristic, Constantinian, and imperial expressions of anti-Semitism developed and culminated in Nazism. I was told by the publisher that there would be no honorarium, that Christians would not read the book, only Jews would read it. In Germany, it has been translated by people from the Bonhoeffer circle, but, indeed, in America, my invitations to speak come almost entirely from the Jewish community and not from Christians. In the book, I said nothing about the connection between my analysis and the state of Israel, but the fallout from the book dragged me into the arena of forging a stance toward the state of Israel.

In thinking about the founding of Israel, we must remember that the land was not empty. In order for the Jews to settle there, the Palestinians had to be displaced. The Palestinians have become the Jews of the Middle East. There is a great irony in this: the mirror image of two peoples alienated from each other and still almost shaped by each other. Each side has a complete world view that is absolutely counter to that of the other side, although these two worlds exist only five miles from each other. Each has its own history and formal justifications, and each indeed has rights, but the problem is how to bring these two sets of rights together.

The solution would seem to lie in the emergence of some kind of middle ground where these two peoples can modify the totality of each of their claims and share the land together. That kind of middle ground has to be created by Palestinians and Israelis. The forces of self-critique that would make it possible have to emerge from within. Christians or Americans of whatever side are outsiders with a very limited role, and must not imagine themselves to be the righteous vindicators of one side or the other, in effect aggravating the polarization.

These were the rather abstract ideas I had about the situation when I had the occasion to travel to Israel with a women's group. We were whisked from Gaza to the other end of the country and heard from a number of people at high levels of government. We had an hour-long personal interview with Begin in which he insisted that never, never would Palestinians live in the hills where they could fire right into the windows of the Knesset. We got a good idea of the

Israeli point of view, both the self-defense and the idealistic aspects.

Then a group of us went to visit some Palestinian moderates; we also had contact with some Israeli peace people, those who were never introduced to our official group and who were very much at ease with the Palestinians. Among those we met was Samaya Khalil, who runs a women's center that tries to find training for Palestinian women who have lost their husbands through the war, and also tries to place Palestinian children whose parents have been jailed or killed. We asked Mrs. Khalil about the Palestinian refusal to accept the very existence of the state of Israel and their determination to push Israel into the sea. She told us that since 1973 the Palestinians have begun to change, to accept the reality of Israel and of the two-state solution. She herself had been so very much against this position that when her son first proposed it to her, she refused to see him for three months, even though he was in prison. Now, however, she saw that most Israelis were also refugees and did not have a homeland to go back to. She could accept an Israeli state within the 1967 borders, but she wanted a Palestinian state as well on the West Bank and Gaza. She could accept that those Jews who had suffered under Nazism needed a homeland and had no other place to go, but she wanted a limit to Israeli expansion. As she saw it, there was no need for Jews who did not need a homeland to come to Israel, especially those who were doing well in America. We also met Israelis who had a similar point of view.

There are critical forces on both sides that are ready for peace, but on both sides those forces have been suppressed by their own militants, who have not allowed these moderate voices to speak. American Jews who have tried to put forth peace positions have also been silenced. The suppression is helped along by the desire on the other side not to hear the moderates; by pushing everything to the extreme, both governments justify their own intransigence. It may be that now the critical forces in Israel and in the American Jewish community are being unleashed.

23

Suggestions from the Working Group on Political Strategies

"Don't just do something, sit there." This saying from Zen Buddhism lends support to strategists who see the need not merely to plan action but to pause long enough to examine a particular problem from a broader perspective. This saying also explains why the group on political strategies chose to start with an analysis of the patriarchy and its distinguishing features, since this is the larger context in which women's struggle for equality and justice is taking place. In the process of articulating dissatisfactions with the patriarchal system and its values, the group began to formulate an alternate feminist vision of social interaction. If we begin with an analysis, it is because we recognize that we, too, can oppress by jumping in too quickly.

A Critique of Patriarchy

Features of the Patriarchal System

- Normative
- Exclusive, hierarchical
- Impersonal, alienating

Features of the Proposed Feminist Alternative

- Pluralistic
- Inclusive, egalitarian
- Personal, integrating

Patriarchy is a normative system; it assumes that there is only one system, which everyone must follow—namely, the system of the one in power. In this system, minorities are relatively powerless and voiceless.

Patriarchy values exclusivity. It sets up separate spheres of influence for men and women, for rich and poor. People are isolated in their separate, ranked categories in such a way that they fail to recognize common bonds.

The patriarchal style is impersonal and alienating. The patriarchs speak of abstract and legal categories, and they so value the mind over the body that they alienate people from their emotional life and their existential life story.

The feminist vision is pluralistic. Because it strives for unity rather than uniformity, it affirms diversity. To this end it works to build coalitions with constituencies that reflect the diversity of the human race and human concerns. Similarly, feminists envision an ethic that challenges the poor and powerless to define the good and work together to attain it. This "good" will vary according to the group formulating it—Hispanics, Blacks, refugees, women, migrant workers. This avoids the patriarchal approach of allowing the ruling group to legislate what is supposedly normative for all.

The feminist vision also recognizes the need to be pluralistic with regard to decision-making, which means following democratic process as well as consensus. Consensus has become a popular way of arriving at a decision, but sociologist Irving Louis Horowitz points out its shortcomings in his study "Consensus, Conflict and Co-operation" (*Social Forces* 41, December 1962). He explains how consensus can be used so that the minority is controlled by the majority. Since the aim of consensus is to reach an agreement, the social pressure to conform tends to increase. By the end of the discussion, it is likely that dissident voices will either be silenced or relegated to the fringe. According to Horowitz, consensus *emerges* when the participants are basically united. When participants are not predominantly of like mind, then arriving at a consensus can become an exercise in manipulation, which in the end establishes a norm.

By contrast, the model of cooperation focuses on procedural steps for mediating differences rather than quashing them. If a small group is already committed to some common goal and an agreement emerges from the group discussion, that is true consensus. But if there are diverse people in the group and it reports only what everyone agrees on, a great deal will be left out. In fact, some views are certain to be marginalized. A grassroots group with no immediate common interest, should shift to another decision-making model. In a diverse group, consensus easily becomes oppressive because it leaves out the interest of the minority, who by definition will never have consensus on their side. When building coalitions with diverse and sometimes hostile groups, it is important to use democratic processes—which are more in line with the cooperation model described by Horowitz—to arrive at limited agreements for limited time periods and to allow full scope for minority reports.

The feminist vision is inclusive. Inclusivity calls for making connections of all kinds—for example, making the connection between an immediate local concern about unemployment and international issues like the sweatshops in Korea, along with national and international governmental policies. Or it could mean helping others to see the connection between the cutback in student loan funds and the army's need for recruits. Let the feminists bring together issues the patriarchs prefer to separate.

In the face of alienation, a feminist vision is personal. It deals with persons with personal histories instead of retreating to safe abstractions. Why not talk about lesbians instead of lesbianism? about women who undergo abortions instead of the abortion issue? about divorced men and women instead of the problem of divorce? Do you know their stories? Once you put a personal face on an issue, you cannot look at it in quite the same way.

Concern for the person also calls on feminists to be against structures, not against individuals. The point is to be against nuclear arms, not to boycott the home of a worker in a nuclear plant. In the case of the war in Vietnam, the goal was not to attack individual soldiers but to challenge the institutional forces that promoted the war. The task is to liberate individuals and groups from oppressive structures.

Recovering the Cultural Sphere

The feminist goal can be nothing less than the recovery of the government, the political process, and the media, three spheres which at present are largely controlled by the multinational corporations. In Brazil, for example, the multinationals spend millions on education that prepares people for jobs in their industries. Thus the people become dependent on American industry. Consciousness-raising must go on at all levels. It may begin in small face-to-face communities where the poor, the unemployed, Blacks, and Hispanic refugees come together to tell their stories and form common bonds as they break down myths and stereotypes. In other words, story-telling is a political activity, "Oh, that happened to you! I thought that only happened to lazy people who got fired." Story-telling breaks down the myths about the American dream that everyone who works hard is going to get their share of the pie sooner or later. The more people listen to each others' stories, the more likely they are to see the need for social change.

Building Communities and Networks

Form communities around justice issues; do not let people work alone. Start with minimal grass-roots activities around a concrete, local interest—a street lamp for the corner, a playground for the children on the block. Start with small things where people can experience some success and excitement about achieving their goal. Even if they do not succeed, they will be encouraged and will see that they have to do more work.

Creating alternative institutions at the grass-roots level that mobilize self-help resources is a useful strategy so long as those institutions are also linked to the fight for more resources. It is useful to develop food co-ops, cooperative day care, etc., but these groups should also demand resources from the state. Do not get caught in an either/or mentality.

From these concrete local projects, try to spiral upward to national issues, emphasizing the relation between local, national, and international needs. Then form coalitions with other groups. It is important in building coalitions not to put down more conditions than are necessary. Do not demand that others accept your whole agenda if you are going to work with them. It may be necessary to build some subcoalitions as a first step. Maybe not everything has to be worked out in public at a national level.

When forming coalitions, a preferential option for the poor means that the poorest and the least empowered are asked to help set the agenda.

Make use of the media. If the majority of the people you want to reach are not highly educated and will not come to educational institutions, make use of existng channels, e.g., the churches, cartoons and comic books, television and radio.

Use the electoral process for access to the media. Where possible, work within the political primaries to get a candidate that represents your group; where that is not possible, get a coalition to run a representative candidate. The National Organization for Women (NOW) succeeded in putting through its leader as a vice-presidential candidate as a way of showing that there were a lot of people whose interests had to be taken into consideration.

Two Immediate, Concrete Steps

- Join the local chapter of NOW, which is the political arm of the women's movement.
- Make use of WOMEN USA, the hotline set up by Bella Abzug and others, to help mobilize women for political action. Those who call their toll-free number (800-221-4945) will be given concrete suggestions for immediate action, particularly on current legislation.

Above all, it is important to remember that there are many places to insert oneself: either at the local level, building base communities for consciousness-raising, or at the level of networking, coalition-building, or linking base groups. Without this kind of political organizing, women cannot hope to challenge the multinational control of institutions that most affect our lives.

Part VI

Lesbianism and Homophobia

LESBIANISM IS CLEARLY one of the connections between women that embody Adrienne Rich's description, "most feared" and "most potentially transformative." No candid observer can overlook the wealth of poetry, art, music, literature, and scholarship with which the lesbian community has enriched this culture. In recent years, an outburst of creative energy has flowed from the affirmation of self and other as the lesbian community has emerged into public view. Concomitantly, there has been a rethinking of all women's relationships and fresh insights into the ways in which the label lesbian has been used to divide women. But at the same time, homophobia—the fear of homosexuality—has intensified and has presented major barriers to women's bonding.

As Patricia Broughton has insisted, "Until every woman is free, no woman is free. There are no liberated women until all women are liberated from the fear of lesbianism. The problem is not lesbianism, but heterosexism or homophobia and the oppression of lesbians." At this conference we shared experiences as women who were fearful of lesbianism and women who had made the often painful journey to self-definition as lesbians. We explored our own attitudes, looked at the pros and cons of a political definition of lesbianism, and considered the potential of lesbianism as a force for women's spirit bonding. Few conclusions were reached, but the discussion makes clear that the definition of lesbianism and the analysis of heterosexism are major issues for the 1980s.

This part includes a prose poem by Lynn Wilson on the fear, anger, and joy of being lesbian; a Christian perspective by Letha Scanzoni; a political perspective by Mary Hunt; and a transcript of the discussion.

My Voice . . . and Many Others

LYNN WILSON

Normally, when people get together and lesbians share their personal experience, they tell part of their own, specific history. Rather than tell my story, I decided to draw from my experience and from the experiences of other lesbians, trying to reveal some of the fear and the anger, and then to look at how those feelings might be transformed into the "connections" Adrienne Rich speaks of, connections that bind women and create broader possibilities. This is my voice, and many others'.

I am afraid

I fear that I could be detained like my Cuban sisters when they came to this country. I fear that I could lose my income. When I can't touch, talk to, or sit by another lesbian, I am afraid. I am afraid that straight women will always be afraid of being called a dyke.

As a woman, I am afraid to be raped; as a lesbian, I am afraid of being raped because someone wants to prove I'm not a lesbian. I am afraid that I might choose chemical abuse or suicide as many of my lesbian

and I am angry

I am angry I have to hide pictures, records, books that might reveal too much when certain people come to visit. I am angry when our churches and society want to understand me and they ask gay men. I am angry that you assume I don't want children. I am angry that we listen to other people's stories and weep, and no one weeps for us.

I am angry that current lesbian resources are going out of

Lynn Wilson

sisters do. I am afraid of imprisonment, torture, and death. I am afraid of losing family and friends, either by not sharing my whole self with them or by sharing myself with them.

I am fearful of being betrayed by other women who say it's O.K. I am afraid my windshield could be bashed in someday by someone in my neighborhood. I am afraid of my own homophobia against myself and my friends. I was afraid when I came out that I'd have to let my hair grow.

I am fearful if I choose monogamy you'll think I haven't let go of the patriarchy. And if I choose nonmonogamy, you'll see me as promiscuous.

print. I am angry that nobody asks about the person most important to me. I am angry when I hear story after story after painful story of other lesbians. I am angry that I as a lesbian who is not out am labeled "dyke" by others because I'm a feminist. I am angry that as a lesbian who is out, when I suggest to women a get-together, my motive is read as sexual.

I am angry that as a Peace Corps volunteer, if I had been open about my lesbianism, I would have had to sign a piece of paper saying I would abstain from sexual intimacy for two years. I am angry that people don't believe I'm a celibate lesbian. I'm angry that as a sexual lesbian others see sex as a primary focus for me.

I'm angry that I can't see many of the role models we have because they have been erased from history.

But in all that anger and fear, there can be a positive side. There *is* a positive side. There *is* potential to transform and stimulate women's culture in general, whether all the women are sexually oriented toward women or not. Women can expand and explore—not just lesbians, but other women too—regardless of whether they are sexually active. We have discussed the power of politics. There is a power of life-style as well, and lesbians, because we are in the process of questioning authority and tradition, can be free to explore it, and then share that exploration with other women. There is a striving for personal wholeness in terms of health and in terms of integrating various facets of our lives. There is a new women's culture: music, theater, philosophy, and—who knows?—maybe even mathematics. What lesbians have to share involves learning new dimensions of power, initiating, and learning to lead.

25
A Religious Perspective
LETHA DAWSON SCANZONI

Is the Homosexual My Neighbor?, the book I coauthored with Virginia Ramey Mollenkott, comes from the Jewish and Christian ideal of neighbor love: "You shall love your neighbor as yourself [Lev. 19:18]."

Religious persons and groups throughout history have tried to dodge this responsibility of neighbor love by raising the question, "Who is my neighbor?" In that way, barriers can be put up and people can be put into categories. And if a decision is made that persons in one category are neighbors and those in another category are not, then maybe one does not have to love certain persons or groups. Lesbians and gay men have been especially singled out as somehow less deserving of neighbor love in the eyes of many sincerely religious people. Our book explores that sad fact; it is aimed at a religious audience to show, among other things, that the Bible has been wrongly used to clobber people rather than to lift up and liberate the oppressed. Rosemary Ruether made a remark that is apropos. She said that if you want to use the Bible to hit people over the head, you have to keep it closed!

If we open the Bible, we may be surprised to see how deeply embedded are the concepts of love, justice, and compassion for all persons. I speak out of my Christian faith and out of loving concern for my gay brothers and sisters—those persons whom I have come to know and appreciate during my efforts to understand the topic of homosexuality in theological perspective. It has been a gradual pilgrimage for me—not without struggle, as is always true of rethinking and growth. But what I have come to realize is that the basic issue is *human personhood*.

This emphasis on human dignity, worth, and personhood is what I like religious audiences to see. We are talking about human beings, not abstractions. It is easy to intellectualize and speak in the abstract; the topic can seem more remote that way. Thus discussions may be centered around such questions as how homosexuals got that way, rather than on what it means to *be* a homosexual person in a homophobic society. Questions are seldom raised about why heterosexuals are as they are; in other words, the focus needs to be on the much broader topic of human sexuality in general and what is and is not known according to modern scientific research. One result of some analytic approaches is that parents of gay men and women worry that they may have done something to "cause" their offsprings' sexual orientation. They need reassurance, information, and understanding—not blame![1]

When lesbians and gay men are talked about in the abstract and are viewed as impersonal stereotypes, it is easy to ignore them, disregard them, even hate them. But when the topic is brought close to home through dealing with specific human beings, something happens inside. Suppose you know a person very well and are quite close to her or him. It may be a friend or relative. Then one day you discover that this person belongs to a category you consider to be wrong or stigmatized. The category does not have to be homosexuality. Perhaps you find the person has been divorced or has had an abortion, and you have religious scruples about these things. Social psychologists point out that you will be likely to do one of two things: either you will mentally push the person away from you, out to where the subject has always been for you; or you will bring the subject up close to you, where the person has always been before telling you the news, and you will begin to take a new look at the topic, being open to see things you had not seen before but that now you want to see because this person matters to you.

Let me give a few illustrations by looking at homosexuality in terms of human personhood—seeing lesbians and gay men as human beings with the same needs, concerns, and feelings as anybody else. That should be obvious, but so often it is not, because homosexual persons are viewed as abstractions, not as individuals, by many religious people who are therefore able to distance themselves mentally from the hurts many gay people feel because of society's insensitivity.

One example of human pain concerns the report I read of a dying lesbian in a hospital's intensive care unit. The hospital said that only members of her immediate family were permitted to visit. But the person the woman really yearned to see was the lesbian partner with whom she had lived for twenty years, who was as close as a spouse would be in a heterosexual relationship. Yet that woman was not allowed to be with her when she was dying.

Or take the matter of child custody. A 1979 law journal told the story of a woman whose husband abandoned her during her second pregnancy. In fact, he was so unconcerned about providing for his family's needs that he denied paternity when the divorce was filed, hoping thereby to avoid having to pay child support. The woman was a lesbian, but in the seven years in which she reared her two little girls alone, she never lived in the same house with her lesbian partner. She was a model of devoted motherhood and good citizenship, attending a community college and leading a scout troop; she excelled in a Parent Effectiveness Training program and was asked to teach one of the courses. During all that time, the woman's former husband had nothing to do with her and their daughters, providing no finances or emotional support and not bothering to visit even when the younger girl was stricken with an illness that was nearly fatal.

Yet when the father sued for custody of both girls some time later, he was granted it, solely on the basis of the mother's lesbianism. This decision was made in spite of strong positive testimony on the woman's behalf by schoolteachers, the children's school principal, and a court-appointed psychiatrist, who not only stated that the children were well adjusted but also warned that the younger child would be harmed psychologically if removed from her mother's home, the only home she had ever known. Even the judicial decision gave recognition to the woman's warm and loving relationship with her daughters and acknowledged they were given adequate care. Even so, her lesbianism was determined to be enough reason to move the children to their father's care.[2]

Then there is the question of gay rights: the right to have a job, to have a home, to have access to public accommodations. I was in Bloomington, Indiana when a gay rights ordinance was passed. The newspapers were filled with letters full of rage and fear, the majority coming from religious people. They said things like, "Run the Sodomites out of town." Such a letter was reprinted as a full-page advertisement several days after it appeared on the letters-to-the-editor page. The ad was paid for by churches that solicited more than three thousand signatures, with as many appearing on the advertisement as could be crammed into the space. Many gay persons were becoming frightened. One said to me in a phone interview for an article I wrote for the *Christian Century* (October 13, 1976), "I don't understand why Christians hate us so much." Her question grieved me. Of course, Christians were not a monolithic group, but it certainly must have looked that way at the time. I found myself wanting to be a bridge between the gay community and the pastors and church members who showed such deep-rooted homophobia. I talked with persons on both sides of the controversy and also with those religious leaders who took a more compassionate and accepting attitude toward gay men and women and saw that civil rights for all people is a *justice* issue. This was the beginning of my involvement with this issue, except for writing a section on the topic in a college text I coauthored, which was published in its first edition that same year.

Christians seem to have four basic attitudes about homosexuality: condemnation, change, celibacy, and commitment.

Condemnation. I once heard a radio sermon in which the preacher claimed that "God's opinion of the gay community" was shown in the destruction of Sodom and Gomorrah. The raining down of fire and brimstone on these ancient cities, according to this radio preacher, "proved that God is willing to send an atomic bomb on the gay community." In the minds of those who condemn homosexuality in this extreme way, it is a sin, period—a sin so bad that God gives up those who are homosexual. Some of the pastors I spoke with during the Bloomington controversy said, "Of course I love homosexuals, because I love all sinners."

Change. According to those Christians who emphasize a change approach, if you are a born-again Christian, you will simply cease being lesbian or gay. Or if you are already a believer and are struggling with homosexual desires or behavior, then you need a service of healing or exorcism or spiritual discipline and prayer so that you can be changed into a heterosexual. These people neglect current pyschological and sociological research and an awareness that homosexuality is a state of being, an orientation, something within a person's makeup. The example I like to use with Christians who take the change approach is left-handedness. I ask, "Do you think a religious conversion will change a left-handed person into a right-handed person? Or does conversion change what they will want to *do* with their hands?"

Celibacy. Those religious persons who teach that celibacy is the way to deal with homosexuality usually recognize the homosexual *orientation;* they know that to some persons the erotic feelings and romantic love feelings that seem natural are directed toward persons of the same sex. Since they believe that the Bible is against this, or that natural law is against it, they insist on celibacy. It is all right to *be* homosexual, but not all right to express one's sexuality in sexual acts, regardless of the context or meaning of such expression. Homosexual "marriage" is not considered an option.

Committed relationships. Some Christians reason that if we are called to love our homosexual neighbors as ourselves, then it would be unfair to insist on a double standard of ethical conduct that would provide heterosexuals with a legitimate outlet for expressing sexual love (marriage) but would deny such an outlet for homosexuals. Christians of this persuasion believe that committed monogamous relationships between two lesbians or two gay men could be analogous to heterosexual marriage and could be considered morally right. Some gay persons object to calling an ongoing covenantal relationship a homosexual *marriage,* while others prefer that term because it acknowledges that their love partnerships are on a par with those of heterosexuals.

These attitudes define a continuum on which are found most Protestants and Roman Catholics. Celibacy for homosexual persons appears to be becoming the predominant position among Catholic spokespersons, although a small number have voiced an acceptance of committed relationships. Celibacy is, of course, a more enlightened position than condemnation, because it shows an awareness of a homosexual "nature" or orientation even though it cannot go so far as to accept its expression. The position of lifelong celibacy for gay men and lesbians is also held by large numbers of Protestants. The author of a new book from England entitled *Homosexuals in the Christian Fellowship* believes that the celibate position is the only one. He also is aware that Paul talked about the "gift" of celibacy, acknowledging that celibacy is not for everyone. Therefore, concludes this author, a homosexual person can know by virtue of simply *being* homosexual that he or she has been called by God to a life of celibacy and has been given the *gift* of celibacy to enable him or her to live it. (As I read that, I wondered why God did not simply make them asexual; that would be a lot simpler!) Of course, an individual, whether homosexual or heterosexual, may voluntarily choose celibacy for religious or other reasons. But this is quite different from requiring a whole category of persons to remain celibate for life with no option for expressing their sexuality, in contrast to the option of marriage that society encourages for heterosexuals.

These, then, are the four main positions held by Christians today. Those who hold the last—the moral permissibility of committed couple relationships—arrive at it by comparing modern social and behavioral science with distorted scriptural interpretations, exploring anew what scripture does and does not say, and then working toward (as I have tried to do) a recognition that if the homosexual person is truly my neighbor, I am not going to hold a double standard that heterosexuals may act one way, but homosexuals must act another way.

26

A Political Perspective
MARY E. HUNT

The lesbian question has not yet been integrated into most feminist analysis, either in this conference or in feminist theory in general. I invite those who are working on feminist analysis to look at how heterosexism functions in order to link it with racism, sexism, classism, and the other forms of oppression.

I was brought up as a good Roman Catholic girl in the 1960s; being lesbian was not my mother's dream for me. I am what I call a post-*Rubyfruit Jungle* lesbian feminist. *Rubyfruit Jungle* is a very entertaining, sometimes poignant novel by Rita Mae Brown that came out in the early 1970s. I remember going to a women's bookstore in Cambridge and asking for "Ruby Mae Fruit" by Rita Brown Jungle. I really did not want the clerk to know I was lesbian, and in my confusion I could not even remember the title. The book was written from a feminist perspective, and went around feminist circles like wildfire. It was a far cry from *The Well of Loneliness* by Radclyffe Hall, which greeted an earlier generation with the news that being lesbian meant being doomed to butch/femme roles and a tragic ending.

For many in my generation, coming of age after Simone de Beauvoir, Betty Friedan, and Kate Millet meant knowing that it is possible to love women as well as men. Coming of age after Stonewall, the beginnings of the gay liberation movement in New York City in 1969, when gay men fought back against police who raided their bar, meant coming of age at a time when in some places like Berkeley and Boston lesbians and gays could be proud instead of being closeted. *Rubyfruit Jungle* is now sold in airports and train stations. People are beginning to talk about and treat lesbian and gay questions in the public forum in a way not unlike what happened in the

1960s when "sexuality" became an acceptable topic for discussion and in the 1970s when women's concerns, particularly about abortion and child care, were brought to public attention.

Two basic themes are under discussion, namely, heterosexism and lesbianism. Definitions for words like these arise out of a specific context. Our context is that of a heterosexist, patriarchal society, namely, one in which male and heterosexual experiences are normative so that men's and straight people's experiences, values, and norms take precedence almost to the exclusion of women's and homosexuals'. Women have begun to understand and name patriarchy, but we are only beginning to realize the far-reaching implications of heterosexism. In fact, the word itself is new for many of us.

Heterosexism means discrimination and prejudice against same-sex relationships. It has the same dynamics as sexism or racism in that it is based on a dualistic notion, heterosexual/homosexual, with nothing in between. In that dualism one member is valued more highly than the other, i.e., heterosexuality is not only different from but is better than homosexuality; or, put another way, heterosexuality is rewarded and homosexuality is punished. It is safe to say that there is a normative character to heterosexual feelings, behavior, and experience in a patriarchal culture that discourages the expression of same-sex love and mitigates against taking it seriously. For example, I recall saying to my mother, "I love so and so," to which she replied, "No, Mary, you are going to *love* a man. You just *like* her." And I insisted, "No, I really love her." Now I know and can say that I really did, that it was probably a real love experience, not simply an adolescent crush nor a case of narcissism. But I did not know that then, or at least that information was not widely available.

Homophobia is akin to heterosexism in that it connotes a fear of homosexuality whether in oneself or in another. Homophobia is powerful in church and society where some people are too frightened to talk about and listen to the variety of ways people can love. Homophobia keeps many of us from learning about the unknown, from facing the unacceptable. Studies show that few people are exclusively heterosexual or exclusively homosexual by nature. Most people fall somewhere in between, in a middle range of bisexuality. The choices people make are conditioned by the society in which they live, which is why it is not surprising that most people are heterosexual. No one has been able to prove anything much more substantive than this. Whom a person loves remains one of the mysteries of the universe that not even careful feminist analysis can unravel. By our analysis and strategies, we can, however, change some cultural structures so that heterosexism will one day be as anachronistic as we wish sexism to become.

This is the goal I have in mind when I say that in a heterosexist patriarchal society it is healthy, good, and natural for all women to love women. But not all women must choose intimate companions who are women in order to be feminist, because love is a gift that comes in all different packages. Women need to take their relationships with women as radically seriously as they have been taught by this culture to take relationships with men. Then and only then will women be open to loving specific individual persons, whether female or male, for who they are in and of themselves. Then the way is open to relationships not based primarily on sexually based definitions but on the bonds of friendship of which humans are capable. But those who behave in this countercultural way risk being called outlaws. Feminist insight in all its countercultural splendor leads to an analysis of heterosexism as a socioeconomic and political structure that excludes lesbians and gay men just as effectively as sexist structures exclude women.

Why bother when we have enough to worry about as feminists? Because the results of heterosexism have meant that some women and men have never loved at all. Another consequence has been that many people who have loved have never been able to talk about it, have never been able to name the very special persons in their lives. As a result they have never been held accountable for whom and how they love. A third result of heterosexism has been that many female/male relationships have been misunderstood. Some people have married when they knew in their hearts that it was not for them, or, often more painfully, they discovered well into their married life that one or the other was after all not heterosexual. Pressures to conform and marry have been so strong that many have acted precipitously and lived to regret it. Dealing with heterosexism will not eliminate these problems, but it may reduce their incidence. A fourth result has been the continued devaluation and separation of women from one another. If in fact I do not have the *potential* to love a woman in a committed relationship, then it is hard to love all women as sisters. It is hard even to love myself as a woman, because women are the quintessential objects in a patriarchal, heterosexist society and therefore are not worthy of love. Women are labeled and separated once again when one is called lesbian, the other straight, and devalued and valued respectively. These consequences make it imperative that women seek to transform heterosexism along with sexism.

The definition of lesbian is mired in a patriarchal, heterosexist context as well. As such it is typically understood to mean a woman who relates sexually to other women and not to men. But this definition emerges from a male-centered logic by which all women are defined not only by their sexual status but by their relationships with men. The litany goes something like this: a married woman sleeps with a man, a divorced woman used to, a separated woman might sleep with a man again, a single woman would like to, a lesbian woman does not sleep with a man, and nuns are not supposed to talk about any of it. These are the patriarchal definitions given to all women. Differences are of degree and not of kind. All are defined in a relational, dependent way. They are totally inadequate definitions, clearly in need of revision, expansion, and justice. Hence, I try to redefine all women, beginning with the word lesbian since it is used about me, in an effort to move us all away from being patriarchal objects of whatever sort. By so doing I do not mean to homogenize away our differences, but to have us name them ourselves instead of having them named for us. At the same time, I stress our similarities in an effort to overcome the divide-and-conquer technique that has been used so effectively against us.

Three recent social movements have helped women to move toward a renewed understanding of lesbianism. There has been a sexual revolution in the 1960s. It was not completely positive for women, but at least it has freed us to talk publicly about sexuality. That is new in the past twenty years. There has been a women's movement, which has helped us to claim our values and dignity as women. We are now understood to be more than the sum of our sexual preference and marital status. We are complex, sensitive human beings capable of being and changing and evolving as women. There has been a lesbian/gay movement. It has brought to the attention of the media in recent years that homosexuals, both female and male, are not very different from others in society. They come in all sizes and shapes; they live in a wide variety of ways. It is harder to spot one than most people thought a decade ago.

These movements have been helpful in evolving a new definition of lesbian, which is still under discussion among lesbian feminists and which I personally affirm. No longer is a lesbian defined as one who does not sleep with men, nor even as one who sleeps with women. Rather, a lesbian is understood as a woman who, in a heterosexist patriarchal context, with all its weight to the contrary, takes her relationships with other women radically seriously. This means that she lives in nonexploitative, loving, committed, mutual relationships with women just as she has been taught to live with men. Her intimate companion may be a woman, but the burden of the definition does not rest on that information. This is not to say that whom she sleeps with is unimportant. Rather, it is to say that it is not of primary importance, especially because it is used to divide women from one another.

Some have asked if this means that all women must be lesbian-defined in order to be feminists, if it is a political rather than a relational definition, and especially what it means about loving men. The questions indicate serious consideration, and this is new for most women, of the insight that heterosexism is limiting and objectifying in all relationships. These questions are aimed, as is my definition, at struggling to eliminate the problem. I suggest a first step in a long, complicated, and as yet unexplored process. It is by no means all that is necessary, but it is a start. I suggest that powerful bonding, overcoming some divisions, will result when we acknowledge that loving women without patriarchally preconceived categories that amount to limits is important for all of us. This radical act does not imply that each woman will live with an intimate companion who is another woman; nor does it mean that women cannot love men as we have been taught. But it means that just as we say as feminists that what happens to one happens to all, so too are we trying to move toward a day when the word lesbian will not divide but unite us.

Further, the word lesbian has come to include an orientation toward community, a community of women striving to live beyond patriarchal structures. It is curious that in so many cities when people speak of "the women's community" they mean a group that is usually predominantly lesbian. It is interesting to note, however, that lesbians do not claim it as such but rather invite inclusivity. This is an effort to break down false barriers between and among women. When the ultimate patriarchal epithet, dyke, can no longer be hurled at any woman regardless of whom she loves, then more time can be spent refining the labels. Until then married, single, separated, divorced, heterosexual, and lesbian women, not to mention women in religious communities, are all prevented from being free.

Lesbianism frees women to love whom they will in what I call the deepest mystery of the universe. It is a happy experience for some of us to love women in committed, ongoing relationships as intimate companions. And for others who find the same degree of fulfillment with men it is also a happy experience. But it will be a happier experience for all of us when we can make those choices and live them out on their own merits without worrying about their being labeled and defined for us. Everyone experiences various types of friendship with men as well as with women, with children and adults, with people from other races and cultures, without being able to explain why and surely without having to defend them as real. This ought to be the goal when it comes to intimate companions as well, since all these relationships are part of the mysterious workings of love in the cosmos over which no one of us has ultimate control.

As women move from the invisibility and discrimination of heterosexism, we can develop what I call unlikely coalitions, basd on love and justice, that will help us to move beyond the differences of race and class, of age and physical differences, of sexual preference and the mysteries of love. Our history will be read as that of a movement that gave credit to the women who fought for child care, abortion rights, alimony, equal pay, and above all the right of all women and men to love.

27
Discussion*

MARY HUNT: In *Signs* [Summer 1980, vol. 5, no. 4] Adrienne Rich has an article on compulsory heterosexuality. I recommend it for an understanding of some of the issues under discussion.

A: I want to tell a brief story. I am the minister of a Unitarian church in Florida. When I applied for the position I was called for a week of interviews, which went very well. At the end of the week, one of the strongest women in the community, who was on the search committee, made an appointment to discuss a serious question, something that was really troubling her. She knew that I was a lesbian, she had firsthand knowledge from someone who *knew* (who knew more about me than I did myself). She asked, "Are you or are you not a lesbian." I replied, "I cannot answer that question." At the time my deepest relation was with a woman, but it was not a genital relation. I also said that I loved women and that politically I considered myself a lesbian, but she left feeling disturbed and the situation was never resolved.

When I first went to my present church, my male friend and I had agreed to stay apart for a year to establish our identities. But because of this incident, we changed our plans and got married. I am now in my fourth year in that church. Many single women, many wealthy women, have joined the church. There is a lot of fear among the men, just about my being a woman, and a rather powerful woman. The women come and tell me about their situation and ask me out. The lesbian women are afraid to be part of a service on lesbianism, and are even afraid to have me do a service on

---

*This discussion followed the presentation of the panel on lesbianism and homophobia. The comments of the various participants are indicated by letters of the alphabet; the panelists are identified by name.

255

this issue. As it is, they can be hidden and the men can overlook them. The people who are afraid of them can pretend that they are not there—they are invisible. There is a fear that if we talk about it, something bad will happen.

HUNT: To be lesbian or gay in Florida must be frightening, more so than in San Francisco or New York or Chicago, where there are larger gay communities.

Your response to the woman on the search committee was a good one. One could answer the question, "Is it a boy or a girl?" by asking, "Why do you want to know? So you can discriminate?" If you use this response, it does tend to bring people up short, and then it may be possible to begin another kind of conversation: What are you really asking? What are you asking about yourself? What do you want to know about me other than a label for which you will have your own content?

It is important to provide space—literally to provide physical space in the churches—for lesbians and gays so that they can begin to do the research that needs to be done with the help of people in pastoral positions. But if you get the kind of feedback you just described, it takes a very courageous minister to go ahead with a public forum.

LETHA SCANZONI: You also need space for parents of gays to discuss the question, because the parents tend to feel guilty. Pastors can help them by leading a discussion based on some of the new literature for parents of gays.

B: There is great pain in coming out to one's family—that is a universal experience of lesbians and gays. I hope our coming out in this generation will ease that pain for the next one.

C: I am worried about Mary Hunt's definition of lesbianism, taking relations with other women seriously. I take very seriously all the relations I have with other women; I love women more all the time, and they are important in my life. Isn't that definition hiding something? Doesn't it show that you don't want to assume your position? In our present experience, we have to talk about gays and lesbians. We hope a time will come when nobody will discuss those preferences. If we use your definition, I think it tends to blur things.

HUNT: My definition is strategic. The goal is that we will move toward a time when the person I love is simply the person I love, a time when that person's gender will not be an issue. We have to move strategically toward that goal in a patriarchal, heterosexual culture. It would be hard to say that in the U.S. and/or Latin America we are anywhere close to that. I am trying to work out not simply a concept, but a concept that is strategic, i.e., that helps us to move toward the goal we have in mind. That is a different way of approaching a definition, although I suspect that most definitions involve an implicit strategy as well. This definition is based on context, on hearing from people who are being named what content they give to the word used to define them.

According to a patriarchal heterosexist definition, a lesbian slicks back her hair, drives a truck, and chews gum. Of course I am exaggerating to make a point, but surely the definition is not complimentary and above all bears little resemblance to what most women about whom it is used would say about themselves. I suspect they would say something more akin to what I have said, and so perhaps I am raising the typical feminist question about how we distribute power, in this case the power to name. What would come from many lesbians, I think, is a definition that takes the sexual component seriously but does not give it primary importance. After all, it is not in the interests of lesbians to be divided from other women, but neither is it in the interests of other women to be divided from lesbians.

C: I think it is important that in your approach to the problem you make use of irony.

LYNN WILSON: Lesbians have been defined only in sexual terms and not in terms of the rest of their lives. This definition is asking people to look at lesbians as something other than primarily sexual beings.

D: When I lived in Wichita, a homosexual rights ordinance was passed by the city council. The man on the council with the swing vote was immediately put out of office. A coalition on the right forced a referendum. Their slogan was "Sin has no rights." For months the issue was debated in the Wichita papers, twenty letters a day. The fear and hate that were expressed still frighten me. I appeared on a panel, arguing for the ordinance from a biblical point of view, and in the next newsletter from the biggest evangelical church in town, they tore my speech apart sentence by sentence. What it came down to was that you do not love sinners, and the article ended with "She is unchristian" in capital letters!

I also want to mention a terrific resource: *Nice Jewish Girls,* edited by Evelyn Beck. It opens up the issue in the Jewish community and includes chapters by lesbian Jews of Color that explain the interstructuring of the various forms of oppression. Another resource is *This Bridge Called My Back,* an anthology that deals strongly with the lesbian issue among Women of Color.

E: When I came forward for ordination as a single woman who had been involved in feminist work for many years, lesbianism was a major issue that was never talked about. Someone said to one of my friends, "I'm anxious about E's life-style." "Well, she does jog, and sometimes I think her vegetarianism is a bit excessive," my friend replied. When I was going through the procedure I was turned down twice. I went to some women friends to talk it over and learned a wonderful response. When anyone asks whether I am a lesbian, I look them in the eye and say, "I usually do not talk about my sexual preference except with people who want to sleep with me. Would you like to sleep with me?" I've only used it twice, and it's wonderful!

F: What about committed lesbian or gay relationships? Aren't they just an imitation of heterosexual marriage?

SCANZONI: The reasons usually given for commitment in heterosexual relationships have to do with having children. I have discussed the ethics of commitment with lesbians and gay men, and many of those in ongoing relationships tell me that this is their ideal. The research that Alan Bell and Martin Weinberg did at Indiana University for the Kinsey Institute suggested that this was the goal of many homosexual persons—not in order to imitate heterosexual marriage, but for deeply felt psychological reasons. To be intimately known by one other person with whom you have a continuous relationship, with a shared past and a shared dream of a future—

this was the ideal. Others do not agree, and there were many whom Bell and Weinberg found to be perfectly healthy psychologically in what they called "open relationships." There are many life-styles, including "swinging single" gays. There is not one gay community, but many gay communities. Some couples live together for years, sharing a household like a heterosexual couple. Others have open relationships, others have swinging life-styles, some are celibate; some have problem relationships, just like straights. It is not a matter of imitation.

HUNT: Commitment is an ideal for many people. The discussion in the lesbian and gay community has just begun, and the studies are limited. Also, given the mores in our culture, more people would report their committed relationships than their one-night stands. The biggest division is between women's and men's experiences. The differences at this level of understanding are pronounced. The taboo on discussion has prevented most of the best and brightest from bringing their insights to bear on this question. The churches have been notoriously negligent in providing any supportive structures for people to talk values. Alternative communities are beginning to do this, and in the wider women's community, communities of accountability are developing in which we can deal with this question.

G: I am uneasy with the political definition. I don't want to cheapen another woman's choice by calling myself by exactly the same name.

HUNT: I understand that anxiety about a "cheapened" definition of lesbians. But it is important to realize that all definitions are political, i.e., that they arise from the *polis* or the context in which they are used. And it is important to realize that they are used to wield power. If we were in a situation of serious, up-against-the-wall repression of lesbians, then identifying with the definitions I am suggesting would not cheapen anyone. I am confident that many of my friends would be there with me. In calling for a whole new understanding of what lesbian means, I am arguing simply that the old definition is locked into a patriarchal heterosexist society. As we begin to change that context, we unlock the definition as well. It is a dialectical process: unlocking the definition will, I hope, change the context because we will feel freer to love whom we will. We will evaluate that love on the basis of its qualities of mutuality and faithfulness, not on the basis of the gender of the persons involved. This is the strategic reason to highlight the changing definition, but people will need time to consider it, understand it, and perhaps incorporate it into their working vocabulary.

H: Lesbians and nuns are two groups of women that have a women's culture. I would love to see them come closer together. When I had to teach a marriage course, I became much more aware of a very bad tradition of sexuality in Christianity, which leaves us in a dilemma. I look at 42nd Street in New York City, and that is a bad tradition too. The question of sexuality is being raised in a deeper sense than ever before.

I: Does Wicca have trouble with homosexuality? The Craft is based on the idea that sex is inherently sacred, good, to be valued. Everybody's sexuality is sacred. You are supposed to find out what yours is and live it out honestly for what it is, not to fit it into someone else's formula. Part of immanence is valuing things for themselves, valuing sexuality because it feels good, because it is a means of connecting deeply with another human being, with nature, with all sorts of things. Our connections in the Craft with nature are inherently sexual. Lesbianism and homosexuality raise the question of whether sexuality is valued for itself or because it is good for procreation. How much do we have to define it and control it before we can let ourselves do it?

In World War II, homosexuals were required to wear a pink triangle and had to go first to the death chambers, so I think it is very important to expand the definition. They were the first to go because they were invisible—hardly anyone knew about them.

J: I know there are many women in this group who have found that celibacy is also a way of liberation and a contribution to the transformation of society. There has been a backlash against celibacy, and it is not easy to speak about it. Free choice has a place.

K: I think it would be a mistake to compare lesbian culture and nun culture. We should not overlook that nun women's communities are not independent women's communities but are governed and controlled by boards that are patriarchal.

HUNT: Celibacy is not a sexual preference; rather, it is what one decides to do with one's sexuality. Celibacy in the Roman Catholic tradition is typically understood to imply heterosexual celibacy. But of course there is homosexual celibacy as well, although the weight of sexuality has so fallen on the side of heterosexuality in our culture that it is difficult for some people to imagine homosexual celibacy. Awareness of this choice is growing among the members of Catholic religious orders, however, especially among lesbian sisters.

L: I take issue with Mary Hunt. In political situations where people are asking about your preference in order to discriminate, I hope everyone will be lesbian as a political imperative. But that is separate from the relationship between sexuality and identity. A political definition is fine for the outer world, but we should not let it obscure the fact that sexual orientation is very important to identity. I know I was bisexual (AC/DC) and insisted for a time that I did not really want to define myself. The definition of myself as lesbian cost me in my family and in my life, and has also clarified certain things. It is a very complicated question. I think I am now lesbian. That has changed a certain focus in my life. Being lesbian is almost an epistemological position that goes beyond commitment. I don't know of any vision of sexuality, sexual community, and relationships that satisfies me. For me, it was a question of coming to terms with a part of myself of which I was most afraid. Most of us have the feeling that you are not born one way or the other—you are made. People are then uncomfortable to think that they could be unmade. That is part of where homophobia comes from. The other in yourself is terrifying, and it is very important to face it.

Part VII

Resources from Various Traditions

AS THE CONFERENCE confronted the interlocking web of oppressions, which seemed to expand and multiply in all-encompassing strands as the analyses proceeded, it was easy to feel overwhelmed, helpless, despairing. How to reclaim our personal power? How to help empower one another? Where to turn for resources? The questions sprang readily to mind, and we turned to a variety of traditions in search of ways to use the past to provide energy for an alternative future.

The panelists came bearing gifts from the religions of the ancient Near East, from the Bible, and from the Wicca tradition, which is reemerging today. All agreed on the importance of religion, the necessity for women to know and reclaim their history, the equally great need to subject our respective traditions to searching critique, the prime importance of finding ways to use our differences to empower rather than destroy one another. Within these common orientations, however, differences emerged around issues of monotheism and polytheism, immanence and transcendence, acceptance or rejection of the biblical traditions, reformist or radical approaches.

Mary K. Wakeman turns to the ancient, powerful mythic themes—the battle with the monster, the journey to the underworld, the sacred marriage—themes that have been used to oppress, but that also contain seeds of liberation. These themes are to be found not only in the literatures of Sumer, Babylon, and Egypt since the third millennium B.C.E., but also in the Bible and in the consciousness of modern people. Differing with those who see in biblical monotheism only a legitimation of patriarchy, hierarchy, and dualism, Wakeman offers a reading of biblical literature in terms of an evolution from kingship to peoplehood to personhood that affirms diversity and mutuality. In her view, monotheism leads to persons, persons lead to diversity and to a mutual empowerment that is necessarily pluralistic. She brings her analysis to bear on practical suggestions for empowering one another today.

Judith Ochshorn, out of her familiarity with the history and sacred texts of the ancient Near East, traces the relations of gender, power, and divinity as conceived by these cultures. Suggesting that much of the scholarship in this field has been biased by sexist and monotheistic assumptions, she finds liberating models in polytheism: these divinities are not locked into sex-stereotyped roles—there are warrior Goddesses and earth Gods; sexuality, female as well as male, is valued; while Goddesses are mothers, their activities are not limited to motherhood but extend over a wide range of public and private concerns. She finds in these cultures powerful models of women's engagement in the public activities of the community and an absence of deterrents to women's autonomy.

One of the issues that has put obstacles in the way of women bonding is whether the biblical traditions can be of use to feminists. Opinions have diverged sharply, from those who insist that retranslation and reinterpretation will purge the texts of patriarchal overtones, to those who would use the prophetic voices to critique and reject portions of scripture, to those who regard the Bible and biblical religions as irredeemably patriarchal. Elisabeth Schüssler Fiorenza would place herself with the prophetic voices, insisting that a feminist theology must be a theology of liberation that is critical of both the biblical and the Goddess traditions. Building on the often-quoted phrase from the "Redstockings Manifesto," "Until all women are free, no woman is free," she argues that if there are no free women, there can be no feminist theology or religion free from patriarchal ideology, whether Jewish, Christian, or Wicca. She points out that all these theologies have failed to deal sufficiently with the political-social-economic base of women's oppression, and therefore have failed to appeal to poor and Third World women. Images have an emotional resonance that analysis lacks, and are therefore a tremendous resource to energize a movement. In her desire to "reclaim the center" for women, Fiorenza rejects the biblical image of Eden (Eve, mother of all the living, safely ensconced in Paradise—an image she associates with the Moral Majority), and also the image of exodus (calling women to leave behind the oppression of patriarchal home and church). Rather, she puts forth the image of the *ekklēsia* or gathering of women, a community always in process, always in need of reformation, and therefore able to admit its complicity in racism and classism, to take responsibility for naming and changing these oppressive structures, but at the same time able to find support and cause for celebration in women of the past and present who have acted in the power of the life-giving spirit.

Starhawk, speaking out of her experience of the rebirth of the Wicca tradition (which she explains as the old religion of the Goddess, rooted in the pre-Christian, tribal traditions of the West), sketches her vision of the immanence of the Goddess. She sees immanence as powerful in building community, enabling people to recognize the sacred in one another and to devise participative, collaborative ways of acting. For her, immanence is a way of empowerment that moves her and her group into direct political action for social change. A gifted maker and facilitator of rituals, she describes some of her experiences in antinuclear protests, where rituals became a means of expressing shared meanings, generating energy, and unifying and giving courage to a group. She too finds contemporary meaning in the journey to the underworld: blockading a nuclear plant takes on the meaning of standing literally at the gates of death and risking the journey into imprisonment. The same small groups—covens, affinity groups—that find mutual empowerment through ritual provide a wide range of practical supports that make direct action possible: nonviolence training, visits to jailed members, care for jailed members' homes or families.

All four writers contribute suggestions for how women can use their differences to empower rather than destroy one another. Ochshorn urges the value of pluralism; Starhawk describes the transformative power of ritual and direct action based on small, supportive groups; Fiorenza warns women against either ignoring differences or excluding one another as not "the truly true feminists," rather than continuing to explore differences and share strengths. Wakeman sketches the most detailed description of feminist process. The personal disciplines required—honesty with self, openness, accurate and empathetic listening, tolerance for conflict, patience in negotiating differing needs—seem at least as demanding as the asceticism of the desert fathers!

Part VII concludes with the paper from the working group on feminist education, since it also deals with practical processes for moving toward mutuality in educational settings.

28
Affirming Diversity and Biblical Tradition
MARY K. WAKEMAN

Too often, biblical tradition has had the effect of inhibiting the ability to imagine a social order that affirms diversity. The idea of one God, one world, has been used to rationalize the exclusion of people with different opinions, or to justify the attempt to annihilate those who have other ideas about how to live. But ancient Near Eastern and biblical traditions can be reread to support women in envisioning a state of political, psychological, and spiritual diversity and to assist us in imagining the possibility of letting others be other without feeling threatened by it. An affirmation of diversity is rooted in biblical tradition, if that tradition is read as an account of cultural transformation—from kingship to peoplehood to personhood.

I speak as a White, Protestant, middle-class, middle-aged, educated American woman from New England. Affirming diversity involves acknowledging all these various aspects of oneself, while taking responsibility for sorting out the particular strengths and weaknesses of one's own history and tradition. What differentiates us is also what can make us valuable to one another. My fascination with the Bible and the ancient Near East is an attempt to get at the roots of power and authority for myself, both as a participant in the dominant Western culture and as an agent of social change. Like the biblical prophets, we can use the energy of the tradition for change when its power over us as tradition is broken. The way to let the past go is to use it for what it is good for: getting on.

I want to present a schema of three mythic themes (the Journey to the Underworld, the Battle Against the Monster, Sacred Marriage) in three time periods (the ancient Near East, the

Mary K. Wakeman

biblical period, and the present). All three themes refer to three dimensions of experience—spiritual, political, psychological—and there is a rough correspondence between the three time periods and the three forms of polity, i.e., kingship, peoplehood, personhood. The purpose of this analysis is to make the past lend its weight to, rather than dragging against, such developments in the present as the civil rights movement, the human potential movement, the current wave of feminism, the antinuclear movement, and other ways of reclaiming personal power and the ability to empower one another.

Three Myth and Ritual Themes in the Ancient Near Eastern City-State

As kingship developed in the city-states of ancient Sumer, it expressed the power in the idea of unity, as the authority of one ruler extended over an ever wider area, bringing communities of people who were not otherwise related to one another into economic and military alliance. Three themes appear in the myth and ritual context that supported the authority of the ancient city-state king.

The Journey to the Underworld: There is a story about how Dumuzi, the king and the spouse of the Goddess Inanna, dies in order to take her place in the underworld, where she has gone to challenge her older sister's power, only to fall victim to it. Thus human mortality is made meaningful, as it is necessary to the ongoing cycles of life that had been suspended in Inanna's absence. She is allowed to return to life on condition that someone take her place, and the king, as representative of the human, mortal community, does so.

The Battle Against the Monster of chaos: In the Babylonian version of the story, the God Marduk defeats Tiamat and her monstrous horde and creates the universe out of her parts. Tiamat, primordial watery being, mother of the Gods, represents the old, decentralized order. The order Marduk establishes is monistic and hierarchical, in which the labors of humanity are a service to the Gods as represented in the king.

The Sacred Marriage recreates harmony between human and divine worlds, between culture and nature, combining submission to and victory over nature, or death, in a way that deifies the king. As the king marries the Goddess, his power to impregnate, to make fruitful, the female divine power acknowledges symbolically the necessity of human labor to bring forth agricultural abundance from the earth.

By means of the ritual celebration of these themes during the New Year festival, the ancient Near Eastern city-state king was authorized by the Gods to command the people to do his will. He had power. The people were essentially his slaves in service to the Gods. These themes characterize male puberty rites of passage, to assist with the tasks appropriate to adolescence: facing sex and death. By means of rites that effect a death to the old and a second birth into a new state of consciousness, rites that celebrate heroic self-assertion over old dependencies (the ability to carry out conscious intention in spite of unconscious, involuntary impulses), a boy is transformed into a man. He can safely risk access to women in confidence that their power will not overwhelm his, as his mother's had done.

It is likely that the degree to which the king was free to act on his own initiative fluctuated greatly, but there is no question that these rites of passage give men in traditional societies access to spiritual power, in varying degrees according to individual temperament. Reference to these initiation themes in the periodic renewal of the king's power argues for their having lost their mooring in the religious life of the people as life-crisis rites. Appearing in the calendrical rites of societal renewal at the turn of the year, the rites served to set the king apart from ordinary people, draining off spiritual power from them to make the king their center. As Jackie Di Salvo explains ("Class, Gender, and Religion"), the power of spirit was substituted for the worship of authority.

At the same time, the rites may have retained their spiritual effectiveness for the king as an individual. To make the king's role humanly viable, the rites had a twofold task. On one hand, they had to provide periodic reminders that the king was an ordinary person who experienced helplessness, who suffered as the target of people's resentment when his efforts to alleviate the suffering of his people through providing order inevitably failed. This was effected through the ritual expression of humiliation, as the king, with the help of a priest, was divested of all his royal insignia (robe, crown, scepter), made confession of his innocence, and was slapped in the face. On the other hand, lest he be overwhelmed with the responsibility he had to take, not only for social injustices but also for natural disasters over which he had no control, the rites provided divine sanction, as the support of the Gods was ritually enacted in a procession of the priesthoods of the various temples. With the king at their head, they proceeded out of the gate of the city into the surrounding countryside and eventually returned, a sign that the king's ability to maintain order in the midst of chaos was given by the Gods and could be trusted. It was the heroic valor displayed in this symbolic battle to which the Goddess responded. In becoming her spouse, he who had been the scapegoat of the people received superhuman status. Sacred marriage celebrated the human powers of initiative and justified the exercise of managerial power over a society of workers.[1]

The Biblical Period

Israel began when the peasantry of various Canaanite states succeeded in supporting one another to throw off the power of kings, who were exploiting them to support their interstate wars. For example, Judges 4 and 5 recount a battle in which the peasants unite to overcome the kings of Megiddo and Taanach. Israel's origins as a peasant revolt, bonding across city-state lines in covenant relation to one God whose kingship liberated them from the city kings (Joshua 24), provided a basis for a pluralistic conception of power, where the plurality of the people substituted for the plurality of the Gods in polytheistic society.[2] The gradual amalgamation of power in the city-states of ancient Sumer was reflected in the formation of a pantheon of Gods and Goddesses. These had originally expressed the forces of nature as they were experienced by diverse population groups. As those groups were brought together under one rule, relations among the Gods came increasingly to express power relations within the human community. The people themselves lost power to the rulers, but there was preserved in the "assembly of the Gods" an intuition of the power they might yet exercise. Once people found that together they could throw off the domination of rulers, the notion of unity needed projection onto the divine realm as a binding force. The fact of Israel's existence was proof of God's existence. The concepts of God and People were reciprocal. In ancient Israel, no human was *by nature* authorized, but authority was subject to whether the people accepted it or not, as contrasted with the city-state ideology of slavery. "Man is created out of the blood of the rebel god to serve the gods," says the Babylonian creation story, in support of the idea that the king is authorized by the Gods. In serving him, the people are fulfilling their destiny. In ancient Israel, to say that a leader was chosen by God was to say that people recognized power in him and were therefore willing to follow him.

Having begun as a liberation movement, Israel was able to maintain its existence for two hundred years without a king. But with the conquest of Jerusalem and the establishment of a temple and palace there, it became a state much like the other states, until it was engulfed by the Assyrian and Babylonian empires. The prophets, however, were able to use the tradition of liberation to construct a new identity for Israel as a people when they had lost land, king, and temple.

There are two ways to view the nature of political power. One is monistic: people are dependent on the government; the other is pluralistic: the government is dependent on the people. The achievement of the biblical writers, as they reflected on their history, was the recognition that people give their rulers power. The contrast between state and nation—the institution of kingship on one hand and the biblical discovery of peoplehood on the other—has to do with the location of power and authority. (Power is the ability to realize intentions; authority is the right to command.) In both cases the ancient records were kept by the ruling class; the religious ideas preserved in these records served to legitimate the authority of the rulers or leaders. The unity of God, meaningful in the ritual support it gave the kings in Jerusalem (where God had put his name), began to take on new implications. Israel was boldly redefined as dependent not on its king or priests or any other known form of political organization, but solely on the *Word* from a God whose power was universal: the biblical prophets' interpretation of events saw the reality of Babylon's expansion through to its conclusion in Israel's destruction without being seduced by Babylon's power.

The Old Testament is largely the work of the so-called Former and Latter prophets (the Deuteronomic history, Joshua through 2 Kings, the books bearing the prophets' names) working in exile in Babylon to save Israel. They put together bits and pieces of the old Israelite state ideology and the religious ideas that had supported the power of the Israelite king (some of them related to the three mythic themes), along with the grand idea of God's kingship that had supported the formation of the original federation. Once the prophets had let go of the interpretive frameworks of kingship and covenant (they simply were not adequate to the realities of international empire-building that they experienced), they had pieces that they could put together in new ways to forge a new framework to accommodate what was actually happening. The prophets' job was to face the loss of Israel as an independent state and to redefine Israel as a people with a special role to play among the nations under God's universal governance.

Amos picks up on the victorious warrior theme, but in such a way as to turn inside out the assumption that the political viability of Israel is the measure of God's power. "The day of the Lord . . . is darkness, and not light [Amos 5:18]" for the rulers who get rich at the expense of the poor. "You only have I known [Amos 3:2]" affirms the special privilege of a people who bear witness against themselves (Josh. 24:22) rather than relying on fate (heaven and earth) or natural disaster to judge them. The privilege is the possibility, held out by this view, of making sense of historical experience as a way to keep from being overwhelmed by it.

Through the inverted image of Sacred Marriage, where it is God who is husband to the people, Hosea adroitly differentiates Israel from Canaan, reinterprets the covenant relation so as to define God's power as relatively independent of Israel's, and at the same time, in himself as faithful husband, suggests a model for the new leadership.

The image of the nations coming up to Zion to receive Torah from Israel as the priestly nation (Isa. 2, Mic. 4) is an international extension of the original covenant federation model. As that covenant had been modified to accommodate kingship, so the "everlasting covenant, my steadfast, sure love for David" is extended (Isa. 55:3–5) to give Israel the preposterous role of royal commander among the nations!

The theme with the most promise, because it is both plausible and powerful as a metaphor for the people of Israel, is the underworld journey. Jeremiah picks up the language from the psalms that had originally expressed this dimension of the king's role (ensnared in a pit, led like a lamb to slaughter, wounded and in pain, mocked and despised, confessing his innocence and pleading for vengeance on his enemies as the powers of evil). Its application to Jeremiah's situation dislocates kingship from the house of David, and prophecy from its context in covenant. What remains is God's universal rule, and the figure of his spokesman, not as faithful husband, priest, or warrior, but as the mediator whose responsibility for his people enables his suffering for them to be redemptive. This is the figure that is developed as the "suffering servant" in 2 Isaiah, to make a pair with King Cyrus of Persia, the victorious warrior anointed by God to shepherd the nations (Isa. 44:28).

The one who has power is God, who is realizing intentions in time. The knowledge of those intentions belongs to the spokes*men*, the word-makers, those who speak in public to interpret what is happening so as to create a history for people to identify with. What it means to be a people is to share a history: to maintain identity across change, in time. (I suggest that there is a correlation among the ideas of monotheism, nationalism, history, and time.) It is the people who know this history who have authority, the educated elite, and they are male, because authority is male, as a legacy from the institution of Sacred Marriage. (Remember that the king, as male representative of the relatively puny human community, gained authority through marriage to the more powerful divine realm, which was, again for historical reasons, female.)

Monotheism expresses fascination with the possibilities of power conceived hierarchically, particularly of peoples having power over one another as this was happening in the ancient Near East in the first millennium B.C.E. Power itself, measured by the increase in numbers of people coming under one rule, was what was real, and what was worshiped. The will to power was projected into the divine realm. Relation to it is still made through historical enactments in which can be recognized idolatrous forms of the kingship themes. Sacred Marriage justifies sexual hierarchy. As the king becomes God, the people become his bride (Hosea). Ephesians 5:22–23 instructs, "Wives, be subject to your husbands, as to the Lord. For the husband is the head of the wife as Christ is the head of the church, his body, and is himself its Savior." The Battle justifies historical war between nations, as the forces of chaos are equated with historical rivals who fight over access to resources, the right to control one another, or over competing ideologies. The Underworld Journey justifies ego-centered consciousness. It represents the developmental ordeal that results in alienation, in breaking the sense of connection with nature, other people, and repressed parts of oneself. These are the idolatrous forms that we are familiar with today.

But there has continued to be a liberating element in the

biblical tradition of a God who delivers from bondage. The liberating element in kingship was the establishment of order in chaos. (The slave state was an emergency strategy to reduce the suffering brought on by the population explosion that resulted from dependency on agriculture in the great river valleys.)[3] The liberating element in peoplehood, community bonding across kinship lines on the basis of a shared history, was the possibility of identity that transcended the family, clan, and tribal loyalties of ordinary people. The one God says that anyone who has transcended clan loyalties can speak, appear in public, give the community a sense of direction, and be a truth-teller about the community's actual experience, so as to keep tradition and experience from slipping apart.

The achievement of centralized powers of organization of society and self was worshiped, as were all tools before they became merely useful. The singularity of God in the Bible had its precedent in the singularity of the king as a unifying idea in the states of the ancient Near East (particularly ancient Sumer). The idea of that single God gave identity to Israel in its formation. As Israel ceased to exist as a state, the idea of God was universalized so as to preserve Israel's identity as a people, although they had no power. Projecting the will to power into the divine realm made it possible to appropriate power personally in the form of ego-centered consciousness that seems to be a necessary stage in the developmental process. Monotheism leads to persons. But the problem of the singleness of God is that it seems to imply a hierarchical order where some people have power over others. Once everyone has power, structures that give some people power over others can be seen to shut off access to essential revelation. If today people could trust the sense of connection our heightened awareness of global crisis brings with it, we could take the same delight in discovering how we are different and what promise of solutions this offers, as we now do in finding things we have in common. Affirming diversity must mean recognizing God in one another. Mutual empowerment is necessarily pluralistic: heterarchical or many-centered. The overarching vision is unitary, but as elusive as the elephant we blindly try to describe to one another.

The Present: Political and Religious Forms for Mutual Empowerment

The sense of being a person rests on what monotheism has achieved. Ego boundaries allow one to be aware, to sense one's connection with others, and at the same time to maintain partiality.[4] For historical reasons (some of which have been sketched here), personhood was defined as male, but all have inherited it. Everyone is a king in the sense that all are both free to act and also responsible. Judith Ochshorn's analysis is helpful here in reminding us that power, as it was developing in the ancient Near East, was not gender-specific.[5] Except for the king's role, men and women of the upper classes engaged equally in managing affairs of state. Now all have power as centers of initiative.

A reinterpretation of the kingship themes expresses what it means to be a person. The Battle is a metaphor for impassioned caring, an expression of the partiality (uniqueness) of persons that balances the sense of relatedness; it is because the personal is partial that it is valuable. The Underworld Journey has to do with the transition from ego-centered personality (the heroic warrior mentality, appropriate to adolescence, that is unaware of its own partiality, that sees things in terms of black and white, us and them, that assumes a norm and asserts, "I'm it") to recognizing one's own partiality, recognizing the fact that one's self is participatory in character rather than self-made, and submitting to the sense of connection that orients people in deciding how to use their resources. The Marriage, finally, is the integration of partiality and the sense of connection in personal wholeness, the psychological autonomy that enables individuals to act effectively in light of the whole.

Politics. It is hard to separate the political and the religious implications because politics is becoming, once again, religious. Who are "the public"? Each person is a whole state, if not an empire. What mode of government could do justice to the variety of human concerns? How can people institute politically the awareness that human life is embedded in the life of the planet? The diversity of structures of interpretation among human beings (ways to think and experience the world) goes so deep as to affirm that there are many Gods present, many beliefs on which life depends.

The experience of personhood is different from ego-centered consciousness in its awareness of otherness, its sense of the reality and value of others, and of human interdependence. Differences in the way people feel about things is an important part of reality. As sexuality is protected (as "a wildlife preserve"[6]) by relegating it to the private realm, people hold one another responsible publicly for levels of self-revelation that used to be kept private or perhaps even unconscious. Just as ancient Israel was advised by the prophets to look at what was happening on the international scene, so the only way to know God/Reality today is to listen to one another and to other forms of life in the world. The biblical writers were struggling to accommodate history: changes in time as a continuous medium. We must now find ways to take into our consciousness that others—whose histories and therefore consciousness ("The mind is by nature historical," says Hannah Arendt) are very different from ours—are equally real and legitimate. "Our equality lies," says James Ogilvy, "not in our univeral inclusion in one family (the universal brotherhood founded in the childish faith in the One Father) but in our universal marginality. Relative to some others we are each the other."[7]

Maybe "political" and "religious" can be separated by focusing on a description of feminist process as a way to raise the questions about what is required for people to be able to work together, and then see what kinds of rituals might foster the qualities needed. Ynestra King, in a recent flyer passed out by the War Resisters League, says: "Feminist process, which grows out of our politics, demands (1) participation by everyone in meetings or actions, (2) concern with the experience of each woman in the group, (3) rotation of leadership and public roles, (4) adherence to consensus decision-making."

What do each of these demands require of us? (1) Each person contributes necessary information about reality, but only if there are ears willing to hear. "Listening itself is a revolutionary activity"[8] as, in Nelle Morton's phrase, we "hear one another into speech." What was not there appears, as we are ready to see it. "Taking issue" as a mode of discourse assumes that we share the same assumptions and can help one another make our thoughts clear and distinct by picking them apart (using logic as a tool to build "solid" arguments), whereas—given my conviction that our thought-worlds are fundamentally different in structure—what helps me think is an open ear. (2) In addition to what I think, you will need to know what has happened to me, but in order for me to be able to tell you the truth about that, I may need to face some fears I have about myself. With (1) and (2), you experience my partiality. (3) Leadership is a role anyone can play. Essentially, it involves gathering the best thinking of members of the group, thinking about the group as a whole, and suggesting policy for the group. It is good for each person to learn the role, and it is good for the group, because each person brings something different to it. Its purpose is undermined by people who assume that the leader is different in kind (a God) rather than "one from among your brethren [Deut. 17:5]" out of a desire to be taken care of. The notion of leading assumes a sense of connection. (4) Whereas authority is given to personal experience, power inheres in the *group process* through which intentions are realized. A fair tolerance for conflict and willingness to suspend the urge to resolve it too soon is required of everyone. Accepting real difference allows the possibility of making sense of and for one another: the power of persons is interdependent. Working groups must be small enough so that it is possible to arrive at consensus about what makes sense through sensitivity to one another's legitimate concerns. If we see ourselves as citizens of the world, we can accept organization in nations, cities, neighborhoods, families, and what Mary Hunt calls "unlikely coalitions" as useful levels, each appropriate to a particular kind of relationship (coalition for specific issues, family for emotional support, neighborhood for experiencing God in persons, city for "appearing in public,"[9] nations for cooperative management of resources, etc.), keeping clear our sense of direction in relation to the planet as a whole.

Religion. To work together, women need to be able to hear, to tell the truth, to think well about people whose concerns are different from our own, to acknowledge and tolerate conflict within and among ourselves, to face our fears and embrace them as useful directives of attention, to delight in our differences as revelation. The rituals that foster these qualities of personhood are perhaps more appropriate to the tasks of middle age: rituals that enable self-acceptance, the opening of closed doors on our own anger and violent propensities; rituals that encourage us to acknowledge our genuine motivations rather than judging them; and valuing the resources we have so that we may dispose them wisely with a sense that time is finite, because that sense gives us power to act.

Looking at these now in relation to the three themes, self-acceptance is a backward journey into the underworld to reappropriate the spiritual energy tied up in repressed anger. We discover there, along with our own capacity for evil, a sense of connection with all the evils in the world and the people who perpetrate them. Having faced this worst fear of finding that the enemy is ourselves, perhaps we can better tolerate fear for what it is—a feeling useful for directing our attention to a hurt that needs healing. Discovering what one is really willing to "go to battle" for is often in itself an experience of embattlement, of being torn between conflicting issues (what are the priorities of a Black, working, lesbian mother?). Tolerance for conflict begins at home, and we need ritual ways to help one another with it.

Physical pain is practically unsharable. Emotional pain is all too sharable, so historically we have found ways to insulate ourselves from one another's suffering. But psychological separateness brings with it the possibility of opening up to one another the emotional component of our partial experience as the means of becoming able to see, of adding to our own experience of "the world," of what it is to be human, of God. Women need regular, ritual ways to assist one another in clearing ourselves of emotional overload so that we can tell the truth, and hear it when it is told to us. Not every encounter with another human being necessarily gives us a glimpse of God, although potentially it could. Sometimes we are telling the truth, sometimes we are wallowing around in a bunch of garbage—paranoia, victim patterns, helplessness. There needs to be a support group of our "own kind" where we can go and dump our garbage without hurting anybody, and in that process, come to see the truth. There need to be mixed-group meetings where it is possible to speak, and to hear, the diversity of the truth without jumping to premature conclusions.[10] The saving word is what we appear in public with, as we tell the truth about our experience, share our histories, and show how we feel so as to regain our mutual sense of direction. We have the only power there is, personal power. We can choose to abdicate it, by asking "What can *I* do?" or we can exercise it in action that issues from a truly sacred inner marriage when we reorient ourselves in light of what we know and direct what resources we have toward ends we care about, in awareness that impassioned caring is a precious resource that must be nurtured in ourselves and in all others.

Reclaiming Our Past
JUDITH OCHSHORN

The reemergence of feminism in the 1960s stimulated a far-ranging critique of patriarchal attitudes and institutions. Among them were those aspects of Judaism and Christianity that seemed to exclude and demean women, or to justify the treatment of them as inferior to men, or to portray God as masculine. Generally, the feminist critique has emphasized the authority of female experience over some of the androcentric stories that continue to be told as sacred,[1] but its content has varied widely. What unites the divergent positions is the conviction that religion is basic to culture and exercises an enormous influence, whether as institution or as expression of personal belief.

In the West, an overriding concern with justice, wisdom, and compassion has been conceptualized by both Jews and Christians, in different ways, as the province of God (although women and men frequently have had different access to that province). Since feminism springs from precisely such concerns, it is no accident that many feminist theologians who articulate female experience and consciousness (as distinct from male-biased perceptions) are also activists. In one way or another, they seek to engage women's consciousness in the creation of a future that is more just, wisely ordered and compassionate than the present—one that is nonexploitative, nonracist, and nonsexist, and that honors diversity, pluralism, and the full personhood of women and men.[2]

Overcoming the Burden of Women's Socialization

While these are goals that many feminists might share, the problem for women is how to overcome the burden of our

Judith Ochshorn

historical experience and the effects of our socialization, both of which have been deeply internalized by most of us. To use Jean Paul Sartre's phrase, we need to achieve an existential leap out of the present, but how is this to be done? There are two difficulties involved. The first is that the ideology we have internalized is often confusing, indeed in conflict with our life experiences. For example, women as a sex have long suffered from the onus of inferiority and incompetence in the public sphere under custom and law. However, our long experience as economic producers who also function competently in a variety of other ways seems at odds with our alleged inferiority. The second difficulty is that every culture has its own rewards and punishments for conformity to and deviance from prescribed behavior; these rewards and punishments are substantial, and they tend to inhibit most the less-powerful groups, among them women. Therefore, although women have ample motivation to advocate change, in order to move ahead we must first devise strategies to rid ourselves of our negative self-images. Then we will be able to translate the ethical insights that often flow from the experiences of marginality and oppression into shared social goals. We must also reassess what is judged as moral. Since our religious legacy helps to formulate even as it reflects, legitimizes, and promotes ethical values in society, it is in this area that it particularly invites our scrutiny.

Among the many salient factors in female socialization is a widespread lack of knowledge about women's own history—in itself a potent instrument of oppression—and, until recently, a lack of alternative models to what has been defined for us as our history. Along with the ideology of inferiority and incompetence, many of us have been powerfully socialized to intellectual passivity, or excessive deference to traditional, "expert" opinions about the content and meaning of our history, which then can be made to illustrate and vindicate current definitions of what is normal and ethical for women. Deference to the "experts" is often coupled with a disinclination on the part of many women for autonomous identification of our own priorities and for active attempts to realize them in our personal and public lives.

Thus, as a first step, it seems critical that women recover and understand their past—not only, as George Santayana remarked, because those who fail to learn from the past are doomed to relive it, but also because such knowledge might effectively counter female socialization and provide a means of empowerment. If women themselves choose what in their religious traditions is important to appropriate as truly liberating and what deserves rejection as continuing to oppress, if they define for themselves what accords with female experience, such action could initiate a long step toward autonomy; it would probably prove redemptive in confirming women's strengths, help to establish a new measure of morality, and offer possible models for a more humanely structured world.

An Alternative Model: Gender, Power and Divinity in the Religions of the Ancient Near East

One alternative model may be found in the visions of the divine and the accompanying cultic practices of polytheistic religions that flourished throughout the ancient Near East from the third through the first millennium B.C.E. In order to appreciate the significance for women of these models, we must consider them with an open mind as possible parts of our religious legacy, and lay to one side as at least suspect many of the expert assessments of them. Obviously, historical investigations are colored by what researchers expect to find, and work on the ancient Near East is no exception. Many of the accounts of the archaeological discoveries of these cultures in the last century or so have been interpreted by scholars through a bias in favor of monotheism. Consequently, the religious beliefs and sacred rites of that time and place are often trivialized, treated not in their own right or as examples of what is humanly possible, but as important primarily for the light they shed on the milieu out of which Judaism and Christianity evolved.

While no one today would characterize these ancient civilizations as primitive, there is a term, mythopoetic, often applied to their thought processes, which sets their apprehension of reality apart from (or perhaps as more innocent and superstitious than) the empirical, rational tradition that presumably has typified Western thought since the time of the Greeks. Of course, there is much that is mythic and poetic in the Bible, and much that is less than empirical and rational in some of our Western literature (e.g., in polemics on the nature of women in the writings of Thomas Aquinas, Martin Luther, John Milton, Sigmund Freud, and a host of others). Moreover, it is hard to see in what sense those polytheistic cultures were nonempirical or nonrational, since they invented language; built pyramids (historians still do not know how); traded extensively; made use of navigation and astronomy; developed irrigation systems; authored fairly elaborate codes of civil statutes; produced impressive theologies, art, and poetry; and are even believed to have lived in peace with one another for a long period prior to the third millennium B.C.E..

Furthermore, many of the analyses of ancient Near Eastern polytheism are flawed by projections of more modern sexual stereotypes onto these earlier cultures. The Jungians and neo-Jungians seem to assume that traits of femininity and masculinity have always existed in the psyche as nearly polar opposites exemplified in the feminine and masculine archetypes. Some scholars, by an equally fanciful assumption, conflate all the ancient female divinities into fertility or mother Goddesses, regardless of how their own cultures viewed them. Perhaps most misleading in the appraisals of polytheistic religions are the beliefs that gender and power have been inextricably linked in human history, or that history has always exhibited sexual hierachies of superordination and subordination, or that the advent of monotheism signified tremendous ethical progress for humanity.

However, if we try to look at the surviving sacred texts of polytheism through the eyes of those who wrote them and believed in their efficacy, if we discard the prejudice that has informed some of the commentaries about them, and use gender as a basic category of analysis, quite a different picture emerges.[3]

To an extent that seems incredible today, the continuity of established patterns in nature and the social order was believed to depend on the active and constant intervention of the divine, which determined the course of human events from the most mundane and personal to the largest communal undertakings. The polytheistic conception of the divine rested on a belief in the existence of many Goddesses and Gods, most of whom were endowed with a plurality of attributes. While differences between the sexes were recognized (i.e., the requirements for reproduction were known), these differences were considered secondary to the satisfaction of individual and community needs and the guarantee of survival, stability, and prosperity to the community of worshipers.

Although Goddesses and Gods were portrayed as animating all nature, no particular part of nature was seen as the exclusive residence of female or male divinities; no connection was drawn between human biology and nature. There were both Goddesses and Gods of the earth, the sun, and the moon, at times within the same divine pantheons. Since deities of both sexes were described as benign, malevolent, or capricious in their actions toward humanity, the divine in nature was sometimes revered as the source of an adequate food supply, sometimes feared in those regions like Sumer where the weather could be violent and unpredictable, but neither reverence nor fear was predicated on the gender of the divine.

If the divine was believed to be immanent in nature, it was also portrayed as transcendent. Despite the anthropomorphic characterization of divinities, their lives and activities transpired on a grander, more powerful and qualitatively different scale than that of humans, but their attributes were not clustered along sexual lines. Rather they were seen as functioning in ways indispensable to the survival of the human community; Goddesses and Gods shared in rough equivalence the powers of wisdom, justice, social order, fertility, victory in war, and the like. Indeed, divine power was so little contingent on gender that the sex of some deities changed as their worship spread from place to place. The Canaanite Goddess Anath and the Mesopotamian Goddess Ishtar were also worshiped under a male guise, and a number of major Egyptian and Mesopotamian deities were sometimes described as bisexual, such as the Gods Osiris and Nanna.

When a moral consensus developed, at least as early as the third millennium B.C.E. in Egypt (as evidenced in the wisdom literature), and at least by the second millennium B.C.E. in Mesopotamia (as attested by hymns and prayers addressed to deities for relief from personal affliction), both Goddesses and Gods were viewed as dispensers of judgment, compassion, and mercy in response to the solicitations and behavior of their worshipers. Furthermore, the Egyptian texts that delineated the sacred rites performed for the dead and the Mesopotamian exorcism literature that described the rituals employed to combat sickness indicate that both Goddesses and Gods were appealed to, evil spirits of both sexes were seen as the source of disease and expelled, and both women and men were the beneficiaries of such rites. These rites continued in use in virtually unchanged form for thousands of years.

Polytheistic attitudes toward Goddesses in their sexual/reproductive aspects perhaps stand in sharpest contrast to subsequent images of the female in dichotomized, purely sexual terms—as carnal seductress or asexual, spiritualized madonna—that were to dominate Western thought and literature. Produced by an educated, elite minority that appears to have been obsessed both with a fear of female sexuality and with anxiety about passing on property to legitimate heirs, these images present a view of women that is simplistic and biologically reductionist. These notions bore scant relation to the lives of most people, and they used different standards for women than for men. The nature of women came to be identified with their sexuality and reproductive capacity; motherhood, simultaneously idealized and used pragmatically, came to be equated with feminine aspirations; a mind-body split was accepted as part of a natural hierarchy, with the male sex associated with the superior, rational elements, and the female sex with the inferior, material elements; and virtue in women came to consist of chastity, either in virginity or monogamy. Wife, mother, virgin, widow—these were the acceptable female roles, all prescribed by men.

Polytheistic religions did not usually confuse Goddesses with real women, but the qualities of the former sometimes spilled over into attitudes toward the proper roles of the latter. In the nonmonogamous families of the divine, typified by shifting affections and incest, in which the concept of illegitimacy was alien, the active sexuality of both Goddesses and Gods was valued. Whether the creation of the universe was accomplished by the parthenogenetic activity of a female or male deity, that initial act was followed by the sexual unions of Goddesses and Gods, which accounted for the further creation, organization, and maintenance of nature and society. Both the feminine and masculine were believed to be indispensable, and no artificial dichotomy was established between the rational and material aspects of existence.

Significant Aspects of Ancient Polytheism for Modern Feminists

There were several significant consequences of these views. The first was the absence of pejorative attitudes toward divine sexuality in general and female sexuality and reproduction in particular; no stigma of shame, sin, uncleanness, or ritual impurity was attached to women's sexual functions. On the contrary, two thousand years of Sumerian poetry celebrated the beneficent results of divine female sexuality in the Sacred Marriage, in which the commanding roles and active sexuality of the Goddesses Inanna and Ishtar, in their "intercourse" with kings, resulted in the fertility of the land rather than in divine offspring; in the stability of the throne, or social order, through the divine legitimation of the king's fitness to rule; and in the survival and success of the human community through the divine promise of victory in battle.

The second consequence was that divine motherhood was revered when it benefited the human community. When the Goddess Isis (whose name originally meant "the throne") conceived and bore her only child Horus, he symbolized the peaceful union of Upper and Lower Egypt in the figure of the pharaoh, who was seen as the God incarnate at his assumption of the throne. In most instances, however, the great ancient mother-Goddesses had few but very important offspring. The Sumerian Nammu, for example, bore only An and Ki, but they were the sky and earth. Even Goddesses like the Canaanite Asherah, who personified the reproductive principle itself after she mothered seventy deities, was actively involved in Baal's struggle with El for the kingship of the Gods, and competed sexually with the Goddess Anath for the affection of Baal. In other words, polytheistic religions did not exalt motherhood as the greatest achievement of all Goddesses, or limit the appropriate field of their action only to maternity, or preclude their active intervention in the most critical concerns of society at the same time that they were also mothers.

A third consequence was the occasional importance of same-sex bonding in pursuit of important social goals. At times Goddesses and Gods functioned autonomously, such as Inanna and Rā; at times, in conjunction with divinities of the other sex, such as Isis and Thoth, Baal and Anath; at times, with divinities of the same sex. In some of the same-sex bondings the relationships were varied but intense and productive for humanity: in the mentor relationship of Thoth and Osiris, in the sibling relationship of Isis and Nephthys, and in the mother-daughter bonding of Demeter and Koré. These various affiliations indicate that there was no gender-specific preference for the primary support and reinforcement of indispensable divine activity; it is one of the few places where female affiliation is approved without ambiguity.

The foregoing might be merely interesting were it not that these androgynous attitudes toward the divine were reflected in the cults of societies that were religion-centered, in which religion was frequently the matrix of culture and was interwoven with the political and economic life of the community. While some sacred rites were celebrated only by women, others only by men, most often persons of both sexes participated as initiates, celebrants, and priests, even at the highest echelons of the priesthood, which entailed secular retinues, land, and power. For instance, during the Old Babylonian period, the records from Mari in the north and Sippar in the south attest the heavy involvement of temple personnel in public affairs, in both the economy and politics, at a time when women, like men, served the temples as priests, oracles, diviners, ecstatics, scribes, judges, witnesses of legal documents, buyers and sellers of land and houses, and the like.

In addition, either the central rituals of purification were required of both sexes, or neither sex was viewed as particularly impure. Since celibacy was sometimes required of both women and men, sexuality itself rather than female sexuality was viewed as contaminating. By the second millennium B.C.E., Akkadian wisdom literature neutrally referred to the *Ishtaritu*, or holy women of Ishtar, as poor choices for wives because they were vowed to a God and therefore were nonmonogamous (suggesting that men did marry them).[4] By the first millennium, the sexual aspects of the divine came to be celebrated by sacred prostitutes of both sexes (though the later label of them as prostitutes may be erroneous in light of their roles in cult).

In short, except for those ritual proscriptions placed on women due to their biology—at times of menstruation, miscarriage and childbirth—which surfaced in the second millennium among the Hittites, Canaanites, and Assyrians, for most of that three-thousand-year period, across cultures where Goddesses and Gods were worshiped, both women and men played prominent and public roles in cult. Toward the end of the second millennium, when some cultures such as Assyria became more male-dominant, and women apparently began to be excluded from their many roles in Assyrian temples except as priestesses, women came to dominate widespread popular cults. Thus, they dominated the cult of the dying young God of vegetation, and there is a long history of easy coexistence of official and popular religion. And in the mystery cults that sprang up around the Mediterranean in the first millennium—the Isaic, Dionysian, and Eleusinian—while each centered around the worship of a female or male deity, both priests and priestesses officiated over the sacred rites engaged in by women and men of every class. Indeed, the popularity of these mystery cults may yet be correlated, at least in part, with the changing status of women in some of the official religions, and the practices of mystery cults may be found to conform closely to the long, androgynous tradition in the ancient Near East.

What can be learned from all this? Which values can women fruitfully appropriate as part of our history from the enduring polytheistic traditions, and how can we use them to construct a new measure of personal and social ethics? If women adopt as a moral touchstone the androgynous values implicit in the religious vision of ancient Near Eastern polytheism, which in practice appeared to permit the full participation of women and men in public cult or assumed the equal potential and capabilities of both sexes, it might clarify ways we could move in the direction of a life-affirming, nonexploitative future. The following preliminary strategies are mandatory, if not exhaustive.

1. While monotheism by no means introduced the notions of moral concern and consensus, it did make them more central than did polytheism. Justice, wisdom, and compassion not only became the preeminent attributes of God but also the highest virtues for members of the human community. The definitions and practical applications of these attributes and virtues, however, were frequently closely linked to gender. Thus, following the androgynous model (and the lead of Mary Daly in her earlier work), morality must be redefined in ways that assume the full personhood of both sexes. The belief that justice, wisdom, and compassion are of value in themselves must be disengaged from the patriarchal context of the biblical tradition and reimaged in nonsexist, nonracist, nonexploitative fashion.

2. The long, peaceful coexistence of official and popular religion might teach women to honor pluralism and value diversity in people, cultures, and varieties of religious experience.

3. While the God of monotheism is pictured as both immanent and transcendent, it is as the latter that he initiates some of the most culturally crucial events of the divine-human covenant. In this time of global ecological crisis, it is important that

human beings abandon a paradigm of the divine as above nature, existing eternally whether the natural universe lives or dies; rather let us return to the earlier reverence for all nature as sacred, and to the belief that the welfare of human society rests on the right functioning of nature.

4. There are a number of beliefs and practices that must be rejected out of hand as unrealistic, irrational, nonempirical, and punitive. Among them are the mind-body dichotomy; ambivalence toward women; fear and restriction of female sexuality; definitions of the nature of women in solely sexual or reproductive terms; the idea of complementarity, or that women and men are by their natures fit for different but equal roles; any suggestions that men are somehow fitter to deal with large moral, intellectual, or public issues and that women are happier when they apply themselves to more specific, private, equally important but more material tasks such as household chores and family nurturance; and a polarization of femininity and masculinity, either as sanctioned by the divine or as structured in more prosaic, secular sex roles, even when these are elaborated as feminine and masculine archetypes.

The mind-body dualism is psychologically unhealthy as well as inaccurate and male-biased; complementarity has never meant equality for the one who complemented the other. Women have always been more than walking wombs, just as men have always been more than public figures; men are also sexual and play a role in reproduction. Some women are intelligent enough to function well in the public sphere just as some men are intelligent enough to care for children. The polarization of feminine and masculine traits does not in fact correspond to the complexities of human experience. Demonstrably, in different eras and cultures, sex roles have varied, and there have been different normative expectations of behavior for females and males.

5. Women must define our own sexuality and modes of sexual expression, retain control over our own bodies and reproduction, and be free to exercise a range of sexual choices, including sexual preference. Historically, the denial of such rights to women has often marked their diminished status and opportunities.

6. Women must recognize that the emphasis by some, at-

tractive as it may seem, on a special, more moral female nature or culture is the product of historical, patriarchal oppression. While some women might think and act differently than men today, and possibly even in more gentle and nurturant ways, it seems unlikely that these behaviors result from biological differences. Based on the evidence from cultic life in the ancient Near East and on more recent examples, it appears that women are capable of as wide a range of behavior as men when both sexes are afforded equal opportunities or when women have adopted roles deviant for their own time.

7. Perhaps what the polytheistic religious model most cogently offers as an alternative is an example of female as well as male engagement in the central public concerns of the community, underscored by a conspicuous absence of a number of deterrents to female autonomy. As far as modern scholarship can tell, women were not regarded as merely complementary to men. Motherhood itself was not exalted, nor were women defined as only sexual beings or reproducers. Mind or spirit and body were not dichotomized.

If everyone embraced an androgynous model for women and men, it would not and could not eliminate all differences between the sexes. Some of those are real. But it might empower us as women to overcome our socialization to passivity, enabling us to establish our own political priorities and act on them with autonomy and comfort. In the process, it might enhance the humanity of men.

Claiming the Center: A Critical Feminist Theology of Liberation

ELISABETH SCHÜSSLER FIORENZA

The Song of Questions

Mother, asks the clever daughter,
who are our mothers?
Who are our ancestors?
What is our history?
Give us our name. Name our genealogy.

Mother, asks the wicked daughter,
if I learn my history
will I not be angry?
Will I not be bitter as Miriam
who was deprived of her prophecy?

Mother, asks the simple daughter,
if Miriam lies buried in sand,
why must we dig up those bones?
Why must we remove her from sun and stone
where she belongs?

The one who knows not how to question,
she has no past,
she has no present,
she can have no future
without knowing her mothers,
without knowing her angers,
without knowing her questions.

The Jewish feminist writer E. M. Broner, who together with Naomi Nimrod created the Passover Haggadah from which this song of questions is taken, says about their process: "We used the male Haggadah as the spine of our ceremony, and within it, reincorporated women. We dug up Miriam's bones from the desert. And we asked questions."[1] Because our religious experiences are diverse and the monster of patriarchy is many-headed, there ought to be diverse articulations of feminist theo-(or thea-)logy. Yet there is a curious tendency among feminist scholars in religion to dichotomize our efforts and present our options in a dualistic fashion.

I have circumscribed my own feminist theological questions as a "critical feminist theology of liberation."[2] Since such a theology is formulated in Christian terms it has been classified as reformist in distinction to radical or revolutionary feminist theology, which defines itself as post-Christian or post-Jewish.[3] Needless to say, as is the case with all classifications, these labels may fit or not fit actual articulations of feminist theology. While reformist feminist theologians supposedly take their criterion for *human* liberation from within the Jewish or Christian traditions, revolutionary feminist thinkers allegedly derive it from "women's experience, seek *women's* liberation, and advocate a female ascendancy principle articulated in the Goddess."[4] I stress that a critical feminist theology of liberation does not fit either the reformist or the revolutionary "box." I understand a critical feminist theology of liberation to be concerned with the liberation struggle of *all* women, to derive its criteria from women's experience and not from the tradition, and to claim the center of biblical religion for women rather than to subscribe to a female ascendancy principle. I explore this topic not for academic reasons but in order to move beyond the present dichotomy and the mere tolerance of women's differences. By clarifying our understanding of feminism and patriarchy and by discovering why to be a Christian feminist is not a reformist contradiction, women may recover the creative function of difference in the interdependency of our common struggle.

A Critique of Some Feminist Theologies

In her novel *Movement*, Valerie Miner captures the life of a woman who is involved in the struggle of various movements and committees to end injustice during the 1960s and early 1970s. Toward the end of the book the woman reflects on her situation.

> Struggle. Where was the sisterhood now? Susan wondered sometimes if feminism was the ultimate in female masochism because there seemed to be nothing beyond the struggle. She had been retained as a good fighter, a prolific petitioner. Now brittle with fatigue, she contemplated how she gave her loneliness to group consciousness, her anger to organized protest, her oppression to revolutionary retribution. So what if she were free from sexist family, teachers, husbands, boss, critics? What was salvation if there was no afterlife? She was free from all that, free for. . . ?[5]

The goal of feminist liberation is expressed as freedom from the domination and exploitation of men.

The Black poet June Jordan articulates the goal of feminist liberation not so much as freedom from men but as a movement into "self-love, self-respect, and self-determination." Such a self-love and self-respect has the strength to love and respect women "who are not like me" and to love and respect men "who are willing and able, without fear, to love and respect me." She defines the struggle not so much in terms of feminist group consciousness, organized protest, and revolutionary retribution, but in terms of survival: "And it is here, in this extreme, inviolable coincidence of my status as a Black feminist, my status as someone twice stigmatized, my status as a Black woman who is twice kin to the despised majority of all the human life that there is, it is here, in that extremity that I stand in a struggle against suicide."[6] That the progress of women's liberation has to be measured on the liberation of those women who suffer double or triple oppression in a patriarchal society was already articulated in the Redstockings Manifesto (April 1969), one of the earliest statements of the women's liberation movement.

> We define the best interests of women as the best interests of the poorest, most insulted, most despised, most abused woman on earth. Her lot, her sufferings, and abuse is the threat that men use against all of us to keep us in line. She is what all women fear being called, fear being treated as, and yet what we all really are: ugly, dumb . . . bitch, nag, hag, whore, fucking and breeding

machine, mother of us all. Until every woman is free, no woman will be free.[7]

If self-love, self-respect, and self-determination of the most despised and abused women on earth is the yardstick for our liberation, then we have to insist that there are no liberated women until *all* women are free from oppression and exploitation. In other words, there is no totally liberated consciousness or sisterhood as long as any woman is not free to love and respect herself as well as to determine her own life. If there are no "free women," however, there can be no feminist theology and religion free from patriarchal ideology. The task of feminist theology is not freedom from patriarchal religion but the articulation of women's self-love, self-respect, and self-determination in a religious context. Yet as religious women we have to be careful not to mistake such a feminist politics of identification as altruism or as an "option for the oppressed." When Third World American feminists point out that European-American women react to their challenges with guilt and evasiveness, but not with support and solidarity in their struggles, then they highlight that we have not yet learned to perceive in other women's oppression and struggles for liberation the different dimensions of our own alienation and our own liberation struggle.

Much feminist theological writing accepts a twofold presupposition: that the root of women's oppression is dualistic thought or patriarchalism as a mind set or projection, and that the monotheistic religions of Judaism and Christianity constitute the bedrock of Western patriarchalism. This hierarchical pattern of Western society, culture, and religion is characterized by the split between subject-object, superior-inferior, spirituality-carnality, life-death, mind-body, men-women. As monotheistic religions, Christianity and Judaism have provided the ultimate rationale for Western patriarchy. They have fashioned an absolute transcendent God in the image of men and have declared women as "the other" who cannot image or represent God. According to Rosemary Ruether:

> The meaning of the feminine thus becomes modeled in classical spirituality on the images of the lower self and world. Autonomous spiritual selfhood is imaged (by males, the cultural creators

of this view) as intrinsically masculine, while the feminine becomes the symbol of the repressed, subjugated and dreaded "abysmal" side of "man."[8]

From this basic dualism between a righteous God and sinful man all the other dualisms develop. Therefore, a paradigm shift is called for: the transcendent Father God needs to be replaced by the immanent Mother Goddess, the religious imagination and projection of males needs to be supplanted by women's spirituality rooted in the procreative powers of the female body.

Feminist theology has therefore paid much attention to the functioning of androcentric God-language and patriarchal dualisms but has not been sufficiently attentive to the complexities of women's life and oppression, especially that of Women of Color and of poor women. Insofar as feminist theology has taken as its starting point patriarchalism as a dualistic mind set but not patriarchy as a socioeconomic-political system within capitalistic and socialistic modern societies, it is in danger of formulating its feminist strategies and religious frameworks in terms of the oppression of women by men and to understand women's liberation struggle as a struggle of women against men. Neglected thereby is the experience of Third World women, who have consistently refused to define their own liberation struggle as a struggle against men of their own race or class.

Moreover, as Judith Plaskow has pointed out, such dualistic patterns of thought have crept into feminist religion and theology even though feminist thinkers have set out to move beyond dualisms.[9] Plaskow takes motherhood as a test case and outlines its complex nature in the life of working-class women in order to insist that we must "hold together in praxis and in theory what is held together in women's experience." Neither the feminist identification of women with motherhood and nature nor the feminist transcendence and negation of women's bodiliness does justice to the complexities of women's experience. The mind-body dualism that identifies men with civilization and women with nature is not overcome in a feminist theology that elevates and celebrates the identification of women with nature as female metaphysical ascendancy. This dualism is equally perpetuated by feminist thought that values women's freedom and personhood over their female physicality. Both feminist proposals overlook that nature and motherhood are human constructs and institutions, on one hand, and that women's physicality is a "resource rather than a destiny," and the ground "of all we make ourselves to be," on the other hand.

Historical Roots of Patriarchy

A historical exploration of patriarchy might help clarify the complexity of women's oppression and not simply reduce it to the male-female, culture-nature dualisms, or to the religious projections of men. It might also enable us to recognize in the oppression of Women of Color and poor women our own exploitation and abuse as women. Aristotelian political philosophy is concerned with the relationships between rulers and ruled in household and state. In distinction to the Sophists, Aristotle stresses that the patriarchal relationships of the household and the city-state are based not on social convention but on nature. He therefore insists that the discussion of political ethics must begin with household management and marriage, which he defines as the union between the "natural" ruler and "natural" subject. Against those who argue that slavery is against nature, Aristotle points to the rule of the soul over the body.

> It is manifest that it is natural and expedient for the body to be governed by the soul and for the emotional part to be governed by the intellect, the part possessing reason, whereas for the two parties to be on equal footing or in the contrary position is harmful in all cases. Also as between the sexes, the male is by nature superior and the female inferior, the male ruler and the female subject. And the same must necessarily apply in the case of humankind generally; therefore all human beings that differ as widely as the soul does from the body . . . are by nature slaves for whom to be governed by this kind of authority is advantageous (1254ab). Hence there are by nature various classes of rulers and ruled. For the free rules the slave, the male the female, and the man the child in a different way. And all possess the various parts

of the soul but possess them in different ways; for the slave has not got the deliberative part at all, and the female has it but without full authority, while the child has it but in an undeveloped form (*Politics* 1260a).

Since every household is part of the state, the state is jeopardized if the different forms of household rule are not exercised faithfully. The supraordination-subordination relationship is based on property relationships and the definition of nature serves social functions.

That the categories of sexual property and state are the critical elements in classical patriarchy is obvious in Plato's utopian thought. In the *Republic* Plato describes the ideal city-state, which is ruled by the guardians. He understands the city-state as a united patriarchal household in which private property is communalized. Women and children are no longer the property of individual free male citizens but the property of all. Since the private household is abolished, women of the aristocratic class are freed from their "natural" social functions within the private household and therefore can take over their share in the administration of the city-state household. Whereas the split between the public sphere of the city and the private sphere of the household requires the stress on the "natural" differences between men and women, the utopia of a city-state household in which private and public spheres are merged allows Plato to stress that except for procreative differences (the man "mounts" and the woman gives birth and lactates) no other natural differences exist. Plato notes that women in general are physically weaker than men, but attributes this in part to their deficient physical education. Nevertheless, even the female guardians remain the sexual property of all men, although both women and men are restrained in their sexual expressions because of eugenic reasons. Since for the functioning of such an ideal state slaves and metics are crucial, the relative liberation of aristocratic women from patriarchal definition and social function does not lead to the liberation of all women from the oppression of patriarchy.

According to classical scholar Marilyn Arthur, the articulation of the polarity between the sexes is not explicit in the writings of the aristocratic period but only emerges with the introduction of democracy.[10] Whereas in aristocratic society women were an aspect of the world at large and male and female social roles of the upper classes approximated each other, in Athenian democracy women became a subcategory of men because male headship of a household was declared a precondition for citizenship. While previously the inferior status of women was not explicit, now the political and legal structures of the state prescribed women's subservience and excluded them from citizenship. Not polytheistic or monotheistic patriarchal religion but politics and economics were the sustaining rationale for patriarchal oppression and dualism. Explicit misogyny and ideological polarity between the sexes were thus rooted in a contradiction between the social-political structures of Athenian democracy, which restricted full citizenship to free propertied male heads of households, and the democratic ideal of human dignity and freedom first articulated in the middle-class democracy of the city-state. In short, ideological polarity and misogynist dualism as well as the philosophical justification of social roles based on the distinctive "natures" of slaves and women seem to have been generated by a social-political situation where the equality and dignity of all humans was articulated as a principle, but their actual participation in political and social self-determination was prohibited, because they remained the sexual property of men.

The same contradiction between democratic ideals and social-patriarchal structures determines modern society. Susan Moller Okin, a political philosopher, has shown that Aristotelian patriarchal philosophy is still operative in American democratic society and legal-political philosophy.[11] Although the patriarchal family has been modified in the course of history, the split between the public and private spheres has been intensified through industrialization. Political philosophy still works with the Aristotelian premise that the free propertied male is the full citizen, whereas all the other members of the population—women, colonialized peoples, and the "working" classes—support the few propertied, free, usually older White males who determine public and political life and thus exercise full citizenship.

Even though liberalism understands society to be constituted of independent and free persons, it is clear, according to Moller Okin, that in spite of this individualistic rhetoric the family and not the adult human individual is the basic political unit of liberal as well as nonliberal philosophers. Even a liberal feminist philosopher such as John Stuart Mill asserts that since the wife is responsible for the economic and emotional climate of the private sphere, she can only take on outside responsibilities after she has successfully taken care of *her* domestic responsibilities. Whatever public function or profession a woman fulfills, housework and child care is her primary responsibility. Moreover, adult members of a family are assumed to share the same interests. Whenever a conflict of interest arises between wife and husband, the presumption in political and legal philosophy has been that such a conflict must be decided by the male head of the household.

This split between the public and private spheres generates a separate system of economics for women.[12] The women's system of economics is based on the assumption that every family consists of the ideal father earning the living for the family and that therefore all women are either temporary workers or work for pin money because they will get married and become pregnant. Lower wages and lower-level positions for women are justified because women's wages are presumed to be supplementary. Since it is assumed that housework and child care are women's *natural* vocation, women need not be paid or counted in the gross national product. The result of this separate system of economics for women is the increasing feminization of poverty and the destitution of female-headed households. This system is also stamped by racism. All statistics consistently show that Women of Color earn less than their White sisters. The sexist impact is more pervasive than that of racism, however, insofar as all American men earn more than women. Finally, this separate economic system for women sustains female sexual slavery that cuts across all lines of race, class, and culture.[13]

The Patriarchal Co-optation of Christianity

The same basic contradiction between the call to the discipleship of equals and ecclesial-patriarchal structures characterizes contemporary Christianity. This contradiction was introduced toward the end of the first century in the process of ecclesial adaptation to Greco-Roman culture. There is considerable evidence that Aristotle's patriarchal philosophy was revitalized in neo-Pythagorean and Stoic philosophy in reaction to the increased emancipation and independence of women in the first century C.E. It was also accepted by Hellenistic Jewish writers such as Philo and found its way into the New Testament. The "household codes" of the New Testament, which demand subordination and obedience from wives, children, and slaves, participate in this stabilizing reception of Aristotelian patriarchal philosophy and politics in the first centuries of our era.[14]

The Christian missionary movement caused conflict with the existing order of the patriarchal household because it converted *individuals* independently of their social status and function in the patriarchal household. Christian mission evoked social unrest because it admitted wives and slaves as well as daughters and sons into the house church, although the paterfamilias might still be pagan and not have converted to Christianity. The social implications of religious conversion were realized in the house church as the discipleship community of equals. Independently of their fathers, husbands, and masters, women had membership and leadership in the early Christian movement.[15] Even in the beginning of the second century, women slaves were leaders in their communities and expected to be bought free by the Christian community. The pagan accusation that Christian mission was subversive and destructive to patriarchal household structures was still made even in the second century. It was not a misunderstanding or a slander but an accurate perception of the social implications of conversion. The household-code injunctions of the later New Testament writers are therefore best understood as a prescriptive attempt to mitigate the subversive impact of religious conversion on the patriarchal order of the house and of society.

In a similar fashion Judaism was attacked for its infringement on the religious patriarchal prerogatives of the paterfamilias, insofar as it admitted slaves and women of pagan households as God-fearers and converts. How deeply the Romans resented the social disruption wrought by proselytism comes to the fore in the following statement of Tacitus:

> For the worst rascals among other peoples, renouncing their ancestral religions, always kept sending tributes and contributions to Jerusalem. . . . Those who are converts to their ways follow the same practice [i.e., of hating other peoples, being immoral, adopting circumcision], and the earliest lesson they receive is to despise the gods, to disown their country, and to regard their parents, children and brothers as of little account. (History V, 5)

Christian missionary conversions caused even greater tensions between the societal environment and the Christian community, for Christians, unlike Jews, did not belong to an established, albeit often despised religion. The prescriptive household-code texts of the New Testament attempted to soften this political tension by asserting the congruence of the Christian ethos with that of patriarchal house and state. In doing so they not only patriarchalized the early Christian ethos of the discipleship of equals but also the structures of the Christian community.

Insofar as this pattern reinforced the patriarchal submission of those who according to Aristotle must be ruled, the early Christian ethos of coequal discipleship lost its capacity to transform structurally the patriarchal order of family and state. The vision of agape and service, mutuality and solidarity among Christians no longer connoted a new reality but became reduced to mere moral appeal. Submission and obedience but not equality and justice were institutionalized by this patriarchal ethos. Insofar as it was not restricted to the household but was also adopted by the house church, Christian vision and praxis could no longer provide a structural-political alternative to its patriarchal culture. Its preaching of the gospel and its hierarchical-patriarchal structures became a contradiction that robbed the gospel of its historical transformative power.

This same contradiction enables the political right today to co-opt biblical religion against feminist reforms and at the same time inspires Christian feminists to dedicate themselves to the liberation struggles of women in El Salvador, Appalachia, or the South Bronx. The feminist writer Charlene Spretnak, however, overlooks this tension.

> The churches have contributed an enormous amount of money, time and organizing toward the goal of crushing us, especially on the issues of abortion and the ERA. How is it that masses of women follow their lead? *Because patriarchal religion and social structure are believed to have always been the natural order.* Feminism is seen as unnatural, as a threatening aberration. Women whose lives revolve around Judaeo-Christian teachings will never embrace feminism unless we reach them with the historical truth that the system they are holding up is itself the recent aberration.[16]

She argues that only the recovery of the matriarchal religions preceding patriarchal religion will enable women to be true feminists. Yet the historical truth seems to be that patriarchal domination and sexist ideology are perpetuated by social-political-economic forces of Western society that are able to co-opt biblical religion just as easily as they are able to co-opt Goddess religion for their own ends. As long as any woman is enslaved, a feminist religion untainted by patriarchy is not possible.

Biblical Images of Liberation

Images have great power. For almost two hundred years two biblical images have dominated the American women's movement in and outside of organized religion. The image of paradise determines today the arguments and appeals of the so-called Moral Majority, while that of the exodus has inspired radical feminism, calling women to abandon the oppressive confines of patriarchal home and church. The "cult of true womanhood" proclaims that the vocation of women is homemaker and mother. The fulfillment of her true nature and happiness consists in creating the home as a peaceful island in the sea of alienated society, in which children are protected and men can retreat from the exploitations and temptations of the work world. Women must provide in the home a climate of peace and happiness, of self-sacrificing love and nurturing gentility, in order to "save the family." Therefore, the feminine spiritual calling is superior to that of men. This praise of femininity conveniently overlooks that poor and unmarried women cannot afford to stay at home; it overlooks the violence done to women and children in the home, and it totally mistakes patriarchal dependency for Christian family.

The exodus image, however, compels women to leave behind everything they treasure—loving community with men, shelter, happiness, children, nurturance, religion—because all of it has contributed to their oppression and exploitation in patriarchal society and church. Women have to move away from the fleshpots of patriarchal slavery and live "in a new space and time." The image of the exodus calls women to move out from the sanctity of the home, to leave the servitude of the patriarchal family, and to abandon the certitudes of patriarchal religion. The spirituality of exodus overlooks not only that the patriarchal oppression of Egypt is everywhere, but also that God is present not just on the boundaries but also in the center, if God is in the midst of us wherever and whenever we struggle for liberation. These two biblical images—of Eden and of exodus—place women before the alternatives: either to become Martha serving Jesus in the home or to become Miriam, the sister of Moses, leading her people into the desert. They do not, however, lead us into the center of patriarchal society and church, nor bring about God's vision of co-humanity in our struggles and solidarity with one another. The God of Judith as well as the God of Jesus is Emmanuel: God with us, especially with those who are oppressed, despised, and destitute.

Neither the yearning for paradise nor the exodus from Egypt are possible for me, because they take me out of the struggle of my sisters in biblical religion for survival and against patriarchy. For them and for myself I reclaim my heritage because, as artist Judy Chicago says, "Our heritage is our power." Religion, theology, and spirituality can be potent weapons in the hands of patriarchal society. I had the privilege to know and learn how to use them—and I will use them in the struggle for liberation. Yet I can only use them where the enemy is. To paraphrase Karen Brown's powerful statement in "Why Women Need the War God": I did not marry the War God, but

I learned to steal his weapons. To affirm myself as a Christian feminist theologian means, then, first of all to own my complicity in patriarchal oppression. Women were and are not only victims of patriarchy but also collaborators and supporters of it.

To affirm myself as a Christian feminist theologian is an attempt to come to terms with the oppressive aspects of my history and my identity. I cannot say that I am no longer a Christian since I have come to realize the full extent of sexism perpetrated by Christianity in the past and in the present, just as I cannot say I am no longer a German after I have come to realize the horrors of German anti-Semitism climaxing in the Holocaust. Even if I were to become a naturalized American, my language and culture would still betray me as German. Moreover, to become an American would not help me out of my complicity with oppression, since I would then have to own the genocide of Native Americans, the institution of Black slavery, Hiroshima, Vietnam, and El Salvador. I do not want anyone to misunderstand me. I do not speak of collective guilt but of collective responsibility, which gives one the right to challenge and critique one's own people.

To call myself a feminist Christian theologian means, first, a commitment to do all I can to denounce and change the patriarchal structures of biblical religion, my own church, and my own tradition. Feminist theology must therefore first of all be and always remain a *critical* theology of liberation. It seeks to name theologically the alienation, anger, pain, and oppression of women engendered by patriarchal sexism and racism in society and church as well as to provide an alternative Christian vision of liberation. Such a theology is not based on the theological anthropology of the complementarity of the sexes nor on a metaphysical female ascendancy principle. It does not advocate the co-optation of women's spiritual powers by ecclesiastical patriarchy nor the emigration of women from patriarchal society and church. Since it is based on the radical presupposition that gender is socially, politically, and theologically constructed, and that such a construction serves to perpetuate the patriarchal exploitation and oppression of women, it seeks to enable women to explore theologically the structural sin of patriarchal sexism,[17] to reject its internalizations and ecclesial legitimizations, and to become in such a conversion the *synagōgē* or *ekklēsia* of women.

Such a feminist theology conceived as a critical theology of liberation names the oppressive structures of patriarchal religion, of Christian church and tradition, while rediscovering the liberating elements of Christian faith and community that enable women to sustain their commitment to the struggle against patriarchal sexism. Such a theology does not ask only for the reformation of sexist-patriarchal structures, nor does it advocate elitist separation, but it works for the radical transformation of Christian symbols, tradition, and community as well as for the transformation of women. Therefore, it cannot base its theology or derive its liberating vision from the special nature, religious powers, and feminist notion of Woman as the incarnation of the divine feminine principle, but only from women's historical experiences of oppression and their struggles for liberation.

In exorcising the internalized structural sin of sexism as well as in calling the whole Christian church to conversion and repentance, we reclaim our Christian birthright of being the *synagōgē* or *ekklēsia* of women, the gathering of free and responsible citizens who have the power to articulate their own theology, to reclaim their own spirituality, and to determine their own and their sisters' religious life. As church we celebrate our religious powers and visions for change, we ritualize our struggles, and we share our strengths in nurturing one another. Yet I would insist that the *ekklēsia* of women is always also the *ecclesia reformanda* in need of conversion and revolutionary patience with our own failures as well as those of our sisters.

Women as the people of God have a continuous history and can claim Miriam, Judith, Jesus, and the early Christian women disciples as their foresisters in the struggle. This history of women as the people of God must be exposed as a history of oppression as well as a history of liberation and conversion. Women as the people of God, of the past and of the present, have acted and now act in the power of the life-giving Spirit/ Wisdom. Such an understanding of catholic sisterhood that spans all ages, races, and cultures does not need to deny women's hurt and anger or to cover up the injustice and violence done to women in the name of God or Christ. Neither does it need to claim salvific power for women, nor to narrow its understanding of sisterhood to those women who are the truly true feminists. It does not expect salvation from women because it knows too well that as women we have been accomplices in patriarchal racism, that we all have internalized the structural sin of patriarchal sexism, and that women can act against their own self-interest.

Such a solidarity in sisterhood allows women to keep alive and to remember the sufferings and struggles of our foresisters, to learn from their visions and defeats. It allows us to accept all religious women who are "not like us," to respect their beliefs and decisions rather than to declare them as false consciousness. It allows us to treasure and recover our heritage, to celebrate and to rejoice in the victories of all women in the past and in the present. In short, the gospel of the life-praxis, execution, and resurrection of the Jew Jesus does not spell for me salvation by a male savior but the promise that the victims of history will not have suffered for nothing, but that a new creation is emerging that turns their defeat into life. This Christian vision has become for me the sustaining religious experience that allows me to struggle and to work for change with hope, despite all experiences to the contrary. It allows me to move from guilt to solidarity with all those women whose life is devastated by the death-dealing powers of patriarchy: the poor, colonialized, destitute, and dehumanized sisters who struggle for self-love, self-respect, and self-determination as women-people.

We feminists in religion have been caught up in the dualistic alternative of either "the biblical" or "the post-biblical" option rather than having explored how our different religious experiences inform our spirituality, theology, and politics. We tend either to ignore our differences or to hurl patriarchal anathemas against one another. Rather than to celebrate our differences as the source of our common power for change, we tend to get lost in doctrinal quibbles or uncritical emotionalism. Yet as Audre Lorde insists, only within the interdependence of mutual (non-dominant) differences lies that security which enables us to descend into the chaos of knowledge and return with true visions of our future, along with the concomitant power to effect those changes which can bring that future into being. Difference is that raw and powerful connection from which our personal power is forged.[18]

31

Immanence: Uniting the Spiritual and Political
STARHAWK

I am struggling not to remove the idea from its context. Early in the morning I take my dogs down to the beach to run in the summer fog. The ocean whispers; all is soft, gray, and silver-blue. A line of birds skims the waves, winking out of sight as the crests hide it. The tide is running out. There are sand dollars at my feet and the fossils of sand dollars embedded in black rocks.

The thought-forms of immanence are embedded in *context*; they *are* context and content, as this fossil is now also rock.

Let me try again.

Let us imagine that we live in a culture where time is a cycle, where the sand dollar lies beside its fossil (as it does). Where everything is seen to return, as the birds return to sight with the movement of the waves. As I return to the beach, again and again.

Imagine that in that returning nothing stands outside; the bird is not separate from the wave but both are part of the same rhythm. Imagine that I know—not with my intellect but in my body, my heart—that I do not stand separate from the sand dollar or the fossil; that the slow forces that shaped the life of one and preserved the other under the deep pressure of settling mud for cycles upon cycles are the same forces that have formed my life; that when I hold the fossil in my hand I am looking into a mirror.

Or better, imagine that you are with me on that beach; that we are together (as we are); and that when we look into each other's faces, we see (as light is both particle and wave) ourselves mirrored and yet transformed by each other's unique, independent being; that we value the mystery of each other's being, which can never wholly be known, that we honor in each other the richness of our difference, honor that which we cannot predict in each other, that which makes us free.

Starhawk

And let us imagine that we are not alone, that we are together with our friends, our children, the people we love. And because we are aware of the world as returning, the forms of our thoughts flow in circles, spirals, webs; they weave and dance, honoring the links, the connections, the patterns, the changes, so that nothing can be removed from its context.

Even God.

Let us imagine that these children, at least, have never known a God who stands outside the world, that nothing in their minds is receptive to the principle of power-over. That as infants, they learned that the demands, the pleasures, and the innermost beings of their bodies were sacred because these children were honored by their parents; they were fed when hungry, suckled, held close to the bodies of both women and men.

Imagine that their mothers were not—by virtue of being mothers—expected to stay separate from the enterprise and activity of the world; that their fathers also cared for their infant bodies with all the tenderness we expect from women. Imagine that these children were never taught to separate flesh and spirit; never trained to view themselves, their bodies, their excretions with shame; that to their parents, even shit was something sacred, something to be returned in the cycles of returning.

When these children learn, they sit in circles; they move, they dance, they explore, they question, they teach other children what they themselves know. When they grow up to work, their work is not separate from their lives. Because they have no way to hold in their minds the absolute value of an abstract, they do not work for money as if it were a God. Because they themselves are not strangers in the world, they cannot hold the illusion that individual gain is possible at others' expense. They know—in their bodies, in their hearts—that what goes around comes around, that what is taken from the earth must be given back. Though they know that each one of them will die, they do not expect life to end. In their minds there is no Cosmic Referee to blow the whistle and yell "Game's over!" They cannot stand outside the world to own it, to profit from it. They cannot isolate themselves from the pain of other people; they are of the world, of each other.[1]

The vision described above is a glimpse into the world view of witchcraft: the Old Religion, the pre-Christian, tribal tradition of the West. The Craft, as we call it, like similar Native American, African, and other indigenous religions, conveys an attitude toward the spirit that is very different from that found in patriarchal religions. In the Craft, spirit and flesh are one. There are no splits between mind and matter, sacred and profane, culture and nature. For the Goddess, our favorite name for the divine, is nature, culture, human beings: she is manifest in the physical world. The purpose of our rituals, our spiritual discipline, and the communities we create together is not to transcend the world but to experience more deeply the immanence of the Goddess in ourselves and all beings around us.

"Witch" itself comes from the Anglo-Saxon root *wic*, meaning to bend or shape. The wicces (pronounced witches) were the wise women or men of the village, who could bend and shape the subtle energies that move through physical beings. They were the herbalists, the healers, the counselors, the medicine women and men, the priests and priestesses.

When Christianity first spread through Western Europe, it coexisted with the Craft on friendly terms. Many of the major pagan festivals, such as Halloween, to take the most familiar example, were simply given a Christian gloss that allowed the old customs to continue. So people continued to welcome their ancestors on the Eve of All Hallows, to burn the Yule log at Midwinter, to celebrate spring's return with candles on the second of February, and to dance the maypole on Mayday. The round of the year and the cycle of the seasons was marked with communal festivals that helped assure harmony between human beings and the life of other beings around.

Not until the sixteenth and seventeenth centuries did first the Catholic and then the emerging Protestant churches begin extensive persecutions of witches. Thousands, more likely millions, of women and men were imprisoned, tortured, hanged, or burned in the centuries we call the Burning Times, and the negative stereotypes we today associate with the word witch are the legacy of the propaganda of that period. The persecutions helped destroy peasant resistance to the takeover of their common lands and traditional rights. They helped drive women out of the professions of healing and midwifery. And they cemented the hatred of women and sexuality onto the foundations of modern Western culture.[2]

The Craft survived only in fragments, in secret traditions passed down in families or shared among isolated, small covens—groups of thirteen or fewer members that form the traditional congregational unit. Much knowledge was lost. Only in the latter part of the twentieth century have witches felt safe enough to begin practicing their religion openly, writing about it, teaching it.[3]

What is it like to be a woman and a feminist practicing and living a tradition of immanent spirituality in the United States of the 1980s? For me, living the tradition has three vital aspects. The first, of course, is closest to what is usually thought of as religion—the rituals, the seasonal cycles, the meditations and ceremonies. The Craft is a religion of experience, and ritual—not beliefs, dogmas, theologies, or scripture—is the heart of what we do. Because we conceive of the Goddess as constantly alive in us, she is constantly inspiring. Our rituals are constantly recreated and always allow room for free, spontaneous, personal expression. The group I work with in San Francisco is committed to a collective, nonhierarchical approach to ritual-making, which involves everyone in participation and leadership.

Ritual builds community, and community is an equally vital aspect of a living religion of immanence, for the Goddess is manifest in the relationships we have with one another, the love, the friendship, the comfort, the spiritual and material help we can give one another. Because each one of us *is* the Goddess, a world view of immanence can furnish no support for the concept of authority, for the belief that some people have the right to wield power over others. We strive to build our community on a basis of equality, with each member equally valued.

Finally, the Goddess manifests in action in the world, action to change conditions that destroy the lives and potential of millions of human beings today, that poison the earth whom we hold sacred and threaten its destruction. For me, a commitment to the Goddess at this time in history must mean a commitment to action in the political sphere, to work and struggle for social change. For when spirit is seen as manifest in the material world, then the spiritual and the political cannot be seen as separate.

I tell my personal story not because I am unique but because, as we say in the feminist movement, the personal is political. The themes of ritual, community, and action that weave throughout my own past decade are representative of movements and changes that have affected many women's lives, and which, I believe, are shaping the decades to come.

I was raised in the Jewish tradition, received a long and extensive Jewish education, and was very religious as a child. As I grew older, however, I found that my deepest moments of connection happened not in conjunction with formal prayer or study, but in nature, and in the discovery of my own sexuality. When at the age of seventeen I met a group of witches who talked to me and my friends about the religion, I felt that for the first time my own true experience had been named as spirituality. The imagery of the Goddess was completely new to me, and I found her tremendously empowering. To acknowledge my own body, my emotions, my sexual desire, my intellect, my capacity for leadership as manifestations of the spirit affirmed their worth and allowed me to grow with a sense of my own value.

When feminists debate the historical meaning or present-day appropriateness of Goddess symbolism, they often forget to recognize the tremendous healing power the imagery of the Goddess has had for women. Patriarchal culture is a constant blow to every woman's sense of worth, a message reiterated over and over again that true value is not found in woman. The imagery of the Goddess asserts that women are the very shape and embodiment of value.

Throughout the 1970s, many women—and men—began to come together in community centered around the rituals and imagery of the Goddess. For me, this community first took the form of a coven. My coven eventually developed into a work collective, called Reclaiming, which offers classes, workshops, and public rituals in the Goddess traditions. Reclaiming has expanded over the past year, and is now a network of work groups, covens, and households that all see themselves as part of a broad community attempting to live their spirituality and their politics.

Since the Goddess manifests in the world, the *thea*logy of immanence is of the concrete rather than the abstract. In Reclaiming, we constantly wrestle with issues of *thea*logy and politics in very practical terms. How much shall we charge for our classes? How do we make them available to people who have little money? Shall we invoke the God in a public ritual—and if so, what aspects shall we name? How do we train new teachers? How do we teach in ways that empower our students and do not reinforce patterns of authority?

In the Craft spirituality develops not as a series of answers, but through our attempts to look at all the implications of each thing that we do. For us, it cannot be separated from the way we make decisions or from the practical work that we do.

Nor can we see our spirituality as separate from our politics. In the late 1970s and early 1980s, many of us in the Craft community found ourselves drawn back into active involvement with a variety of political issues. As a group, we had continuously worked on feminist projects, but Ronald Reagan's election and the right-wing backlash it portended propelled us into antinuclear and disarmament work as well.

In September 1981, a group of us from Reclaiming participated in the blockage of the Diablo Canyon nuclear power plant in California. We were able to bring ritual to the camp, to the action itself, and to the jail.

Since then, we have been continually involved with the planning and organization of many forms of nonviolent direct action, working with the Livermore Action Group to try to convert the Livermore Weapons Lab to peace research, doing nonviolence training and coalition-building with a variety of different groups.

Action has become for me a personal vision quest. There is a saying in the Craft, "Where there's fear, there's power." The fear we face in an action is not occult or psychological. It is a very real fear of very concrete things: police, jail, physical pain and damage. We face that fear in an effort to act against the larger fears—of nuclear war, of the slow erosion of human rights, of the destruction of the environment, of the conditions that destroy and oppress human beings. Facing the real fears, moving through them to act, we find deeper courage and power.

One small example: Witches often do rituals outdoors, in the parks, on the beach, in public places. We have no temples or protected worship grounds, so our rituals are often on public display. Many of us have often felt shy or inhibited about dancing, chanting, and being in ecstasy within sight of casual passersby. Over the past year, however, we have done rituals overlooking the Diablo plant with helicopters circling above us and searchlights glaring on our circle. We have done many rituals in jail, under the gaze of prison guards. And we have found that we can tap a deeper level of power, one that is not disturbed by other people's eyes or judgments, one that is connected with a willingness to be who we are and express what we feel whatever our circumstances. With that willingness came the realization that to do ritual publicly was itself a form of direct action, that for people to happen upon a group of us chanting to the ocean or a ring of women dancing in the park was consciousness-raising, that we could use these opportunities to talk to people and share a vision of a world in which ecstasy and closeness would not be out-of-the-ordinary sights.

Political action has also strengthened our community. We have needed to give each other support in very tangible ways: watering the plants, walking the dogs, caring for the kids, waiting throughout the night for one of us to be released from court. That support has built trust. We have learned that we can depend on one another, and that we are far stronger as a community when we do help one another. Now, many of us are moving toward living collectively, toward developing households that reflect our spiritual and political values.

Our rituals have also changed. When we attempt to raise power in an action that includes people from many religious traditions, we find ourselves, to quote Mary Hunt, "declaring a moratorium on God and Goddess language." Instead, we name the things—the elements, the earth, our own names—that to us are manifestations of the deity, and to which all people can feel connected, regardless of the name they prefer for spirit.

We also find ourselves moving more and more away from rituals that are led or prewritten, and into ways of evoking spontaneity and creativity from those who come. For example, over the years the way we cast the circle—the traditional beginning of a ritual—has changed. Casting the circle involves calling in the four directions, each of which corresponds to an element and an aspect of human life. Years ago, one priestess would always cast the circle. Later, we began to rotate the task. Eventually we would ask four different people each to call in one of the directions. In larger, public rituals, four different covens might each prepare an invocation for one of the directions. Now, however, we often ask the people who come to the ritual to find the direction to which they feel most drawn. They then form a group, create an invocation, and share it with the rest of us, so that each person has a chance to create, perform, and appreciate others. Or a facilitator may simply name the direction and the element, and ask people to share spontaneously the images, colors, and qualities it brings to mind. As voice after voice is heard, a group poem is created, and so the circle is cast by all of us.

Immanence-based spirituality could perhaps be defined as the attempt to live in the world we envision while acting to change the world that is, to heal its hurts, to redress its injustices, to prevent its destruction.

Action is power. In this conference we have shared ideas, hopes, pain, anger, vision. If we can take with us a renewed commitment to action, we will strengthen the power we hold together, the power to shape the world.

32

Suggestions from the Working Group on Feminist Education

From the Redstockings Manifesto: "Until all women are free, no women are free." In response to this week, we have begun a rhetorically circular model:

Assumptions: A feminist perspective on education assumes:

- the value of lifelong learning
- the value of cooperative models and mutuality in relationships
- the value of nonverbal along with verbal articulation
- an awareness of the oppression inherent in institutional education
- that feminist strategies are bound into this specific moment in culture and herstory, and therefore, that strategies must reflect the need to compromise without being compromised

Purpose: The purpose of this working group has been to begin the exploration of the impact of feminist perspectives on lifelong learning.

Components: A feminist perspective on education requires:

- an understanding of education as empowerment of the whole person—affective, cognitive, physical, and spiritual
- continual reassessment and development of critical consciousness

- development of an awareness of diversity and unity; encouragement of a possibility of choice in living out the dialectic
- equal attention to process and content, i.e., the process reflects content and the medium is the message; more specifically, a feminist perspective on education suggests a balance between experience and theory, i.e., a participatory process of learning that is inclusive of the whole person
- a process that is inherently nonracist, nonsexist, nonheterosexist, nonimperialist, nonclassist
- an interdisciplinary focus, i.e., an understanding that bridges departmental categories and builds networks among institutional members

Strategies: A grocery list—shop where-when-how-as you like it:

- Put students in the position of the teacher—how would you teach this?
- Enable students to develop an evaluation process for their own work.
- Allow, insofar as possible, student choice of materials and goals.
- Exercise: In dyads, have students interview one another concerning their own goals, reasons for presence in the group, etc. Repeat the exercise later in order to note possible changes.
- Have students draw a map of their environment/space/world.
- Have students give people directions to their houses from the university/school/center.
- Take care that nonsexist, nonracist, nonclassist, nonheterosexist resources are used.
- Support publishers who work out of cooperative modes and support feminist perspectives.
- Encourage "functional schizophrenia." Exercise: Write a love letter. How would you write the same letter if you knew it would be seen by (a) your parents; (b) your best friend; (c) your clergyperson?
- Exercise: To acknowledge attention lapses, try Fantasy

Fix: Encourage/allow thirty-second centering exercises, i.e., "For the next thirty seconds . . ."
- Free-writing exercise to aid the focus of energy: For a period of time, have people write with three rules: (a) the pen never stops moving on the paper; (b) *anything* that comes into one's mind must be written down; (c) *no one* sees it but the author. This can be followed by brief reflection on the relative usefulness of ideas by having students circle ideas for their own future consideration.
- Use participation games in the classroom/meeting place that foster increased awareness and experience of the inequities in the world, i.e., Baldicer, Becoming a Person.
- Use participation games in the classroom/meeting place that enhance an awareness of the uniqueness and value both of self and of others in the group. See *Ways to Enhance Self-Esteem in the Classroom* by Jack Canfield.
- To raise consciousness about personal power and powerlessness and to encourage responsibility: Using the three categories of self, community, and world, solicit descriptive adjectives. Compare for positive and negative values. Discussion can lead to a sense of interconnectedness among the areas for the individual and interconnectedness among group members.
- Inner/outer journey toward relinquishment: Pedagogy for the nonpoor. Exercise: Spend a day in the city with only a dollar. Reflect on the experience to see what you might do as a result.

Poem by Carol Feiser Laque*

In my dream, I'm a high soprano singing of woman.
In my dream I'm building America with my own hands.
In my dream I'm a teacher on a prairie playground of children and tumbleweed.

*"This never happened to me before in my creative life," Carol Laque remarked about this poem. "After our discussion, the group said, 'Someone should write a poem about this,' and asked me to do it. I found a quiet place and wrote this."

In my dream I live in the inner city borrowing tomorrow from evening shadows.
In my dream I keep every human life burning like a candle in my soul.
In my dream I survive the holocaust and like Anne Frank my diary is sacred.
In my dream I dance about joy and terror, about wickedness until my dance is dawn and dusk.
In my dream I am a stone thrown upon still waters.
In my dream I am the ghost of Indian and Aboriginal children who were never born.
In my dream my leaves burst into bloom and fall—only to bloom again because I am the Tree of Life.
In my dream I hunt despair like a wild animal and destroy her with the eyes of faith.
In my dream I am a river running to the ocean and then rising heavenward.
In my dream I am rain and the time of falling down.
In my dream I am full of my own wars, so the blood of others is not shed.
In my dream I am the ripeness of heavy fruit.
In my dream I am noon and midnight loaning songs for the price of experience.
In my dream I am a young girl's story written on the wind.
In my dream I plant a handful of seeds every day for the rest of my life.
In my dream the last seed I plant is Death itself.

Part VIII

Envisioning an Alternative Future

EVERY CRITIQUE IMPLIES an alternative, but it is not easy to draw out the positive implications from a criticism of the existing state of affairs, still less to clothe them with sufficient concreteness to arouse and direct energies for change. There is a tendency to pour new content into old thought forms rather than to shift the paradigms themselves. And the imagination is notoriously weak when it comes to clothing concepts with flesh and blood. Some feminists have attempted utopias—one thinks of Charlotte Perkins Gilman's *Herland*—and certainly women need more work of this kind to stir their imaginations.

This section offers both conceptual guidelines and some concrete models to aid the envisioning of an alternative future.

Rosemary Radford Ruether analyzes two models that dominate thinking about possible futures: the linear trajectory, moving onward and upward toward a limitless goal; and the cyclical model, which tends to repeat certain proven patterns. While both have biblical roots—in the apocalypse and in Eden—both reappear in secular guise in the nineteenth and twentieth centuries. On one hand, Ruether criticizes the linear model—whether in its secular form of endless technological progress or in its Marxist form of social revolution and the classless society—as too absolutist, expecting a solution "once and for all." On the other hand, those who long for Eden out of their vision of a simpler life can fall into a romantic idealism.

Finally, Ruether finds in the biblical notion of a year of Jubilee the germ of a viable model that combines the strengths of the linear and the cyclical. The year of Jubilee was ordained every fifty years to get society off to a fresh start—debts were canceled, captives freed, the people renewed their determination to live in justice and charity with one another. She suggests that many of the characteristics of the good society can be named—a human scale, a just sharing of material goods, a measure of self-determination for each person, work that utilizes head and hands. But this order cannot be realized once and for all; rather, each generation must use its limited energies to move toward the ideal in its concrete historical circumstances. The cycle does not return to the same place; the trajectory becomes a modest spiral.

Carol Coston, speaking out of her ten years' experience at Network, a Catholic social justice lobby, takes hold of the problem at the other end. Noting how strongly feminist analyses have pointed to the need for new economic structures, she introduces in some detail three going concerns, which in quite different circumstances have developed models of economic democracy: the Mondragon experiment in Spain with its eighty producer cooperatives; the Scott-Bader Commonwealth, described in *Small Is Beautiful;* and Network, a nonprofit educational and lobbying organization. She focuses on the specific mechanisms these enterprises have devised to put into practice their basic values of participation, self-determination, stewardship, and integration. She concludes with some practical suggestions for ways women can bond to build alternative enterprises that would be both economically healthy and socially responsible.

33

Envisioning Our Hopes: Some Models of the Future
ROSEMARY RADFORD RUETHER

How do we envision our hopes? What patterns shape our imagination when we speak of the need to build a better world? It is important to look at these models because, to a large extent, they both shape and limit our ability to imagine something different. Our projections generate contradictions that we do not understand until we look at the unconscious patterns that we use to imagine alternatives to the present.

The dominant model that has shaped the Western imagination about the future for the last two hundred years has been some version of secular messianism. This model has, of course, much older roots in the Judeo-Christian tradition of messianic hope. But only in the last two centuries has the notion that humans themselves could shape the ideal future become a prominent force in human affairs. Secular messianism shapes the imagination to think in terms of a linear trajectory or flight forward and upward from a bad past and present to a utopian future.

Several assumptions have been contained within this model of secular messianism. One assumption is that linear change, change as upward mobility, is good. Cyclical patterns of change are bad. Biblical professors, among others, promulgated this dogma. Linear is biblical and good. Cyclical is pagan and bad. Second, linear change is a flight from the finite into the infinite; the old Christian idea of flight from the created into the infinite or transcendent world has been laid on its side. But the secular messianic flight into the future is still understood as a flight from the limited into the limitless.

Third, the better future is seen as coming about through the

Rosemary Radford Ruether

conquest of nature. Nature is the static, evil pole to be overcome through historical transcendence. When one rereads the Protestant theologians of the last two centuries, it is startling to see how consistently nature is defined negatively.[1] This trajectory into the future is seen in moral terms. Evil is conquered; good is established. Finally, it is a monolinear change. There is only one line into the future, one correct direction, not a plurality of possibilities. The end is once and for all, another favorite expression of modern Protestant theologians.[2] There is one paradigm and one future solution.

Three different versions of the secular messianic myth have shaped modern imagination: progress, revolution, and apocalypse.

The progress model was particularly prominent in the nineteenth and early twentieth centuries. It is still evoked today, but with considerably more ambivalence. Progress understands the conquest of nature as a project of endless expansion of scientific knowledge and technological productivity. Scientific knowledge will gradually unveil all the secrets of nature and thus give humans (White elite males) increasing mastery over nature. This scientific knowledge will be implemented through technology. As a result of science, expressed in technology, all that has enslaved humanity—ignorance, superstition, poverty, disease—will be progressively conquered. In the writings of the Marquis de Condorcet at the end of the eighteenth century can be found the dream of progress at its most ambitious. Eventually the limits of human mortality will be overcome. Science and technology will conquer the last enemy, death itself.[3]

Today this ideology of progress appears under the guise of developmentalism. Having ceased to believe in progress in the first world, it is now being exported to the Third World! Developmentalism, as it was promulgated in the 1950s, would direct the rich nations to help the poor nations to industrialize. The assumption is that there is one typology of how to industrialize, represented by Western Europe and the United States. These nations represent advanced stages of this trajectory of industrialization, while the poor nations are poor because they are underdeveloped. The rich nations get the poor nations on the bandwagon moving in the same direction as themselves.

In the mid-1960s, Third World thinkers began to criticize this myth of development.[4] They pointed out that development does not work in the Third World because it is carried on under conditions of exploitation of labor and the material resources of colonized regions. Far from trickling down, such development gushes up. The gap between rich and poor is increased rather than overcome. Industrialization under conditions of neocolonialist dependency cannot be universalized to include everyone; it is structured to create superprofits for the multinational corporations. Moreover, it runs increasingly into ecological contradictions. It is based on monopolizing and using up finite resources on behalf of the rich, not on building a base for sustainable life for future generations. Developmentalism points to its own collapse in mass poverty, pollution, famine, and warfare.

The second pattern of the future in modern society is revolution. The revolutionary model, as carried out by Marxist ideology, recognizes a truth that progress does not: progress does not work for the vast majority of the world because it monopolizes ownership of the means of production by the capitalist class. Therefore, it is necessary to carry out a revolutionary overthrow of this ownership class and reorganize the ownership of the means of production in the hands of the workers themselves. It will then be possible to create an alternative form of industrialization or development from the bottom, on behalf of the vast majority who are presently poor.

This model has been in action in recent years in China, Cuba, and Nicaragua, and it represents the aspirations of many other peoples around the world. The old liberal dream of satisfying the basic needs for education, medical benefits, food, clothing, and housing for all is carried out in a way that starts with the poorest and most needy. The results are impressive, particularly when contrasted with the situation in these countries before the revolution. Mass literacy campaigns have overcome massive illiteracy. New medical systems have been established to deliver basic medical care to the poorest throughout the countryside, rather than monopolizing an advanced medical care system in the cities for an urban elite. In Cuba, the government concentrates on building a system that can produce housing and basic foodstuffs and goods for everyone at a minimal level. If more affluent people want more than that, they have to pay a much higher price.

But there is a flaw in the revolutionary ideology that even the best of the Marxist states does not seem to be able to overcome. The system is based on the unification of all the functions of the revolutionary system in the hands of one party, the managers of the revolution, who are simultaneously the army, the government, and the economic directors. This concept of the state is called totalitarianism. It rejects the liberal suspicion of putting too much power in the hands of one group—the classical concept of checks and balances. Reliance on the all-controlling revolutionary party absolutizes the revolutionary process as monolinear and once and for all. The good revolution is set against the evil counterrevolutionaries.

Of course the threat of counterrevolution is real, both from within as internal subversion by the remnants of old ruling classes, and from without, by global capitalism. Paranoia is justified, particularly in the Caribbean and Central American struggles; paranoia is simply a way of saying that they are out to get you. But this real threat of subversion accelerates the tendency toward rigidity in the revolutionary party. This type of political system and ideology does not seem to be able to filter out the difference between subversion and criticism. It is not able to leave a space for pluralism, for civil and intellectual freedom. The party develops an infallibility complex. It is all-knowing; it alone has the correct line to the future. This dogmatism has fossilized the Communist parties of Eastern Europe particularly, which have expended their efforts in the last decades to suppress constructive efforts at internal renewal of socialist ideology and practice.

The third model of the future that has shaped the modern imagination is that of the apocalypse. Apocalypticism is the particular temptation of the 1980s, especially today among the liberal left. There are many valid reasons for such attitudes of doom and gloom. Tracing forward into the future the present trajectories of militarism, ecological destruction, overpopulation, and pollution seems to lead only to the inevitable unleashing of the four horsemen. The bowls of wrath are filled to the brim and are about to be spilled out over the world.

But there is also a psychological attraction to the apocalyptic scenario. It will all blow up, and then it will all be over. All will be returned to the peace and quiet of primordial death. Maybe the blowup will also return humanity to its primordial beginnings. New life will begin in the radioactive sea, and perhaps it will start over again in a better way. There is a kind of relief of tension in the final big explosion that ends it all. At cocktail parties each person adds another piece to the picture of inevitable disaster. Eyes begin to glisten as the picture of inescapable catastrophe builds up. What is going on here? Apocalypse allows one to be both radical and passive at the same time. One can prove that one knows how bad it is. But since it is so bad, there is no use trying to do anything about it.

Besides this left-wing apocalyptic thinking, there is also a right-wing version of the apocalypse abroad in the land. It is called Armageddon. This scenario is cultivated particularly by evangelical militarists. According to this myth God is preparing the instruments of destruction for His enemies. Nuclear war is the means by which God will destroy the evil ones. Nuclear holocaust will break out, of course, in Israel, since that is God's chosen land for the final struggle between good and evil. The elect will be wafted up into the air in a process called "the rapture." Christ will lead the heavenly hosts in wiping out the armies of the godless nations, the Communists. The earth will be cleansed by fire. And then the elect will descend again to inhabit an earth purified of all evil. One might think that few could take such a drama seriously. But, in fact, there are a number of its devotees in the Reagan administration, such as the secretary of the interior.[5] It is unnecessary, such people believe, and even unfaithful to God's plans to try to avert nuclear war or to conserve natural resources.

In addition to these various types of secular messianism, an alternative model of change has shaped Western imagination in the last two centuries, this one also having ancient cultural roots. It is built on the myth of the utopian beginning rather than the utopian end of history. Once there was a time when men and women were equal, there was no hierarchy, no class structure, no urban civilization. People lived in harmony with nature, and nature gave forth her fruits spontaneously without labor. This myth of Eden draws on the idealization of preagricultural hunting and gathering societies, plus the memory of babyhood in all of us.

The myth of the return to nature, or to earlier, simpler human societies, was cultivated by romanticism in the nineteenth century and continues to have great influence, particularly on the ecological movement and some branches of the women's movement. Out of this romantic imagination, scholarship has reconstructed many of the evidences of the earlier societies of both preurban and early urban cultures. The sources for the cultures and religions of these pre-Judeo-Christian peoples in the Mediterranean world and in Europe were discovered and translated. Ancient paganism was seen as the religion that put human society in harmony with nature, in contrast to dualistic religion promoted by Christianity. Romanticism idealizes the groups that have been suppressed in Western culture: women, peasants, Native Americans, Blacks, and South Sea Islanders. These "nature people" are in touch with their bodies and the earth; they are endowed with "soul," rather than with alienated intellect.

Romanticism directs its followers toward a dismantling of the large structures of modern technology, urbanization, and centralized political power. It suggests a return to simpler, more familial structures where there is an integration of head and hand, culture and agriculture, work and play. Utopian socialists explored this kind of reconstruction of more organic communities in the nineteenth century, and twentieth-century ecologists have been taking up this quest with new emphasis on alternative technology based on renewable energy sources, such as sun, wind, and water. Romanticism also values the human capacities suppressed by lopsided, left-brained male culture. It cultivates the intuitive, the artistic, and the poetic, rather than linear rationality.

These romantic traditions contain much that is good and valuable, and they have been rightly taken up by feminism, which recognizes romanticism as valuing those capacities traditionally denigrated by masculinity. There are two deformations of the romantic tradition that one must guard against, however. I name these deformations not to reject the romantic tradition as a whole, but rather to identify them in order to be able to defend what is indispensable for feminism in the romantic tradition. These two deformations have occurred in various forms within movements inspired by the back-to-nature ideology. For want of better terms, I call these deformations two-spheres romanticism and fascism.

Two-spheres romanticism appears whenever members of an alienated elite from the possessing classes, usually male but sometimes female, wish to embrace the sphere of the repressed while retaining their own privileged way of life. They then refashion the places to which women, peasants, Native Americans, Blacks, and South Sea Islanders have been restricted as vacationlands for themselves. The whole romantic remodeling of the patriarchal ideology of womanhood and the home has been the most pervasive expression of this two-sphered ideology. The home is idealized as the Garden of Eden, an oasis of tranquility, harmony, and loving relationships. Women are to be strictly segregated in this home and garden to cultivate the paradise of love and peace in opposition to the real world of materialism, strife, and technological rationality. Men then repair to this paradise to renew their spirits and to gain respite from the battle.

Tourism is another version of this same delusion. The "natives" are set aside on their islands of "primitive" culture to provide R&R for weary urbanites from advanced industrial cultures. One goes camping in national forests or flies to Hawaii or Fiji in order to relax and renew one's spirits by returning to what one imagines to be simple life-styles, dancing on the beach in a grass skirt and barbecuing under the palm trees. One seldom has any perception of how the natives are being exploited to provide entertainment in this vacationland experience.

What is wrong with the home-and-tourism ideology is not the instinct to return to simpler and more loving life-styles. The problem is that a delusion is created by setting up islands where the privileged play at returning to nature, islands whose sociology is unrecognized. The real world of alienated existence is reinforced rather than challenged by constructing a separate, compensatory sphere to which the elite repairs on its off hours.

If the romantic critique of alienated, technological civilization is to be taken seriously, the two spheres must be dismantled. Models must be developed for constructing the organic community as a new system that replaces the present system, rather than just serving as a refuge from it. To construct an alternative community of new social relations, new technology and new relations to nature are a beginning. Even these alternative communities cannot remain utopian, but have to serve as a base for organizing politically to dismantle the larger systems of destruction that surround them.

A second deformation of the romantic tradition is fascism, a more virulent form of the mentality that wishes to retain the privileges of technological civilization while fantasizing the recovery of organic community. Fascism exalts the technological and warfare state in totalitarian form but attempts to transform it into the organic community by massive ideological indoctrination. Rather than dismantling the real structures of alienation, a marginal group is chosen as scapegoat for modern alienation from what is imagined to be an earlier, happier period of the society. If only this group of aliens can be purged from the society, it is said, the earlier familial community will be restored. Members of the scapegoat group are seen as pests or as a disease in the body politic, causing all the problems of modern urban life. Purging them (killing or expelling them) from the society is presented as curative. European fascism fastened on the Jews as the scapegoats in the fascist project of recovery of organic community. Modern America would probably focus on homosexuals, although gays are only the most provocative target on the hit list. Feminists, non-Whites, Jews, poor people, and Communists are also despised. But gays are the group that can most openly be stigmatized as the disease that has caused the loss of paradise (patriarchal, small-town, White America).

Feminists need to guard against versions of both these deformations. They too could play at feminist back-to-nature, without serious efforts to reconstruct the system. Although women are not in the positions of power to do the fascist scapegoating of the enemy on a large scale, they could develop their small-scale version of it within the women's separatist community. Males would then become the demonic aliens, whose very nature is defective and lacking the full humanity possessed by women. Men would be seen as unsalvageable as human beings, naturally tending to alienated, destructive forms of existence. Women would be able to construct the organic community only by purging themselves of relations with males.

In this way women would fail to take responsibility for their own human ambiguity and project the negative side of themselves on men. They would identify a particular social construct (in which some males—elite White males—have had privilege) with the nature of men as such, and imagine that women would automatically create the organic community if only they could do it without the presence of men. There are enough truths in this to make the project of the better community of women appear plausible. But it fails to reckon with the fact that whenever cohumanity between human groups is systematically denied, the separatist group loses its own capacity for humor and self-criticism. In projecting the negative capacities of human nature on the other, the separatists become rigid and hostile to outsiders—not only to men, but to other women who do not share the same opinion. The separatists begin to duplicate some of the oppressive, dogmatic patterns they have denounced in the others. Moreover, a real reconstruction of the whole cannot take place from a separatist stance, but only when the alternative group sees itself as an attractive paradigm on behalf of the whole.

The patterns of change in recent culture have both attractions and defects. There is an alternative that has some promise of uniting the strengths of the models of both future historical hope and back-to-nature, without some of their flaws. This alternative also appears in the Bible, but it is distinct from the messianic millennarian tradition: the tradition of the Jubilee found in Leviticus 25:8–12. It is not necessary to take the prescriptions of the Jubilee literally, but rather to look at it as an alternative model for imagining change that combines the linear and the cyclical.

In the Jubilee tradition, change is seen not as one big cycle, or one big, once-and-for-all leap into the future, but as a series of periodic restorations and renewals that correct the specific deformations that have occurred in a particular period. The Jubilee tradition assumes that there are certain just and harmonious patterns of relationship among humans and between humanity and nature that make for life as God intended it. These are described in terms of the free peasant society of small landholders of ancient Israel as opposed to the systems of slave-holding, big landowners of the ancient Near East. In the good society, everyone would have their own lot of land sufficient to support their families, their own vine and fig tree. No one would be enslaved to another. No one would be overburdened by debts that would cause them, gradually, to lose their land and then their freedom. The land and animals would not be overworked.

But human sinfulness causes a drift away from this intended state of peace and justice. Debts pile up. Some people have their land expropriated by others. Great landlords arise; tenant farmers fall into serfdom or are sold into slavery. Nature is overworked. So, on a periodic basis, every fifty years, there must be a revolution. Every seven times seven years, there must be a call to "proclaim liberty throughout the land [Lev. 25:10]." This corresponds to a revolution every two generations (time for you and then your children to grow up). The accumulated overload of debts must be liquidated (forgiven). Those who have been sold into captivity must be released. The land that has been expropriated must be returned to its original owners. The land and animals are allowed to rest. Humanity and nature recover their just balance.

Although modern people might want a few more urban and

technological amenities, they too have an idea of what makes for a just and liveable society. That idea includes a human scale of habitats and communities, the ability of people to participate in the decisions that govern their lives, work in which one can integrate the intellectual and the physical, a just sharing of the benefits of production, a balance of urban and rural environments, technologies based on renewable energy sources that do not pollute the environment, and so on. In this sense, the vision of the good society is not arbitrary, but there are some rules in the nature of things that shape the ability of people to live justly with one another and nondestructively with nonhuman nature. This base in human and natural ecology is the point of reference for criticizing and changing alienated systems.

But the important insight of the Jubilee tradition is that it cannot be done once and for all. To be human is to be in a state of finite process, to change and to die. Both change and death are good. They belong to the natural limits of life, and human beings need to seek the life intended for them by God within these limits. But this return to just ways of living with one another and with nature is never a cyclical return to what existed in some idealized time in the past. Each new achievement of liveable, humane balance will be different, based on new technologies and new cultures, belonging to different moments in time and place. It is a historical project to be undertaken again and again in changing circumstances.

The mandate is not to create the revolution once and for all, but to create the revolution for this generation, so that people can pass on to their children a world where they too can live and change, where they can die of old age, rather than of bombs and poisoned gas. Only when human beings overcome the tyranny of the absolutizing imagination can we turn our finite energies (which are the only kind of energies we have) to doing what we need to do for our time and for our generation.

34

A Feminist Approach to Alternative Enterprises
CAROL COSTON

Several challenges have emerged during this conference. One, of course, is women's need for self-determination and some kind of economic independence. Second, as Jamie Phelps has said ("Racism and the Bonding of Women," pp. 70–74), and as the Black community has been saying for years, there is a need for employment, housing, and education. Yolanda Tarango and Ada Maria Isasi-Diaz spoke of people coming to the U.S. from the Hispanic tradition—the Mexican Americans, the Cubans—people fleeing from Haiti and similar places (" 'Las Marías' of the Feminist Movement," pp. 85–88). Again, employment is a key problem.

Another challenge is to find alternatives to all the "isms" that are bothering women—sexism, racism, militarism, classism. The final challenge, as Mary Hunt has said ("Political Oppression and Creative Survival," pp. 164–72), is trying to find a way to deal with social structures and to build new communities.

What alternative enterprises would be appropriate to a feminist perspective? In a more humane world of work, there would be diverse groups of women bonding in economic, social, and spiritual support; they would create cooperative enterprises. Some of these would be owned by women, others by women and men, but all of them would share the values of participation, self-determination, stewardship, and integration. These businesses would make products that were nonviolent, that would not exploit the environment. The work would be done in an environment that emphasized the quality of life. Flex-time arrangements for families would be encouraged. There would be ongoing education, there would be time and

Carol Coston

space for the aesthetic and the spiritual, there would be support systems such as child care, health care, pensions, and so on.

The salary scale in these enterprises would be adequate, but it would not create a class system. In *Three Guineas* (first published in 1938), Virginia Woolf responds to three people, each requesting a donation for a worthy cause: a women's college, a society for advancing women in the professions, a society for the prevention of war. Taking seriously the question of how to prevent war, she analyzes the class structures, the values, and the prejudices of the culture, and concludes that she will not give money to any of the three groups unless they take the lessons that "the uneducated daughters of educated men" have learned—poverty, chastity, derision, and freedom from false loyalty. Her definition of poverty would apply to a salary scale in alternative enterprises: "By poverty is meant enough money to live on. You must earn enough to be independent of any other human being and to buy that modicum of health, leisure, knowledge and so on that is needed for the full development of body and mind. But no more. Not a penny more." She also states: "By chastity is meant that when you have made enough to live on by your profession, you must refuse to sell your brain for the sake of money."[1] (Perhaps we should send this definition to the Vatican as they revise canon law.)

The profits from these enterprises would go to the worker owners, to ongoing research and development, and to local community needs. In these enterprises the division of labor would be structured horizontally, decided collectively or by delegated representatives, and there would be creative ways to handle and share more tedious tasks. (For background read Charlotte Perkins Gilman's *Herland,* a description of a feminist utopia with creative ideas for building an alternative future.[2])

One enterprise that succeeded using such an approach is the Mondragon experiment, which took place in the Basque region of Spain. It began with the inspiration of a Catholic priest who in his seminary studies recognized that the Church's social encyclicals offered principles to create an alternative economic system that was different from either capitalism or socialism. In the 1940s, Father José Maria Arizmendi returned to Mondragon and established a technical training school. The areas he wanted to emphasize were worker ownership and worker management. This is a key difference between his vision and some of the cooperatives that had been tried earlier in England. One English cooperative, for example, was doing quite well and wanted to expand, but instead of keeping the shares among the workers, the cooperative offered shares to outside buyers who wanted to increase their own incomes and had no concern about the quality of life in the work place. Within a couple of years the enterprise had ceased to function. Father Arizmendi insisted that the cooperative be kept in the hands of the workers.

The cooperative started in 1954 with five of his graduates who had gone to engineering school, then came back and tried his ideas out in a local factory. The owners of the factory were not impressed, nor were they cooperative, so the five men got together and with Arizmendi's backing were able to obtain enough money to start manufacturing little cooking stoves. From this they moved to electrical products and then to a casting shop and foundries, which became support industries for the factories. By 1981 there were more than eighty cooperatives—worker-owned producer cooperatives, employing some 17,000 people, which is about 12 percent of that region.

The finances are such that each worker has to buy a personal share, now something like 2,000 pounds. If the worker does not have that money in his or her family, it can be borrowed from the Caja Laboral Popular—the Bank of the Working People—which was established as a secondary cooperative specifically to be a support system. It now has 300,000 depositors.

The salary scale was set so that the highest-paid worker earns no more than three times the lowest. The lowest paid in these particular cooperatives made more than the pay scale in a similar enterprise in the surrounding area. The middle pay scale was about the same, and those that worked in the top management received much lower salaries than in comparable businesses. A local community that does not have a huge disparity in salaries is free of class structures as well. At the end of any given year, the profits are divided 70-20-10. Seventy percent goes to a fund that is kept for the worker owners until they leave the cooperative, so that it continues to accrue and earn interest; the fund is deposited in the Caja Laboral Popular. Twenty percent is put into a reserve fund that serves as a buffer for emergencies, and 10 percent goes into local community projects.

Each worker has equal voting rights. At a general assembly held once a year, workers elect their board, usually around twelve people. The board of directors—composed of workers—then hires the manager. The manager is responsible to the board and can be fired by it. Members meet weekly and are not paid any extra for being on the board. The board rotates some new members each year, so that change is possible and more people learn to take leadership. The workers also elect a social policy advisory board that operates by departments. Each of the worker groups—the secretarial pool, the truck drivers, the foundry workers—elects to the advisory board one of its members; the board then sets questions of policy and makes recommendations on the conditions of the work place, according to the members' particular experiences. Another essential support system is social security. Because they were worker-owners they were not eligible for Spain's social security, so they developed a system of their own. They also have an education system that enables high-school students to learn the cooperative model. The students buy shares so that not only are they making money according to their cooperative standings at the end of the year, but they also experience the values of cooperative management, which eliminates middle management and encourages individual responsibility.

Another component of the Mondragon experiment is research and development, which serves all the cooperatives. It does anticipatory planning for new products and lines up the type of scientific research needed to develop them.

The Mondragon experiment works. Experts from the London School of Economics, among others, have visited Spain to evaluate the experiment according to economic criteria. Mondragon comes off as well as or better than similar-sized capitalist corporations in terms of profit alone, but when the other social factors are considered it comes off even better: the quality of life, the work relationships, the contributions to the local environment, the technical training, and the support systems.

The second model is described in E. F. Schumacher's *Small Is Beautiful*[3]—the Scott Bader Company. It began with a man who inherited a factory that made polyester resins. When he reached retirement age he did not want to desert the factory. He remembered how it was when he was a worker, not an owner, and he wanted to do something creative with it—he wanted to "fit industry to human needs." The values he tried to incorporate as he transformed this factory into a worker-owned enterprise were a sense of freedom, happiness, and human dignity—without loss of profit.

The finances were shifted by a transformation from family ownership into incorporation. The salary range is seven to one, before taxes; the highest-paid worker cannot earn more than seven times the lowest paid. As to profits, 20 percent is bonuses to workers, 20 percent goes into charitable projects outside the company, and the remaining 60 percent is used for taxation and self-financing.

The management style is different from Mondragon's. The owner converted the business from private ownership to become the Scott Bader Commonwealth, which was then vested with ownership of the firm. The workers were given the authority to run the business. The new partners, who were the former employees, established a constitution that articulated their freedoms, responsibilities, and restrictions. The constitution says that because of work relationships and quality of life the plant size has to be limited to no more than 350 workers, and that the members of the commonwealth cannot be dismissed by their coworkers, the partners, except for gross personal misconduct (it does not say how that would be determined, or by whom). The board is fully accountable to the commonwealth, composed of the workers, and therefore they can confirm the board people, their appointment, and their rate of remuneration. A final restriction in the constitution is that no products are to be sold for war-related purposes.

The third alternative model is a nonprofit organization called Network. This model also began with a vision and some agreed-upon values; the programs and financing and everything else flowed from that. The vision was that the organization would be a network of sisters. Today Network has evolved into a Catholic social justice lobby. Membership is open to and encouraged for all sectors of people who are interested in this particular social justice tradition, which comes from the Catholic social encyclicals.

In the beginning, each staff person took the time to write out her own vision of what a just world would look like. That was very important, because one can be overwhelmed by issues such as the MX missile, voting rights, the federal budget, etc., unless one has some analysis or critique to guide choices on the positions one is going to take publicly. The values that emerged from all the visions were participation, cooperation, stewardship, mutuality, and integration.

Network produces publications, workshops, seminars, action-alerts, and so on. All the products are based on the principles and values found in the social justice teachings, the experiences of women, and the cries of the poor. This is undergirded by political reflection, which is part of a sense of stewardship about resources, part of an attempt to be integrated.

How are the finances at this point? We started with $159 in 1972, and our budget this year is almost $230,000. Forty-five to 50 percent comes from membership fees, about 40 percent from ongoing sustaining donations from religious communities (particularly of women), an annual fund drive, the donated services of the staff who started out working for little or nothing, and fees from our workshops.

All the work at Network is considered equally important, therefore there is equal pay for work of equal value. We are moving toward equal pay for all staff members. Those who are in religious communities will get a raise in salary, because we found a two-tier salary scale was problematic. Those who have dependents, such as a divorced woman with children or an elderly parent, receive an additional amount.

The management style is participative and circular. The goals of Network—educating, publishing, lobbying, and so on—are our central mission, and everything we have to do to make that happen is equally important. So publications, research, lobbying, administration, promotion, development, and organizing are symbolized by interlocking circles. Any important decisions, such as salary, new staff, new programs, and so on, are made by the entire staff at annual planning days and at subsequent meetings. It is everybody's organization, and we take responsibility accordingly.

Having shared my vision of alternative work places and some actual models, I suggest some strategies. First, some of us within the various communities represented here at this conference need to learn more about cooperatives and collective models throughout the world, as expressed in diverse cultures. The cooperative movement is small in the United States, but there are a number of cooperatives in Canada, Yugoslavia, England, and so on from which data needs to be gathered. Special attention should be paid to the Mondragon cooperatives.

Second, we need to develop a pool of women with technical training. We need people who can travel to where new groups are forming to pass on their technical training, and also to form a network that will eventually connect all the groups. We need marketing analysis; we need to learn about financing, cooperative values and management, research and development.

Third, it would be an interesting challenge to locate an area or a region where worker-cooperatives could be attempted on a small scale. We might start where interest and support bases are already in place, such as active community organizations and consumer cooperatives.

Finally, we have a political task: to encourage other women and men to transform the work environment by offering examples of alternative enterprises that are both economically healthy and socially responsible.

Part IX

Rituals and Celebrations

IN THIS VISION of women bonding, modes of communication beyond the verbal played a significant part. We were sure that we wanted to share in this way, although we had some difficulty naming what we wanted to do. The conference program listed two "liturgical consultants"—Julia Upton and Diann Neu—but it soon became clear that "liturgy" carried too many distinctively Catholic connotations to be appropriate to our diversities of background and belief. "Worship," with its strong implication of a transcendent being to be worshiped, also presupposed too much. Finally, we settled for "rituals" or "celebrations," not making any sharp distinction between the two terms, but meaning by them actions performed by a community, having enough formal or solemn character to lift them out of the daily routine, and at the same time striking a festive note of praise and rejoicing.

We knew what we wanted our rituals to accomplish: uniting and energizing the group, increasing and deepening the store of shared meanings, enabling individuals to draw upon their physical, emotional, and imaginative powers as well as their analytic skills. We have often observed that in meetings where the participants join together in celebrations, communication flows more easily, a climate of mutual trust is formed more readily, and people are better able to work through conflicts of principle or policy. Somehow, sharing hopes and fears in a context of ritual both expresses shared meanings and contributes to making new meanings. Ritual uses concrete physical things—water, bread, fire, flowers, fruit, the human body—to call into play the whole person. Coparticipants in a ceremony, by their very presence, affirm one another, and can move beyond affirmation to celebration of one another's gifts and strengths. At its best, ritual can enable people to touch the depths of reality together, an experience that is a powerful means of bonding.

Of course, to exercise such healing and energizing power, ritual must be authentic, reflecting the real thoughts and feelings of the participants. Hence, it must provide space for spontaneous expression as well as some recognizable and comfortably familiar structure. But it must also be rooted in a tradition. Rituals cannot be made out of whole cloth, so to speak. Part of the power of ritual lies in its resonance, its use of elements that evoke communal as well as personal memories, that place the participants in the line of the generations that have gone before. Two sources of resonance that are readily available are the great natural symbols—water, fire, bread, wine; and the religious traditions that are alive in this culture. The Jewish and Christian traditions pose grave problems for those who reject sexism, misogyny, and patriarchy, and yet they offer indispensable starting points for future developments.

It was no easy task the ritual planning team took on. The nine team members included representatives of Catholic, Protestant, Jewish, and Wicca traditions. In the materials that follow, Diann Neu, Julia Upton, and Ellen Umansky reflect on their experience of trying to provide structure as well as spontaneity, to respect diverse traditions while achieving some authentic unity. They suggest guidelines for planners and also include the bare outlines of two specific rituals; one uses the symbol of water as cleansing and healing, the other uses the structure of the traditional Jewish sabbath meal as a vehicle to affirm the different traditions of the participants. The outlines are the skeletons, the bare bones, to which the feelings, thoughts, songs, poems, prayers, and dances of the participants gave flesh and blood.

An important experience for many of the participants in the week was the series of Wicca rituals, which Starhawk facilitated after the close of the formal program each evening. Some of the elements of these rituals are described in her books *The Spiral Dance* and *Dreaming the Dark*.

35

Guidelines for Planners of Rituals

DIANN NEU AND JULIA UPTON

Ritual is the means by which members of the human community savor an event or a passage that has significance in their lives. Using symbols that express a reality beyond what they signify, we come together around that focal point and allow ourselves to be centered by it.

Thus, as the anniversary of my daughter's birth approaches, I want to pause and savor the significance of that event in her life, in my life, and in the lives of those whom she has touched. Around that event swirls a rhapsody of past, present, and future, all of which come together in the ritual moment. The birthday cake is more than food, and the candles more than light, for in the ritual we experience a transformation of ordinary things into vehicles of the sacred, and thus the full impact of the event penetrates us more deeply than it would without the ritual.

At Women's Spirit Bonding we wanted the community present to experience the full impact of the presentations, the events, and the environment of each day's activities. For that reason, we built into each day a time for ritual activity—a time for savoring the significance that the day had had in our lives.

Because the women gathered at Grailville came from widely diverse religious and nonreligious backgrounds, we decided to use only universal symbols in our rituals, except for the ritual meal. Symbols such as water and fire break through the lines of religious traditions and speak to the human community words of healing, cleansing, comfort, warmth, wholeness.

We came to the conference with no prepackaged rituals, and instead each day formed an ad hoc group of women who wanted to participate in planning the day's celebration. Each day's group was different, as was each day's ritual. This was not always easy, but it was honest; the rituals were not superimposed on the conference, but rather flowed with and from the events of each day.

Finding symbols and creating rituals that spoke to all and were relevant to our experience together was a challenge, an almost impossible task. The results were uneven, yet the efforts were rewarding.

Some guidelines that we found helpful in creating feminist rituals:

1. Invite each planner to share her feelings, insights, reactions to the day's input. Each is part of the community. If we are in touch with ourselves and listen to one another, we can highlight common reflections that may be helpful for the celebration.
2. From what has been heard, begin to name the energy in the group. State what needs to be celebrated.
3. Suggest the symbols, music, readings, poems, dances, prayer forms that express the central theme of the celebration. Be sure to use inclusive language and symbols.
4. Identify what environment/setting enhances the celebration.
5. Plan the structure of the celebration so that leadership for various parts is shared. Be sure that participants are actively involved in sharing a meaningful part of their lives. Try to strike a balance between structure and spontaneity, words and music, dance or other movement and rest, speech and silence.
6. Lift up and affirm diverse elements and traditions in a healing way.
7. Gather in a circle. If the group is large, move from one large circle to smaller ones, each with a celebration leader, and back to the large circle.

The following outline for a ritual based on the natural symbolism of water grew out of the day devoted to women and poverty.

36

A Ritual of Water

SETTING A large open space indoors; in its center a table covered with a cloth on which are a large bowl of water surrounded by thirteen empty bowls and thirteen towels. Rugs on the floor mark out places for small groups.

OPENING: The group forms one large circle, chanting the following song:

> I am a circle, I am healing you
> You are a circle, you are healing me.

READING: Ecclesiastes 3:1–8 (A time for everything).

INTRODUCTION: To focus the day and give the structure of the celebration.

ACTION: "I am a circle" is sung as thirteen women come forward, forming a circle around the table in the center. Each takes an empty bowl, scoops some water into it from the large bowl and moves to one of the rugs where smaller groups have formed and where she serves as celebration leader.

NAMING: The leaders invite each woman to sing her name; the small groups respond by chanting the name, continuing until each one has sung her own name. (Quiet time)

GRIEVING: The leaders invite each one to think of times of grieving, burdens that bind, what we have lost or fear losing. Each one is invited to put her body in a grieving position—hands over face, bent-over body, arms clutching knees in a fetal position—and to speak her grief in a word or phrase.

HEALING: When all have finished, the leaders let the water flow through their hands. A sound like a waterfall fills the room. Each one is then invited to receive the healing power of the water—drinking it, sprinkling it on another, letting it flow through her fingers, washing her hands and face.

When everyone has received the water, the small groups are invited to stand and begin reconnecting with the total group. Each leader returns her bowl to the central table, waiting silently, facing outward, until all have assembled. Then the thirteen celebration leaders turn toward the table and simultaneously pour the water from their groups back into the central bowl.

SONG: With the sound of water flowing, the Black spiritual "A Wonderful Change" is intoned and taken up by the group.

> A wonderful change has come over me (repeat)
> You've called my name and set me free (repeat)
> Change, change I'm so glad you've changed me (repeat)
> Change, change I'm so glad you've changed me (repeat)
> A wonderful change has come over me (repeat).

CLOSING: A celebration leader invites all to embrace as a sign of peace.

37

Reflections on the Creation of a Ritual Meal

ELLEN M. UMANSKY

How can we use traditional forms in an authentic way? That was the question the ritual meal posed for me. I did not want to create a nondenominational ritual that would gloss over or ignore the differences that existed among us. If the group at Grailville represented anything, it was not "woman" but "women"—Jewish, Christian, Black, White, Hispanic, lesbian, heterosexual, bisexual, American, non-American, rich, poor. My hesitation over creating a ritual meal was not rooted in the idea of worshiping with non-Jewish women. Rather, it lay with the idea—the fear, really—of being asked or expected to worship as anything other than a Jew.

Yet, to have created a Jewish ritual meal (a suggestion made by a member of the committee) would have been as inauthentic as creating a nondenominational one. As a group, we were not Jewish. Moreover, what had emerged during the week were not simply religious differences but differences that were racial, cultural, economic, even sexual in nature. If we were to have a ritual, then, that would enable us to celebrate together, we needed to express not only what united us but also what divided us. We needed to make our differences and our commonalities clear.

The decision to structure the meal around the Jewish sabbath celebration was mutual, based on the fact that our celebration was taking place on the eve of the sabbath and that the symbols Judaism uses either did hold or could hold meaning for all of us. The ritual followed the order of the sabbath meal: the lighting of the candles, the blessing over the wine, the washing of hands, the blessing over the bread, and then the sharing of food. In addition, we attached special significance to the number eighteen—eighteen candles, eighteen bowls of water, the eighteen women whose names we invoked—because the number eighteen in Hebrew spells out *chai,* the Hebrew word for life.

While the structure of the ritual was Jewish, the content went beyond that of a Jewish sabbath celebration, reflecting the many concerns that had been expressed during the week. The lighting of the menorah, the seven-branched candle holder, by seven women of different backgrounds expressed some of the major particularistic concerns raised during the week. The singing of "Shalom Aleichem," which echoes both the Hebrew and Arabic greetings of peace, underscored our common hope for the future. The lighting of the eighteen additional candles, one for each table, reflected our need to name our foresisters. In the seven blessings over the wine (seven symbolizes wholeness or completeness), we used words that were virtually identical in content, yet the different languages in which we spoke again reflected the difficulties of communication. Perhaps most symbolic of our reaching out to one another, attempting to transcend the very real tensions that had surfaced during the week, was our washing the hands of those next to us at table. Having thus symbolically cleansed ourselves and others of prejudice, fear, and hatred, we listened while women from four different traditions blessed four loaves of bread. Thus cleansed and renewed, we began to break bread together. After the meal, we regrouped into one large circle, embracing and joining one another in song and dance.

Our meal began with a voicing of our differences in the many languages used, the varied hopes and fears expressed. It ended with gestures of unity, reminding us that in listening to one another's voices and trying to understand one another's concerns we had taken one small step toward becoming sisters.

38
A Ritual Meal

SETTING: A dining room with eighteen tables, each set for a festive meal, with individual place settings, flowers, a whole loaf of wheat bread, and a pitcher of wine. On the center table, the menorah (the seven-branched candle holder), eighteen single candle holders, eighteen bowls of water, were set out.

OPENING: Having assembled outside, all entered the room together, forming a large circle around the tables while singing:

We are women's spirit bonding
and we are singing, singing for our lives (repeat)
  (Adapted from Holly Near's "Singing for Our Lives")

CANDLE-LIGHTING:

Menorah: Seven women, representing seven perspectives that had emerged in the group—Jewish, Black, Hispanic, Arabic, lesbian, poor, non-American—circled the center table. Each lit one candle while intoning a prayer for peace. The traditional sabbath melody "Shalom Aleichem" was sung by a solo voice, as others joined in humming the melody.

The eighteen single candles: Eighteen women came forward to the central table. Each spoke the name of one of our foresisters, cited her contribution, and lighted a candle to recall her spirit. The litany included figures from a more or less distant past—Lilith, Isis, Judith, Mary Magdalene, Brigid of Ireland, Catherine of Siena, Soeur Marie de l'Incarnation of Quebec; nineteenth-century women whose hidden histories have been recovered by feminist scholarship—Margaret Fuller, Olympia Brown, Mary

McKillop, Nellie McClung, Rosa Luxembourg, Mother Jones, Sojourner Truth; and women of our own century—Radclyffe Hall, Bertha Pappenheim, Dolores Huerta and Lolita LeBron, Ita Ford, Maura Clark, Dorothy Kazel and Jean Donovan, who met their death in El Salvador; the Mothers of the Plaza de Mayo in Buenos Aires; Rosa Parks; and Maggie Kuhn. When all the candles had been lighted, each woman took her candle and the placard bearing the name of the woman she had invoked to one of the dining tables. The participants seated themselves at the table of the woman most important to them, while singing "We are women's spirit bonding."

BLESSING OF THE WINE:

Seven women blessed the wine in seven different languages, beginning in Hebrew with the core blessing of the Jewish tradition and passing the cup around the circle:

> Brucha ya Shechinah, malcha ha alam Baray pri ha' gafen.
> Blessed are you Shechinah, Queen of the Universe, who has brought forth the fruit of the vine.
> The other languages used were Arabic, Creole, English, French, Gaelic, and Spanish. Women at the tables were invited to take a cup of wine, offer a blessing, and drink.

WASHING OF HANDS:

One person blessed the water and invited each woman to wash the hands of those at her table as a sign of reconciliation and healing. A person from each table received a bowl of water from the center table and returned to her place to begin the hand-washing.

BLESSING OF THE BREAD:

Circling the center table, four women from the Jewish, Christian, Unitarian, and Goddess traditions blessed the bread, each using gestures and prayers from her tradition. Women at the tables were invited to take their loaf of bread, offer a blessing, break the loaf, and eat.

SHARING THE FOOD:

> The blessing of food was offered. One person at each table became the server, bringing the main dishes from the kitchen.

CLOSING:

> When all had finished eating, the music began spontaneously, continuing to the end of "Song of the Soul" by Cris Williamson, when everyone stood up and danced. For the final sending forth, each woman was invited to offer an embrace of peace to continue the bonding.

Epilogue

We were ambitious enough to speak of "Women's Spirit Bonding." Here we assess the results of our efforts: What obstacles to bonding did we identify? What factors could we point to as aids to bonding? How far were we able to frame alternative visions? What practical suggestions can we offer for starting to move away from the "isms" and toward the alternatives?

Obstacles to Women Bonding

Our sense of urgency gave added impetus to our desire for bonding and sharpened our analyses of the barriers in our way. It is a truism that the "isms"—racism, classism, nationalism, imperialism, heterosexism—put major roadblocks in the way of women bonding. Our discussions rendered more acute our perceptions of how these "isms" have operated and are operating within the women's movement, even within our own conference.

First, racism. In putting forth the view that feminism offers an all-encompassing perspective on reality as well as an immense potential for transforming action, we faced the charge that in the United States feminism is a White middle-class movement, often both racist and anti-Semitic in practice. "Reflections on a Process" by Cheryl Giles and Nancy Richardson (pp. xxii–xxviii) examines in some detail how the total group struggled with these issues. Although we were not able to deal with racism as effectively as we would have liked in the context of the total group, we did considerable analysis in the base and working groups of the barriers to bonding from the perspectives of both Black and White women.

One of the major insights that emerged is the difference in historical consciousness between Black and White women. In the forefront of the consciousness of Black women is the long history of the exploitation of People of Color by Whites: in the African slave trade, in the practice of slavery in the United States, in the misery of Reconstruction, in the continuing racism in this country in both North and South. Black women are familiar with the history of co-optation of Blacks by White political movements seeking to further their own goals. Thus, after the Civil War the Republican Party pushed for Black male suffrage not out of a concern for human rights, but to assure their control of the South by adding two million Black males to the voting rolls. Black women are well acquainted with the history of the relations between White and Black women in this country—the harsh treatment their foremothers received at the hands of the slaveholders' wives; the often poorly paid drudgery of Black domestics serving White women employers. They called attention to the racist and elitist arguments used by

White feminist leaders, even such great figures as Elizabeth Cady Stanton, Susan B. Anthony, and Charlotte Perkins Gilman. They pointed to the willingness of the turn-of-the-century suffrage movement to sacrifice solidarity with Blacks for the sake of winning support from conservative White southern women and men. They judged the feminism of the 1970s as another instance of co-optation—in this case White middle-class women inviting token Black women to join in activities aimed primarily at enabling White feminists to enter the American mainstream. White women, who are otherwise highly educated and aware, are either totally ignorant of this unhappy past or barely advert to it as something that once existed but has now been overcome. This difference in consciousness between Black and White women is a major obstacle to bonding. In the light of history, Black women have little reason to trust White women who speak of sisterhood.

Racism has deep roots that continue to poison the atmosphere in the women's movement today. Among current manifestations of racism that we noted were these: the assumption, often unconscious, by White women that their agenda has universal validity for all women; the haste of White feminists to underline commonalities and ignore differences in the experience of White women and Women of Color; the inability of White women to hear the agendas of Black women, particularly their agendas around the Black family; the expectation that People of Color will take the responsibility of educating Whites, raising consciousness, identifying the problem, providing solutions, and above all giving absolution; the reluctance of White women to accept Black leadership and the tendency to treat Black women as junior partners who are expected to defer to the superior analysis of their White seniors; the use of "plantation politics," e.g., playing one Third World group off against another—Blacks against Hispanics, educated Blacks against working-class Blacks, etc.; the failure of White feminists to make racism an explicit part of their analysis, even when insisting on the interstructuring of the oppressions.

Out of their historical experience, White women have internalized attitudes that hinder bonding. Women of the middle and upper classes frequently find themselves in a position that can be described as "privilege without power." Socialized to passivity, dependence, and acceptance of blame, they may find it difficult to recognize themselves as either oppressed or oppressor. In comfortable financial circumstances, enjoying a secure family life or a privileged professional position, such women may resist seeing the elements of oppression in their situation—"I've never been discriminated against!" "I'm not a women's libber!" However, those who have discovered themselves to be oppressed, powerless, or dependent on husband or father or social approval are often unable to confront their complicity in the oppression of Women of Color. Or, when challenged in specific instances, they may succumb to guilt and paralysis. In the opinion of Third World women, White women generally lack sensitivity to cultural differences vis-à-vis Blacks, Hispanics, Asians, and Native Americans. Class and race prejudices—often unconscious—can lead to ignoring or downgrading differences rather than valuing them as possible sources of enrichment. If White women are to find ways to bond with Women of Color despite the "isms," they must say with Delores Williams, "Fuck the guilt"; they must eschew defensiveness, make fresh commitments in the light of new levels of awareness, and get on with the struggle.

"Anti-Semitism: The Unacknowledged Racism" by Judith Plaskow (pp. 89–96) is representative of recent work by Jewish women who are calling attention to the subtle anti-Semitism in the women's movement. Because so many women in the movement come from Christian backgrounds insensitive to the anti-Semitism in the New Testament and in Christian traditions, there are failures both of omission and commission: omission when the movement fails to speak out against anti-Semitic incidents and policies; commission, in the overt form of anti-Semitic jokes, or in a kind of unconscious Christian imperialism, which leads feminists to speak of the Judeo-Christian tradition as if the Christian interpretation of the Old Testament as foreshadowing the New were the only one. Plaskow expressed her resultant sense of alienation, not feeling at home in the Jewish community because of her feminism, but not at home in the feminist movement because of increasing evidence of anti-Semitism. The Hispanic women expressed a similar sense of alienation, for them a kind of triple jeopardy:

suspicion of their feminism in the Chicano community; charges of cultural illiteracy from the Latins of Mexico and Central America; invisibility among White feminists.

Another obstacle to bonding is the horizontal violence endemic in oppressed groups, whether in the Black ghettos or in the trashing that takes place in feminist groups. Victims making victims is the other side of divide-and-conquer, and arguments about who suffers the worst oppression simply feed into this destructive dynamic.

The lesbian group pointed out that the problem is not homosexuality, but rather homophobia (the fear of same-sex relationships) and heterosexism (making heterosexual relationships normative). Homophobia and heterosexism often devastate women's groups. Somehow many women seem to need other women not simply to affirm their own choice of life-style but to adopt it. This demand is equally destructive whether it comes from heterosexuals, who insist that their choice is the norm and other life-styles are deviations to be more or less tolerated, or from homosexuals who insist that lesbians are the only true feminists.

While we recognized the crucial importance of classism and imperialism as dividing women, we were not able to devote much time to explicit analysis of these two factors. Rather we concentrated on the interlocking and mutually supportive character of what we called "the web of oppressions." Racism and sexism have been used consistently in this country to split the working class and to weaken seriously the labor movement. While the servant girl and the society woman were able to stand shoulder to shoulder for a brief time on the picket lines and in the jails at the height of the suffrage movement, once the vote was won women tended to divide again along class and race lines. If we fight sexism without at the same time fighting racism, we will succeed in gaining new places for White women but not for Women of Color. Whatever our intentions, our actions in fact contribute toward White supremacy. Also, by accepting the preferential treatment accorded White women by the White male system, we end up supporting the sexism as well as the racism of the system. Capitalism and imperialism combine to move industries out of the United States to the Mexican border and to southeast Asia, where the garment and electronic industries employ large numbers of young women as cheap labor. While theoretical understanding of the interlocking character of the various systems of oppression is growing among feminists, we have not yet found adequate ways as a movement to join effectively in the struggle of poor, Black, and Third World women.

Factors Identified as Aids to Bonding

"Until we find each other, we are alone," writes Adrienne Rich in her powerful poem "Hunger." What can help us to find one another across the multiple barriers of race, class, ethnicity, heterosexism, religion?

Face-to-face meeting and dialogue is a sine qua non, although difficult to achieve because so many who are needed in the dialogue lack the necessary time and money. And if we think of bonding internationally, we Americans lack the language ability for communicating easily with women from other cultures. Too often we ask the other to speak our language, instead of reaching out in theirs.

Such meetings need to take place in a favorable physical environment. The planning group for our conference, after experience with urban hotels, college campuses, and retreat centers, chose Grailville for many reasons. The rural setting kept us in close touch with the natural environment (quite unlike the air-conditioned, neon-lighted, windowless hotel rooms) and offered possibilities for solitude and for a variety of activities—sunning, swimming, gardening, sketching, walking in the woods between sessions. Not least important was the fact that Grailville is a women's place, owned and run by women, who emphasize simplicity, wholesome food, and integrity of design and materials in daily surroundings.

The dialogue that leads to bonding proceeds by sharing personal histories. "What is unique about feminist theology is not its use of the criterion of experience but rather its use of women's experience," writes Rosemary Ruether in *Sexism and God Talk*. Women have come to affirm their own experience as a source of truth, a revelation of the holy, a theological locus, if you will, out of the experience of "hearing each other into speech." After centuries of having internalized the image of women as intellectually incapable, telling one's story to an attentive, respectful listener is the beginning of learning to trust one's own perceptions. The listening ear, the empathetic response, the clarifying question—these are the means by which women are empowering one another. Reflecting together on the shared experiences has brought a wealth of insights, the power to name self, world, oppressions. "I tell stories to myself in poems and prose," Delores Williams writes in "Women as Makers of Literature" (pp. 139–45), "to see who I am, to explain the world to myself." Out of such sharing, women find the courage to ask the nonquestion, to think the unthinkable, to say clearly and in public, like the little child in the fairy tale, "But the emperor has no clothes on."

Humor, the ability to take ourselves with a grain of salt, to laugh at our own foibles and limitations, is another force for bonding. The Women in Pain group could begin their litany with a skit.

> JANE: What did you do at the first meeting of the workshop on women in pain?
> GROUP: We cried a lot.
> JANE: What did you do at the second meeting of the workshop on women in pain?
> GROUP: We laughed a lot.
> SUSAN: Pardon me for using up your air, but I did need to breathe just a little.

Working together on a joint task is another powerful means of bonding. In the conference working groups, we tested our patience in listening to differing viewpoints until we reached a mutual understanding. Any honest attempt to carry out a common work can become a force for bonding, and is a good way for women of different backgrounds to begin to build bridges.

Rituals and celebrations are another strong means of bonding. Because rituals appeal to the senses and the emotions as well as to abstract understandings, they involve the whole person. Because they can be planned so as to give everyone an active role and a voice, they imply mutual recognition and affirmation. Because they provide a way symbolically to lift up and affirm differences, they can express a unity in diversity without watering down the separate elements. The section on ritual elaborates on these ideas.

The very identification of our own oppressions can become a means of bonding. Judith Plaskow asks poignantly if the knowledge that we have all been slaves in Egypt can become a bridge to one another. And Mary Wakeman, building on the work of James Ogilvy, remarks that perhaps our equality lies not in our universal inclusion in one family, but in our universal marginality. Relative to some others, we are each the other. Wakeman argues that affirming such diversity means recognizing God in one another. Mutual empowerment is necessarily pluralistic. We discover a universe of many centers of power and initiative, rather than a hierarchy emanating from a single source of power; the operative image is that of a web or network with many intersections rather than a pyramid with one all-powerful ruler on top.

In this universe, our problem becomes how to deal with the multiplicity of differences, all of which are to be valued. Two ideas emerged during the week with particular force: a theology of immanence, touched upon by Wakeman and elaborated particularly by Starhawk ("Immanence: Uniting the Spiritual and Political," pp. 310–17); and an outline of feminist process adverted to by many of the speakers and developed rather fully in the last section of Wakeman's paper ("Affirming Diversity and Biblical Tradition," pp. 267–80). Seeing God/dess in the other, seeing the other as sacred, is the theological basis for respecting differences. The disciplines of participative process translate this respect into practice. Among the disciplines Wakeman lists: to be able to hear, to tell the truth, to think well about those whose concerns are different from our own, to acknowledge and tolerate conflict within and among ourselves, to face our fears and embrace them as useful directives of attention, to delight in our differences.

Alternative Visions

Looking through the work of the various contributors, it is evident that each one offers glimpses of an alternative future, caught in a fleeting image or perhaps sketched in more or less tentative strokes. These intimations toward a viable future come from women of diverse backgrounds and very different starting points. We cannot point to a consensus as to what the new world, or the new church, should look like, or how we might move toward it. Still less can we put all the pieces together into one comprehensive picture. Rather we would tend to agree with Karen McCarthy Brown ("Why Women Need the War God," pp. 190–201) that "the wholeness of life does not surrender to rigorous thinking." Too great an insistence on a comprehensive system or on clarity of perceptions can lead to sacrificing the fullness of vision. Yet despite all the diversities, there is a common realization that women's power, women's freedom, and women's bonding are essential for a more human and viable world.

Perhaps we can highlight some of the elements common to these various intimations of a viable future. First, a nonhierarchical concept of reality: That all is connectedness is a theme central to Ynestra King ("Making the World Live," pp. 56–64). She sees all life as an "interconnected web," in which everything we do to nature has a reaction somewhere. Or as Starhawk explains it in her vision of immanence, "What goes around comes around . . . what is taken from the earth must be given back." In the web of connectedness, there can be no higher and lower; all are interdependent. For King, since all is connectedness, the evils of racism, of structural poverty, and of the neocolonialization of poor nations by wealthy ones are not single issues but are from the first interrelated and to be fought simultaneously. Using a different image of connectedness, Letha Scanzoni, in her rejection of the "great chain of being" ("The Great Chain of Being and the Chain of Command," pp. 41–55) sees reality as a cosmic dance, full of spontaneity, individuality, freedom, and creativity, "all inspired by one and the same spirit."

This vision of interdependence involves a life lived in harmony with nature, in which humans take their place on earth not as lords of creation but as one species among millions of others. Starhawk's vision of immanence reinforces this notion. For her there is no way for humans to see themselves as standing outside the world to own it or exploit it. For King, ecofeminism is both a vision of harmony and a careful, ecologically sound practice: using renewable sources of energy, conserving natural resources, using alternative technologies, planning for a sustainable future.

A third element in the images of the future is a radical pluralism, the richest possible diversity in both nature and human society. Mary Wakeman in her reading of the Old Testament finds affirmation of the diversity of personhood. She insists that we can "use the energy of the tradition for change when its power over us as tradition is broken. The way to let the past go is to use it for what it is good for: getting on." The theme of differences not as threats but as enrichment is taken up by Judith Ochshorn ("Reclaiming Our Past," pp. 281-92), who sees as a major task for feminism to honor pluralism and value diversity. And Elisabeth Schüssler Fiorenza ("Claiming the Center," pp. 293-309) asks if the women's movement can learn to "celebrate our differences as the source of our common power for change."

Interdependence involves a life lived in harmony with one another, in a world of peers who relate in mutuality and are skilled in developing a flexible, negotiated order rather than drilled in obedience to a chain of command. Many voices spell out what mutuality will demand of the women's movement: respect for the other, "going out of our minds" to enter the world of the other, recognition of the right of the other to set her own agenda in the light of her experience and the experience of her community (a point stressed particularly by the panel on racism), the difficult disciplines of tolerating conflict and working through disagreements if we are ever to build those "unlikely coalitions" that can move us toward the future. Mutuality means too that the political strategist burning with eagerness for action and the woman in pain seeking healing must give each other freedom and affirmation. The panel on racism, the heated discussion of Israel and Lebanon, the milder discussion on lesbianism and heterosexism—all kept us aware that the road we travel to women's bonding and the emergence of a more just world requires courage, honesty, listening, accountability, and the continued search for visions that empower and give hope.

Another facet of the future: healing the mind-body split.

Liberation requires self-love, self-respect, self-determination. Delores Williams describes her journey toward self-determination as a process of woman inventing herself, using poem and story as ways of assessing her past, lamenting its tragedies, and affirming its strengths and hopes. Self-love implies accepting and affirming all the parts of oneself, body and spirit, sexuality, negative experiences, and special gifts. Fiorenza points out that self-love orients us to the struggle and enables us to enter into truly mutual relations. We fight not out of altruism, but out of perceiving in other women's oppression the different dimensions of our own struggle. The best interests of women, in the words of the Redstockings Manifesto, are the best interests of the poorest, the most alienated and abused of women.

Mary Buckley ("Women, Poverty, and Economic Justice," pp. 3–10) and Jackie Di Salvo ("Class, Gender, and Religion," pp. 11–34) address the need for a new economic order that would put people before profits and meet the basic needs of the masses before producing luxuries for the few. Such an order implies collective responsibility for the production and distribution of goods, a kind of economic democracy necessary to the genuine functioning of political democracy. Di Salvo sketches the outlines of a socialist feminist vision, with collective ownership of the means of production, abolition of the sexual division of labor, the socializing of the domestic sphere and the participation of men in child care and housework. Along with collective responsibility for the nonproducers—children, the aged, the disabled—she advocates the European concept of the social wage. Under this notion, people have a rightful share in the resources of the society their labor has helped to create. Their share is returned to them not as charity but as entitlements, in the form of public housing, medical care, a mother's allowance, etc. The profound restructuring of society these dreams imply will require a merger between the struggles of women and those of all oppressed people and will involve vast political and cultural changes as well as a new economic order. Carol Coston ("A Feminist Approach to Alternative Enterprises," pp. 336–43) approaches the question of economic democracy concretely. She does not attempt to deal with the future of society as a whole; rather she puts forward three experiments in the world of work that have tried to embody a genuine spirit of equality among the workers in pay, in ownership, and in management.

The picture that emerges is of a world of decentralized communities, using only those technologies that are ecologically sound, relating to one another as peers, forming loose networks for mutual support with other similar groups. Thus, Starhawk speaks of the intimate community, whose members in the tradition of immanence see the Goddess in each other and join in rituals and in practical work. These covens (in another context these might be thought of as base communities) reach out to other groups and form coalitions for political action against the destructive powers of war and the unjust distribution of the world's resources. Buckley, DiSalvo, and King stress the need for autonomous women's groups in the political realm and in the churches to keep women's issues clearly in focus. From the biblical tradition, Rosemary Ruether ("Envisioning Our Hopes," pp. 325–35) draws the image of the year of Jubilee, not a final, apocalyptic new heaven and earth, but rather a humbler, more limited vision of human communities striving to live justly with one another and nondestructively with nonhuman nature. She describes her vision of a just, liveable society in some detail. Its ingredients include

> a human scale of habitats and communities, the ability of people to participate in the decisions that govern their lives, work in which one can integrate the intellectual and the physical, a just sharing of the benefits of production, a balance of urban and rural environments.

Inherent in the notion of the year of Jubilee, which recurred every fifty years, is the need for renewal. Whatever peace and justice a human society attains is not a "once and for all time" achievement, but rather a fragile arrangement that will need to be reshaped in the changed conditions of each succeeding generation.

What would happen to war in these visions of a possible future? All the contributors reject nuclear war out of hand, but they disagree over whether war can be totally eliminated. Mary Condren ("Patriarchy and Death," pp. 173–89) and Carol Christ ("Feminist Liberation Theology and Yahweh as Holy Warrior," pp. 202–12) find the origins of war in the patriarchal glorification of death-defiance and death in battle "for God and country." Both Christ and Condren point to patriarchal socialization as perpetuating militarism through the stress on proving manhood through violence. They call for women to bring into the public realm the traditional female virtues of sustaining and enhancing life. Brown speaks eloquently of the necessity of owning our anger on the personal level. On the societal level, she and Di Salvo both hold that under some circumstances, violence may be necessary to throw off oppression. Whatever the disagreements over whether women need the War God, there was general agreement with Brown's statement that "the great obscenity of nuclear war lies . . . in its abstraction. . . . The possibility of nuclear holocaust . . . has taken us quantum leaps away from a position where our leaders can imaginatively grasp the havoc they are capable of causing in the world. Humankind is in grave danger."

Finally, out of the chorus of diverse voices comes the strong affirmation of the unity of the personal, the spiritual, and the political. Mary Hunt, in outlining her political strategies ("A Political Perspective," pp. 249–54) appeals to the concrete values and actions that make the transcendent mystery real to us and ground our commitment to struggle for justice and love. Starhawk, out of the nondogmatic Wicca tradition with its meditative nature rituals, appeals for direct political action as a way to shape a more human world. Di Salvo, basing herself on her understanding of Marxism, calls on the Marxists to recognize the importance of spirituality for making the revolution. Elisabeth Fiorenza grounds her struggle against patriarchy in the heart of biblical religion. For her the Jew Jesus does not speak of salvation by a male savior but of the promise that the victims of history will not have suffered for nothing, that a new creation is emerging that turns their defeat into life. In the midst of patriarchal domination and ideology, of the oppression of the capitalist class system, of the political and economic forces that have co-opted Christianity, she sees feminism at its deepest as a movement of change. She emphasizes the image of the *ekklēsia* of women, acknowledging their complicity in patriarchal oppression, keeping alive the memory of the sufferings and triumphs of their foresisters, struggling in solidarity with women devastated by poverty, colonialism, racism, and classism, drawing strength from the power of the life-giving spirit and the hope that suffering and defeat can be turned into life.

The web of connections, the cosmic dance, the structures of economic democracy, the Goddess world of immanence, the year of Jubilee and the *ekklēsia* of women—these are some of the images that gave us glimpses into a future where human potentialities could expand in a fullness of compassion and creativity.

Where Do We Go from Here?

Feminist theology is a critical theology of liberation: the vision must be tested in action (praxis), and reflection on action expands and corrects the vision. The working groups chose different starting points, but whether they began with political strategies or personal pain or theological questions, all agreed in seeing action as grounded in a spiritual vision and seeing spirituality as leading to personal and political action.

The practical suggestions are diverse and on many different levels. They are inspired by the conviction that action can open up new possibilities, that we need not have a perfect scheme before we can move. A brief summary of some specific recommendations follows.

Continued consciousness-raising. In the words of a Hispanic participant, we need to "go out of our minds" in order to respect, enter into, and understand the culture of the other. We must learn to see the culture of the other as having value for our own survival and enrichment, must learn to delight in differences as much as we now delight in commonalities.

Integrating the shadow side of ourselves. We cannot come to wholeness without owning our anger and other negative emotions and finding appropriate ways to express them. We must also own our complicity in the oppression of others. It is not possible to grow up in a racist, classist, imperialist, heterosexist society without absorbing those values. The crucial question is what do we do when we become aware of these distortions in ourselves? Evasion, guilt, inaction—these are no solution. Rather we must commit ourselves to the struggle and use our resources accordingly.

Building face-to-face communities of support. In the present reactionary climate we all have special need for small, face-to-face communities for nurturance. These go by many names from the *comunidades de base* in the Hispanic culture to the Wicca covens. What they have in common is that they are small, the members are personally known to one another, they have listened to one another's stories, they have built a degree of mutual trust, they are prepared to stand by one another in practical ways when some members move into action. Thus, Starhawk describes some of the West Coast groups who consciously decide to engage in nonviolent direct action that involves risks both of physical injury and of jail sentences. The support group prepares for the action by nonviolence training; they support one another during the demonstration; those who are jailed know that they can count on other group members while they are "inside" to take care of what they have left behind, whether it be an apartment, a pet, or a family member. Increasingly such small groups are forming loose networks that can be mobilized for particular actions.

Building "unlikely" coalitions. Coalition-building requires political analysis and skills. Coalitions are nonutopian, pragmatic vehicles; it is not necessary to agree with the entire platform of the other group as long as the coalition is not inspired by sheer opportunism. The parties need to have a clear self-interest that can be achieved by the coalition, and this often works best in multiissue coalitions.

Building a broad-based feminist agenda. Among the issues to be included:

- speaking for nature, encompassing an ecological perspective
- speaking for the right of women to define and express their own sexuality, and therefore speaking for freedom

of choice in regard to abortion and for the rights of homosexuals
- bringing a feminist perspective to the peace movement. The urgency of the nuclear threat tends to trivialize all other issues, but it is important that as feminists we incorporate the issues of sex and race into our dealings with peace issues.

Considering direct action as a tactic. See Ynestra King's paper for a discussion of direct action as empowering the individual, and Starhawk's paper for a discussion of practical, concrete methods.

Beginning to build alternative enterprises. To continue to struggle against the mainstream, one must have a reasonably assured economic base. Carol Coston's paper suggests some models for alternative enterprises and indicates a few first steps that could be taken.

This book focuses primarily on what feminists are bringing to theology: the critique of age-old traditions; the recovery of a lost heritage; the trust in women's experience as a source of theological insight; the beginnings of a new vision of reality, a new framework of ultimate meaning and value. We have not touched except indirectly on what feminist theology might bring to feminism. The theological task is to examine the ultimate questions of meaning and value. The way we image the world and our place in it affects everything else: our self-understanding, the quality of our relationships, the structuring of our institutions, the use we humans make of planet Earth. We believe religious feminists have gifts to bring to the women's movement and to our task of reconstituting the world. The gathering and explication of these gifts are yet to come.

Janet Kalven

Notes

Epigraph
1. Susan Griffin, *Woman and Nature* (New York: Harper & Row, 1978), p. 190. Copyright © 1978 by Susan Griffin. All rights reserved. Used by permission of the publisher.
2. Meridel LeSueur, "Hush My Little Grandmother," *Rites of Ancient Ripening* (Minneapolis: Vanilla Press, 1977). Used by permission of the author.
3. Karen Voss, San Francisco, unpublished diary. Used by permission.

1. BUCKLEY: Women, Poverty, and Economic Justice
Much of the material in this chapter has appeared in "The Growing Impoverishment of Women," *The Ecumenist,* October 1982, and is used by permission of Paulist Press.
1. The U.N. Commission on the Status of Women reported at the conference in Copenhagen in July 1980 that although women constitute 51 percent of the world population, are one third of the formal labor force, and do four fifths of all informal work, they receive only 10 percent of world income and own less than 1 percent of the world's property.
2. *National Advisory Council on Economic Opportunity Final Report: The American Promise—Equal Justice and Economic Opportunity* (Washington, DC, September 1981), pp. 7–32; *The Inequality of Sacrifice: The Impact of the Reagan Budget on Women* (Washington, DC, May 6, 1981), mimeographed pamphlet with data supplied by thirty-nine endorsing and resource organizations; Barbara Ehrenreich and Karen Stollard, "The Nouveau Poor," a special report in *Ms.,* July/August 1982, pp. 217–24; Frances Fox Piven and Richard A. Cloward, *The New Class War* (New York: Pantheon, 1982), pp. 16–19; *The State of Black America,* James D. Williams, ed., National Urban League, January 22, 1980.
3. See note 2.
4. Adrienne Rich, *Of Woman Born* (New York: W. W. Norton & Co., 1976), p. 44.

5. Zillah Eisenstein, *The Radical Future for Liberal Feminism* (New York: Longman, Inc., 1981), pp. 14–15. See especially chapter 2.
6. Comment of William Tabb, professor of economics, Queens College, Queens, NY, quoted in Ehrenreich and Stollard, "Nouveau Poor," p. 224.
7. Kenneth Clark, in William K. Tabb, *The Political Economy of the Black Ghetto* (New York: W. W. Norton & Co., 1972). The following materials are also helpful: Emma Rothschild, "Reagan and the Real America," *New York Review of Books*, February 5, 1981; Bella Abzug, "Forming a Real Women's Bloc," *The Nation*, November 21, 1981; Elisabeth Schüssler Fiorenza, "Sexism and Conversion," Network 9 (May/June 1981); Lisa Leghorn and Mary Roodkowsky, *Who Really Starves? Women and World Hunger* (New York: Friendship Press, 1977).

2. DI SALVO: Class, Gender, and Religion

1. Karl Marx, *Economic and Philosophic Manuscripts*, edited by Dirk J. Struik, translated by Martin Milligan (New York: International Publishers, 1964), p. 144.
2. William Blake, "Nobodaddy," in *The Poetry and Prose of William Blake*, rev. ed., edited by David V. Erdman and Harold Bloom (New York: Doubleday, 1970), p. 659. Copyright © 1965 by David V. Erdman and Harold Bloom. Reprinted by permission of Doubleday & Co., Inc.
3. On the religion of the earth Goddess see Joseph Campbell, *The Masks of God: Occidental Mythology* (New York: Viking Press, 1964); Robert Graves, *The White Goddess* (New York: Farrar, Straus & Giroux, 1966); Janel Ellen Harrison, *Prologomena to the Study of Ancient Greek Religion* and *Themis* (Cambridge, England: Cambridge University Press, 1903); Merlin Stone, *When God Was a Woman* (New York: Harcourt Brace Jovanovich, 1976) and *Ancient Mirrors of Womanhood*, 2 vols. (New York: Sibylline, 1980); Rayna Rapp, "Women, Religion and Archaic Civilization," *Feminist Studies* 4 (1978); Judith Ochshorn, *The Female Experience and the Nature of the Divine* (Bloomington, IN: Indiana University Press, 1982). For the role of women in prestate and state societies, see George Thomson, *Studies in Ancient Greek Society*, 2 vols. (New York: Citadel Press, 1972); Frederick Engels, *The Origin of the Family, Private Property and the State* (New York: International Publishers, 1974); Eleanor Leacock, *Myths of Male Dominance: Collected Articles on*

Women Cross-Culturally (New York: Monthly Review Press, 1981); *Toward an Anthropology of Women,* edited by Rayna R. Reiter (New York: Monthly Review Press, 1975); Karen Sacks, *Sisters and Wives: The Past and Future of Sexual Equality* (Westport, CT: Greenwood Press, 1979); *Becoming Visible: Women in European History,* edited by Renate Bridental and Claudia Koontz (Boston: Houghton Mifflin, 1977); Elise Boulding, *The Underside of History: A View of Women Through Time* (Boulder, CO: Westview Press, 1976); and *Women and the State in Pre-Industrial Societies,* edited by Christine Gailey and Mona Etienne, forthcoming. For an opposing view, see *Women, Culture and Society,* edited by Michelle Z. Rosaldo and Louise Lamphere (Stanford, CA: Stanford University Press, 1974).

4. Alexander Heidel, ed., *The Babylonian Genesis* (Chicago: University of Chicago Press, 1951), p. 40.
5. Robert Harper, *The Code of Hammurabi* (Chicago: University of Chicago Press, 1904).
6. Karl Marx, "Contribution to the Critique of Hegel's Philosophy of Right," in *Marx and Engels on Religion* (New York: Schocken Books, 1964), p. 41.
7. Blake, "The Four Zoas," in *Poetry and Prose,* op. cit., pp. 320–21.
8. Norman O. Brown, *Life Against Death* (Middletown, CT: Wesleyan University Press, 1959), p. 45.
9. Karl Marx, *Capital,* quoted in T. B. Bottomore, ed., *Karl Marx: Selected Writings in Sociology and Social Philosophy* (New York: McGraw-Hill, 1956), p. 255.
10. *Marx and Engels,* op. cit., p. 42.
11. Ibid.

4. SCANZONI: The Great Chain of Being and the Chain of Command

Some of the material in this paper was originally published in an article by the same name in *The Reformed Journal,* October 1976, and is used by permission.

1. C. S. Lewis, *A Preface to Paradise Lost* (New York: Oxford University Press, 1961), p. 73 (emphasis added).
2. For a detailed study of this concept, see Arthur O. Lovejoy, *The Great Chain of Being: A Study of the History of an Idea* (Cambridge, MA: Harvard University Press, 1936).
3. E. M. W. Tillyard, *The Elizabethan World Picture* (New York: Vintage Books, n.d.); Roland Bainton, *The Medieval Church* (New York: D. Van Nostrand Co., 1962), p. 28.

4. Quoted in C. A. Patrides, *Milton and the Christian Tradition* (London: Oxford University Press, 1966), p. 67.
5. From Alexander Pope's *Essay on Man*, as quoted in Lovejoy, *Great Chain*, op. cit., p. 206.
6. Soame Jenyns, *A Free Inquiry into the Nature and Origin of Evil* (London, 1757), pp. 28–29, as quoted in David Brion Davis, *The Problem of Slavery in Western Culture* (Ithaca, NY: Cornell University Press, 1966), p. 361 (emphasis added).
7. Gottfried Wilhelm von Leibniz, *Théodicée*, as quoted in Lovejoy, *Great Chain*, op. cit., p. 206.
8. Source unknown. Quoted in Lovejoy, *Great Chain*, op. cit., p. 207.
9. Davis, *Problem of Slavery*, op. cit., p. 68.
10. Gordon Turnbull, *An Apology for Negro Slavery; or The West-Indian Planters Vindicated from the Charge of Inhumanity* (2d ed., London, 1786), pp. 34–35, as quoted in Davis, *Problem of Slavery*, op. cit., p. 392.
11. Winthrop D. Jordan, *White over Black* (Chapel Hill, NC: University of North Carolina Press, 1968), Penguin Books paperback ed., p. 227.
12. Edward Long, *The History of Jamaica* (London, 1774), as quoted in Davis, *Problem of Slavery*, op. cit., p. 461.
13. William Wilson, *Power, Racism and Privilege* (New York: Macmillan, 1973).
14. Steven Goldberg, *The Inevitability of Patriarchy*, expanded ed. (New York: William Morrow & Co., 1974).
15. Thomas Howard, "A Dialogue on Women, Hierarchy, and Equality," *Post American* (later renamed *Sojourners*), May 1975, pp. 12–13.
16. Elisabeth Elliot (Leitch), *I Am Somebody* (Elgin, IL: David C. Cook Publishing Co., 1975), the curriculum book for the Sunday school Lifestyle course series.
17. This drawing appears in the basic course book for Bill Gothard's Institute in Basic Youth Conflicts, massive seminars that are held in major cities, charge a high fee (which includes materials not available to the general public), and often attract crowds of twenty thousand or more for each session.
18. Larry Christenson, *The Christian Family* (Minneapolis: Bethany Fellowship, 1970), pp. 17–18.
19. C. S. Lewis, *Preface to Paradise Lost*, op. cit., pp. 73–74.

20. Stephen B. Clark, *Man and Woman in Christ* (Ann Arbor, MI: Servant Books, 1980), pp. 21–24.
21. Ibid., p. 25.
22. Alexander Pope, *Essay on Man*, IV, ii, 49ff., as quoted in Lovejoy, *Great Chain*, op. cit., p. 206 (emphasis added). Also see Jordan, *White over Black*, op. cit., p. 483.
23. Jordan, *White over Black*, op. cit., p. 228.
24. Erich Fromm, *Escape from Freedom* (New York: Holt, Rinehart, & Winston, 1941; Avon paperback ed., 1965).
25. Peggy Reeves Sanday, *Female Power and Male Dominance: On the Origins of Sexual Inequality* (New York: Cambridge University Press, 1981), p. 231.
26. Elizabeth Rice Handford, *Me? Obey Him?* (Murfreesboro, TN: Sword of the Lord Publishers, 1972).
27. Bill Gothard, *Supplementary Alumni Book*, Vol. 5 (Institute in Basic Youth Conflicts, 1979).
28. Peter L. Berger and Thomas Luckman, *The Social Construction of Reality* (Garden City, NY: Doubleday, 1966; Anchor Books paperback ed., 1967).
29. Nelle Morton, unpublished sermon entitled "Hearing to Speech," presented at Claremont School of Theology, Claremont, CA, April 27, 1977, as quoted in Carol P. Christ, *Diving Deep and Surfacing: Women Writers on Spiritual Quest* (Boston: Beacon Press, 1980), p. 7.
30. Anne Wilson Schaef, *Women's Reality* (Minneapolis: Winston Press, 1981).
31. Kristin Lems, "Women Walk More Determined," from her album *Oh Mama!* (Carolsdatter Productions, P.O. Box 2267, Sta. A, Champaign, IL 61820). Quoted by permission.
32. Berger and Luckman, op. cit., p. 108.
33. James I of England commanded the Bishop of London to instruct the clergy "to inveigh vehemently against the insolence of our women" for their way of dressing. Referred to in "Letter to John Chamberlain," January 25, 1620, as quoted in Carolyn Merchant, *The Death of Nature* (San Francisco: Harper & Row, 1980), p. 166.
34. Letter to the *Greensboro* (NC) *Daily News*, June 1, 1982.
35. Elisabeth Elliot (Leitch), "Feminism or Femininity?" *Cambridge Fish*, Winter 1975–1976, p. 6.
36. Cris Williamson, "Song of the Soul." © 1975 by Bird Ankles Music. All rights reserved. Used by permission. Sung on the Cris Williamson album, "The Changer and the Changed" (Olivia Records, Inc., 4400 Market St., Oakland, CA. 94608).

5. KING: Making the World Live
   1. Simone de Beauvoir, *The Second Sex* (New York: Random House Modern Library, 1968), p. 144.
   2. Sherry B. Ortner, "Is Female to Male as Nature Is to Culture?" in *Woman, Culture and Society*, edited by Michele Zimbalist Rosaldo and Louise Lamphere (Stanford, CA: Stanford University Press, 1974), pp. 71–72.
   3. Ibid., p. 80.
   4. Ibid., p. 75.
   5. Ibid., p. 87.
   6. Adrienne Rich, *Of Woman Born* (New York: W.W. Norton, 1976), p. 285.
   7. Adrienne Rich, *On Lies, Secrets and Silence: Selected Prose 1966–78* (New York: W. W. Norton, 1979), p. 279.

Introduction to Part III: Racism, Pluralism, Bonding
   1. Miriam Schneir, ed., *Feminism: The Essential Historical Writings* (New York: Vintage Books, 1972), pp. 93–94.
   2. Gloria T. Hull, Patricia Bell Scott, and Barbara Smith, eds., *All the Women Are White, All the Blacks are Men, but Some of Us Are Brave: Black Women's Studies* (Old Westbury, NY: Feminist Press, 1982).

7. PHELPS: Racism and the Bonding of Women
   1. James Boggs, *Racism and the Class Struggle* (New York: Monthly Review Press, 1970), pp. 147–48.
   2. John Henrik Clarke, *Black-White Alliances: A Historical Perspective* (Chicago: Institute of Positive Education, n. d.), pp. 1–5.
   3. Ibid., p. 9.
   4. Quoted in Vincent Harding, *The Other American Revolution* (Atlanta: Institute of the Black World; Berkeley, CA: University of California Press, 1980), p. 56.
   5. Ibid., pp. 66, 69, 71.
   6. Ibid., p. 64.
   7. Angela Y. Davis, *Women, Race and Class* (New York: Random House, 1981), p. 59.
   8. Ibid., p. 71. The chapter is replete with similiar quotations, illustrating some on the permeation of the suffrage movement by racism.
   9. Ibid., pp. 44–45.

8. JOHNSON: **A Historical Addendum**
   1. Quoted in Gerda Lerner, *The Grimké Sisters from South Carolina: Pioneers for Women's Rights and Abolition* (New York: Schocken Books, 1975), p. 52.
   2. Quoted in Eleanor Flexner, *Century of Struggle: The Women's Rights Movement in the United States* (New York: Atheneum, 1971), p. 48.
   3. Lerner, *Grimké Sisters*, op. cit., p. 162.
   4. Ellen DuBois, ed., *Elizabeth Cady Stanton, Susan B. Anthony: Correspondence, Writings, Speeches* (New York: Schocken Books, 1981), p. 8.
   5. Angela Y. Davis, *Women, Race and Class* (New York: Random House, 1981), p. 39.
   6. Ibid., p. 51.
   7. Dubois, *Stanton, Anthony*, op. cit., p. 81.
   8. Davis, *Women, Race and Class*, op. cit., pp. 44-45.
   9. Ibid., p. 78.
   10. Ibid., p. 82.
   11. Judith Papachristou, ed., *Women Together: A History in Documents of the Women's Movement in the United States* (New York: Knopf, 1976), p. 57.
   12. Flexner, *Century of Struggle*, op. cit., p. 144.
   13. Davis, *Women, Race and Class*, op. cit., pp. 125-26.
   14. DuBois, *Stanton, Anthony*, op. cit., p. 92.
   15. Davis, *Women, Race and Class*, op. cit., pp. 8-11.
   16. Ibid., p. 18.
   17. Ibid., p. 19.
   18. Miriam Schneir, ed., *Feminism: The Essential Historical Writings* (New York: Random House, 1972), p. 25.
   19. Ibid., p. 94.
   20. Gerda Lerner, ed., *Black Women in White America: A Documentary History* (New York: Random House, 1973), p. 567.
   21. From *And Still I Rise* by Maya Angelou. Copyright © 1978 by Maya Angelou. Reprinted by permission of Random House, Inc.

10. PLASKOW: **Anti-Semitism**
    1. Rosemary Radford Ruether has always insisted on a complex analysis of oppression. See her *New Woman/New Earth* (New York: Seabury Press, 1975), particularly part 2.
    2. Elizabeth (Vicki) Spelman made this point in a paper deliv-

ered at the 1981 National Women's Studies Association Conference.
3. Maurice D. Atkin, "United States of America," *Encyclopedia Judaica,* vol. 15, p. 1636.
4. Robert Weisbord and Arthur Stein, *Bittersweet Encounter* (New York: Schocken Books, 1972), p. 15.
5. In ibid., Weisbord and Stein stress this point.
6. Letty Cottin Pogrebin, "Anti-Semitism in the Women's Movement," *Ms.,* June 1982, pp. 68-69.
7. Ann Wilson Schaef makes this point for female and male culture in *Women's Reality* (Minneapolis: Winston Press, 1981).
8. Lucy Dawidowicz, *The War Against the Jews 1933–1945* (New York: Holt, Rinehart & Winston; Philadelphia: Jewish Publication Society of America, 1975).
9. Jean-Paul Sartre, *Anti-Semite and Jew* (New York: Schocken Books, 1965), p. 69.
10. Pogrebin, "Anti-Semitism," op, cit., p. 66; Evelyn Torten Beck, ed., *Nice Jewish Girls: A Lesbian Anthology* (Watertown, MA: Persephone Press, 1982), particularly the introduction and first section.
11. Quoted in Pogrebin, "Anti-Semitism," p. 49; a fuller, pseudonymous report on the Copenhagen conference appears in the #8 issue of *Lilith.*
12. Lucy Dawidowicz, "American Jews and the Holocaust," *New York Times Magazine,* April 18, 1982.
13. Alice Walker, "One Child of One's Own: An Essay on Creativity," *Ms.,* August 1979.
14. Esther Ticktin, "A Modest Beginning," *Response,* Summer 1973.
15. Cherríe Moraga in Beck, *Jewish Girls,* op. cit., p. xxi.

11. GOLDEN: **White Women and Racism**

1. Michelle Russell, "Rapunzel, Let Down Your Hair: An Open Letter to White Women in the Academy," *Politics and Education,* March/April 1979, p. 41.
2. Bell Hooks, *Ain't I a Woman: Black Women and Feminism* (Boston: South End Press, 1981), p. 12.
3. Russell, "Rapunzel," op. cit., p. 41.
4. Johnnie Tillmon, "Welfare Is a Woman's Issue," *Liberation News Service,* February 26, 1972.
5. Quoted in Hooks, *Ain't I a Woman,* op. cit., p. 127.
6. Ibid., p. 149.

13. GRANT: A Black Response to Feminist Theology
    1. Jacquelyn Grant, "Black Theology and the Black Woman," in *Black Theology: A Documentary History 1966–1979*, edited by Gayraud S. Wilmore and James H. Cone (Maryknoll, NY: Orbis Books, 1979).
    2. Langston Hughes, "Evil," copyright 1942 by Alfred A. Knopf, Inc. Reprinted from *Selected Poems*, by Langston Hughes, by permission of the publisher.
    3. Quoted in Jurgen Moltmann, *Religion, Revolution and the Future* (New York: Scribner's, 1969), p. 35.
    4. Angela Y. Davis, *Women, Race and Class* (New York: Vintage Books, 1983).
    5. Harmon Deborah Hines, "Racism Breeds Stereotypes," *The Witness*, February 1982, p. 7.
    6. Lucille Clifton, "To Ms. Ann," in *An Ordinary Woman* (New York: Random House, 1974), p. 25. Used by permission.
    7. Toni Morrison, "What the Black Woman Asks About Women's Liberation," *New York Times Magazine*, August 22, 1971.
    8. Michelle Russell, "Women, Work and Politics in the U.S.," in *Theology in the Americas*, edited by Sergio Torres and John Eagleson (Maryknoll, NY: Orbis Books, 1976), p. 349.
    9. Myrtle Gordon, "Bigotry 'Fashionable' Again," *The Witness*, February 1982, p. 8. Used by permission.

15. WILLIAMS: Women as Makers of Literature
    1. Zora Neale Hurston, *Their Eyes Were Watching God* (Champaign, IL: University of Illinois Press, 1978).
    2. Margaret Atwood, *Surfacing* (New York: Popular Library, 1981).
    3. Quoted in Philip S. Foner, ed., *The Voices of Black America* (New York: Simon & Schuster, 1972), p. 103.
    4. Doris Lessing, *The Summer Before the Dark* (New York: Knopf, 1973).

17. HUNT: Political Oppression and Creative Survival
    1. See, for example, Perry Deane Young, *God's Bullies* (New York: Holt, Rinehart & Winston, 1982).
    2. See, for example, Sheila Bolotin, "Voices from the Post Feminist Generation," *New York Times Magazine*, October 17, 1982.

3. Sheila Collins, "To the Youth of Nicaragua," in *Struggle Is a Name for Hope*, edited by Renny Golden and Sheila Collins (Minneapolis: West End Press, 1982), p. 47.

18. CONDREN: **Patriarchy and Death**

1. Plato, "Phaedo," in *The Dialogues of Plato*, vol. 1, translated by B. Jowett (New York: Random House, 1937), p. 451.
2. Elizabeth Fisher, *Woman's Creation* (New York: Doubleday, 1979), p. 191.
3. Ibid., p. 193.
4. Mary O'Brien, *The Politics of Reproduction* (London: Routledge & Kegan Paul, 1981), p. 29.
5. Ibid., p. 57.
6. Ibid., p. 60.
7. As Margaret Mead has observed, "The recurrent problem of civilization is to define the male role satisfactorily, whether it be to build bridges or raise cattle, kill game or kill enemies, build gardens or handle bank shares, so that the male may in the course of his life reach a solid sense of irreversible achievement of which his childhood knowledge of the satisfactions of childbearing have given him a glimpse." *Male and Female* (New York: New American Library, 1959).
8. G. W. F. Hegel, *The Phenomenology of Mind*, translated by J. B. Baillie (New York: Harper & Row, 1967), p. 233.
9. Simone de Beauvoir, *The Second Sex* (New York: Bantam, 1961), pp. 58–59.
10. Carol Ochs, *Behind the Sex of God* (Boston: Beacon Press, 1977), p. 94.
11. Amaury de Riencourt, *Sex and Power in History* (New York: Delta, 1974), p. 39.
12. Ibid., p. 39.
13. Quoted in O'Brien, *The Politics of Reproduction*, op. cit., p. 41.
14. Quoted in Mircea Eliade, *Myths, Dreams and Mysteries* (New York: Harper & Row, 1967), p. 155.
15. Quoted in R. C. Zaehner, *The Teachings of the Magi* (New York: 1956), p. 43.
16. Quoted in Mary Daly, *The Church and the Second Sex* (New York: Harper & Row, 1975), p. 85.
17. G. W. F. Hegel, *Reason in History*, translated by Robert S. Hartman (Indianapolis: Bobbs-Merrill, 1953), p. 92.
18. Derek Bok, speaking in defense of a controversial proposed appointment in *The Harvard Independent*, September 1979.

19. Nancy Jay, "Throughout Your Generations Forever: A Sociology of Blood Sacrifice" (Ph.D. diss., Brandeis University, 1980), p. 116.
20. O'Brien, *Politics of Reproduction,* op. cit., p. 121.
21. Fisher, *Woman's Creation,* op. cit., p. 156.
22. Thomas Kinsella, *The Tain* (Dublin: Dolmen Press, 1977), pp. 6–8.
23. Mircea Eliade, *Rites and Symbols of Initiation* (New York: Harper & Row, 1975), p. 7.
24. Ibid, p. 25.
25. Ibid., 27.
26. Ibid., p. 30.
27. Ibid.
28. Ibid., p. 106.
29. Ochs, *Sex of God,* op. cit., p. 23.
30. David Bakan, *They Took Themselves Wives* (New York: Harper & Row, 1979), p. 137.
31. Charlotte Perkins Gilman, *His Religion and Hers: The Faith of Our Fathers and the Work of Our Mothers* (London: T. Fisher Unwin, 1924), p. 160.
32. Quoted in O'Brien, *Politics of Reproduction,* op. cit., p. 25.
33. Ibid., p. 27.
34. E. Troeltsch, *Christian Thought: Its History and Application* (New York: Meridian Books, 1957), pp. 55–56.
35. Quoted in J. V. Nef, *War and Human Progress* (Cambridge, MA: Harvard University Press, 1950), p. 406.
36. Fisher, *Woman's Creation,* op. cit., p. 54.
37. Carol Gilligan, "In a Different Voice: Women's Conception of Self and Morality," *Harvard Educational Review* 47 (1977): 515.
38. Arthur Schopenhauer, *Essays,* translated by T. B. Saunders (London, 1951), p. 65.
39. Amaury de Riencourt, *Sex and Power,* op. cit., pp. 325–26.
40. David Starr Jordan, *War and the Breed* (Boston: Beacon Press, 1915), p. 169.
41. J. Glenn Gray, *The Warriors* (New York: Harper & Row, 1970), p. 46.
42. Quoted in Susan Griffin, *Ramparts,* September 10, 1971, pp. 26–35.
43. Robert Lowie, *Crow Indians* (New York: Holt, Rinehart & Winston, 1956), p. 44.
44. Jay, *Blood Sacrifice,* p. 168.
45. Eliade, *Rites and Symbols,* p. 134.

46. These connections on military equipment were first made in Mary Daly's class on feminist ethics, Boston College, 1980.
47. Quoted in Donna Warnock, "Patriarchy Is a Killer," in *Reweaving the Web Of Life*, edited by P. McAllister (Philadelphia: New Society Publishers, 1982), p. 22.
48. Dexter Master, *The Accident* (New York: Knopf, 1965), p. 41.
49. William Lawrence, a science writer, quoted in Robert Jay Lifton and Richard Falk, *Indefensible Weapons* (New York: Basic Books, 1982), p. 90.
50. Quoted in Jonathan Schell, *The Fate of the Earth* (New York: Avon Books, 1982), p. 149.
51. David Martin, *The Religious and the Secular* (London: Routledge & Kegan Paul, 1969), p. 44.
52. Quoted on Irish radio during the Falklands crisis.
53. This idea was first suggested to me by Monica Sjoo, a Swedish artist now living in Britain.
54. G. W. F. Hegel, *Reason in History*, translated by Robert S. Hartman (Indianapolis: Bobbs-Merrill, 1953), p. 89.
55. Pierre Teilhard de Chardin, *The Future of Man* (New York: Harper Colophon Books, 1964), p. 151, quoted in Lifton and Falk, *Indefensible Weapons*, p. 193.
56. Harry S. Truman, *Years of Decision*, vol. 1 of *Memoirs* (Garden City, NY: Doubleday, 1955), p. 421; quoted in Martin J. Sherwin, *A World Destroyed* (New York: Vintage Books, 1977), p. 221.
57. Quoted in *Newsweek*, July 28, 1980.

19. BROWN: Why Women Need the War God

1. This title is a self-conscious play on the title of an article by Carol Christ, "Why Women Need the Goddess," which appears in *Womanspirit Rising: A Feminist Reader in Religion*, edited by Carol P. Christ and Judith Plaskow (New York: Harper & Row, 1979). I give this title to my article as a way of saying thank you to Carol. I have learned from her.
2. The accepted spelling for the African deity is Ogun. In the new official orthography of Haitian Creole, the name is Ogou. I have chosen to use the Creole spelling throughout the paper so as not to confuse typesetters and readers.
3. Sandra T. Barnes, "Ogun: An Old God for a New Age," ISHI Occasional Papers in Social Change no. 3 (Philadelphia: Institute for the Study of Human Issues, 1980). Most of what I have to say here about the history and current state of the Ogou cult in Nigeria is derived from this work.

20. CHRIST: Feminist Liberation Theology and Yahweh as Holy Warrior

1. See Rosemary Radford Ruether, "Religion for Women: Sources and Strategies," *Christianity and Crisis*, December 10, 1979, pp. 307–11.
2. Adrienne Rich, "The Phenomenology of Anger," in *Diving into the Wreck* (New York: W. W. Norton, 1973), p. 29. Used by permission.
3. Marija Gimbutas, "Women and Culture in Goddess-Oriented Old Europe," in *The Politics of Women's Spirituality*, edited by Charlene Spretnak (Garden City, NY: Anchor Books, 1982), pp. 22–31.
4. See for example George Ernest Wright, *The Old Testament and Theology* (New York: Harper & Row, 1969), especially chapter 5, "God the Warrior," pp. 121–50; Patrick D. Miller, Jr., *The Divine Warrior in Early Israel* (Cambridge, MA: Harvard University Press, 1973); Rudolf Smend, *Yahweh War and Tribal Confederation: Reflections upon Israel's Earliest History*, translated by Max Grey Rodgers (Nashville: Abingdon, 1970).
5. All biblical quotations are from the Revised Standard Version with "Yahweh" substituted for "Lord."
6. Adrienne Rich, "Natural Resources," in *The Dream of a Common Language: Poems 1974–77* (New York: W. W. Norton, 1978), p. 67.) Used by permission.
7. Rich, *Diving into the Wreck*, op. cit., p. 29.

25. SCANZONI: A Religious Perspective

1. Another useful resource is Mary V. Borhek, *Coming Out to Parents: A Two-Way Survival Guide for Lesbians and Gay Men and Their Parents* (New York: The Pilgrim Press, 1983).
2. *Family Advocate*, Winter 1979, p. 21.

28. WAKEMAN: Affirming Diversity and Biblical Tradition

1. See Henri Frankfort, *Kingship and the Gods* (Chicago: University of Chicago Press, 1948); Thorkild Jacobsen, *The Treasures of Darkness* (New Haven, CT: Yale University Press, 1976).
2. For the full development of this thesis see Eric Wolf, *Peasants* (Englewood Cliffs, NJ: Prentice-Hall, 1966); George E. Mendenhall, "The Conquest of Canaan," in *The Biblical Archeologist Reader 3*, edited by E. F. Campbell and David

Noel Freeman (New York: Doubleday-Anchor, 1970); Norman Gottwald, *The Tribes of Yahweh* (Maryknoll, NY: Orbis Books, 1979).
3. Morton H. Fried, *The Evolution of Political Society* (New York: Random House, 1967).
4. As Carol Gilligan writes: "We know ourselves as separate only insofar as we live in connection with others, and we experience relationship only insofar as we differentiate other from self." *A Different Voice* (Cambridge, MA: Harvard University Press, 1982), p. 63.
5. Judith Ochshorn, *The Female Experience and the Nature of the Divine* (Bloomington: Indiana University Press, 1981).
6. Dorothy Dinnerstein, *The Mermaid and the Minotaur* (New York: Harper & Row, 1976), p. 73.
7. James Ogilvy, *Many Dimensional Man* (New York: Harper-Colophon, 1979), p. 79.
8. Ricky Sherover-Marcuse, in her Unlearning Racism workshops.
9. Hannah Arendt, *The Human Condition* (Chicago: University of Chicago Press, 1958), pp. 50ff.
10. The process by which Mary Abu-Saba and Judith Plaskow came to discuss their concerns for Israel and Lebanon is a good example ("Women Responding to the Arab-Israeli Conflict," pp. 221–33). One person who listened said that it had been for her "a sacred experience."

29. OCHSHORN: **Reclaiming Our Past**
1. See Karen Brown's "Why Women Need the War God" (pp. 190–201) and the introduction to Carol P. Christ and Judith Plaskow, eds., *Womanspirit Rising: A Feminist Reader in Religion* (New York: Harper & Row, 1979).
2. See Mary Wakeman's "Affirming Diversity and Biblical Tradition" (pp. 267–80).
3. Citations of original sources for the discussion of polytheism that follows may be found in the notes to Judith Ochshorn, *The Female Experience and the Nature of the Divine* (Bloomington: Indiana University Press, 1981), chapters 2, 3, 4.
4. Robert H. Pfeiffer, trans., "Akkadian Proverbs and Counsels," in *Ancient Near Eastern Texts Relating to the Old Testament*, 3d ed. with supplement, edited by James B. Pritchard (Princeton, NJ: Princeton University Press, 1969), p. 383.

30. FIORENZA: **Claiming the Center**

1. E. M. Broner and Naomi Nimrod, "A Woman's Passover Haggadah," *Ms.*, April 1977, pp. 53–56. Also in *The Ceremonial Woman*. Used by permission.
2. Elisabeth Schüssler Fiorenza, "A Feminist Theology as a Critical Theology of Liberation," *Theological Studies* 36 (1975): 605–626.
3. See especially the introduction to Carol P. Christ and Judith Plaskow, eds., *Womanspirit Rising: A Feminist Reader in Religion* (New York: Harper & Row, 1979).
4. See Sallie McFague, *Metaphorical Theology* (Philadelphia: Fortress Press, 1982), pp. 145–192.
5. Valerie Miner, *Movement* (Trumansburg, NY: Crossing Press, 1982), p. 180.
6. June Jordan, *Civil Wars* (Boston: Beacon Press, 1981), p. 143.
7. Redstockings, *Feminist Revolution* (New York: Random House, 1976), p. 205.
8. Rosemary Radford Ruether, *New Woman/New Earth* (New York: Seabury Press, 1975), p. 74.
9. Judith Plaskow, "Woman as Body: Motherhood and Dualism," *Anima* 8 (1981): 56–67.
10. Marilyn B. Arthur, "Early Greece: The Origins of the Western Attitude Toward Women," *Arethusa* 6 (1973): 7–58.
11. Susan Moller Okin, *Women in Western Political Thought* (Princeton, NJ: Princeton University Press, 1979).
12. See *Fact Sheets on Institutional Sexism* (New York: Council on Interracial Books for Children, January 1982); L. Leghorn and K. Parker, *Woman's Worth: Sexual Economics and the World of Women* (Boston: Routledge & Kegan Paul, 1981).
13. Kathleen Barry, *Female Sexual Slavery* (New York: Avon Books, 1979).
14. For a fuller discussion see Elisabeth Schüssler Fiorenza, "Discipleship and Patriarchy: Early Christian Ethos and Christian Ethics in a Feminist Theological Perspective," in *The Annual of The Society of Christian Ethics 1982*, edited by L. Rasmussen (Waterloo: CSR, 1982), pp. 131–72.
15. See Elisabeth Schüssler Fiorenza, *In Memory of Her: A Feminist Theological Reconstruction of Christian Origins* (New York: Crossroad, 1983).
16. Charlene Spretnak, ed., *The Politics of Women's Spirituality* (Garden City, NY: Anchor Books, 1982), p. 336.

17. See Elisabeth Schüssler Fiorenza, "Sexism and Conversion," *Network* 9 (1981): 15–22.
18. Audre Lorde, "The Master's Tools Will Never Dismantle the Master's House," in *This Bridge Called My Back: Writings by Radical Women of Color*, edited by Cherríe Moraga and Gloria Anzaldua (Watertown, MA: Persephone Press, 1981), pp. 98–101. The book is a must for anyone interested in women's struggle for liberation and the possibility of women's spiritual bonding. See also Bettina Aptheker, *Woman's Legacy: Essays on Race, Sex, and Class in American History* (Amherst, MA: University of Massachusetts Press, 1982).

31. STARHAWK: Immanence

1. Excerpted from Starhawk, *Dreaming the Dark: Magic, Sex and Politics* (Boston: Beacon Press, 1982), pp. 15–17.
2. For a fuller explanation of the history of the Burning Times see Starhawk, *Dreaming the Dark*, pp. 183–219.
3. The history and philosophy of the Craft are more fully explained in Starhawk, *The Spiral Dance: A Rebirth of the Ancient Religion of the Great Goddess* (San Francisco: Harper & Row, 1979).

33. RUETHER: Envisioning Our Hopes

1. Reinhold Niebuhr, *The Nature and Destiny of Man*, vol. 1 (New York: Charles Scribner's Sons, 1949), pp. 104–12.
2. See Tom Driver, *Christ in a Changing World: Toward an Ethical Christology* (New York: Crossroads, 1981), pp. 57–81.
3. Antoine-Nicolas de Condorcet, *Sketch for a Historical Picture of the Progress of the Human Mind* (1793), especially the Ninth and Tenth Stages; see Rosemary Radford Ruether, *The Radical Kingdom: The Western Experience of Messianic Hope* (New York: Harper & Row, 1970), pp. 44–46.
4. See Gustavo Gutiérrez, *A Theology of Liberation* (Maryknoll, NY: Orbis Books, 1973), pp. 22–37.
5. Daniel Maguire, *The New Subversives* (New York: Crossroads, 1982), pp. 8, 63.

34. COSTON: A Feminist Approach to Alternative Enterprises

1. Virginia Woolf, *Three Guineas* (New York: Harcourt Brace Jovanovich, 1963), pp. 145–46. She continues: "By derision . . . is meant that you must refuse all methods of advertising merit, and hold that ridicule, obscurity and censure are pref-

erable, for psychological reasons, to fame and praise. . . . By Freedom from unreal loyalties is meant that you must rid yourself of pride of nationality in the first place; also of religious pride, college pride, school pride, family pride, sex pride and those unreal loyalties that spring from them." Having learned these lessons, which British law and custom make easy for women, they will be able to enter the professions without being contaminated by them. They will be able "to rid them of their possessiveness, their jealousy, their pugnacity, their greed," and thus be in a position to help "to abolish the inhumanity, the beastliness, the horror, the folly of war" (pp. 146, 151). Used by permission.
2. Charlotte Perkins Gilman, *Herland* (New York: Pantheon, 1979).
3. E. F. Schumacher, *Small Is Beautiful: Economics as If People Mattered* (New York: Harper & Row, 1976).

DATE DUE

WITHDRAWN
from
Funderburg Library

FUNDERBURG LIBRARY
MANCHESTER COLLEGE